Songs for Life

Leader's Edition

Text illustrations: Paul Stoub

Unless otherwise indicated, Scripture quotations are from the HOLY BIBLE, NEW INTERNATIONAL VERSION, copyright © 1973, 1978, 1984, International Bible Society. Used by permission of Zondervan Bible Publishers.

Definitions in the signing index are from the following three sources:
American Sign Language Concise Dictionary, Martin L. A. Sternberg. New York: Harper & Row Publishers, Inc., 1990.
Religious Signing, Elaine Costello. New York: Bantam Books, 1986.
The Joy of Signing, Lottie L. Riekehof. Springfield, MO: Gospel Publishing House, 1978.
Used by permission.

Library of Congress Cataloging-in-Publication Data
Songs for LiFE: leader's edition.
      p.   cm.
      Part of the LiFE (Living in Faith Everyday) curriculum, published in cooperation with the Reformed Church in America.
      Includes indexes.
      ISBN 1-56212-114-6
      1. Hymns, English—Juvenile—Instruction and study. 2. Christian Reformed Church—Hymns.
3. Reformed Church in America—Hymns. I. Christian Reformed Church. II. Reformed Church in America.
MT898.S67   1995
782.27—dc20   95-22552
                                          CIP
                                          MN

ISBN: 1-56212-114-6

10 9 8 7 6 5 4 3 2 1

Leader's Edition

CRC Publications
Grand Rapids, Michigan

Contents

SONGS WITH SONG NOTES

Meeting with God's People

Singing God's Story

Living in God's World

A WORSHIP EDUCATION CURRICULUM

The Elements of Worship

The Christian Year

Living in God's World

INDEXES

Acknowledgments

Harry Boonstra wrote the units on the Christian Year (Units 8-14), and also the notes for the illustrations. Boonstra is theological librarian at Calvin College and Seminary, Grand Rapids, Michigan, where he teaches a course on worship. He is also associate editor of *Reformed Worship*.

Emily R. Brink wrote "Worship Education in the Gathering Time" (p. 324) and served as editor for both editions of *Songs for LiFE*. She also edited the *Psalter Hymnal*, and continues as editor of *Reformed Worship*. Brink is music and liturgy editor for CRC Publications.

Laurie Dekker is one of the writers of the song notes. Dekker is minister of music at Fellowship Reformed Church, Holland, Michigan. She is also director of the Holland Youth Chorale.

Norma deWaal Malefyt was a member of the *Songs for LiFE* hymnal committee and is one of the writers of the song notes. She is director of music at Hillcrest Christian Reformed Church, Hudsonville, Michigan, and coauthor of *Lift Up Your Hearts: Resources for Planning Worship.*

David J. Diephouse wrote the units on the Elements of Worship (Units 1-7). Diephouse is professor of history at Calvin College, Grand Rapids, Michigan, where he also teaches a course on worship. He is a member of the Christian Reformed Worship Study Committee.

Lynn Frens is one of the writers of the song notes. She has taught music at the elementary, secondary, and college levels in Illinois and Michigan. She is currently a children's worship leader at Faith Community Christian Reformed Church, Wyoming, Michigan.

Joanne Hamilton was a member of the *Songs for LiFE* hymnal committee. She recently moved from an administrative position in a Christian school in Ontario to Massachussetts, and is chair of the music committee at Norfolk Federated Church in Norfolk, Massachussetts.

Fran Huberts was a member of the *Songs for LiFE* hymnal committee. She teaches music at Cambridge Christian School, Cambridge, Ontario, and often leads workshops for music teachers in Ontario.

Charlotte Larsen was a member of the *Songs for LiFE* hymnal committee. She wrote all the lesson plan material (p. 326), including the model plans at the end of each unit. Larsen is director of music at the Ann Arbor, Michigan, Christian Reformed Church.

Nancy Mulder wrote "Teaching Songs to Children" (p. ix) and is also one of the writers of the song notes. Mulder is a former music teacher for elementary and middle school and for many years was children's music leader at Bethel Christian Reformed Church, Zeeland, Michigan.

Bert Polman was chair of the *Songs for LiFE* hymnal committee. He wrote the units on Living in God's World (Units 15-21). Polman is professor of music at Redeemer College, Ancaster, Ontario. He was also a member of the committee that prepared the 1987 *Psalter Hymnal*.

Kathy Sneller chose the signing motions for the songs and organized the signing index. Sneller is a children's worship leader at Eastern Avenue Christian Reformed Church, Grand Rapids, Michigan.

Richard Van Oss was a member of the *Songs for LiFE* hymnal committee and is one of the authors of the song notes. Van Oss is music director at First Reformed Church, Holland, Michigan, and a middle school teacher in Ravenna, Michigan.

Key to Music Terms, Symbols, and Abbreviations

c.	for Latin word (*circa* = "around") meaning "around a certain date"
Capo	for guitarists, to indicate an alternative key; see chart on page 430
CM	common meter (poetry in four-line stanzas, each with the following number of syllables: 8,6,8,6)
CMD	common meter double (eight lines)
D.C.	for Italian words (*da capo* = "the head") meaning "go back to the beginning"
Fine	Italian word meaning "the end" (pronounced "FEE-nay")
LM	long meter (poetry in four-line stanzas, each with eight syllables)
LMD	long meter double (eight lines)
ostinato	a persistently repeated pattern
patsch	tap hands on thighs (patschen is plural form)
SM	short meter (poetry in four-line stanzas, each with the following number of syllables: 6,6,8,6)
SMD	short meter double (eight lines)
⌐ ¬	introduction marks for an accompanist

Preface

Welcome to the Leader's Edition of *Songs for LiFE,* a hymnal for children of all ages, especially those in preschool through sixth grade. The Leader's Edition includes the entire hymnal as well as resources for using the hymnal in a worship education curriculum for children.

This hymnal and worship education project began with a vision of providing a resource for the "gathering time" in church-education programs, the time when all the children sing together as a group before dividing into smaller groups. Most church-education curricula provide abundant resources for those smaller group sessions, both for children and leaders. But they have seldom addressed the needs of children and leaders who sing and worship together. Therefore, we developed *Songs for LiFE* as part of the new LiFE curriculum (Living in Faith Everyday) published by CRC Publications in cooperation with the Reformed Church in America. A committee of six—three from the United States and three from Canada—worked for three years to develop the contents of the hymnal. Although it is a part of an entire curriculum, *Songs for LiFE* is intended for use in other settings as well: families, children's choirs, day schools, private study on keyboard, and as a supplementary pew hymnal.

Released in 1994, *Songs for LiFE* includes 252 songs carefully selected from different lands and cultures. You will find historic hymns of the faith, new psalm settings and Scripture choruses, and simple call-and-response songs. The keyboard arrangements are usually simple, with autoharp/guitar chords included. Many songs include descants and instrumental accompaniments.

The Leader's Edition incorporates the entire hymnal. However, the pages are larger to accommodate notes for every song. The song notes include information on the text such as Scripture references and ethnic origin; suggestions for teaching the song and using instruments; and ideas for having the children sing in congregational worship. Several songs have signing motions or additional musical accompaniments. A metronome marking with a suggested tempo is included on the top of every song page.

After the hymnal with song notes comes a worship education curriculum. The resources in this section will help gathering time leaders develop a plan for singing together, worshiping together, and learning something about what it means to worship God. Twenty-one units, from two to four weeks long, provide a structure for choosing songs according to particular themes. The themes include the elements of worship, the Christian year, and living in God's world. Several of the units on the elements of worship are also found in the worship committee manual *Lift Up Your Hearts: Resources for Planning Worship* (CRC Publications). The correlation is intentional: congregations that use both resources will have a consistent approach to planning worship.

Finally, the Leader's Edition contains a wealth of indexes. In addition to the typical hymnal indexes, there are many more, including descriptions of all the signing motions recommended on the song pages. The thematic approach, along with a complete Scripture reference index, will give ample opportunity for worship planners to involve children in congregational worship.

Our thanks go to the many people who helped prepare this collection of songs and resources to give expression to our faith and bring praise to God. May these songs help us live in faith every day, and may many of these songs become for us songs for a life of worship.

Emily R. Brink, *editor*

Introduction: Teaching Songs to Children

Using the Leader's Edition of *Songs for LiFE* assumes a measure of musical training and a desire to worship together with children. Some congregations enjoy a wealth of musical talent, trained musicians, and willing leaders for teaching songs to children. Others may have few members with a background in music or in teaching. This introduction is intended to give encouragement and support to those with little background. For those with more training in music education, the ideas presented here may offer some good reminders and new ideas about teaching songs to children.

Basic Qualifications

Jesus summarized the law in terms of loving God above all and our neighbor as ourselves. The first qualifications for being an effective children's leader are similar.

1. *A love for God.* 1 Corinthians 10:31b makes a good motto: "Whatever you do, do it all for the glory of God." The gathering time can be a time for your own spiritual growth as you worship together with the children.

2. *A love for children.* The gathering time is an opportunity to show your love for the children, giving them a firm foundation that will forever affect their lives. Realize the important role music can play in children's lives, and be committed to helping them grow into a closer relationship with Jesus Christ. Learn something about the different characteristics of children at different ages. Every child is created in God's image.

3. *A love of singing.* Children will model their love of singing after those who lead them. Realize the importance of singing together as a community-building activity that joins us together as no other activity can. Teaching children to sing prepares them for a life of worship.

4. *Musical knowledge and skills.* These include the following abilities:

   - to sing on pitch, and to be willing to sing unaccompanied
   - to sing with a clear natural tone, using good enunciation
   - to hear when children sing on or off pitch
   - to read music, both pitches and rhythms
   - to be able to cue children clearly for entrances and cutoffs

   If you have all these skills except for the ability to read music, you could still lead children in the gathering time together with a pianist. In order to be an effective team, you will require more preparation and a willingness to share leadership in learning new songs.

5. *A creative bent.* An active imagination, and your willingness to use it, is crucial. Children love to be challenged with creative ways of learning and doing.

6. *Commitment to preparation.* As in all teaching, time spent in preparation is usually at least double the time spent with the children. It goes without saying that you cannot teach a song unless you know it well.

7. *Leadership skills.* These include the ability to develop a relationship of mutual enjoyment with children. You will need the support of parents, church school staff, the congregation, pastors, worship committee members, and other musicians.

Helping Children Use *Songs for LiFE*

Depending on their ages, the children you lead may or may not be using copies of the *Songs for LiFE* hymnal. Younger children who do not yet read need to learn by rote, perhaps with the aid of charts. Older children, though, will benefit greatly from learning to use the hymnal. They will be able to learn songs more quickly, and so can also sing more songs. Teach children how to "read" a hymnal, taking advantage of the information available to them.

Parents may already have helped children learn how to read the lines of text in stanza arrangements. Remember that when looking at a song with several stanzas, a child's first inclination is to read the lines in order under each other. Older children can help the younger ones by tracing the lines with their fingers.

Encourage children to notice who wrote the song. You may wish to mention something about the author or composer, or the date the song was written. Some songs were even written by children! Older children will also enjoy learning about the meter and tune name. The numbers simply refer to the number of syllables of text in each phrase. Sometimes the tune name has special meaning, which the song notes will point out. All that information on the bottom of the page is there for a purpose!

Unlike the children's edition of the hymnal, this Leader's Edition also includes a metronome marking at the top of the song page.

Introducing a New Song
Because the gathering time is usually very short, there is no time to lose. The way you introduce and present a new song is crucial—be sure you know the song well and have thought through ways to introduce each specific song. The song notes will be very helpful. Here are a few ideas to keep in mind.

- Use visuals to arouse interest. Every age truly appreciates seeing something, but visuals are especially important for younger children who cannot read. A visual can be any appropriate object, such as a candle, crown, flower, or toy. Let very young children hold and touch the objects. A poster is another kind of visual. Make your posters big and bright, using pictures and symbols but very few words.

- Tell a (very brief) story about the composer, about the background of the song, or about

an experience you had that makes it meaningful to you.

- Mention key words and ideas in the text that help children understand why they are learning this particular song. If the song is based on a Bible story, encourage older children to help by finding it in the Bible.

- Sing the song for the children. If a recording is available, perhaps you could play it while the children are settling down before you actually begin. But when teaching it, your singing is far preferable to listening to a recording. Children want and need to connect with you.

- Continually encourage the children as they are learning the song. Tell your singers the song is especially for them. Plenty of encouragement will motivate children to really concentrate and learn the song.

Teaching the Melody
After you have introduced the song, spend additional sessions concentrating on the words, rhythms, and melody. Often it is best not to separate the words from the melody; they are, after all, a unit. So teaching the text in its rhythmic and melodic context makes good sense, especially if broken down into manageable units like pairs of phrases or just a refrain. Some songs include words that need explanation; as you teach the song, make sure the children understand what they are singing.

Some melodies are so simple that, after hearing them once or twice, the children can begin to join in. Other melodies are longer, more complex, or have tricky spots, either in the pitches or in the rhythms. Those songs need some study to determine just where the tricky spots are and how to teach them. Often the song notes will refer to the basic structure of the piece using alphabetical letters. For example, a song in ABA form might have three sections of text but only two different sections of music to learn.

One excellent method is to "line out" the song; that is, sing the song phrase by phrase, instructing the children to echo each phrase after you. After learning shorter phrases, combine them, using longer lines. Learn simple refrains or repeated parts first, remembering that you may want to teach only these parts to very young singers.

From the start, model good posture, good breathing, and good enunciation of the text. Since children will imitate you from the very beginning, always pronounce the words correctly and musically when you sing. That is, use good, rounded vowels, and enunciate all consonants, especially beginning and ending ones. As you teach the song, remind the children that they do not sing only for themselves; their singing communicates to others and to God.

Encourage your singers to produce a "sweet" sound, and allow no "playground voices." Work on singing with an open throat, resonating the sound in the head (singing in the upper register), always encouraging mouths open wide, with the lower jaw dropped. Since good singing is also dependent on good breathing, always give clear cues to breathe. Children should be ready to sing: mouths open, eyes round and sparkling, alert and anticipating. You can include visuals to illustrate how to produce a good sound. Keep little surprises in your pockets, and pull them out as the need for them arises. Rubber bands (used to demonstrate open mouths), puppets, tennis balls (cut slit for mouth, and draw eyes and nose to demonstrate open mouth and alert faces), and pipe cleaners (used to demonstrate posture), all are handy little tools.

To teach the melodic direction of the melody, you may wish to trace the up and down movement by tracing the melody with your hand. Children will benefit from noticing when the melody leaps up, or floats down, or climbs, for example. Explain that you are "drawing" the melody with your hands—not teaching more motions! If some of the melodic patterns are still tricky, concentrate on the pitches without the words by humming or singing a phrase on a neutral syllable such as "tah" or "lah." If some of the rhythms are tricky, it may help to speak the text rhythm or clap out the patterns. The echo method could be used here too, with the children speaking or clapping patterns after you.

To help children sing phrases rather than individual notes, encourage them to think in longer lines and phrases, perhaps by pulling an imaginary or actual scarf through your fingers.

As you teach melody and rhythm, be active! Practice hand clapping, finger snapping, and thigh patting. Make sounds that reflect the music; that is, tap fingers together for a softer moment, or fill in a syncopation (shifted accent) with a clap. Use space by clapping high, low, left, or right. (Remember to teach the students to mirror: always do the action on the same side as the leader.) As you get active, teach your children to remember these rules:

- Listen louder than you sing.
- Sing louder than you clap.
- Clap softer than you sing or listen.

An easy way to add variety is to change your singing formation. Try singing in a circle. Young children sing best this way. With a larger group, assign groups to face each other as they sing. On occasion, perhaps when preparing for a processional, lead the singers through the rows or around the room.

Learning a song need not be tedious. Make it an enjoyable time for you and your students.

Teaching and Memorizing the Words

Younger children who do not read will need to memorize the words. Older children who are holding copies of *Songs for LiFE* should also be encouraged to memorize some songs. In all fairness, do not ask children to memorize a song unless you also have it memorized! If you would like to rely on the hymnal as you sing, so would they, if they can read.

The question method is one of many tools you can use to help children learn a text. Sing the song, asking the children to listen for something specific. Either ask everyone the same question or include variety by assigning each row or age group to listen for something different. Ask a question about the text, evoking an answer that is a specific word or phrase from the song. Or instruct children to listen for a specific word or phrase and count how many times they hear it, and/or to stand every time they hear it. Remember to help young children with these activities by holding up your fingers and giving them clear cues.

Use your imagination when teaching the words of a song. One way to incorporate action into the learning is to use motions that correlate with words, or learn the signing motions based on American Sign Language. Signing and singing are two separate languages, and each will help reinforce the other. Movement is another way to use action in your teaching. For example, if the song says "step," let everyone take a step, or if it says "turn," instruct everyone to turn. As you enjoy motions and movement, be wholehearted! If hands must point up, arms should fully stretch out, not just halfway. Train everyone to mirror your motions. Movement can lead to another help for learning songs: dramatization. Your singers can have great fun becoming actors and actresses, especially if you ask for their suggestions.

"Visuals" are another great tool for teaching the words of a song. Design signs with symbols or pictures that correlate with the words. Any size poster board works well; attach a slender piece of smooth wood with masking tape to make an excellent "handle" for your sign. Be imaginative also in your use of the signs. For example, encourage students to hold them up at the proper time, arrange them in the proper order, or march with them. Young children especially enjoy this.

Song charts (posters that review the complete song) give singers a good overview of the entire text. If you are working with older children who can read, include some words and assign singers to fill in blanks or put the phrases in the correct order. Poster board is good material, but overheads also work well. Remember to remove the charts after they have been used—they should not become a necessary crutch!

Flannel boards are also good visuals. They work especially well for story songs. Ask children to help illustrate the story as the song is sung.

Any appropriate object can serve as a visual. Display objects in the room or let various children hold them. Little play people, a globe, a prism, rocks, a crown, and stuffed animals are just a few examples. Puppets are a favorite for children of all ages. These fun creatures can be bought, sewn, or simply made out of paper bags. Puppets can do all sorts of things: ask questions, sing, or act silly. Children can help animate the puppets.

As you teach the text, keep your mind and the minds of the children alert. Do this by thinking about what you are singing and by including plenty of variety. Think of as many ways as possible to repeat words and phrases and still keep the children's attention. Have them echo words or phrases, complete a phrase, or fill in blanks. Divide the group in half, instructing one half to begin a sentence, the other half to end it. As you sing, take advantage of repeated words or phrases: ask the group to always respond in the same way when they appear. Remember that young children enjoy repetition—they actually look forward to singing the same song each week!

Working with an Accompanist

Children (and adults) often enjoy singing as they work or play or ride in the car. No accompaniment is available then, nor is it necessary. Develop the confidence to sing without accompaniment. Teaching a song to young children will be simpler if they concentrate only on listening to your voice.

That said, an accompanist provides musical interest and can be a great aid in teaching as well. Guitar or autoharp are actually better instruments than piano for providing simple accompaniments that support children's voices. If you do need some additional help in teaching the melody, the accompanist can play the melody on the piano or on another treble instrument such as the violin or flute. As the children are learning the melody, the pianist can gradually add accompaniment, taking care to support, not dominate, the children's singing. Pianists should play lightly and musically. It is important not to add too much variety in accompaniment while learning a song.

One of the basic requirements of working with an accompanist is to make introductions clear and concise. No matter how simple they may be, always plan introductions. Especially for younger children, a single starting pitch is often just fine. Introduction marks (⌐ ¬) are provided for almost all of the songs; they can be shortened but seldom lengthened. Look at the accompanist when directing the beginning of the introduction but then look immediately to the children, establishing eye contact so that you come in together. Use the same introduction consistently so that children will be prepared to come in when you give them a cue.

The rhythm of the song begins with the introduction. When you cue the children to begin, they simply join the rhythmic flow that has already begun. That same rhythmic flow should last through the entire song; don't stop and start at the end of each stanza. The best rule of thumb at the end of stanzas is to conduct one extra measure to give the children time for a good breath to begin the next stanza.

Also work on endings. Help the children hold out longer notes and help them finish together at the conclusion. Give clear cutoff motions with a little preparatory motion as a signal. Practice endings just as you practice beginnings. Train your singers to "keep the mood": the song is not concluded until the accompaniment is finished.

Be sure to communicate and discuss plans and goals with your accompanist. Give him or her a simple copy of your plan and briefly explain what you expect. Provide necessary copies of the songs, including introductions, interludes, and endings, all well-marked. Everyone will benefit if you spend some time rehearsing together so that you are truly working together as a team. With encouragement and some coaching, middle school and high school pianists often make wonderful accompanists. Be sure to give them the music well in advance to provide ample preparation time. Remember to thank your pianist and other guest musicians, and help your group appreciate them as well!

Children as Accompanists

Reward children for learning a song by adding another layer of interest: instruments! Even the youngest children can play a variety of rhythm instruments. Be keenly aware of the different sounds made by different instruments, and use them according to the sense of the song text. Don't buy cheap toys; invest in real instruments. A good set of rhythm instruments includes tambourines (small ones are just fine), triangles, rhythm sticks, finger cymbals, a small hand drum, bongo drum, and maracas. Teach young singers how to properly play and hold instruments. It is a good idea to let children try each instrument first before playing with the group.

Tone bells, handbells, or Orff instruments (such as xylophones, metallophones, and glockenspiels) work especially well with older children. If Orff instruments are new to you, try to attend a workshop to get a good introduction to using these wonderful instruments. Purchasing Orff instruments for your church would be a major investment, but well worth it if used on a regular basis. Children love playing them, and congregations delight in hearing the creative patterns that lend a gentle and delightful accompaniment without obscuring children's voices.

As with rhythm instruments, let children play the instruments alone first. Make sure players know how to hold mallets and how to strike the instruments, pretending they are striking a raindrop off the tip of their finger. Most important, remember to give constant encouragement to help build confidence.

Other types of instruments to include are students' own band or orchestra instruments. They are good for easy descants, or they can play another second part, either aiding a certain group or playing the part alone. These instruments can also help on a round or with the introduction. Many songs include chords for the guitar or autoharp, and you should also try to use these instruments. When you give students the opportunity, you will be surprised at their ability!

Keep in mind that the suggestions given above about planning introductions are even more important when involving children as accompanists.

More Ideas and Suggestions

Teaching songs to young singers always includes words, melody, and rhythm. Harmony, however, is a musical quality that average young voices cannot grasp quite as easily. One way to introduce your singers to this musical component and have a great deal of fun with it is by teaching them rounds and canons. A few basic hints will help you accomplish your task.

First, make sure everyone knows the complete song well. Begin singing the round in a very simple manner: instruct the complete group to be part 1, and assign part 2 to a single leader or the pianist. Then assign a part to the adults sitting with your children. Finally, divide the children, making sure each group has an equal amount of strong singers. Listen to each group sing alone first; if necessary, space the groups apart. Use piano, instruments, or leaders to help each group. As you direct, be sure to cue in each group, including the repeats and endings. Do your homework ahead of time and know where each group makes its entrance. Especially help each part hold out longer notes so they receive their full value, always keeping a steady main beat. Make sure everyone has proper instructions: how many times the song is sung, and how to conclude the round. A round can be effectively concluded either by having each part finish alone or by having each part repeat the last phrase, so that everyone finishes together. By singing rounds and canons, children can experience the joys of harmony at a very early age!

Be sure to encourage solos or small group singing as well. A good time to do this is when there are added stanzas or a new idea in the middle of a song. Singers from grades 3-6 are often able to take part in this, but young singers should not be ignored.

Motivate your group to constantly improve by evaluating them. In the Olympics a "10" is the best score. Don't be afraid to rate your group's singing. Set goals for them and tell them what they have to do to earn a certain number.

Finally, treat your singers as a team. Constantly remind them that every single member is important, and help them realize that what each person does or doesn't do really counts. Just as every successful sports team needs a good coach, so does a good singing team. Be an honorable coach: stay qualified, introduce and motivate, teach words, melody, and rhythm, and always reinforce proper singing techniques!

Good singing technique also includes undivided attention. Do not start singing without it. A wonderful tool to use now and then that will help singers project their voices is a target. Assign anything in the room to be the target or make one from construction paper with a heart in the middle. Attach it to the wall and instruct the group to sing to the target or "sing to the heart."

Be sure to enforce one basic rule of singing: no gum chewing or candy eating. This rule applies to everyone, including the accompanists and leaders.

You will undoubtedly add to these ideas and suggestions. Following is a brief summary of tips:

1. Stretch your imagination to its limits at all times.

2. Use repetition in a creative way, employing as much variety as possible.

3. Be totally committed and full of boundless energy.

4. Show personal interest in your singers. Learn their names; let them know they are a team of special people.

5. Be complimentary.

6. Use all of your available resources, including other leaders, older students, people from your congregation, and parents.

7. Know the songs well before you teach them to the children.

8. Write out a good plan for each session. Don't be afraid to include small details,

even writing out some of your exact words. Think every minute of your session through. Practice it from start to finish, making sure you are completely prepared. Make extra copies of your plan for your accompanist and anyone else involved with the session. Practicing with your accompanist will make things proceed in a much smoother fashion.

9. Always give good cues. Either conduct simple beats or show the melody direction.

10. Enjoy your singing and make learning fun!

May the Lord bless you as you work in God's kingdom, using music to help children know Jesus, and guiding them as they grow into a closer relationship with him. "Whatever you do, whether in word or deed, do it all in the name of the Lord Jesus, giving thanks to God the Father through him" (Col. 3:17).

Songs
with
Song Notes

Meeting with God's People

A Psalm for Singing

♩ = 132

Songs for LiFE begins with an invitation to sing "unto the Lord," the "Rock of our salvation" (Ps. 95). Explain that God is often referred to as a rock. Rocks are strong, and rocky places, like those in Israel, make good hiding places. So it makes sense that rocks are often used to symbolize God's unfailing strength as a refuge.

Sing this song joyfully with strong voices! The melody is made up of fast-moving notes followed by long-held notes. Make sure the children sing through each phrase on one good breath, holding the long notes, and breathing only when there is a period or exclamation point. On the first section, encourage the children to hold the long notes by clapping on beats 2 and 3.

The first section may also be sung in canon on the repeat. Group two begins when the first group reaches ②. The canon can follow all the way through the section or you may prefer a unison ending (beginning at "unto the Rock"); that may be a more satisfying ending.

For a more elaborate treatment, get two copies (for conductor and accompanist) of the original anthem (in F). The middle section is in two parts (one could be played by an instrument), and the ending is extended. The children could still sing from this hymnal.

In congregational worship, sing as a gathering song, call to worship, or introit. Try pairing with another gathering or praise song in the key of D (7, 8, 9) or in G (2, 10-14).

May be sung in canon on the repeat

Come, let us sing un-to the Lord! Come, let us sing un-to the Lord! And let us make a joy-ful noise un-to the Rock of our sal - va - tion! The Lord is a great God and a great King o - ver all the earth. The Lord is a

Words: Psalm 95:1-3; adapted from the anthem *A Psalm for Singing*
Music: Charles Kirby II, 1975; arranged by Norma de Waal Malefyt, 1992

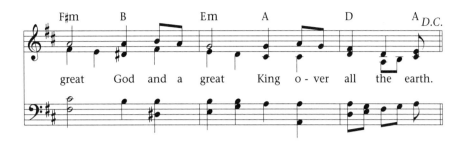

great God and a great King o-ver all the earth.

♩ = 132

Come, Let Us Gather 2

♩ = 132

Round

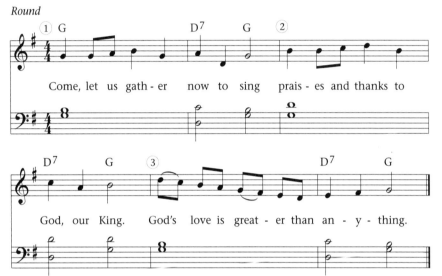

Come, let us gath-er now to sing prais-es and thanks to God, our King. God's love is great-er than an-y-thing.

Orff instrument patterns

Triangle or soprano glockenspiel *Alto xylophone*

Alto glockenspiel *Bass xylophone*

Words and Music: traditional; arranged by Richard L. Van Oss, 1991
Arr. © 1994, CRC Publications

This traditional round is a reminder to praise and thank God for his love, which "is greater than anything."

Sing with strong voices, learning the melody well before trying it as a three-part round. Point out that the first and second phrases have the same rhythm. The melody in the second measure drops all the way down to D; the fourth measure drops only a third.

Three C instruments could join the voices in the round. In addition, rhythm instruments could repeatedly play the ♩♩♩ pattern found in measures 2, 4, and 6. You may also want to experiment with other rhythm patterns.

In congregational worship, sing as a gathering song, introit, or call to worship. First sing all together and then perhaps as a round, with a leader bringing in the adult choir, children's choir, and congregation. Sing two or three times, and perhaps pair with another song in G (e.g., 12, 15, or 19).

3 This Is the Day

𝅘𝅥 = 132

Arrange some smiley faces around your room to introduce this joyful song celebrating this day of the Lord (Ps. 118:24). Why are we happy? Because God made today (st. 1), he rose again (st. 2), and sent his Spirit (st. 3). Create other stanzas to the song as well:

These are our friends,
    that the Lord has made;
we will rejoice
    and be glad with them.

At the beginning or end of the Christian year, substitute "year" for "day" to rejoice in the year God has created.

This melody can easily be taught by following *Leader* and *All.* After children know the melody, divide into two groups and sing antiphonally, with all on the higher middle section and the final phrase. Have fun with clapping on every beat or on beats 2 and 4. Or try this variation: *hands, hands, thighs, thighs* or *hands, hands, thighs, snap.*

Add the different instrumental rhythm patterns one at a time. Children find them easier to play when making sound patterns on the beats such as

- *triangle:* "shh, shh, shh, walk"
- *tambourine:* "this is the day, shh"
- *maracas/sand blocks:* "happy singing, happy playing"

Sing in congregational worship on any occasion for praise, as a call to worship, or opening hymn. Children will enjoy singing antiphonally with the congregation.

Words: stanza 1, Psalm 118:24, paraphrased by Les Garrett, 1967; stanzas 2-3 traditional
Music: Les Garrett, 1967

THIS IS THE DAY
Capo 1

this is the day, this is the day that the Lord has made.
this is the day, this is the day when he rose a - gain.
this is the day, this is the day when the Spir - it came.

Rhythm patterns
Triangle   Tambourine   Maracas/Sand blocks

♩ = 108

Come into His Presence 4

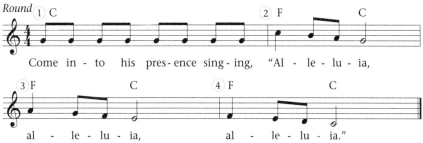

Round
Come in - to his pres - ence sing - ing, "Al - le - lu - ia,

al - le - lu - ia,   al - le - lu - ia."

Other stanzas may be added:

Come into his presence singing,
   "Jesus is Lord." *(Easter, Ascension)*
   "Worthy the Lamb." *(Lent)*
   "Glory to God." *(Christmas)*

Final stanza each time (especially appropriate to sing as a round):

   Praise the Lord together singing, "Alleluia . . . ."

Words and Music: anonymous

People come to worship with many different feelings. Some of those feelings are expressed in the various stanzas of this song. Have the children suggest other verses to reflect how they feel, such as "Come into his presence singing, I love you Lord."

This song may be sung as a four-part round. Unaccompanied is best, but light accompaniment on guitar or autoharp may be used. Ask one child to keep the beat on a G using a tuned bell, choir chime, handbell, or Orff instrument.

This would make a good processional (in unison) as the children enter the worship center. Have the children sing as a call to worship; on the final stanza, bring in different groups until all are singing in a round.

Based on Psalm 122, this is a song the Israelites sang together with friends and family as they journeyed from their villages to Jerusalem to worship God in the temple. They were glad because when they worshiped and obeyed God, they would find true peace and justice. Explain to the children that "justice" (st. 3) means "being fair." Justice and peace come when all people of all races and all colors, rich and poor, close by and far away, are treated fairly. Creation also needs to be treated fairly.

The refrain is simple enough to teach by rote to even the youngest children; have them repeat each short phrase after you. Ask older children or soloists to sing the stanzas with clear and confident voices, perhaps different groups on each of the three stanzas. Keep the beat going—the refrain starts right after each stanza. The descant instrument—any C instrument (flute, recorder, violin, or oboe)— could help the children by playing along on the melody. When the melody is secure, add the descant.

In congregational worship, sing as a call to worship or as part of the Scriptures for the day. Invite all to sing the refrain with (perhaps different groups of) children singing the stanzas. Or ask a child to read the psalm directly from the Bible, with all the children singing the refrain before the reading of verse 1 and after verses 2, 5, and 9.

5 In the House of Our God

♩ = 108

Refrain

In the house of our God, in the house of our God,
we give praise to the Lord in the house of our God.

1 I was glad____ when they said: "Let us go____ to God's house!" and now with joy we are stand - ing.
2 Je - ru - sa - lem is built as the cit - y of our God; and here the peo - ple are sing - ing.
3 It is here that we find peace for our fam - i - lies and friends; and here we find true____ jus - tice.

Repeat refrain

Descant
Refrain

Words and Music: Christopher Walker, 1990, based on Psalm 122
© 1988, 1989, 1990, Christopher Walker. Published by OCP Publications. All rights reserved.

Capo 5

♩ = 69

Come Bless the Lord

Words: Psalm 134:1-2
Music: traditional, arranged by Emily R. Brink, 1992
Arr. © 1994, CRC Publications

Capo 3

How can a person bless the Lord? By praising him! Bless and praise mean the same thing here. This song is taken directly from Psalm 134:1-2. (Ask one of the children to read this for your group.) In Bible times, worshipers sang this psalm as they were about to leave the temple after the evening service. They sang to the Levites who were staying on temple watch through the night.

Introduce the song by singing it. Then ask

* How many times do you hear "bless the Lord?"

* Who are the servants of the Lord? (The Levites)

* Why lift up your hands? (That was a posture for prayer.)

A good way to memorize the words is to speak the beginning of each line, omitting the last word. Instruct the children to finish the phrase. Repeat, omitting more and more words for the children to include.

Learn the main melody (without the descant) first. To help children hold the long notes, try these motions:

1. Hand motions: show each phrase with a long, moving, hand motion, alternating hands for every phrase. Pretend everyone is pulling long scarves through the air. (Take a scarf and demonstrate.)

2. Stepping motions: take a step (in place) for every beat of the echo part. Step in place, or have fun moving first left, then right.

After children know the melody, introduce the descant with piano or flute. Ask a few older children to sing it; show them with your hand motions that sometimes the echo simply repeats, other times it is higher or different. Sing twice: first, all on the melody, then in two groups, with a smaller group on the echo/descant, along with instrument.

In worship, sing as a gathering song of praise or a concluding blessing, perhaps following a verbal blessing using the words of Psalm 134.

7 Allelu

♩ = 76

1 Come and bless, come and praise, come and praise the liv-ing God.
2 Come and seek, come and find, come and find the liv-ing God.
3 Come and hear, come and know, come and know the liv-ing God.
4 Al - le - lu, al - le - lu, al - le - lu - ia, Je - sus Christ.

Al - le - lu, al - le - lu, al - le - lu - ia, Je - sus Christ.

Seasonal verse:

5 Come behold, come and see,
   come and see the newborn babe.
   Allelu, allelu, alleluia, Jesus Christ.

This song is an invitation to "allelu" God. *Allelu* (Greek) or *hallelu* (Hebrew) means "praise," and *Jah* means "God." The whole word "Alleluia" means "praise God." This song lists several ways to "praise the Lord." Did you know that fourteen Psalms begin with "Praise the Lord!" (NIV)? Others end with those words. Stanza 1 is a reminder to do just that. Stanza 2 is based on Matthew 7:7: "Ask and it will be given to you; seek and you will find; knock and the door will be opened to you," or Isaiah 55:6: "Seek the Lord while he may be found; call on him while he is near."

The music is easy to learn. Point out that the first half of the song has the same melody as the second half except for the last note. Try dividing the children into two groups. Group 1 could sing the first measure, group 2 the second, and both groups sing the third and fourth measures. The "allelus" could be performed in the same manner. Add rhythm instruments playing the rhythm of the first measure throughout.

This song makes a good opening or call to worship. Sing stanza 2 before a prayer; stanza 3 before the Scripture lesson or sermon. Stanza 4 makes a good response to the assurance of pardon, the offering, or the benediction.

Words: Mimi Farra, 1971
Music: Mimi Farra, 1971; arranged by Norma de Waal Malefyt, 1992

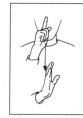

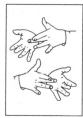

Come   *Bless*   *Praise*   *God*   *Allelu*   *Jesus*   *Christ*

See Signing Index for stanzas 2-5.

♩ = 116

I Will Sing, I Will Sing 8

For piano or Orff instruments

1 I will sing, I will sing a song un-to the Lord.
2 We will come, we will come as one be-fore the Lord.

I will sing, I will sing a song un-to the Lord.
We will come, we will come as one be-fore the Lord.

I will sing, I will sing a song un-to the Lord.
We will come, we will come as one be-fore the Lord.

Al - le - lu - ia, glo - ry to the Lord.

3 In his name, in his name we have the victory. (3x)
  Alleluia, glory to the Lamb.

4 Allelu, alleluia, glory to the Lord. (3x)
  Alleluia, glory to the Lord.

Fingertips on palm:

Words and Music: Max Dyer

Children of all ages will enjoy singing this energetic praise chorus. Each stanza has only one line of text, followed by the repeated refrain line (notice the new last word in st. 3).

Children will enjoy creating new stanzas as well; for example "We will go, we will go to serve the living God" would be a good ending stanza.

Mastering the syncopation will be the main challenge in learning this song. Accent all the quarter notes, especially the tied notes, where the word jumps ahead of the regular beat in joyful eagerness. It may be easier for the children to tap the same syncopated melodic rhythm while they sing instead of the regular rhythmic pattern given below the music. Ask some children to tap the pattern while the others sing, then switch groups. Eventually, some of the children may be able to combine the singing and tapping patterns.

This song needs little accompaniment. Tap finger tips on palms or pat thighs (patsch) to encourage a brighter, lighter tone (rather than clapping). Tambourine, hand drum or other percussive instruments could also play this ostinato pattern. Instead of keyboard, try Orff instruments or cello (plucking) on the bass line, with guitar or autoharp on the chords. Also consider adding a flute or recorder on the melody line with the lower Orff xylophone playing the bass line.

Whatever you choose, sing at a cheerful tempo.

Sing this chorus as an opening song of praise or as part of a series of praise songs within a service. It is placed here between two other songs in the same key that could be linked together.

Psalm 100 is one of the first psalms children commit to memory. This song captures the simple praise of that psalm. It is full of thanksgiving and the joy of entering into God's presence.

The traditional tune reflects the joy of the words. It should be sung joyfully and with spirit. Clap two eighth notes on beat 4 of each measure that begins "he has made me glad." In addition to those suggested, other rhythm instruments could be played on every beat by the youngest children. Have a recorder or flute play along on the melody also.

This song could be sung by two groups alternately singing the phrases. Group 1 would sing the first phrase, group 2 the second, and so on, with both groups singing together on the last phrase only or starting at "he has made me glad." Try singing antiphonally with the two groups not standing next to each other.

This song would make a wonderful processional, an introit, or call to worship. To extend your praise, try pairing it with 8, which is in the same key.

9 I Will Enter His Gates

♩ = 132

Words: from Psalm 100
Music: traditional, arranged by Christopher Norton
Arr. © 1989, Harper Collins Religious, London. Used by permission.

will re - joice, for he has made me glad.

He has made me glad; he has made me glad. I

will re - joice, for he has made me glad.

Rhythm Patterns

Over 400 years ago, William Kethe, a minister, wrote Psalm 100 in his own words. Christians around the world have been singing his beautiful poetry ever since. To introduce this text, ask one of the children to read the related verses from the Bible. Then ask questions to determine key words for each stanza. For example,

- What words remind you of happiness? st. 1 (v. 1-2)

- What words remind you of creation? st. 2 (v. 3)

- What words remind you of worship? st. 3 (v. 4)

- What words remind you of God's care? st. 4 (v. 5)

Children will likely know this famous hymn tune, found in most hymnals. It first appeared over 400 years ago in the Genevan Psalter, a songbook used by John Calvin to help people sing the psalms. Because it is often sung with Psalm 100, this melody has been given the name OLD HUNDREDTH. Children can find that name in the lower right hand corner of the song page.

This song can be sung at any time as a call to worship or song of praise. It is possible to build an entire service on Psalm 100 using the themes listed above. Each section could begin by singing the related stanza. Conclude the service with the doxology (11).

10 All People That on Earth Do Dwell

♩ = 72

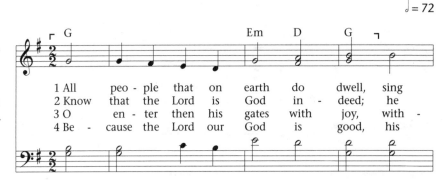

1 All peo - ple that on earth do dwell, sing
2 Know that the Lord is God in - deed; he
3 O en - ter then his gates with joy, with -
4 Be - cause the Lord our God is good, his

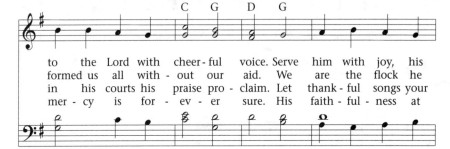

to the Lord with cheer - ful voice. Serve him with joy, his
formed us all with - out our aid. We are the flock he
in his courts his praise pro - claim. Let thank - ful songs your
mer - cy is for - ev - er sure. His faith - ful - ness at

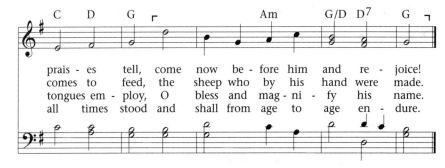

prais - es tell, come now be - fore him and re - joice!
comes to feed, the sheep who by his hand were made.
tongues em - ploy, O bless and mag - ni - fy his name.
all times stood and shall from age to age en - dure.

Words: Psalm 100; versified by William Kethe, 1561
Music: Louis Bourgeois, 1551

LM
OLD HUNDREDTH

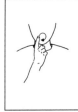

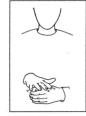

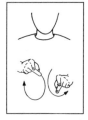

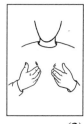

Praise   *God*   *Whom*   *Blessings*   *Flow*   *Creatures (1)*   *(2)*

Praise God, from Whom All Blessings Flow 11

Praise God, from whom all blessings flow;
   Praise him, all creatures here below;
Praise him above, ye heavenly host;
   Praise Father, Son, and Holy Ghost. Amen.

Words: Thomas Ken, 1709
Music: OLD HUNDREDTH, see no. 10

Originally one stanza of another hymn (see 78), these words have become loved as a doxology set to the tune OLD HUNDREDTH (see 10). A doxology is a song of glory to God, often sung at the conclusion of worship or of a section of the service. This doxology may be the best known hymn in the English language. (Words to be signed begin on previous page.)

♩ = 60

Jesus, Jesus, Praise Him 12

1 Je - sus, Je - sus, praise* him in the morn - ing,
praise* him at the noon - time; Je - sus, Je - sus,
praise* him when the sun goes down.

* 2 love him   3 serve him   4 thank him   5 trust him

Words and Music: traditional American

Open your session with this lively praise song and encourage your children to joyfully worship Jesus anytime—morning, noon, and night. Young children will enjoy making up additional stanzas as well. Teach it by rote, one phrase at a time. Use simple motions (arms left, overhead, right) to depict the sun rising, overhead, and setting.

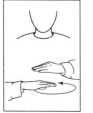

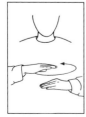
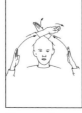

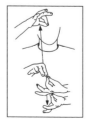

Below   *Above*   *Heavenly host*   *Father*   *Son (Jesus)*   *Holy Ghost*

Mary's song of praise on learning she was to become the mother of Jesus (Luke 1:46-49; see 14) has become one of the most loved and sung hymns of the church. For us, Mary's song is a hymn of praise to Christ, "the Lord who is my Savior." To help the children understand the word "magnify," explain that a magnifying glass makes things look bigger. We use the word when we want to say that our God is very large and great.

The Community of Taize is an ecumenical monastic community and retreat center in France. The brothers there developed a style of worship and prayer that continues to draw thousands of visitors, especially young people, from all over the world. To accommodate the lack of a common language for prayer, Jacques Berthier created a style of song in Latin that is short, repetitious, and often in canon. On the repetitions, variety comes from the descant parts, which can be layered on in various combinations. As people brought these songs back to North America, many were translated into English (see 124, 134, and 168).

You can sing this Magnificat in many ways, ranging from simple unison to a double four-part round (eight parts!). Begin by singing one phrase at a time, the children repeating after you. Sing the dotted rhythms crisply, distinguishing them from the regular eighth-note rhythms. When children know the melody, add an instrument on the descant part. Or try singing as a two-part round, dividing the children into two groups. Guitar and string bass would provide a de-

13 Magnify the Lord

♩ = 96

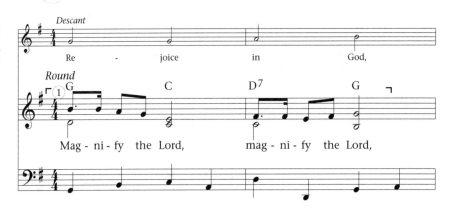

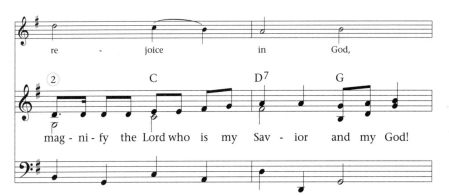

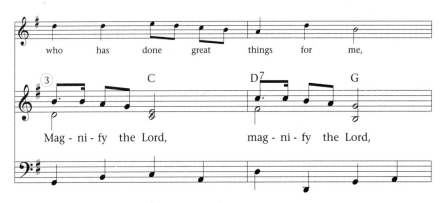

Words: Bert Polman, 1985; based on the Song of Mary, Luke 1:46-49
Music: Jacques Berthier, 1984
Music © 1984, G.I.A. Publications. All rights reserved.

MAGNIFICAT

who   has   done   great   things   for   me.

mag - ni - fy   the Lord who   is   my   Sav - ior!

lightful accompaniment to the harmonies produced by the round.

Sing in congregational worship for any time of praise. The children begin in unison. Then, if your congregation knows it well, have the children repeat as a two-part round, adding the congregation as the third and fourth parts, perhaps layering the adult choir on top of that with the four-part descant! Add instruments on any and all parts.

Magnificat 14

My soul praises the Lord;
 my heart rejoices in God my Savior,
because he has shown his concern for his humble servant girl.
From now on, all people will say that I am blessed,
 because the Powerful One has done great things for me.
 His name is holy. *Refrain (no. 13)*

God will show his mercy forever and ever
 to those who worship and serve him.
He has done mighty deeds by his power.
He has scattered the people who are proud
 and think great things about themselves. *Refrain*

He has brought down rulers from their thrones
 and raised up the humble.
He has filled the hungry with good things
 and sent the rich away with nothing. *Refrain*

He has helped his servant, the people of Israel,
 remembering to show them mercy
as he promised to our ancestors,
 to Abraham and to his children forever. *Refrain*

Words: The Song of Mary, Luke 1:46-55 (New Century Version)

Here is the text of the song Mary sang when she learned she would become the mother of Jesus. The title comes from the Latin word *magnificat*, from which we get the English word "magnify." For hundreds of years, Latin was the language of the church, so composers who wrote music for Mary's song used Latin. Mary's song was so well known that just the first word was enough to identify it; and it was so important that it was (and still is in many churches) sung every afternoon.

In congregational worship, ask one child to read the text, interspersed with the singing of "Magnify the Lord" (13). This combination of reading and singing ties the whole text of Mary's song together with the joyful "exclamation" of praise based on just the first part of that text.

Psalm 8 is a song of praise to our Creator. The first stanza (v. 1) says that all of creation speaks of God's glory. The sun, moon, and stars are "singing" right along with us, "How great your name!" Stanza 2 (v. 4) marvels that God has asked us to take care of creation. What an assignment! Another stanza (covering v. 2) would also have been appropriate:

Infant voices chant your praise,
telling of your glorious ways;
weakest means work out your will,
mighty enemies to still.

Isn't it amazing that God uses children to conquer enemies?

Begin teaching the refrain. Perhaps the youngest children will learn only the refrain and the final phrase of each stanza. Sing one line at a time, and have the children repeat after you, singing brightly with strong voices, especially on the words "How great your name!"

This could be sung as the opening song in congregational worship or as a song of praise in any part of the service. For congregational singing, have the children sing one stanza.

15 Lord, Our Lord, Your Glorious Name

Words: from Psalm 8; versified in *The Psalter*, 1912
Music: William F. Sherwin, 1877

77 77 4 with refrain
EVENING PRAISE

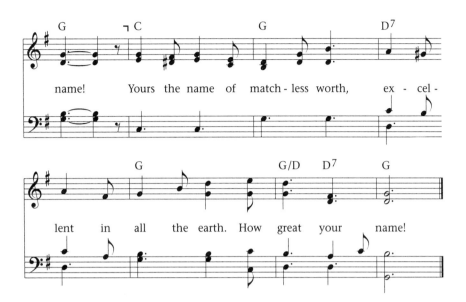

name! Yours the name of match-less worth, ex-cel-

lent in all the earth. How great your name!

♩ = 92

King of Kings and Lord of Lords 16

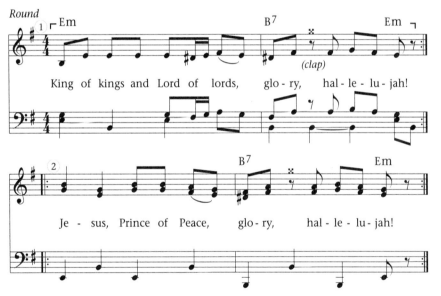

King of kings and Lord of lords, glo-ry, hal-le-lu-jah! *(clap)*

Je-sus, Prince of Peace, glo-ry, hal-le-lu-jah!

Words: Sophie Conty and Naomi Batya, 1980
Music: Hebrew folk song

KING OF KINGS

Jesus has many names in Scripture. This short praise chorus includes three important ones: King of kings, Lord of lords, and Prince of Peace.

Teach one measure at a time, and be sure to repeat each line. Then divide the group into two parts for singing in a two-part round. When the children know the song well, try singing in the style of an Israeli dance: begin slowly and sing three times, a bit faster each time.

Sing as a response to any Scripture reading that uses these names of Christ. Try pairing this song with 17 (in the same key) and/or 18, which also praises the King of kings.

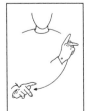  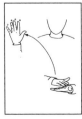 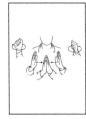 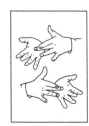 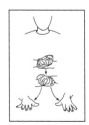

King *Lord* *Glory* *Hallelujah* *Jesus* *Prince of Peace*

Psalm 98 invites us to "sing to the Lord a new song." This Brazilian folk hymn begins by doing just that. Stanza 2 goes further, encouraging us to "shout." Why? Because God "gave us the Spirit." But the climax—the reason for our singing and shouting—comes in stanza 3: "For Jesus is Lord!"

Together, these three stanzas celebrate the Trinity; each opening phrase is sung three times. Try reading one phrase from each stanza, and you have the whole song in a nutshell: "O sing to the Lord" (st. 1), "who gave us the Spirit" (st. 2), "For Jesus is Lord! Amen! Alleluia!" (st. 3). Each stanza ends with a little refrain that ties it all together.

The tune is infectiously joyful, tumbling down the chords, then winding up to fall down again. Treat the word "sing" almost like bells, with a bright ringing "ee" sound followed by a good "nng" sound. Swing with a feeling of one large beat per measure. Accompany with guitars, even bass guitar on the bass part if possible, to capture the song's South American flavor. Also add castanets and other rhythm instruments. For a more involved keyboard accompaniment, try the anthem published by the Choristers Guild.

You may want to teach the final phrase first, and perhaps teach the other phrases to different groups, all joining each time on the refrains. Once they know it, try at least the first stanza in Spanish. The children will love it!

In congregational worship, sing as a call to worship or for any time of joyful praise, especially on Ascension or Pentecost. Try pairing this song with 16 (in the same key) or 18.

17 O Sing to the Lord / Cantad al Señor

♩. = 54

Spanish words:

1 Cantad al Señor un cántico nuevo. (3x) ¡Cantad al Señor, cantad al Señor!

2 Es él que nos da el Espíritu Santo. (3x) ¡Cantad al Señor, cantad al Señor!

3 ¡Jesús es Señor! ¡Amen, aleluya! (3x) ¡Cantad al Señor, cantad al Señor!

Words: Brazilian folk song; stanza 1 based on Psalm 98:1; translated by Gerhard M. Cartford
Music: Brazilian folk song
English and Spanish trans. © Gerhard M. Cartford; arr. © Editora Sinodal. Used by permission.

♩ = 88

We Will Glorify 18

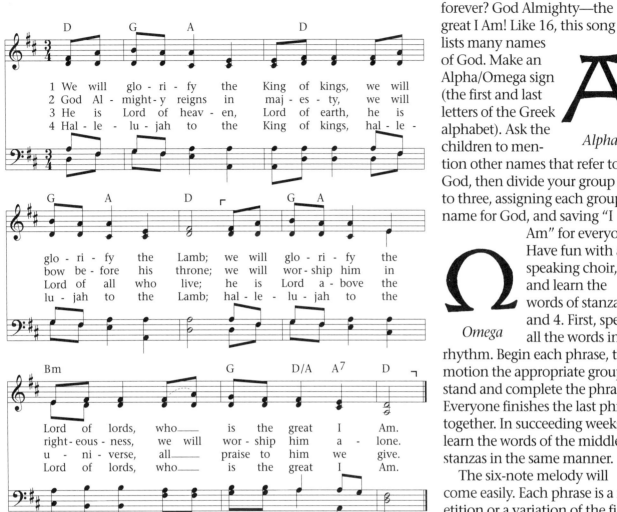

1 We will glo-ri-fy the King of kings, we will
2 God Al-might-y reigns in maj-es-ty, we will
3 He is Lord of heav-en, Lord of earth, he is
4 Hal-le-lu-jah to the King of kings, hal-le-

glo-ri-fy the Lamb; we will glo-ri-fy the
bow be-fore his throne; we will wor-ship him in
Lord of all who live; he is Lord a-bove the
lu-jah to the Lamb; hal-le-lu-jah to the

Lord of lords, who___ is the great I Am.
right-eous-ness, we will wor-ship him a-lone.
u-ni-verse, all___ praise to him we give.
Lord of lords, who___ is the great I Am.

Words and Music: Twila Paris; arranged by David Allen

WE WILL GLORIFY

Who lived before the world was created, lives now, and will live forever? God Almighty—the great I Am! Like 16, this song lists many names of God. Make an Alpha/Omega sign (the first and last letters of the Greek alphabet). Ask the children to mention other names that refer to God, then divide your group into three, assigning each group a name for God, and saving "I Am" for everyone. Have fun with a speaking choir, and learn the words of stanzas 1 and 4. First, speak all the words in rhythm. Begin each phrase, then motion the appropriate group to stand and complete the phrase. Everyone finishes the last phrase together. In succeeding weeks, learn the words of the middle stanzas in the same manner.

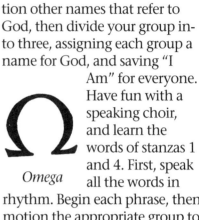

Alpha

Omega

The six-note melody will come easily. Each phrase is a repetition or a variation of the first. Add tone bells at the beginning of each phrase, changing the pattern just a little at the end. Include hand clapping, either using all claps or a pattern: hands on strong beats and thighs on weak beats. Add a tambourine on the half notes.

In worship, sing as a call to worship, or as a conclusion to the Lord's Supper. Include it in Easter or Ascension Day praise.

Glorify

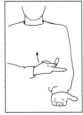

King

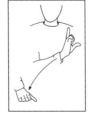

Lamb

Lord

Great

I Am (=God)

Charles Wesley wrote over 6,500 hymn texts! Point out your church hymnal's index, and encourage the older children to look his name up in your pew hymnal before church. Remember to ask what they found next week. (*Songs for LiFE* includes four of Wesley's hymns—19, 122, 172, 180).

Who was Charles Wesley? And how could he write so many hymns? The youngest of eighteen children, Charles was taught by his mother and came to know the Bible well. Later, as a minister in the Church of England, he would often ride horseback to preach in different places. While he was riding, he would write hymn poetry in his head. When he got to the town he would quickly ask for "pen and ink" so he could write down his new hymn.

This hymn is his best-known, written at the age of twenty-one to celebrate the first anniversary of his conversion. Only three of the original eighteen stanzas are included here. The first line was perhaps inspired by the "tongues of fire" at Pentecost, or maybe he got the idea from his spiritual mentor, who said once, "Had I a thousand tongues, I would praise Him with them all!"

Since then, many thousands of tongues have indeed been singing this hymn to praise God. Sing it with joy and exuberance. We use our tongues in praise because wonderful things happen when God speaks. Even the youngest children know the joy of seeing sick people become well. Scripture references include Matthew 11:5, Isaiah 35:6, and Acts 3:8.

In worship this praise song is appropriate for any time of praise, and for Pentecost, profession of faith, baptism, or other times of renewal. When singing the hymn as a congregation, have the children sing one of the stanzas.

19 Oh, for a Thousand Tongues to Sing

♩ = 84

1 Oh, for a thou - sand tongues to sing my great Re - deem - er's praise, the glo - ries of my God and King, the tri - umphs of his grace!

2 He speaks, and, lis - tening to his voice, new life the dead re - ceive; the mourn - ful, bro - ken hearts re - joice; the hum - ble poor be - lieve.

3 Hear him, you deaf; you voice - less ones, your loos - ened tongues em - ploy; you blind, be - hold your Sa - vior come; and leap, you lame, for joy!

Words: Charles Wesley, 1739
Music: Carl G. Gläser, 1828; adapted and arranged by Lowell Mason, 1839

CM
AZMON

♩ = 104

Praise the Lord 20

1 Praise the— Lord, praise the— Lord,
2 Thanks to— God, thanks to— God,
3 Glo - ry to God, glo - ry to God,

for the green - ness of the trees, for the beau - ty
for the gift of friends in Christ, for the church, our
for the grace of Christ, the Son, for the love of

of the flowers, for the blue - ness of the sky,
house of faith, for the gift of won - drous love,
par - ent God, for the com - fort and the strength

for the great - ness of the sea. Praise the— Lord,
for the gift of end - less grace. Thanks to— God,
of the Spir - it, ho - ly God. Glo - ry to God,

praise the— Lord, now and for - ev - er - more.
thanks to— God, now and for - ev - er - more.
glo - ry to God, now and for - ev - er - more.

Words: Nobuaki Hanaoka, 1980
Music: traditional Japanese melody

SAKURA

"Praise the Lord" is a Japanese hymn praising God (st. 1), thanking him (st. 2), and giving God glory (st. 3). Some Asian art is very delicate, rewarding those who look closely. Nobuaki Hanoaka looks closely at nature in stanza 1, praising God not just for trees and flowers, sky and sea, but for their greenness and beauty, blueness and greatness. Stanza 2 is a reflective thank you to God for the church. And stanza 3 is a doxology to the Trinity.

This traditional Japanese melody is built on a scale North Americans seldom hear. With the exception of the E in the last phrase, the melody is pentatonic (five tones). To teach the song, write key words for each phrase on a chart and color code the phrases. Children will then see that there are only four phrases to learn, and the first phrase repeats within itself. With one letter for every two measures, the form is ABCBCAD. All the children should learn the A and D phrases first. Then divide the children into two groups, assigning one the B phrase and the other the C phrase. Teach each phrase by the echo method, singing with sustained and legato tones. Eventually switch the groups.

For accompaniment, add flute and/or violin on the melody. Ask a child to play a drone on the autoharp by pressing both the D major and the D minor buttons at the same time. This way neither the major or the minor chord will be heard—just the open fifth. Strum one stroke per measure. Another interesting autoharp technique is to pluck just the F sharp and G strings back and forth on quarter notes. Add finger cymbals on the fourth beat of every measure with the word "Lord" (four times each stanza). On stanza 3, create a descant by playing just the five pitches of the melody in random order every half note on the highest bell-like instruments you have.

The children could lead the congregation in this gentle song especially during summer or springtime when all of nature is bursting forth. Have the congregation join on the final repeated phrases of each stanza.

Here is another setting of Psalm 100 (see also 9 and 10) by Lucien Deiss, a French Catholic priest recognized for his leadership in the renewal of worship. He versified a number of psalms for congregational singing, which were later translated into English under his supervision. This is one of Deiss's most effective and popular settings. The refrain comes from Psalm 100:1; stanzas 1 through 5 cover the rest of the psalm, and stanza 6 is a doxology.

The melody is "circular"; that is, it should be sung without any pauses between the refrains and the stanzas. Just keep the beat going! Set the tempo with the stanzas, not the refrain; it's easy to rush the stanzas.

The song is intended to be sung "responsorially," that is, by two groups—a soloist or small group leading on the stanzas and everyone "responding" on the refrain. The stanzas could also be sung by different groups of children. The refrain calls for exuberant accompaniment. Hand clapping, a few rhythm instruments, handbells, even brass fit well with the refrain of this ancient Hebrew "cheering" song. The stanzas call for lighter accompaniment; keyboard or guitar would be effective. This is jubilant music—keep the energy and rhythms going!

Liturgically this song is suitable as a processional psalm. Sing for any time of praise, also for Thanksgiving, Epiphany, and missions services. If the children know the stanzas well, have the congregation join them only on the refrains.

21 All the Earth, Proclaim the Lord

♩ = 69

Refrain

All the earth, pro-claim the Lord, sing your praise to God.

1 Serve you the Lord, heart filled with glad - ness;
2 Know that the Lord is our Cre - a - tor.
3 We are the sheep of his green pas - ture,
4 En - ter his gates, bring - ing thanks-giv - ing;

come in - to his pres - ence, sing - ing for joy!
Yes, he is our Fa - ther; we are his own.
for we are his peo - ple; he is our God.
O en - ter his courts while sing - ing his praise

Repeat refrain

5 Our Lord is good,
  his love is lasting;
  his word is abiding
  now and always. *Refrain*

6 Honor and praise
  be to the Father,
  the Son, and the Spirit,
  world without end. *Refrain*

Words: Psalm 100; versified by Lucien Deiss, 1965
Music: Lucien Deiss, 1965
© 1965, World Library Publications, a Division of J. S. Paluch Company, Inc.
Used by permission.

45 64 with refrain
DEISS 100
Capo 3

♩ = 120

We Praise You for the Earth 22

1 We praise you for the earth, for crea-tures
2 We praise you for our homes, for com-fort,
3 We praise you for our friends, who show us
4 We praise you for the church, where we can

great and small, for flowers and trees, for
food, and clothes, for those who share our
how to love each time we play and
hear your Word, for songs to sing, for

brooks and seas; thank you for the earth.
dai - ly cares; thank you for our homes.
ev - ery day; thank you for our friends.
gifts to bring; thank you for the church.

Words and Music: AnnaMae Meyer Bush, 1984, 1991

LIPSCOMB
Capo 3

This delightful song of thanks-giving can be learned rather quickly with a few fun activities. Try enlarging the poster ideas given below and ask the children to identify them. One picture relates to each of the stanzas: the earth, our homes, our friends, the church. As each poster is shown, ask the children to praise and thank God by finishing the following statements: "We praise you for . . ."; "Thank you for . . ."

Create and randomly hang around your room small picture-signs that illustrate the remaining three phrases for each stanza. Taking one stanza at a time, ask children to match the signs to a specific poster, and attach them to that poster. (Velcro works great!) Use the completed posters to review the stanzas. To review each stanza, ask everyone to speak the start and finish, and you speak the middle part.

Let singers arrange the picture-signs in their proper order. Repeat the speaking exercise several times and finally encourage everyone to speak everything. Then start singing the words, following the same procedure as above. For variety, assign solos or an older group to the middle section.

You could pattern a complete Thanksgiving service after this song. Sing each stanza to introduce a section of the service, which would include a banner, appropriate prayers, songs, Scripture, and meditation. At the conclusion, invite the congregation to join in singing the entire song.

The earth   *Our homes*   *Our friends*   *The church*   *The earth*

This is a speech rhythm "song" whose "melody" is speaking voices. The children chant the words in rhythm. When verses are put to rhythm, speech rhythms help children learn Scripture quickly. They also help children pay closer attention to speaking the text clearly, with good articulation, phrasing, dynamics, and voice inflection. These positive results will also carry over into their singing. One warning: accurate reading of the rhythm is essential, and you have to read the rhythm without any help from a melody. But don't be afraid to try!

Marking your score will also help. Highlight entrances of Leader, All, and Solo with different colors. Mark accents and repeat signs. Notice that every section is repeated and that the first section returns in the middle and again at the end (ABACA). All the children can learn the A section; perhaps you could ask some of the older ones to do the B and C sections.

Establish the beat by tapping two fingers in the palm of the other hand. Have the children echo you by phrases, omitting the canon. They will follow your example of dynamics, accents, and repetition, so be sure to follow the markings.

For the canon, note that the first time the line is spoken together, then in two groups on the repeat. Be sure that the leader waits for both groups to finish before proceeding with the final section.

23 Praise the Lord!

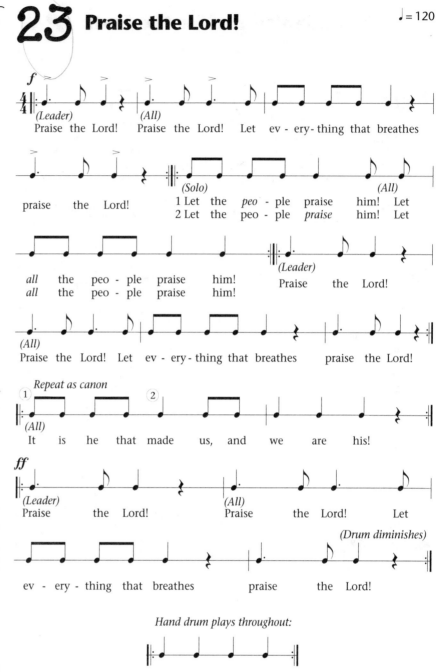

Words: Psalm 150:6; 67:3; 100:3
Music: Betty Ann Ramseth, 1970

Reprinted from *That I May Speak*, © 1970, Augsburg Publishing House. Used by permission of Augsburg Fortress.

A simple accompaniment of the hand drum is sufficient. You may wish to add a cymbal or ringing triangle on the word "praise" in all the A sections of "Praise the Lord!"

This piece would make a wonderful call to worship or song of praise on any occasion.

♩ = 88

Hallelujah, Praise the Lord 24

1 Hal - le - lu - jah, praise the Lord. Praise him with each
2 Praise him in his ho - ly place. Shout his power through
3 Praise him with the pluck - ing string, cym - bal clang and
4 Praise with in - stru - ments of wood, for the Lord is

note and word. Praise him for his might - y ways,
out - er space. Ev - ery - thing that breathes, pro - claim
trum - pet ring, tap - ping foot and clap - ing hand;
just and good. Praise with u - ni - son and chord.

who with love ex - alts our days. Hal - le - lu - jah.
praise and hon - or to God's name. Hal - le - lu - jah.
praise the Lord through all the land. Hal - le - lu - jah.
Hal - le - lu - jah, praise the Lord! Hal - le - lu - jah.

Orff instrument patterns

Alto metallophone

Bass zylophone

Woodblock (st. 3-4)

Words: based on Psalm 150; versified by Marie J. Post, 1974
Music: French, 13th century; arranged by John Ferguson, 1988
© 1974, 1988, 1994, CRC Publications

77 77 4
ORIENTIS PARTIBUS

This song is a versification of Psalm 150, the last psalm in the Book of Psalms and one of the most familiar. "Hallelujah" means "Praise the Lord!" This psalm is full of praise from beginning to end. God deserves our praise because of his mighty ways and love (st. 1) and power (st. 2). "Everything that breathes" (st. 2) is called to praise God: here is an invitation to use every kind of musical instrument.

The French tune is 700 years old. Many hymns and carols have been sung to it throughout the years including "The Friendly Beasts," a song the children may know.

Sing with two strong beats per measure, giving the melody a dance-like bounce. Two Orff instrument patterns are suggested; these could also be played by handbells. Other bell patterns could be made up in keeping with the chordal pattern of F C F. Have recorders, flutes, or violins play along on the melody. Use rhythm instruments to play the suggested pattern or have children compose their own rhythm patterns. Cymbals could play on the first beat of every two measures (the beginning of each line or phrase).

This praise song can be sung in almost any worship service. It is especially useful for a festival-like processional. Try alternating the sung stanzas with instrumental versions.

This song is based on Psalm 22:3, 22-27 and Psalm 145:7. The phrase "in the presence of your people," which occurs also in 52:9 and 116:14, 18, shows the importance of praising and worshiping God with other believers. To help the children understand the phrases "enthroned on the praises of Israel" and "may your name be exalted" have them imagine a king being carried on a chair lifted high so all the cheering crowds can see him.

Although it sounds like Israeli folk music, this song was composed in 1977 by Brent Chambers after attending an evening of ethnic music and dance and named, appropriately, CELEBRATION. In keeping with the style, sing each stanza progressively faster, with great spirit. (This could also be done by repeating stanza 1 several times if the other stanzas have not yet been learned.) Use tambourine on the offbeat (beats 2 and 4) throughout. Children may wish to clap their own rhythm patterns as well. Once children know the melody, have a violin, oboe, or flute play the descant. Another instrument could double the melody line.

Sing as an opening psalm of praise in a worship service. It is especially appropriate when Old Testament festivals or themes are part of the theme of the service. Consider pairing this song with 26, which is in the same key.

25 In the Presence of Your People

♩ = 72, 88, 100

Words: based on Psalm 22:3, 22-27; 145:7; stanza 1, Brent Chambers, 1977; stanzas 2-3, Bert Polman, 1986
Music: Brent Chambers, 1977

CELEBRATION

here   on   earth   and   in   heaven a - bove.

2 All who love you sing your praises
   and proclaim your power,
   for alone you are holy,
   enthroned on the praises of Israel.
   You have not ignored our suffering
   but have heard our cry;
   may your power be exalted
   here on earth and in heaven above.

3 All who seek your rule will praise you
   and be satisfied;
   for alone you are holy,
   enthroned on the praises of Israel.
   All the peoples of the nations
   will bow down to you;
   may your rule be exalted
   here on earth and in heaven above.

Descant

This song, based on Psalm 145:1-3, was written by Casiodoro Cardenas from Ecuador, South America. Originally sung in Spanish, it has been translated for English-speaking people to enjoy as well. You may want to explain the word "exalt" to the children. In this context it means that God is greater than anything and that his name is more important than all others. He is Number One in our lives! He is worthy of all praise and honor because he is so great.

The rhythms of the song give it a South American sound. Use lots of rhythm instruments along with the piano or guitar accompaniment. Four patterns are given for specific instruments, but don't stop there. Sing this song in unison with strong, clear voices.

This song would be most fitting as an introit or call to worship at the beginning of a service, or as a response just before leaving at the end of the service. Consider pairing this song with 25, which is in the same key.

26 I Will Exalt My God, My King
Te Exaltaré Mi Dios, Mi Rey

♩ = 100

Words: Psalm 145:1-3; versified by Casiodoro Cardenas, 1979; composite translation ECUADOR
Music: Casiodoro Cardenas, 1979; arranged by Raquel Mora Martínez, 1979

Although he only lived to be thirty, Joachim Neander wrote about sixty hymns and became the most important German Reformed Church hymn writer of his century. This hymn was published in 1680, the same year he died from tuberculosis. Like many great hymns, it is closely based on the psalms, especially Psalm 150, a psalm of praise, and Psalm 103, which praises the God "who heals all your diseases." (Incidently, an old skeleton was discovered in a German valley where Neander used to walk; it became known as "Neanderthal man.")

This hymn expresses adoration and invitation. Our God is both powerful and personal: stanza 1 ranges all the way from the great "King of creation" to the God who is our "health and salvation." Stanza 2 emphasizes that we must use our "all" to praise God and that all (in heaven and earth) must praise him.

Sing this in a lilting tempo with a strong first beat, almost one beat to the measure. The music is in two sections with the first repeated (AAB). The A section is a very long musical phrase. The B section is made up of three short phrases and is the climax of the song, containing the highest note. You might teach the song in reverse, starting with the final phrases. Teach the song in echo fashion with the children repeating after you.

The invitation in stanza 1 makes this an excellent opening hymn. The children could invite the congregation to join them "in glad adoration." The word "adoration" also links this song with 28; they could be sung as a pair.

27 Praise to the Lord, the Almighty

♩ = 132

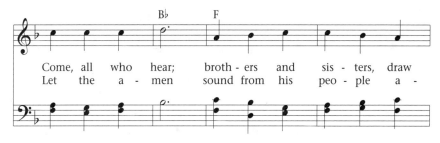

1 Praise to the Lord, the Al-might-y, the King of cre-a-tion! O my soul, praise him, for he is your health and sal-va-tion! Come, all who hear; broth-ers and sis-ters, draw

2 Praise to the Lord! O let all that is in me a-dore him! All that has life and breath, come now with prais-es be-fore him! Let the a-men sound from his peo-ple a-

Words: Joachim Neander, 1680; translated by Catherine Winkworth, 1863
Music: *Erneuerten Gesangbuch*, Stralsund, 1665; arranged by Robert Roth, 1989
Arr. © 1989, Robert Roth

14 14 4 7 8
LOBE DEN HERREN

Father

C   F   C   F

near,   join   me   in   glad   ad - o - ra - tion!
gain.   Glad - ly   for - ev - er   a - dore   him!

♩ = 104

Father, I Adore You 28

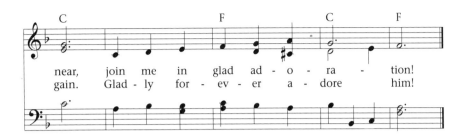

Round

 ① F   Gm   C   F   ②   Gm

1 Fa - ther,
2 Je - sus,   I a - dore   you,   lay   my   life   be -
3 Spir - it,

C   F   ③   Gm   C   F

fore   you.   How   I   love   you.

Words and Music: Terrye Coelho, 1972

664
MARANATHA

Terrye Coelho wrote this song in 1972 while driving her car. Tell the children they too may make up their own songs of praise wherever they are. Point out that each verse begins with one of the three persons of the Trinity.

Part of the joy of this chorus is singing it as a three-part round. Use accompaniment sparingly. Autoharp or guitar are preferable to keyboard. Orff instruments or handbells could also be used. Here are three simple patterns, all playing half notes:

F G C F
A B-flat G A
C D E F

Have a recorder or flute play along on the melody.

Sing before or after a prayer of confession or the congregational prayer. Or link with another song, such as 27. Always sing together first before starting the round.

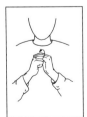

Adore

You

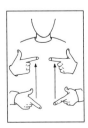

Life

Before

Love

Jesus

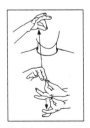

Spirit

This song of praise was written and composed by Natalie Sleeth (for more on Sleeth, see 175). It includes descriptions of who God is and what he is God of. The three initial phrases of each stanza are matter-of-fact statements encompassing all of life and creation. The concluding phrase of each stanza portrays God in a more personal way: God as creator and sustainer, God as companion, God as love, God as King. The refrain is an outpouring of praise to God's name.

The fresh quality of the melody is ideally suited to children's voices, and it includes enough repetition to make learning easy. You may wish to begin by having older children read the stanzas with all the children singing the refrain. Children will also enjoy "signing" the refrain.

Playing the melody quietly while reading the stanza is a good way to introduce the song. The use of motions or charts will also help reinforce the text. Once they know it, the children could sing the stanzas antiphonally (group 1 on measures 1-4, group 2 on measures 5-8), with all singing the refrain.

This song should be sung with sturdiness and dignity. It can be accompanied in a vari-

29 God of Great and God of Small

1 God of great and God of small, God of
2 God of land and sky and sea, God of
3 God of si - lence, God of sound, God to
4 God of heaven and God of earth, God of

one and God of all, God of weak and
life and des - ti - ny, God of nev - er -
whom the lost are found, God of day and
death and God of birth, God of now and

God of strong, God to whom all things be - long,
end - ing power, yet be - side me ev - ery hour,
dark - est night, God whose love turns wrong to right,
days be - fore, God who reigns for - ev - er - more,

Refrain

al - le - lu - ia, al - le - lu - ia, praise be to your

Words and Music: Natalie Sleeth, adapted from the anthem "God of Great and God of Small"

Alleluia

Praise

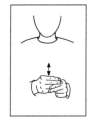
Name

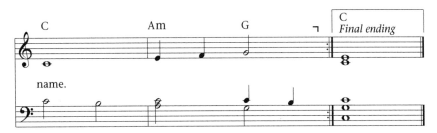

ety of ways. One possibility: use Piano I on stanzas 1-2; Piano II (or organ or guitar) very quietly on stanza 3; then both keyboard parts in a joyful duet on stanza 4. Or use guitar with a solo instrument playing the melody on the stanzas with keyboard joining on the refrains.

In worship settings include this song as part of any celebration of praise.

30 Celebrate

♩ = 76

Make a joyful noise unto the Lord and celebrate! Christians have many reasons to celebrate and this song helps us understand why. Before singing it for the children, ask them how many times they hear the word "celebrate." Then sing it again and ask: What are we celebrating? How do we celebrate? What joyful noise is used in this song?

Begin by learning the opening phrase of the melody. Then sing all the measures in a row that contain the "celebrate (*clap, clap*)" pattern; help the children notice how it rises and falls. Then learn the last phrase, ending with a firm "Praise God, everyone." Add the piano, playing the phrases between. Next, divide your singers into four groups. Teach each group one of the "between phrases." Have fun putting the whole song together as follows:

- Everyone sings the five "celebrate (*clap, clap*)" phrases.

- Everyone sings the concluding "Praise God" phrase.

- Separate groups (stand to) sing the answering phrases between.

After singing the song a few times in this manner, everyone will be able to sing everything. Use rhythm instruments to make other "joyful noises" in place of the claps.

In worship, include this song as a joyful call to praise. Use it to introduce any festive occasion and sing it during the Easter season. Include it as a response to a spoken psalm of praise (such as 100 or 47). A good song to sing in conjunction with this one is "Clap Your Hands" (179).

Words and Music: Joe Pinson
© 1989, Joe Pinson. Used by permission.

♩ = 88

I Sing a Song to Jesus Christ 31

I sing a song to Je-sus Christ, my ris-en Lord, my
Sav - ior; he is the King of ev - ery thing both
great and small, my Sav - ior. I love him so, he
is my God, he lives in-side of me. I sing a song, sal -
va - tion song, to Je - sus Christ, my Sav - ior.

When David Ritsema was nine years old, he composed a "Salvation Song" expressing his faith in Jesus. This simple profession of faith includes the heart of the gospel and a response of love and joy.

There are really only two melodic phrases to learn. The first four measures are repeated with a different ending, and the second and fourth phrases are identical (A A' B A'). Teach the song by echo method, singing one measure at a time, keeping the rhythm going. Each measure repeats the same rhythmic pattern except for the well-placed long note before the final phrase.

Keep the accompaniment simple; perhaps a nine-year-old could accompany on autoharp!

In congregational worship, have the children sing this profession during the Easter season ("my risen Lord"), for Ascension ("King of everything"), or Pentecost ("he lives inside of me").

Words and Music: David Ritsema (age 9), 1989; arranged by Norma de Waal Malefyt, 1992

Natalie Sleeth composed the text and tune of this hymn of praise in 1975 for the children at Highland Park United Methodist Church in Dallas, Texas. This song and eleven of her other compositions, as well as a separate anthem, are included in *Sunday Songbook* (1976). (For more on Sleeth, see 175.)

This song lists various instruments, places, times, and ways in which we can praise the Lord. It suggests how God should be praised, when he should be praised, and where he could be praised. Encourage your children to expand the list. The form of the music is AABA. If you can come up with enough rhyming words, follow Sleeth's basic form as your outline (A: instruments, A: where or when, B: how or when, A: where or when) and create your own verse. Remind the children that praise should occur not only with a loud voice but also "in peace and quiet" and not only in happy times but also "in the time of sorrow."

With the AABA musical form, the children will easily learn the musical sequence within each section. Refer to the chart on the following page when teaching this song. Stars and circles indicate the form of the music. Chart these in contrasting colors (such as red and green). The words and pictures can be printed in black. You may wish to sing this song in canon.

32 Praise the Lord with the Sound of Trumpet

$\downarrow = 72$

Words and Music: Natalie Sleeth, 1975
© 1976, Hinshaw Music, Inc. Used by permission.

PRAISE THE LORD
Capo 5

The piano should lightly accompany the singing of this song. If available, a string bass player could play the lower voice. Any solo or group of soprano instruments could play the top line.

Perhaps the worship leader could introduce the song before it is sung by mentioning that we can praise God "anytime and anywhere" to help the congregation concentrate on the where, when, and how mentioned. It can also be used as a stimulus for seeking additional ways and means to praise the Lord.

dark of night, praise the Lord in the rain or snow or in the
time of joy, praise the Lord ev-ery mo-ment; noth-ing let your

morn-ing light. Praise the Lord in the deep-est val-ley,
praise de-stroy. Praise the Lord in the peace and qui-et,

praise the Lord on the high-est hill, praise the Lord; nev-er
praise the Lord in your work or play, praise the Lord ev-ery-

let your voice be still.
where in ev-ery way!

Verse 1

Verse 2

This German hymn of thanksgiving was written in 1636 by Martin Rinkart as a prayer before meals. Rinkart served as a Lutheran pastor in the town of Eilenburg, Saxony, which was a haven for refugees during the Thirty Years' War. These refugees suffered numerous ills, both financial and physical. In spite of his own frail health, Rinkart officiated at the funeral services of over 5,000 people. During that time he was inspired to write this text. Stanzas 1 and 2 speak of God's protection in the past, present, and future. Stanza 3 is a paraphrase of the *Gloria Patri,* or doxology to the Trinity.

The first two long phrases of music are the same, as is often the case in Crüger's melodies. To help children learn stanza 1, add motions to the text (below).

Now thank we/all our God
clasp hands/spread arms out and up

with heart/and hands/and voices,
cross hands over heart/palms together/cup hands around mouth

who wondrous things has done,
raise left hand in wide arc from right to left

in whom his world rejoices;
raise right hand in wide arc, both hands extended high

who from our mother's arms
cradle arms and rock

has blessed us on our way
move hands beat by beat away from body

with countless gifts of love,
raise arms up and out in wide arc

and still is ours today.
cross arms over heart

In congregational worship, don't restrict the singing of this thanksgiving hymn just to Thanksgiving Day; also sing as a doxology.

33 Now Thank We All Our God

♩ = 56

1 Now thank we all our God with heart and hands and
2 O may this boun-teous God through all our life be
3 All praise and thanks to God the Fa-ther now be

voic - es, who won-drous things has done, in
near us, with ev - er joy - ful hearts and
giv - en, the Son and Spir - it blest, who

whom his world re - joic - es; who from our moth-ers'
bless - ed peace to cheer us, to keep us in his
reign in high-est heav - en— the one e - ter - nal

arms has blessed us on our way with
grace, and guide us when per - plexed, and
God, whom heaven and earth a - dore; for

Words: Martin Rinkart, 1636; translated by Catherine Winkworth, 1863
Music: Johann Crüger, 1647

67 67 66 66
NUN DANKET
Capo 1

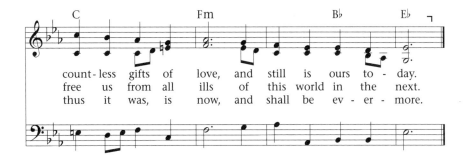

count-less gifts of love, and still is ours to - day.
free us from all ills of this world in the next.
thus it was, is now, and shall be ev - er - more.

♩ = 66

For Health and Strength **34**

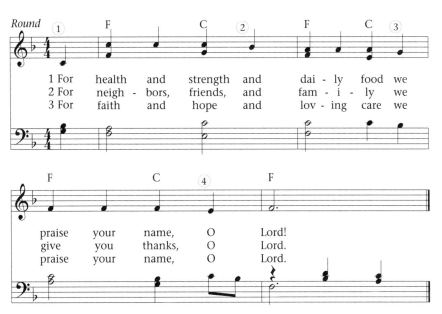

1 For health and strength and dai - ly food we
2 For neigh - bors, friends, and fam - i - ly we
3 For faith and hope and lov - ing care we

praise your name, O Lord!
give you thanks, O Lord.
praise your name, O Lord.

Omit accompaniment when sung as a round.

Words: stanza 1, traditional; stanzas 2-3, Bert Polman, 1991
Music: traditional
Words © 1994, CRC Publications

This traditional round is often used at Thanksgiving but can be sung any time as an expression of praise and thanksgiving. The words are simple and straightforward. You may want to use the text as a springboard to discussing the blessings God has given us.

The melody is simple and easy to learn. After an initial jump of an octave, the melody descends in a stepwise manner until the last note, which goes up a half step. Children will enjoy singing it as a four-part round. Sing a selected verse two or three times or have each of the four groups sing the three stanzas in order. The first three groups may repeat the final phrase after they finish their stanzas until the fourth group finishes.

When sung as a round, the written accompaniment should be omitted; however, a simple Orff or bell accompaniment (C and F) could be used. Autoharp or guitar may also play the F and C chords when sung as a round.

Sing in a service of thanksgiving and praise as an introit, a call to worship, preparation for prayer, or response to prayer.

Young children will enjoy this robust song in praise of God, who is the greatest! Children enjoy talking about their toy or their dad or their bike as the best, the biggest, the strongest. Explain that "handiwork" means "made by God's hand." The things God makes are so great that no one else could make them. Encourage the children to add to the list of what only God can create: people, animals, trees, and so on.

There are only two musical phrases to learn; sing the first section twice at the beginning (following the repeat signs), but sing only once at the end (AABA). Children should stand as they sing so that they have free range of motion to perform the actions. Because it involves movement, this is a good "warm-up" song.

In a worship service, young children could sing this song with the motions as a response to the reading of a creation psalm extolling the greatness of God, for example, Psalm 104, which begins, "O Lord, you are very great." Consider pairing with "There's No God as Great" (240), which is in the same key.

35 My God Is So Great

♩ = 76

(hold up arms and flex muscles)
My God is so great, so strong and so migh-ty! There's

(shake head "no")
noth-ing my God can-not do! (clap, clap)

(hands form mountain peak above head)   (wiggle fingers from left to right)
The moun-tains are his, the riv-ers are his,

(fingers make twinkling stars)
the stars are his hand-i-work too.

Words and Music: Children's folk song; arranged by Charlotte Larsen, 1992

♩ = 84

Jesus Is a Friend of Mine 36

1 Je - sus is a friend of mine. Praise him.

him. Praise him. Praise him.

Je - sus is a friend of mine. Praise him.

2 Jesus died to set us free. Praise him. . . .
3 He gave us the victory. Praise him. . . .
4 Jesus is the King of kings. Praise him. . . .

This delightfully simple song for young children was written by four-year-old Paul Mazak. Paul makes refreshing, concise statements about his relationship with Jesus. His response to each of the four statements is simply, "Praise him." Your children may wish to create new stanzas.

A simple ABA form is used with the first A section repeated (AABA). The faster quarter-note rhythm contrasts nicely with the lyrical "Praise him." Encourage the children to sing smoothly on these longer notes. For variety, divide the children into two groups. For example, a soloist could sing the first phrase with all joining on "Praise him." On the B section (second line), one group could begin and the other echo. Have bells play on the "Praise him" phrases.

This delightful children's praise song would be appropriate almost anywhere in a worship service. Use specific stanzas as a response to Scripture or another song. For example, sing stanzas 2-3 during Easter; stanza 4 at Pentecost. Try pairing it with "What a Friend We Have in Jesus" (52).

Words: Paul Mazak (age 4)
Music: melody by Paul Mazak; arranged by Emily R. Brink, 1992

This song is based on a Dutch children's song, "Klokje klinkt," which means "clocks chime." The original Dutch song told how everybody and everything—even clocks—can praise God. The two words that began the Dutch song are now the tune name, found on the bottom right corner of the song page. (The Dutch "j" is pronounced like an English "y.") Jean Keegstra wrote new words to the tune, making it a prayer for guidance.

There are many ways to sing this song, either simply as written or dressed up like an anthem. Here is one way to make an anthem out of this song:

- *Introduction:* Pianist plays introduction as marked: ⌐ ¬

- *Stanzas 1-2:* Unison, with piano (or organ, guitar, or autoharp)

- *Stanza 3:* For an interlude before starting to sing this stanza, begin the Orff patterns, the top part on bells (glockenspiel), and the bottom part on bass xylophone (or perhaps on keyboard). Once the pattern is going well, bring in the children in a two-part round. After they are through singing, continue the Orff pattern once or twice and then play the final ending.

The children could well lead the congregation in this prayer for guidance as part of the service of confession. Place the words in the bulletin so everyone can participate in the prayer.

37 Lord, I Pray

♩ = 112

Canon (st. 3)

1 Lord, I pray, if to-day some should wrong or trou-ble me, make me kind; bring to mind your for-give-ness makes me free.
2 Should there be joy for me, help me thank you as I should. Let me through all I do praise you, Lord, for all things good.
3 If this day I should stray, show my heart the road to take. Should I fear, please be near; hear my prayer for Je-sus' sake.

Canon accompaniment for keyboard or Orff instruments

Final ending

Words: Jean C. Keegstra-DeBoer, 1949, alt.
Music: Dutch melody; arranged by Grace Schwanda, 1989
Arr. © 1994, CRC Publications

67 67
KLOKJE KLINKT

♩ = 108

We Thank You, God 38

1 We thank you, God, for this new day. We
2 For - give us for the wrongs we do. Come,
3 Please keep us safe with - in your care, for

raise our hearts in prayer to say: May all we think and
clean our hearts and make them new. You of - fer us your
on - ly with your help we dare to do our work and

all we do be pleas - ing, Lord, this day to you.
love al - ways. In thanks we of - fer you our praise.
face our fear. We trust your prom - ise to be near.

The tune title MORNING PRAYER suggests the place in worship of this song, composed by Anna-Mae Bush. It begins with thanks, then moves to petition: help us to please you, forgive us, keep us safe, be near us.

If you are teaching this song by rote, a chart or overhead may be helpful. Start with all the words, then gradually cover the words. Help the children notice that the ending words of each phrase rhyme. Next, elim-inate the middle words and then the ending words. Finally, cover all the words.

Although all the musical phrases are different, the sec-ond phrase is similar to the first, only higher. An autoharp or guitar accompaniment would suit the clear sound of children's voices on this song. For a very simple accompani-ment, try the following pattern on Orff instruments: CCFC (playing half notes).

Children may wish to sing this song as a morning prayer. In congregational worship, sing as a prayer of confession. The stanzas also lend themselves to different parts of the service. Stanza 1 could be sung as an opening hymn of praise, stanza 2 as prayer of confession, stanza 3 as a parting prayer.

Words and Music: AnnaMae Meyer Bush, 1984
© 1984, AnnaMae Meyer Bush

LM
MORNING PRAYER

The text of this Scripture chorus is based on Jeremiah 31:33, God's promise of a new covenant with his people. Explain that a covenant is a sacred promise between two persons. Stanza 1 states God's promise to us; stanza 2 gives our response and promise to God.

Written by June Armstrong as part of a series of songs for the "Children and Worship" program, the melody is accessible to young children's voices. An effective way to illustrate the twofold nature of a covenant is to have a soloist sing the first stanza with the children responding on the second stanza. This song can be accompanied well by guitar, keyboard, or a combination of an autoharp with a recorder doubling the melody line. A recorder or flute could be used on the descant for a haunting effect; using a violin on the descant would give the song a more Israeli folk tune sound. The ostinato patterns printed for Orff instruments work well in combination with an instrumental doubling of the melody or descant.

Consider using this Scripture song as a frame for "You Are Our God; We Are Your People" (203), another song celebrating the covenant. Sing in services that have as their theme the covenant between God and his people or as part of the service of confession.

39 I Will Put My Law

♩ = 60

1 I will put my law in their minds and write it on their hearts. I will be their God, will be their God, and they will be my peo-ple.

2 He will put his law in our minds and write it on our hearts. He will be our God, will be our God, and we will be his peo-ple.

Descant

Orff instruments
Soprano glockenspiel   Alto xylophone   Alto metallophone

Words: based on Jeremiah 31:33
Music: June Fischer Armstrong, 1988; arranged by Richard L. Van Oss, 1992; descant by Roy Hopp, 1992
© 1992, CRC Publications

♩ = 72

Lord, I Want to Be a Christian

40

1 Lord, I want to be a Chris-tian in my heart, in my
2 Lord, I want to be more lov-ing in my heart, in my
3 Lord, I want to be more ho - ly in my heart, in my
4 Lord, I want to be like Je - sus in my heart, in my

heart. Lord, I want to be a Chris-tian in my heart.
heart. Lord, I want to be more lov-ing in my heart.
heart. Lord, I want to be more ho - ly in my heart.
heart. Lord, I want to be like Je - sus in my heart.

In my heart, in my heart, in my heart, in my heart,

Lord, I want to be a Chris-tian in my heart.
Lord, I want to be more lov - ing in my heart.
Lord, I want to be more ho - ly in my heart.
Lord, I want to be like Je - sus in my heart.

Words and Music: African-American spiritual

This African-American spiritual may be over two hundred years old. The simple text begins with a prayer to be a Christian "in my heart." Just saying we're Christians isn't enough; we need to be Christians from the inside out. Being a Christian means to be more loving (st. 2), to be more holy (st. 3), and es-pecially, to be like Jesus (st. 4). Stanzas 2 and 3 may be based on 1 Thessalonians 3:12-13.

As in many spirituals, a "call-and-response" style of singing is appropriate. A soloist could sing the first two lines with everyone joining on the last two lines. If your group is ready for simple two-part singing, try this on the third line: one group sings the melody, and a second group echoes first on the alto pitch (G), then on alto F-sharp. Return to unison for the final phrase. Encourage the children to hold the long notes. This music is reverent and meditative and should not be sung too quickly.

Sing in congregational wor-ship any time a challenge is given, calling for a response of commitment. Or sing at the end of a service of confession or perhaps in response to hear-ing the Word of the Lord.

41 Psalm 51

♩ = 108

Refrain

Cre - ate   in   me   a   clean   heart,   O   God.

Have mercy on me, O God,
    according to your unfailing love;
according to your great compassion
    blot out my wrong-doing.
Wash away all my offenses
    and cleanse me from my sin.   *Refrain*

Surely I was sinful at birth,
    sinful from the time my mother conceived me.
Surely you desire truth in my heart;
    you teach wisdom deep within me.   *Refrain*

Create in me a pure heart, O God,
    and renew a faithful spirit within me.
Do not cast me from your presence
    or take your Holy Spirit from me.
Restore to me the joy of your salvation
    and give me a willing spirit, to sustain me.   *Refrain*

O Lord, open my lips,
    and my mouth will declare your praise.
You do not delight in sacrifice, or I would bring it;
    you do not take pleasure in burnt offerings;
but the sacrifice of a broken and humble spirit,
    O God, you will not despise.   *Refrain*

Psalm 51 is an often-used psalm of confession. And verse 10 is one of the best-known verses. The first part of verse 10 forms the refrain for this responsorial setting of Psalm 51. The music comes from an anthem by the same title.

Responsorial style is similar to the more familiar "responsive" way of reading a psalm. In responsorial psalmody, one person reads (or chants) the text of the psalm, and everyone joins at intervals on the refrain. Traditionally, the refrain is sung first by the cantor, or soloist, and then repeated immediately by the whole group. Thereafter the refrain is sung at indicated intervals. This refrain is short enough that even the youngest child can learn it.

In congregational worship, an older child or teenager could read the psalm text, and all the children could sing the refrain, teaching it to the congregation (no music is needed; they can learn it by rote). Perhaps the children could sign the refrain as well.

Words: Psalm 51:1-2, 5-6, 10-12, 15-17
Music: Carl F. Meuller, 1939

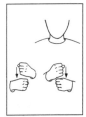

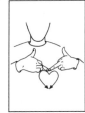
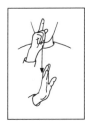

Create   *Me*   *Clean*   *Heart*   *God*

♩ = 88

Restore to Me the Joy 42

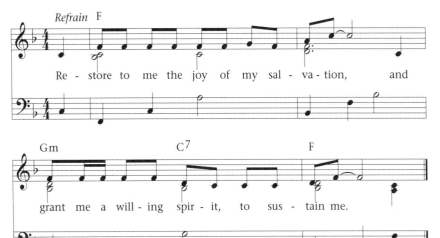

Refrain F

Re - store to me the joy of my sal - va - tion, and

Gm   C⁷   F

grant me a will - ing spir - it, to sus - tain me.

Words: Psalm 51:12
Music: Susan Mulder Langeland, 1993
© 1994, CRC Publications

♩ =92

Lord, Have Mercy upon Us 43

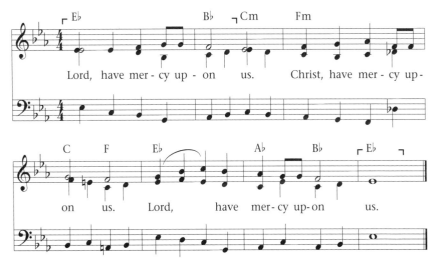

Eb   Bb Cm   Fm

Lord, have mer - cy up - on us.   Christ, have mer - cy up -

C   F   Eb   Ab   Bb   Eb

on us.   Lord,   have mer - cy up - on   us.

Words: Kyrie, from early Christian liturgies
Music: Healy Willan, 1928
Music © 1928, Oxford University Press.

WILLAN KYRIE
Capo 1

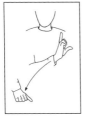

Lord

Mercy

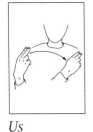

Us

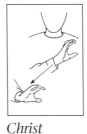

Christ

Like 41, this refrain is also taken from Psalm 51; this time a different verse (v. 12) with a different character. Rather than the single humble petition of the previous refrain, this contains two petitions: that God will restore our joy, and that he will sustain us. So sing with confidence. (But avoid singing too quickly, especially if singing responsorially with the reading of Psalm 51.)

For a third refrain option to the responsorial singing of Psalm 51, here is a setting of the ancient "Kyrie," a Greek word meaning "Lord." These words have been sung in Christian worship for almost two thousand years. Children may enjoy learning them in Greek, the original language of the church:

Kyrie eleison (KEE-ree-eh eh-leh-ee-sohn) Lord, have mercy
Christe eleison (KREE-steh) Christ, have mercy
Kyrie eleison

Explain that "mercy" refers to the undeserved love of God we enjoy in Christ. Feel each phrase by moving your hand in an arc, alternating hands and direction for each phrase. Make the arc a little higher as each phrase builds on higher notes. Ask the children to "draw" the arcs with their hands as well. Sing very smoothly, with a clear tone.

In congregational worship, sing as part of a prayer of confession connected with Psalm 51 or as a response in a litany. Or use as a "frame" for spoken prayers, singing to introduce and conclude the prayer.

Like 43, this is an ancient short prayer for mercy, this time from Latin instead of Greek (see *Words:* at lower left of song page). After Greek, Latin became the language of the church. *Agnus Dei* is pronounced *AH-gnoose DEH-ee*. The *gn* has a soft sound, like the ñ in Spanish for señor.

When Jesus came to be baptized, John the Baptizer said, "Look, the Lamb of God, who takes away the sin of the world!" (John 1:29; see also Isa. 53:7; Rev. 5:6-14). Teach this song with the awareness that Christians have been praying this prayer for almost two thousand years.

Traditionally it is sung three times; the first two times are the same—a prayer for mercy; the third time the final words are a prayer for peace. (Some children may know the Latin words to another song for those final words: "Grant us your peace" in Latin is *Dona nobis pacem*.) Try having one group sing stanza 1, another the identical stanza 2, and everyone together sing stanza 3.

The simple stepwise melody will be accessible to even the youngest children. Ask the children to echo each phrase as you sing it. The melody and rhythm of the "Amen" are more challenging. Encourage the children to imagine they are living back in the 1500s, singing in a chanting style the way children would have then.

Sing in worship during any season of the church year as part of the service of confession and forgiveness or during the celebration of the Lord's Supper. Or choose as a theme hymn during the season of Lent.

44 O Christ, the Lamb of God

♩ = 100

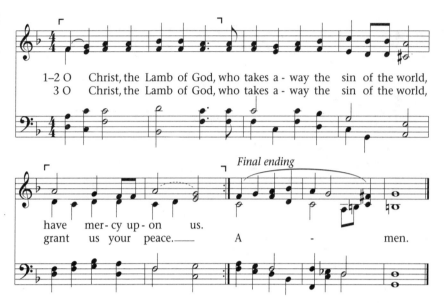

1–2 O Christ, the Lamb of God, who takes a-way the sin of the world,
3 O Christ, the Lamb of God, who takes a-way the sin of the world,

Final ending

have mer-cy up-on us.
grant us your peace.___ A - men.

Words: Agnus Dei (Latin for "Lamb of God"), based on John 1:29
Music: Kirchenordnung, Braunschweig, 1528; harmonized by Dale Grotenhuis, 1984

CHRISTE, DU LAMM GOTTES

Illustration: The Bible portrays Jesus both as a shepherd and a sheep. John the Baptist says of Jesus, "Look, the Lamb of God, who takes away the sin of the world" (John 1:29), most likely a reference to the Old Testament practice of sacrificing sheep in the temple, and to Isaiah 53:7, where the "suffering Servant" is portrayed as a sheep. In the book of Revelation, the Lamb is a sacrificial animal but also a mighty ruler (see 5:6).

♩ = 56

Give Me Peace, O Lord, I Pray 45

1 Give me peace, O Lord, I pray,
2 Give peace to the world, I pray,

in my work and in my play, and in - side my
let all fight - ing stop to - day. May we spread your

heart and mind, Lord, give me peace.
light and love. Lord, give us peace.

Words and Music: Estelle White
© 1976, Kevin Mayhew Publishers. Used by permission. License No. 396070.

This reflective prayer for peace is childlike in its simplicity. The first stanza is a prayer for personal peace; the second focuses on the need for peace in the world and our willingness to spread God's "light and love."

The gentle melody matches the text well. The repetitive phrase structure will help children learn quickly: the first phrase is stated, then repeated one note lower, and then a third time at the original pitch. Encourage the children to sing with their lighter "head" voices and to connect each word to the next as smoothly as possible to help express the peacefulness of both text and melody. Feel the melody flowing in two beats per measure.

The accompaniment can be played by keyboard or guitar, although probably not at the same time. If your older children can handle two-part singing, try teaching them the simple alto part: on phrases 1 and 2, sing the descending scales; on phrase 3, repeat the first descending scale (as seen now in the bass clef), and end with the lowest alto notes in the final phrase.

Sing this prayer at the conclusion of a prayer of confession, following a call to obedience, or in services that focus on peace.

Sing this African-American spiritual and ask the children to identify the most important word (prayer). Then sing it again, asking a number of questions to help the children catch on quickly to the simple message of this spiritual.

- How many times do you hear "standing in the need of prayer"?

- What does "standing in the need of prayer" mean? (Is it joyful praise or a call for help?)

- Who needs prayer?

- Don't any of the other people need prayer?

To get at the call-and-response structure of this song, speak the words, inviting everyone to stand and say the phrase "standing in the need of prayer" every time you stop speaking and fold your hands. Adding the following simple motions is another way to help children learn the text:

extend right arm out, palm up;

extend left arm out, palm up;

point both hands to self;

reach both hands up, palms up;

hold hands together in a prayer position.

Since there are many "r" sounds in this song, ask the children to use soft "r" sounds at the ends of words, even substituting "ah" or "uh" for "r."

Encourage various children to sing the beginning of the phrases solo, with everyone responding on "standing . . . " and the refrain. (Show the melody direction at the phrase endings.) On the refrain, small groups will enjoy singing the echo and older singers can easily learn the harmony. Sing the song fervently, with a little swing, feeling the half note pulse.

Sing as a call to prayer in worship. Or use the refrain alone as a repeated response in a special prayer litany.

46 Standing in the Need of Prayer

♩ = 56

2 Not the elder, nor the deacon, but it's me . . . .
3 Not my father, nor my mother, but it's me . . . .
4 Not the stranger, nor my neighbor, but it's me . . . .

Words and Music: African-American spiritual

Praise God's Name 47

♩ = 108

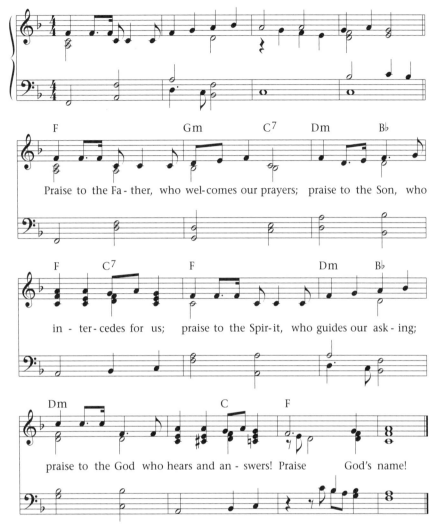

Praise to the Fa - ther, who wel-comes our prayers; praise to the Son, who

in - ter-cedes for us; praise to the Spir-it, who guides our ask - ing;

praise to the God who hears and an - swers! Praise God's name!

Learning this short song in praise of the Trinity will help children understand how God hears and answers prayer. The Father welcomes, the Son intercedes, and the Spirit guides. Tell the children that "intercede" means Jesus, the Son, actually prays for us too!

Each phrase of the song begins with the same rhythmic pattern. The melody should be sung brightly and crisply. Try dividing the children into four equal groups, choosing one child from each group to be the "leader." Have the leaders stand in front of their groups. Teach each group its phrase with all singing the coda. After singing through once, move the leaders one group to the right so that they can help teach the new group their phrase. Then sing the song again. Move the leaders again one group to their right and sing the song again. Repeat this once more. Then move the leaders to their original groups. Everyone will sing all the phrases. You should stand by each leader as his or her phrase is sung.

Sing this song to precede any prayer in a worship service, especially a prayer of thanksgiving and praise. It could also be used during a prayer service.

Words and Music: Dorothy VanAndel Frisch, 1978.

AKRON
Capo 5

48 The Lord's Prayer

♩ = 84

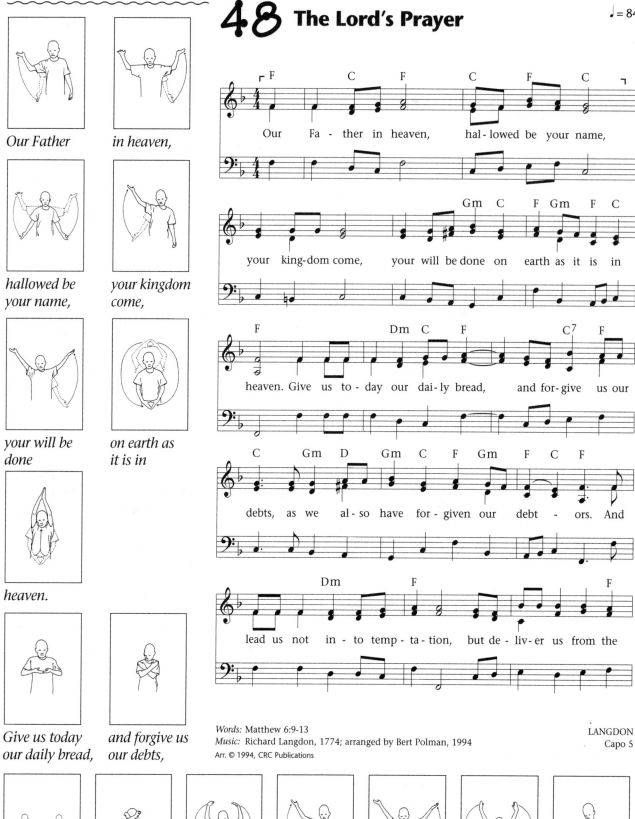

Our Father / *in heaven,*

hallowed be your name, / *your kingdom come,*

your will be done / *on earth as it is in*

heaven.

Give us today our daily bread, / *and forgive us our debts,*

Our Fa-ther in heaven, hal-lowed be your name, your king-dom come, your will be done on earth as it is in heaven. Give us to-day our dai-ly bread, and for-give us our debts, as we al-so have for-given our debt-ors. And lead us not in-to temp-ta-tion, but de-liv-er us from the

Words: Matthew 6:9-13
Music: Richard Langdon, 1774; arranged by Bert Polman, 1994
Arr. © 1994, CRC Publications

LANGDON
Capo 5

as we also have forgiven our debtors.

And lead us not into temptation,

but deliver us from the evil one.

For yours is the kingdom

and the power / *and the glory forever.* / *Amen.*

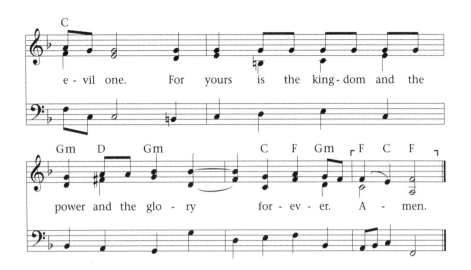

e - vil one. For yours is the king-dom and the

power and the glo - ry for - ev - er. A - men.

♩ = 126

We Can Pray 49

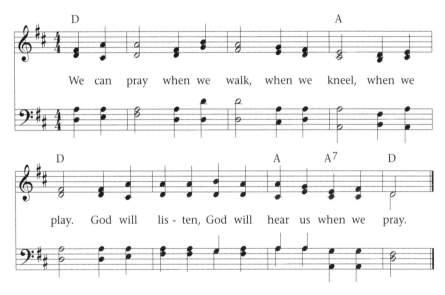

We can pray when we walk, when we kneel, when we

play. God will lis - ten, God will hear us when we pray.

Words and Music: Coby Veenstra, 1985

© 1985, Coby Veenstra-van Duyvenvoorde. Used by permission.

This song teaches children they can pray to God at any time and in any place. Sing the song for your group and ask these questions: When can you pray? What three examples are used in the song?

The song also teaches that God plays an active role in our prayers. Sing it once again, asking, What will God do when you pray?

Ask someone to play the melody on a violin or flute or play the single melody notes on the piano. Before adding the words, ask children to hum along softly, and then sing on "tah." Accompany the song on autoharp or guitar, and use a flute or violin as an introduction and/or conclusion.

Treat this as a theme song for several weeks either before or after praying together as you worship with the children. You may want to offer to lead the congregation in an opening call to prayer with this song.

50 Psalm 25

♩ = 112

Singing the psalms has always been a treasure of the church's worship. This psalm is set in responsorial style. (For an explanation of responsorial style see 41.) The psalm text can be either read or chanted.

The simple melody of the refrain is easily learned by rote. Notice how the initial phrase peaks on the word "lift"; encourage the children to crescendo to that peak and then to sing through to the end of the phrase (the word "soul"). Two keyboard accompaniments are written here: the first is more straightforward and fits a child's hand, the second is more flowing in character and is more difficult. Either accompaniment should be played gently. When played as a duet, the first version should be played two octaves higher than written. Try pairing a child and an adult for the duet.

Another accompaniment for Orff instruments is found below. This pattern should not be played at the same time as the keyboard accompaniments or with the guitar. It does provide a clear foundational pitch for (almost) a cappella singing.

Sing this psalm in worship during the service of confession, as a prayer before the sermon, or as part of the congregational prayer.

To you, O Lord, I lift up my soul;
  in you I trust, O my God.
Do not let me be put to shame,
  nor let my enemies triumph over me. *Refrain*

Show me your ways, O Lord,
  teach me your paths;
guide me in your truth and teach me,
  for you are God and my Savior,
  and my hope is in you all day long. *Refrain*

Remember, O Lord, your great mercy and love,
  for they are from of old.
Remember not the sins of my youth
  and my rebellious ways;
according to your love remember me,
  for you are good, O Lord. *Refrain*

The Lord guides the humble in what is right
  and teaches them his way.
All the ways of the Lord are loving and faithful
  for those who keep the demands of his covenant. *Refrain*

Words: from Psalm 25 (NIV)
Music: Marty Haugen

Capo 1

Orff accompaniment

Duet accompaniment for Psalm 25

Let Us Pray to the Lord 51

Let us pray to the Lord. Lord, hear our prayer.

Alternate Response: Lord, have mercy.

Words: traditional prayer response
Music: Byzantine chant

In peace let us pray to the
  Lord.

Lord, have mercy.

For the peace from above
and for our salvation,
let us pray to the Lord.

Lord, have mercy.

For the peace of the whole
  world,
for the well-being of the
  church of God,
and for the unity of all,
let us pray to the Lord.

Lord, have mercy.

For the faithful who have
  gone before us
and are at rest,
let us give thanks to the Lord.

Al-le-lu-ia.

Help, save, comfort, and de-
  fend us,
gracious Lord. (silent meditation)
Rejoicing in the fellowship of
  all the saints,
let us commend ourselves,
  one another,
and our whole life to Christ,
  our Lord.

To you, O Lord.

At one time in public worship, prayers were sung and even the Scriptures were chanted. This traditional prayer response is set to a historic chant melody.

Sing this response between "sentence prayers" offered by the children. First, hear the spoken prayer, then sing the first phrase unaccompanied and have all the children join on the "Lord, hear our prayer." Don't worry about starting on the exact pitch. In a larger group or congregational set-ting, provide the initial pitch with keyboard or handbell or Orff instrument. The rhythm as notated is only a guide; al-low the syllabic stress of speech rhythm to determine the length of the notes.

In a worship setting an adult choir could continue to hum the final chord (after singing "prayer," simply continue to hum) to accompany the spoken prayers of the worship leader. This can be used as a structure for a prayer of confession or for the prayers of the people.

The litany below is based on litanies from the Eastern litur-gies of St. Basil and St. Chrysos-tom. The person leading in prayer either speaks or chants the petition on G.

Friends are extremely important to children, and they will appreciate this well-known and loved hymn. Joseph Scriven wrote the text in 1855 after experiencing many troubles, including the drowning of his fiancee. He found great comfort in being able to take his troubles to the Lord in prayer. Although small children may not understand some of the text's abstract words, they will all be able to understand that no matter what happens to them, they too can "take it to the Lord in prayer." Jesus will always listen to them.

To teach the text, print each phrase on a strip of colored paper that coordinates with the AABA' melodic form. Leave blanks and hang the phrases up in random order. Sing the song and instruct children to fill in the blanks and arrange the phrases in their proper order. Or print the text on an overhead transparency and gradually cover the key words.

The tune is written in AABA' form, so there are only two long musical phrases to learn. Display the colored papers and sing the song on neutral syllables: "tah" for A and "loo" for B. Ask which phrase is higher and point out the variation at the conclusion.

For a sung or instrumental accompaniment "collage," take advantage of the pentatonic (five tone) tune. The notes and phrases from the song can be combined in many ways. Make patterns with phrases such as "What a friend we have in Jesus," and "everything to God in prayer." Any pattern will work, as long as you use the notes from the song. Instruct children to sing the phrase over

52 What a Friend We Have in Jesus

Words: Joseph M. Scriven, 1855
Music: *The Sacred Harp*, Philadelphia, 1844; harmonized by A. Royce Eckhardt,
    1972; descant by Melinda Ramseth, 1982

87 87 D
BEACH SPRING
Capo 5

pain	we	bear,	all	be -	cause	we	do	not
sor -	rows	share?	Je -	sus	knows	our	ev -	ery
Lord	in	prayer!	In	his	arms	he'll	take	and

car -	ry	ev -	ery -	thing	to	God	in	prayer.
weak -	ness;	take	it	to	the	Lord	in	prayer.
shield	you;	you	will	find	a	so -	lace	there.

and over and combine it with the single melody line, either played or sung. As the singers gain confidence, add more patterns. One group could sing the complete song while others softly sing or play the accompanying ostinato patterns.

To help children feel the triple meter, try this pattern:

beat one: pat thighs

beat two: clap hands

beat three: snap fingers (on eighths)

Be sure to include your instrumental players for introductions and interludes as well as the descant. In worship, include the congregation on stanza 3 in canon with the children leading (conduct the congregation's entrance as well as the children's). Children will also enjoy singing this song in canon on stanza 3 with the adult choir.

53 Kum Ba Yah

♩ = 76

This African-American song originated in the coastal lowlands of South Carolina. *Kum ba yah* is from the Gullah language. It means literally "Come by here." Stanzas 2 through 8 were probably improvised in a service of worship in the tradition of African-American singing. The children may want to add their own stanzas. "Kum Ba Yah" is a prayer offering no specific request other than the Lord's presence. It brings to mind the words of Romans 8:26: "We do not know what we ought to pray for, but the Spirit himself intercedes for us with groans that words cannot express."

The first three phrases are repeated; the final phrase contrasts and brings closure. Teach by echo method. A guitar or autoharp accompaniment would be appropriate. The slow tempo allows for improvisation (adding notes related to the melody and harmony notes) on the long-held notes.

This song is usually associated with informal gatherings and retreats. In congregational worship, it may well serve as a meditative call to prayer.

3 Someone's praying, Lord . . . .
4 Someone's crying, Lord . . . .
5 Someone's hungry, Lord . . . .
6 Someone's hurting, Lord . . . .
7 Someone's dying, Lord . . . .
8 Someone's lonely, Lord . . . .

Kum ba ya means "Come by here."

Words and Music: African-American spiritual; arranged by Norma de Waal Malefyt, 1992
Arr. © 1994, CRC Publications

♩ = 66

Lord, Listen to Your Children Praying 54

Lord, lis-ten to your chil-dren pray-ing,

Lord, send your Spir-it in this place;

Lord, lis-ten to your chil-dren pray-ing, send us

love, send us power, send us grace!

Ken Medema composed this hymn one night while he was meeting with a youth group. They had been talking about a man in the hospital who needed their prayers. During their prayer time, Medema started humming and then singing this song. Soon the kids joined in. This version is only the chorus. The song begins by requesting the presence of the Holy Spirit; its ending calls to mind a familiar benediction found in 2 Corinthians 13:14, "May the grace of the Lord Jesus Christ, and the love of God, and the fellowship of the Holy Spirit be with you all."

Children can easily memorize this song. Be sure to count the beats, taking care to hold the final notes of the phrases for their full duration.

The uses for this song in congregational worship are innumerable: after the spoken portion of a prayer; to "frame" a prayer by singing both before and at its conclusion; to focus the congregation's attention on the presence of God at the beginning of the service. Children may also wish to use this song in their personal devotions or suggest it as a way to end their family devotions.

Words and Music: Ken Medema, 1970

This hymn to the Trinity was written by Elena G. Maquiso, a Filipino. It was translated for the East Asian Christian Conference Hymnal in 1964 by Daniel T. Niles, secretary of the Conference. Bring a globe and point out the Philippines to emphasize that people all around the world are God's children and can sing the same prayers. As you learn each stanza, ask:

- Which person of the Trinity is addressed in this stanza?

- How is this person addressed at the beginning and ending?

As you begin and end each stanza, show the signing motion for the person of the Trinity who is addressed.

Each phrase in this tune repeats the same rhythmic pattern. Teach it to your children by clapping it: alternately pat thighs three times and then clap twice. Ask someone to play it on the piano, and clap the pattern throughout. Let the children sing along with the melody line on two neutral syllables: dah dah di / dah dah. Ask them where the melody is the highest and be careful on the melodic leaps in the fourth measure. Use guitars (or autoharp) and have two flutes or recorders play along on the melody, perhaps with one playing the alto line. For a simple Orff accompaniment, repeat the following four-note pattern, one pitch to a measure: E E A E. The chords are also easy enough for the autoharp. Let the melody flow.

This song is found in the prayer section, but it could have been placed many different places. For congregational worship, sing as an opening or closing song, for Lent and Easter (st. 2), for baptism (st. 3), for Pentecost (st. 3), or with any time of prayer.

55 Father in Heaven

♩ = 96

1 Fa-ther in heav-en, grant to your chil-dren mer-cy and bless-ing, songs nev-er ceas-ing, love to u-nite us, grace to re-deem us; Fa-ther in heav-en, Fa-ther, our God.

2 Je-sus, Re-deem-er, may we re-mem-ber your gra-cious pas-sion, your res-ur-rec-tion; wor-ship we bring you, praise we shall sing you, Je-sus, Re-deem-er, Je-sus, our Lord.

3 Spir-it de-scend-ing, grant us your bless-ing, strength for the wea-ry, help for the need-y; sealed by a-dop-tion, we are God's chil-dren; Spir-it de-scend-ing, Spir-it a-dored.

Words: Elena G. Maquiso, 1961; translated by Daniel Thambyrapah Niles, 1964
Music: Elena G. Maquiso, 1961, harmonized by Charles H. Webb, 1987

Trans. used by permission of Christian Conference of Asia; music © 1962, Silliman University Music Foundation, Inc.; harm. © 1989, The United Methodist Publishing House.

55 55
HALAD

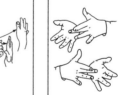

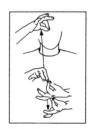

Father   *Jesus*   *Spirit*

Blessed Jesus, at Your Word 56

♩ = 108

1 Bless-ed Je-sus, at your word we are gath-ered
2 Glo-rious Lord, your-self im-part; Light of Light, from

all to hear you. Let our hearts and souls be stirred
God pro-ceed-ing, o-pen lips and ears and heart;

now to seek and love and fear you. By your gos-pel
help us by your Spir-it's lead-ing. Hear the cry your

pure and ho-ly, teach us, Lord, to love you sole-ly.
church now rais-es; Lord, ac-cept our prayers and prais-es.

This song offers a prayer that Jesus may help us listen to and really hear what God's Word has to say to us. We need open lips, ears, and heart (st. 2) to receive God's teaching from the Scriptures. Explain that "impart" (st. 2) means to give. The beautiful rhymed poetry will help the children learn the text.

The melody is in three sections, with the first repeated (AAB). It should be sung in three long lines. Teach the children the words through echo singing, two measures at a time. Be sure to model good breathing and careful enunciation. This song may be accompanied by piano, guitar, or autoharp.

In congregational worship, have the children lead the congregation by singing one of the two stanzas, with all joining on the other stanza. Sing as an opening hymn or as a prayer for illumination before the Scripture and sermon.

Words: Tobias Clausnitzer, 1663; translated by Catherine Winkworth, 1858
Music: Johann R. Ahle, 1664

78 78 88
LIEBSTER JESU

Psalm 119:105 is the setting for "Your Word." Wonder with the children how the Word of God can be a lamp. Talk about what a lamp does (gives light), how feet walk on paths, and how it is very hard to know where we are going if it is dark. The light of God's Word shows us the way— to walk, to live, to follow Jesus.

This echo song is the first of five Scripture songs composed by Frank Hernandez for this hymnal (see 202, 212, 218, 223). He has also produced a recording of them (*Hide 'Em in Your Heart*) sung by Steve Green and children from Christ Community Church in Franklin, Tennessee. Steve writes:

Marijean and I are constantly looking for ways to encourage and strengthen our children in the Lord Jesus.

There are some things that kids are capable of choosing for themselves, but the more foundational choices that result in godly character must be made for them. These include providing them with resources that will nurture their faith in God.

Nothing surpasses the treasure of hiding God's Word in our hearts.

The echo approach and the repetitive phrases makes this song accessible even to very young children. Begin by singing the song, having the children sing only the echo parts. After the children know the song, try dividing into two groups, singing antiphonally on the opening phrases and together on "is a lamp to my feet."

57 Your Word

♩ = 72

Words: Psalm 119:105
Music: Frank Hernandez

Capo 1

58 When We Wonder

♩ = 112

The source of this song is "Long Ago Within the Temple," a song by Flora Kirkland about Jesus as a twelve-year old boy in the temple. This new stanza is a reflection on the amazement Jesus' parents and the temple rulers felt when they listened to this twelve-year-old boy. They were filled with wonder at his wisdom. We too, young and old, are filled with wonder when we meet Jesus.

Sing this song in congregational worship just before the Scripture and sermon.

When we won-der, ask-ing ques-tions, teach us, Lord, your learn-ing youth. Je-sus, help us lis-ten close-ly to your wis-dom and your truth.

Words: Emily R. Brink, 1992
Music: melody from *The Christian Lyre*, 1830; arranged by Robert Roth, 1989
Words © 1994, CRC Publications. Arr. © 1989, Robert Roth. Used by permission.

87 87 D
PLEADING SAVIOR
Capo 5

How Great Is the Love of the Father 59

♩ = 100

1 How great is the love of the Fa - ther, the love he has
2 The world with-out God does not know us be - cause it did
3 What we are to be in the fu - ture as yet has not

shown to us— so great that he calls us his chil - dren, and
not know Christ. Lord, help us to be pure and spot - less, for
been made known, but when Christ re - turns, we shall see him, and

chil - dren of God we are, and chil - dren of God we are!
chil - dren of God we are, for chil - dren of God we are.
then we shall be like him, and then we shall be like him.

The apostle John's first letter contains a passage (1 John 3:1-3) expressing wonder at God's great love for us. This song is based on that passage. Stanza 1 expresses awe at God's choice to call us his children. Stanza 2 is a prayer to live pure lives, like Christ. And stanza 3 speaks of our hope that, when Jesus comes back, we will be like Christ.

James Ward, a performer and songwriter of contemporary Christian music, composed the tune. Its simple, childlike quality fits well with the text. Teach this song by echo method. You may choose to first introduce this song by teaching the children the final repeated phrases. Then sing the other phrases. For a special finale on stanza 3, try teaching the children to sing an octave higher on the last three words, "be like him."

This hymn fits well in many places in congregational worship. It would be especially effective after the assurance of pardon in a baptism service.

Words: 1 John 3:1-3; versified by Edna W. Sikkema, 1986
Music: James Ward, 1985
Words © 1987, CRC Publications. Music © 1987, Music Anno Domini. Used by permission.

97 97 with repeat
ANNO DOMINI

This hymn helps us understand the biblical teaching about baptism. Each stanza starts with the same phrase, taken from John 3:5 and Ephesians 1:13. Stanza 1, based on Titus 3:5-7 and Hebrews 10:14, says that all who believe in Jesus and his promises will be forgiven for their sins. The water used in baptism is a symbol of the washing away of our sins.

Stanza 2, based on Romans 6:3-4 and Colossians 2:12, says that our old sinful way of life has been buried, just as Jesus was buried, and now we have a new way of life, free from sin.

Stanza 3, based on Romans 8:15-16 and Ephesians 4:5-6, tells us that baptism is a sign that everyone who is baptized is one of God's children.

The melody is a folk tune from Scotland. Several other songs have been sung to this tune, including "Morning Has Broken" and "Child in the Manger." Keep the song moving by feeling one beat per measure. A recorder (or other C instrument) could be used to play the melody on the first two stanzas and the descant on the third stanza.

In congregational worship, sing in a baptism service.

60 Baptized in Water

1 Bap-tized in wa - ter, sealed by the Spir - it,
2 Bap-tized in wa - ter, sealed by the Spir - it,
3 Bap-tized in wa - ter, sealed by the Spir - it,

cleansed by the blood of Christ, our King;
dead in the tomb with Christ, our King;
marked with the sign of Christ, our King;

heirs of sal - va - tion, trust - ing his prom - ise,
one with his ris - ing, freed and for - giv - en,
born of one Fa - ther, we are his chil - dren,

faith - ful - ly now God's praise we sing.
thank - ful - ly now God's praise we sing.
joy - ful - ly now God's praise we sing.

Words: Michael Saward, 1981
Music: Gaelic melody, arranged by Norma de Waal Malefyt, 1992
Words © 1982, Hope Publishing Company. Used by permission. Arr. © 1994, CRC Publications.

558 D
BUNESSAN

Illustration: The seashell, primarily as a container of water, is an ancient symbol for baptism. Some churches have baptismal fonts in the shape of a shell. A shell is sometimes used to pour water on the person being baptized. It has also been used as a symbol for immortality—since baptism shows our life in Christ.

61 Jesus Loves Me

♩ = 60

The first stanza of this hymn is likely the first song of the Christian faith that children learn. The first two stanzas in this setting were written by Anna B. Warner in 1859 as part of a novel. At one point in this (now forgotten) novel, a dying boy is comforted by his Sunday school teacher who sings to him four stanzas. The third stanza printed here was rewritten by David Rutherford and published in 1971. This text weaves together some of the most basic truths of our experience as Christians: Jesus loves us (Eph. 5:2, Jer. 31:3), Jesus saves us (Gal. 2:20), and Jesus invites us to come to him (Matt. 18:2-4; 19:13-15).

The Sunday school composer William Bradbury added the refrain lines to these stanzas and wrote the music in 1861. The refrain simply emphasizes that we know Jesus' love from the Bible. The tune is called CHINA in some hymnals, presumably because of its popularity among missionaries to China. Translated into many other languages, this hymn has become an expression of faith among Christian children in many nations. Children enjoy signing the text of the hymn as they sing, and they might also enjoy learning it in a foreign language.

"Jesus Loves Me" could well be used in congregational worship as a hymn of testimony to God's love, at a baptism service, or following a child's profession of faith.

1 Je - sus loves me, this I know, for the Bi - ble
2 Je - sus loves me— he who died heav - en's gate to
3 Je - sus loves me, this I know, as he loved so

tells me so. Lit - tle ones to him be - long;
o - pen wide. He will wash a - way my sin,
long a - go, tak - ing chil - dren on his knee,

they are weak, but he is strong.
let his lit - tle child come in. Yes, Je - sus
say - ing, "Let them come to me."

loves me! Yes, Je - sus loves me!

Refrain

77 77 with refrain
JESUS LOVES ME

Words: stanzas 1-2, Anna B. Warner, 1859; stanza 3, David R. McGuire, 1971; translations: Cherokee, Robert Bushyhead, 1962; Japanese phonetic transcription, Mas Kawashima, 1988; Spanish, *Himnario Metodista*, 1968
Music: William B. Bradbury, 1861; harmonized by Emily R. Brink, 1993

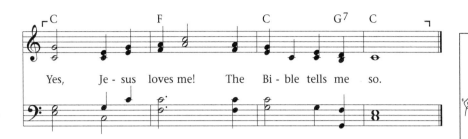

Yes, Je - sus loves me! The Bi - ble tells me so.

Yes

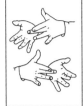

Jesus

Refrain in other languages

Cherokee

Tsis a ki ke yu	(TSEE-sah key KAY you,)
Tsis a ki ke yu	(TSEE-sah key KAY you,)
Tsis a ki ke yu	(TSEE-sah key KAY you,)
a khi no hih se ho.	(a KEY no hee say hoh.)

Japanese

Waga shu Iesu,	(wah gah shoo ee-eh soo,)
Waga shu Iesu,	(wah gah shoo ee-eh soo,)
Waga shu Iesu,	(wah gah shoo ee-eh soo,)
Ware wo aisu.	(wah reh woh ah-ee soo.)

Spanish

Cristo me ama,	(KREES-toe may AH-mah,)
Cristo me ama,	(KREES-toe may AH-mah,)
Cristo me ama,	(KREES-toe may AH-mah,)
La biblia dice así.	(Lah BEE-blee-yah DEE-say ah-SEE.)

Swahili

Yesu anipenda,	(YEH-soo ah͜ nee-PEH-ndah,)
Yesu anipenda,	(YEH-soo ah͜ nee-PEH-ndah,)
Yesu anipenda,	(YEH-soo ah͜ nee-PEH-ndah,)
Biblia yasema.	(Bee-BLEE-yah ya-SEH-mah.)

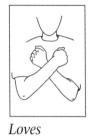

Loves

Me

62 God Claims You

♩. = 60

This song goes a long way toward helping children understand what goes on in baptism. Baptism begins with God's promises to us (refrain). We confess that God's promises last forever (st. 1). And in baptism, parents and the church also make promises (st. 2).

To teach this song, make a display of all your singers' names, using baptism symbols such as shells (see 60) and drops of water as a background. Encourage children to attach a picture of themselves next to their name. Then talk about how each person is a child of God, baptized as a sign of God's promise. Sing the refrain and ask the children what God does for them. When you sing the stanzas, help children understand you are singing to each other as the family of God. Explain that a vow is a promise. Young children will especially enjoy inserting their own names and their parents' names. Have fun together by forming a circle and singing to a special birthday person standing in the middle. Or you could sing to a group, inserting a description of the group, such as "boys of first grade" or "girls of preschool."

This peaceful melody is so soothing, it can almost be called a lullaby. Sing the song gently but also joyfully, feeling one beat per measure.

In worship, invite all the children to come forward to participate in a service of infant baptism; after the baptism they sing this song to the child. Perhaps the whole congregation could join on the stanzas. If more than one child is baptized, simply change the opening rhythm to sing "Children of promise."

*may insert child's name, or sing "Child of promise"
**may insert parents' names "Jeff and Kathy love you so, they vow. . . ."

Words and Music: Stanley M. Farr; harmonized by Emily R. Brink, 1994
Words and melody © 1981, Stanley M. Farr. Harm. © 1994, CRC Publications.

♩ = 96

Lift Up Your Hearts 63

Descant

(Lord!)

1 Lift up your hearts un-to the Lord,

Cm   Gm   Cm   Gm   Cm

1 Lift up your hearts un-to the Lord,   lift up your

hearts un-to the Lord.   Sing al-le-lu-ia, sing al-le-

Sing al-le-lu-ia, al - le - lu-

G   Cm   Gm   A♭

ia;   lift up your hearts un-to the Lord!

E♭   Fm   Gm   Cm   Gm   5 C

lu - ia;   lift up your hearts un-to the Lord!

2 In Christ the world has been redeemed. . . .
3 His resurrection sets us free. . . .
4 Therefore we celebrate the feast. . . .
5 Sing alleluia to the Lord! . . .

Words: stanzas 1-4, early Christian liturgy; stanza 5, Linda Stassen, 1974   SING ALLELUIA
Music: Linda Stassen, 1974; harmonized by Dale Grotenhuis, 1986   Capo 3
St. 5 and Music © 1974, Linda Stassen

The text of the first four stanzas of this popular praise chorus are derived from early Christian liturgies and the "Easter Canticle," which includes references to 1 Cor. 5:7-8 and 15:20-22. The tune and stanza 5 were written by Linda Stassen in 1974. Imagine yourself singing this as part of a choir of Christians of all times and from all places.

The repetition in the text and the short melodic phrases, which move primarily by step, combine to make the song accessible to all children. Once they know it, try these additional stanzas. Encourage children to come up with other ideas as well.

Jesus is risen from the dead. (Easter)

Jesus is Lord of heaven and earth. (Ascension)

He poured his Spirit on us all. (Pentecost)

Jesus is coming back again. (Ascension)

The descant/echo second part imitates the first part initially and again at the close but is fully independent in the middle for the "Sing alleluia" phrases. Wait with the descant voices until the main melody is secure. Then add the descant played by instruments before inviting some of the older children to sing it. Each stanza ends by repeating the initial line of that stanza.

Keyboard or guitar accompaniment is preferred; trumpet, flute, recorder or handbells could be added on either voice part. Sing this at a moving tempo with no breaks between stanzas. Signing would work well on this song, if not on all the text, certainly on "sing alleluia to the Lord."

In worship settings sing prior to or during communion, or as a celebration song during the Easter season. Sing the fourth stanza as an introduction to the "feast" in the Children and Worship program.

64 I Come with Joy to Meet My Lord

When we celebrate the Lord's Supper during Lent, we may remember in solemn tones Christ's sacrifice on the cross. But during Easter and at other times of the year, we "come with joy" to meet Christ at his table because by his sacrifice we are "forgiven, loved, and free." That spirit of joy is the focus of this communion hymn.

Brian Wren, an English minister, wrote this hymn as a summary of a series of sermons he preached on the Lord's Supper. The stanzas progress from the individual "I" (st. 1, 2) to the communal "us" and "we" (st. 3-5). We come one by one to worship, but at the Lord's table we find "the new community of love."

This Appalachian folk tune probably has Scottish or English roots. Folk music was originally passed orally from generation to generation with no written score. Since people heard and performed folk music from memory, you can imagine the number of variations possible! This hymn sounds best sung two pulses per measure with a light feeling. Teach the song by singing one phrase at a time and having the children echo each phrase. Next, echo two phrases at a time. Finally, echo the complete song.

There are many ways to sing this song. Possibilities include choosing a soloist on stanzas 1-2, all children on 3, and congregation on 5. Or have children sing stanzas 1 and 2,

4 And thus with joy we meet our Lord;
   his presence, always near,
   is in such friendship better known:
   we see and praise him here.

5 Together met, together bound,
   we'll go our different ways;
   and as his people in the world,
   we'll live and speak his praise.

Words: Brian Wren, 1968, revised 1977
Music: American; harmonized by Annabel Morris Buchanan, 1938

CM
LAND OF REST
Capo 5

adding the congregation on 3-5. Since the melody is pentatonic, singing in canon (at one measure) is also possible. For example, singing in canon on stanza 2 could symbolize coming all together from different places "far and near," and on stanza 5 it could symbolize going "our different ways."

In a communion service, sing as an opening hymn or during the distribution of the elements. Reserve stanza 5 for the conclusion of the Lord's Supper or sing at the end of the service.

As Your Family, Lord, Meet Us Here 65

♩ = 66

As your family, Lord, meet us here,
    as your family, Lord, meet us here,
    as your family, Lord, meet us here,
    O Lord, meet us here.

At your table, Lord, we are fed,
    at your table, Lord, we are fed,
    at your table, Lord, we are fed,
    O Lord, feed us here.

Fill our spirits, Lord, with your love,
    fill our spirits, Lord, with your love,
    fill our spirits, Lord, with your love,
    O Lord, with your love.

Make us faithful, Lord, to your will,
    make us faithful, Lord, to your will,
    make us faithful, Lord, to your will,
    O Lord, to your will.

As your family, Lord, meet us here,
    as your family, Lord, meet us here,
    as your family, Lord, meet us here,
    O Lord, meet us here.

Words: Anonymous
Music: KUM BA YAH, see no. 53

As your singers enter the room, create a quiet, peaceful atmosphere: softly play the piano or guitar and begin your session by singing this prayer song. Use it to teach children about the Lord's Supper. The stanzas move from adoration to service. Note also that the second stanza changes the pattern at the end. After the children have heard and sung the complete song, ask them,

- How many times is the first line of each stanza sung?

- What words always begin the fourth line?

Explain the first (and last) stanza by telling the children that God, who is present everywhere and at all times, calls his children to worship and enter into his presence. In this song we respond to that call, asking God to declare his presence by entering our hearts and filling us with spiritual food so we can faithfully love and serve him.

The African-American folk tune KUM BA YAH (53) is a perfect match to the mood and spirit of this text. Use a guitar or autoharp for quiet accompaniment.

Sing during a communion service as a response to God's call to worship or during the passing of the elements.

Illustration: The grapes with the wine or juice in the goblet and the sheaves of wheat with the loaf of bread are familiar symbols for the Lord's Supper, as captured beautifully in the following ancient prayer: "As this grain has been gathered from many fields into one loaf and these grapes from many hills into one cup, grant, O Lord, that your whole church may soon be gathered from the ends of the earth into your kingdom."

66 "Holy, Holy, Holy"
"Santo, Santo, Santo"

♩ = 84

The prophet Isaiah saw a vision of heaven: he saw heavenly creatures flying above the throne of God crying to each other, "Holy, holy, holy is the Lord Almighty; the whole earth is full of his glory." Later, in the book of Revelation, the apostle John saw a similar vision, also with creatures calling out to each other, "Holy, holy, holy." The word "holy" tells us something important about God, especially since it is repeated three times. To be holy is to be perfect and pure. Our God is a holy God.

These words from Isaiah 6:3 have been set to music by Christians in every age. They are still part of the historic liturgy for the Lord's Supper, which is why this song is placed in the "Lord's Supper" section. The Spanish word *santo* is very similar to the Latin *sanctus,* which is a name frequently given to these words.

The Latin American tune contains rhythmic elements found in Cuban and Haitian dance forms. Invite the children to clap every quarter note. Use a variety of rhythm and percussion instruments with guitar. If possible, find someone who knows Spanish and learn the Spanish words as well.

In congregational worship, sing as an opening hymn, as part of the Lord's Supper liturgy, or as a doxology. Have the children sing first, followed by the congregation. In Hispanic folk hymn tradition, try pairing this song with others in the same key, such as 16 and 17.

"Ho - ly, ho - ly, ho - ly," an - gel hosts are sing - ing.
"San - to, san - to, san - to," can - tan se - ra - fi - nes.

"Ho - ly, ho - ly, ho - ly is the Lord our God.
"San - to, san - to, san - to, Dios es el Se - ñor.

Ho - ly, ho - ly, ho - ly is God, the Lord of might. Your
San - to, san - to, san - to es fuer - te nue - stro Dios. Tu

glo - ry fills the heav - ens, your glo - ry fills the earth." Ho -
glo - ria lle - na los cie - los, la tie - rra lle - na es - tá." Ho -

Words: based on Isaiah 6:3; English paraphrase by Bert Polman, 1985
Music: Spanish; harmonized by AnnaMae Meyer Bush, 1985
Words and harm. © 1987, CRC Publications

MERENGUE

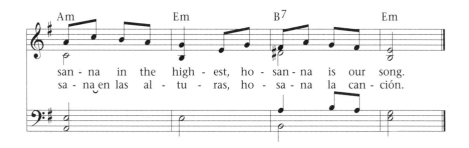

- san - na in the high - est, ho - san - na is our song.
sa - na en las al - tu - ras, ho - sa - na la can - ción.

♩ = 108 **Christ Has Died, Christ Is Risen** **67**

Repeated sections are sung first by leader, then by all.

Christ has died, Christ is ris - en, Christ will come a - gain!

Words: from an ancient liturgy for the Lord's Supper
Music: James A. Kriewald
Music © 1985, The United Methodist Publishing House

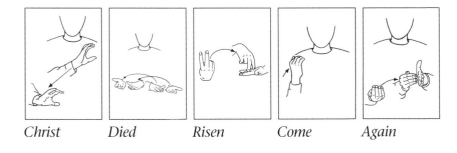

Christ *Died* *Risen* *Come* *Again*

These words, which have been used in the liturgy for the Lord's Supper for centuries, are often called the "memorial acclamation." We remember and we acclaim the central truths of the Christian faith in this very short profession of faith. Adding the signing motions will add to the depth of the profession.

This echo song will be accessible immediately to even the youngest of children. Model for them this firm statement of faith by singing with a clear bright tone. Sing the first phrase clearly and firmly. The second phrase should rise to a bright climax on the high note. And then joyfully sing the conclusion. For a two-measure introduction, ring bells on the pitch G on the first beat of every measure; the bells can play throughout. This music is joyful!

In congregational worship, sing through twice; first the children sing, then they lead with the congregation responding. Sing as a profession of faith, especially during a communion service, or during any service in the Easter season.

Sue Ellen Page was eighteen when she wrote her first composition, "Sing Alleluia." This arrangement is a condensation of her anthem, available from the Choristers Guild. The original anthem has four stanzas with more varied accompaniment and some optional harmony singing.

Each stanza is made up of two identical musical phrases, and the rhyming text consists of several short phrases of a measure each. The song encourages us to praise God for dwelling in and among us (st. 1), to share the good news (st. 2), and to be thankful and show others that God lives in us (st. 3). Explain to the children that the promise mentioned in stanza 3 is the promise of salvation.

One unusual feature of this song is that it switches back and forth between minor and major keys. The stanzas are written in D minor, while the refrain is in D major. Because every phrase is different, the refrain is more challenging. Have the children echo one measure at a time. On the refrain, make sure you model bright high F-sharps.

Sue Ellen Page indicates that the anthem is for "unison treble voices with Organ, Tambourine, and Hand Drum. (Alto Glockenspiel, Soprano Metallophone, Finger Cymbals, Guitar optional)." She also indicates that "organ [rather than piano] is preferred when the glockenspiel and metallophone are used. Guitar is strictly optional and when used must be arpeggiated or

68 Sing Alleluia

♩ = 76

plucked, never strummed." For the metallaphone and alto glockenspiel parts, she has this advice: "Teacher stands with back to class, hands raised, tracing pattern as though playing the instrument. Class joins, singing pitches on a neutral syllable or cue words."

Take care to observe the suggested tempo marking. A bright, sprightly quality can be achieved through clear consonant sounds and a light-sounding voice. Teach the music thoroughly first before adding the suggested accompanying instruments. Begin with the refrain. Next, produce a chart contain-

♩ = 104

Lord, Be Glorified   71

Descant

1 In my life, Lord, I will glo - ri - fy, glo - ri - fy.

D   Bm   G   A   C   A

1 In my life, Lord, be glo - ri - fied, be glo - ri - fied.

In my life, Lord, I will glo - ri - fy you.

D   Bm   Em   A⁷   D

In my life, Lord, be glo - ri - fied to - day.

2 In my song, Lord . . . .   3 In your church, Lord . . . .

Other stanzas may also be added: home, school, class, and so on.

With sweet simplicity this song expresses our desire for God to be glorified in all that we do (Phil. 1:20). Invite the children to add stanzas naming ways they can show honor to God at home, with their friends, in church, at school. Bob Kilpatrick, who wrote this song, sings it with his wife before their concerts as a song of dedication.

The music and words will be easily learned by the children. Sing it to them once or twice, then ask them to join you. After they have the melody down, introduce the descant by having a solo instrument, such as a flute, play the notes. Perhaps some older children can learn the descant separately, then sing in two-part harmony with the main melody. Use a gentle accompaniment and sing meditatively.

In congregational worship, sing this during any time of dedication. Or sing in a service of adult baptism or profession of faith.

Words and Music: Bob Kilpatrick, 1978   BE GLORIFIED

This hymn was first published in *Golden Bells,* a London children's hymnbook. The first four stanzas "catalog" four different ways Christians want to become more like Christ: stanza 1 is a prayer to be filled with the mind of Christ (Phil. 2:5); stanza 2 for the word of God to dwell in us (Col. 3:16); stanza 3 for the peace of God to rule us (Col. 3:15); stanza 4 for the love of Jesus to fill us. Stanza 5 uses the imagery of "running a race" from Hebrews 12:1-2. The first four stanzas are personal expressions, the final stanza is plural; we need each other!

There are a lot of words with no repetition in this text. You may want to choose one or two stanzas to learn, or teach individual stanzas to different groups of children. The text has a richness and depth that will grow with a child throughout life; learning a song of faith for a lifetime is well worth extra time and effort. You may want to make a separate chart for each stanza with key words either pictured or written to help the children learn the words.

The melody has two four-measure phrases. Sing smoothly with good breath support for the long phrases and high pitch in the middle. A keyboard accompaniment would be most effective. Older children may be able to learn the descant which could be played by flute, recorder, oboe, clarinet, or trumpet on the final two stanzas.

72 May the Mind of Christ, My Savior

♩ = 96

4 May the love of Jesus fill me
   as the waters fill the sea.
   Him exalting, self abasing:
   this is victory.

5 May we run the race before us,
   strong and brave to face the foe,
   looking only unto Jesus
   as we onward go.

Words: Kate B. Wilkinson, 1925
Music: A. Cyril Barham-Gould, 1925; descant by Emily R. Brink, 1986
Music used by permission of the estate of A. C. Barham-Gould. Descant © 1987, CRC Publications.

87 85
ST. LEONARDS

In congregational worship, have the children sing one of the stanzas. Sing as an offering hymn, as a dismissal hymn, or as a response immediately following the sermon. For special occasions the "me/my" of stanzas 1-4 could be changed to "you/your" —as a sung blessing on new members of the church, for sending forth missionaries, for ordination of church officers, and for profession of faith.

♩ = 56

I Believe in God 73

I be-lieve in God the Fa-ther. I be-lieve in God the Son. I be-lieve in God the Ho-ly Spir-it. I be-lieve these three are One.

Words: based on the Apostles' Creed
Music: Cary Ratcliff, 1986
© 1986, Cary Ratcliff

87 10 7
KAREN'S CREED
Capo 3

Illustration: These symbols capture our faith in the triune God, summarized in the Apostles' Creed. The creating hand stands for God, the Father: "I believe in God, the Father . . . Creator of Heaven and earth." The cross summarizes Jesus' sacrificial death: "I believe in Jesus Christ . . . crucified." The dove is a biblical symbol of the Spirit: "I believe in the Holy Spirit."

This simple song of profession is based on the Apostles' Creed and focuses on the triune nature of God. To introduce the song you may want to display a symbol that can help the children understand the concept "three in one" (for example, a triangle or a three-way light bulb). Relate the symbols at the bottom of the page to the three persons of the Trinity: Father, Son, and Holy Spirit. The repetition of the text at the beginning of each phrase makes the song easy to learn.

Sing this melody in two rather than in four beats per measure. This gives the song a childlike lilt and grace. Encourage the children to breathe on the quarter-note rest at the beginning of the last line so they can maintain the rhythmic energy generated through the hymn. Once the children have learned the hymn, they could sing it a cappella, or accompanied only with an ostinato pattern in a rocking motif of B-flat F C F. Play it an octave higher than written on keyboard or Orff instruments or even bells. You may also want to sing this song in canon, the second group beginning when the first group reaches the third measure.

This hymn could be sung in worship services that focus on the Trinity or on profession of faith. It could also surround the spoken profession of the Apostles' Creed.

This is a contemporary version of a text written by the English poet Frances Ridley Havergal (1836-1879). Notice the couplets: every two lines rhyme, almost as if every stanza is composed of two small verses. There is no comma after the first phrase in each of the first couplets. Encourage the children to think of the word phrases they are singing; try singing through the long notes at the end of the first phrases, connecting with the second phrase without a breath. To teach the text, prepare a chart or develop motions to help remember the sequence of each couplet: Take my life, moments (st. 1), hands, feet (st. 2), voice, lips (st. 3), love, myself (st. 4).

Timothy Hoekman wrote the tune for this text. The smooth and flowing melody captures well the spirit of dedication and offering of the words. Trace the shape of the melodic line with your hand as you sing, showing how the lines go up and down. Begin each phrase on your right and end each on your left. Sing with a smooth legato. The children can then show the shape of the lines with their hands as they echo you on each phrase.

Keyboard accompaniment will be very helpful in creating smooth connected phrases. Try adding flute or another melody instrument to provide a smooth flowing melodic line and support to the voices.

Sing this song during an offering, in a service of consecration, after a public profession of faith, as a response to a sermon, or as a response to a prayer of commitment. Also encourage the children to use this song in their personal devotions.

74 Take My Life

♩ = 92

1 Take my life that it may be all you purpose, Lord, for me. Take my moments and my days; let them sing your endless praise.
2 Take my hands and let them move at the impulse of your love. Take my feet and lead their way; never let them go astray.
3 Take my voice and let me sing always, only, for my King. Take my lips and keep them true, filled with messages from you.
4 Take my love; my Lord, I pour at your feet its treasure store. Take myself, and I will be yours for all eternity.

Words: Frances R. Havergal, 1874; revised for *Psalter Hymnal*, 1987
Music: Timothy Hoekman, 1979
Music © 1985, CRC Publications

77 77
TEBBEN

♩ = 112

Love the Lord 75

1 Love the Lord, love the Lord, love the Lord with
2 Love the Lord, love the Lord, love the Lord with
3 Seek the Lord, seek the Lord, seek the Lord with
4 Serve the Lord, serve the Lord, serve the Lord with

all your heart. Love the Lord and love each oth-er.
all your soul. Love the Lord with all your be-ing.
all your mind. In God's Word his truth I find.
all your strength. Heart and soul and mind and strength—

I will love the Lord with all my heart.
I will love the Lord with all my soul.
I will seek the Lord with all my mind.
I will love the Lord with all I am.

Words and Music: Austin C. Lovelace, 1978
© 1978, Choristers Guild. Used by permission.

In Deuteronomy 6, God gives instructions for parents to teach their children his laws so they can teach their children from generation to generation. The most basic command is "Love the Lord your God with all your heart and with all your soul and with all your strength." Jesus repeated this commandment, adding that a second like it is to love our neighbors as ourselves. This song (and 76) provides a summary of God's law as found in Deuteronomy 6:5, Leviticus 19:18, and repeated by Jesus in Matthew 22:37-38.

This song by Austin C. Lovelace summarizes Scripture in a clear, concise way that is easy for children to learn. The melody is wonderful for developing children's voices. The outlining of the chords teaches pitch relationship and develops an ear for harmony. Sing the scale passage in the last line smoothly.

Lovelace originally wrote this as an anthem with keyboard accompaniment (available from the Choristers Guild) in which every stanza goes one half step higher (beginning on D-flat, ending in E); if you are interested in that arrangement for the accompanist, the children could still sing this setting.

Sing as a response to the law or in place of the reading of the law. Or sing as a "charge" to the congregation just before the benediction.

Like the previous song, this is based on the summary of God's law as found in Mark 12:30-31, Deuteronomy 6:5, Leviticus 19:18, Galatians 5:14, and James 2:8.

Every hymnal includes hymns by Isaac Watts. You may want to show children the author index of your pew hymnal and ask them to find some (for example, "Joy to the World," 137, and "When I Survey the Wondrous Cross," 166). This short song is part of a poem Watts wrote for the children of Thomas Abney, a family he lived with for many years.

The melody comes from a choir anthem, "Lord, for Thy Tender Mercies' Sake," written by John Hilton (sometimes attributed to Richard Farrant) nearly 450 years ago in the sixteenth century. Have children sing this song at a steady tempo. Accompany with organ or piano. A "C" instrument (flute, violin, recorder, oboe) could play the melody.

Sing in worship as a summary of the law, a response to the reading of the Ten Commandments, or an introduction or response to a prayer of confession. Consider pairing with "If You Love Me" (151) or "Father, I Adore You" (28).

76 Love God with All Your Soul and Strength

♩ = 108

Words: Deuteronomy 6:5; Leviticus 19:18; versified by Isaac Watts, 1715
Music: English, 16th century; adapted by Edward Hodges, 1835; arranged by Emily R. Brink, 1993

Arr. © 1994, CRC Publications

CM
FARRANT
Capo 5

77 Father, We Love You

♩ = 60

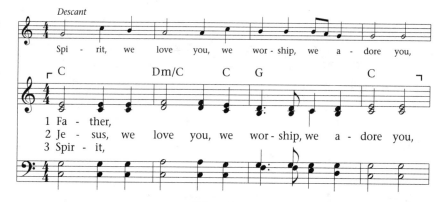

Words: Donna Adkins, 1976
Music: Donna Adkins, 1976; harmonized by Dale Grotenhuis, 1985; descant by Betty Carr Pulkingham

GLORIFY THY NAME

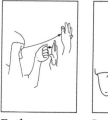

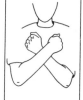

Father   *Love*

glo - ri - fy your name in all the earth,

glo - ri - fy your name in all the earth,

glo - ri - fy, glo - ri - fy,

glo - ri - fy your name, glo - ri - fy your name,

glo - ri - fy your name in all the earth, in all the earth.

glo - ri - fy your name in all the earth.

Written in 1976, this has become one of the most loved of the contemporary praise choruses. It has one stanza for each person of the Trinity: Father, Son, and Holy Spirit. Each begins by telling God how much we love him and continues with the words of Jesus, "Glorify your name" (John 12:28). Each ends by asking that the name of God be glorified "in all the earth" (Ps. 108:5; Isa. 6:3).

Start singing this song softly and build the volume up on each "glorify your name" until the last phrase is quite loud and full. Encourage the children to hold the long notes. A recorder, flute, or other instrument could play the descant on the last verse. You may want to have a few of the older children sing the descant as well.

Sing near the beginning of congregational worship as we enter God's presence, or as a response to a prayer, a sermon, or benediction, especially at a service emphasizing creation or missions. Have the children gather in front to lead the congregation in signing this song.

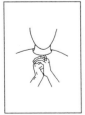 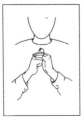 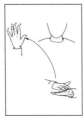 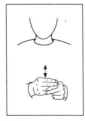 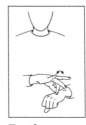 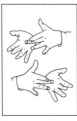 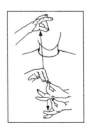

Worship   *Adore*   *Glorify*   *Name*   *Earth*   *Jesus*   *Spirit*

78 All Praise to You, My God, This Night

♩ = 96

Canon

1 All praise to you, my God, this night, for all the
2 For - give me, Lord, for this I pray, the wrong that
3 Lord, may I be at rest in you and sweet - ly
4 Praise God, from whom all bless - ings flow; praise him, all

bless - ings of the light. Keep me, O keep me, King of
I have done this day. May peace with God and neigh - bor
sleep the whole night through. Re - fresh my strength, for your own
crea - tures here be - low. Praise him a - bove, you heav - enly

kings, be - neath the shel - ter of your wings.
be, be - fore I sleep, re - stored to me.
sake, so I may serve you when I wake.
host; praise Fa - ther, Son, and Ho - ly Ghost.

This evening hymn was written over 300 years ago for the boys at Winchester Cathedral School in England by Bishop Thomas Ken as one of a set of three prayers (morning, evening, and midnight). The boys were to sing this in their rooms before going to bed. The first stanza gives thanks for the blessings of the "light" or day and asks God for continued care "beneath the shelter of your wings"; the second asks for forgiveness of sins; the third is a prayer for restful sleep; and the fourth is the famous "doxology" or hymn of praise. It is often sung to the tune OLD HUNDREDTH (11).

The music is the famous "canon" or round written by Thomas Tallis around 1561. Sing any or all of the stanzas in unison or in two-part canon. Note that the accompaniment in the bass clef is a repeat of the melody starting four beats later. When singing in canon, the second group should sing along with the bass clef melody. If possible have two C instruments (flute, recorder, violin, oboe) play the melody in canon as accompaniment. This hymn may also be played in four-part canon with voices and instruments entering every four beats.

At the end of an evening service have the children sing one of the stanzas, the congregation joining on the rest. During the weeks you are learning it, ask your organist to play one of the many available settings for

Words: Thomas Ken, 1709
Music: Thomas Tallis, c. 1561

LM
TALLIS CANON

an offertory or postlude. Stanza 4 is appropriate any time praise is called for. If your congregation needs a change of doxology, try singing the familiar text to this tune for a season.

♩ = 66

Go Now in Peace 79

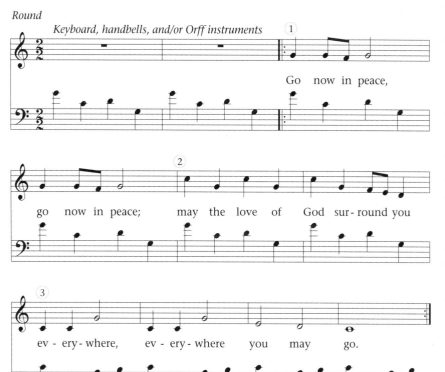

Round

Go now in peace,

go now in peace; may the love of God sur-round you

ev - ery-where, ev - ery-where you may go.

Orff instrument patterns

This piece was written by Natalie Sleeth, a composer of many fine rounds for children (for more on Sleeth, see 175). The words remind children that God's love is always with them wherever they go.

The melody is simple and easy to learn because it has several repeated phrases. Sing each phrase and let the children echo you. Once they know the melody, remind the children to take a breath only where there is a punctuation mark.

The accompaniment patterns may be played on keyboard or handbells as well as on Orff instruments. They are well worth the effort. Choose children with a good sense of beat to play them.

One way to perform this piece is to divide your group into three sections. Start the accompaniment by adding each pattern separately. The entire group should sing all together the first time through. Then start the round (see the numbered entrances) and let each section sing it at least twice. End by having the accompaniment patterns drop out one at a time.

This song is most appropriately sung after the benediction in congregational worship. Or sing at a commissioning service for missionaries or other church workers.

Words and Music: Natalie Sleeth, 1975
© 1976, Hinshaw Music, Inc. Reprinted by permission.

889
GO NOW IN PEACE

Go

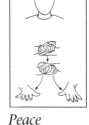

Peace

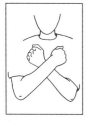

Love

Surround

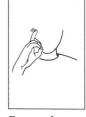

Everywhere

You

Go

80 May the Lord Bless You

♩ = 120

This is a melodic expression of the blessing God gave to Moses to be used by Aaron and his sons when blessing the Israelites (Num. 6:24-25). Tell the children that they may think of God looking at them with love when they hear the words "lift up his face to shine on you." This shortened form of the benediction is often spoken by the minister at the close of a worship service.

The text and the music are repeated except for the endings. The first part is in unison, and the second part could also be sung in unison, although you may want to teach some children the alto part. Learn the melody thoroughly and sing with quiet conviction. The piano score is a broken chord arrangement, reminiscent of a guitar technique that could also be used in place of the given piano score.

For an extended benediction, have your children join the adult choir, which could sing from the published anthem. (This is just the first section.)

You may choose to make this a closing theme song for your singing group for a season. In congregational worship, have the children sing this benediction following the spoken Aaronic benediction by the minister. The minister may raise hands in blessing; have the children give the blessing with the richness of two languages: singing and signing.

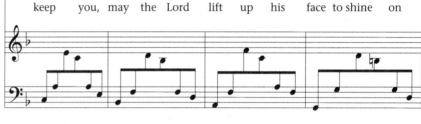

May the Lord bless you, may the Lord

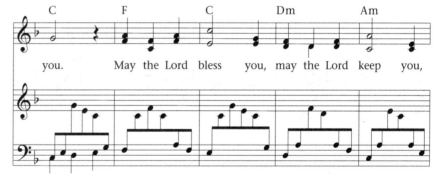

keep you, may the Lord lift up his face to shine on

you. May the Lord bless you, may the Lord keep you,

Words: Numbers 6:24-25

Music: Judy Hunnicutt, from the anthem "May the Lord Bless You"

Capo 5

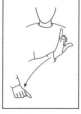

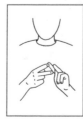

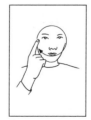
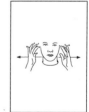

Lord *Bless* *You* *Keep* *Lift* *Face* *Shine*

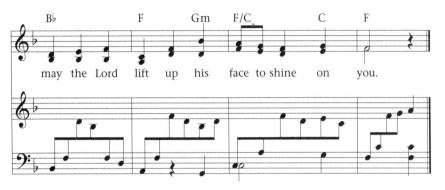

may the Lord lift up his face to shine on you.

♩ = 72

Lord of Our Life **81**

Lord of our life, Lord of our be-ing, stay close to us as we walk with you. Give us your peace, grant us your bless-ing, help us to serve you, Lord, in all that we do.

Words and Music: Loje Braen, 1983

From *Songs of the Spirit*, © 1983 by Loje Braen. Used by permission.

9 9 9 11
DEAN

This quiet prayer for the Lord's protecting presence consists of two similar sentences, each beginning with two short phrases, followed by a longer petition. Let six children hold strips of colored paper to represent the phrases, one color for each sentence: two short strips, one long strip, two short strips, one long strip (see below). Speak the text several times as you point to the strips, asking the following questions:

- What two "L" phrases begin the first sentence?
- What two "G" phrases begin the second sentence?
- How does each long phrase begin?

Ask to whom the song is sung, and explain that "Lord" means master, ruler, God, Jesus Christ. Practice good projection and enunciation by whispering the phrases together.

Using the same strips of paper, echo the melody, again following the structure of two plus two plus four measures. When you reach the last phrase, alter the color of the last paper to illustrate the variation of notes. To emphasize the correct note values, challenge children to sing the counting numbers of each phrase. Breathe only at the beginning of phrases, striving for legato lines.

Sing this prayer at the close of worship or as a response following a spoken prayer or a profession of faith. Let the children sing it first with the congregation repeating it. For personal prayer, children could sing this in first person ("Lord of my life").

This song from Argentina (bring a globe and point out Argentina) is the result of a group effort involving North and South American Christians. The first stanza was written in Spanish and was first translated into English in 1984; the second was written in English. The song combines God's blessing with his call to work for justice and peace. Many children all over the world have a "load of life that is hard to bear" (st. 2). Those "loads" may involve broken families, violence, illness, poverty, and hunger. Singing this song of hope gives us courage and helps us to bear each other's burdens in our own communities and throughout the world.

The Argentine folk melody conveys a strong sense of rhythmic drive. One pattern is repeated for each phrase of the stanzas; another is found in the refrain phrases. All the phrases end with the same syncopated pattern that invites lively rhythmic singing. This characteristically Hispanic rhythm brings a freshness to the music that children will enjoy.

The stepwise movement of the melody makes it easy for children to learn. The text of the refrain will be the most accessible to the younger children. If the children have learned the refrain, encourage them to sing it in Spanish (see below). While keyboard and/or guitar will provide an adequate accompaniment, children will enjoy adding rhythm instruments including tambourine, sticks and maracas, especially

82 Song of Hope
Canto de Esperanza

♩ = 60

1 May the God of hope go with us ev - ery day,
2 God will be our Shep-herd as we go our way

1 ¡Dios de la es - pe - ran - za, da - nos go - zo y paz!
2 Dios se - rá nues - tro pas - tor en el ca - mi - no

fill - ing all our lives with love and joy and peace.
and will not for - sake us when we go a - stray.
Al mun - do en cri - sis, ha - bla tu ver - dad.
no nos a - ban - do - na - rá cuan - do nos per - di - mos.

May the God of jus - tice speed us on our way,
E - ven though the load of life is hard to bear,
Dios de la jus - ti - cia, mán - da - nos tu luz,
La____ vi - da es un - a car - ga pe - sa - da,

bring - ing light and hope to ev - ery land and race.
we must not for - get that God is al - ways there.
luz y es - pe - ran - za en la os - cu - ri - dad.
Pe - ro Dios siem - pre nos a - yu - da - rá.

Words: stanza 1, traditional Spanish, translated by Alvin Schutmaat; stanza 2 by Tom Mitchell, translated into Spanish by Frank W. Roman.
Music: Argentine folk melody
St. 2 © 1993, Choristers' Guild

11 11 11 11 with refrain
ARGENTINA

Refrain

Pray - ing, let us work for peace; sing - ing, share our
O - re - mos— por la paz, can - te - mos—

joy with all; work - ing for a world that's new,
de tu a - mor. Lu - che - mos— por la paz,

faith - ful when we hear Christ's call.
fie - les a— ti, Se - ñor.

on the refrain. Encourage them to make up all kinds of patterns. A trumpet could be added to the refrain. You may want to use Tom Mitchell's anthem, published by the Choristers Guild, for a setting for unison voices, keyboard, optional vocal and instrumental descants, and rhythmic patterns for claves, tambourine, and hand drum.

Sing as a closing song in congregational worship. Or sing as a commissioning song when sending people on work/service/mission projects.

Spanish pronunciation for refrain:

Oh-ray-mohs pour la paz,
cahn-tay-mohs deh too-a-more.
Loo-chay-mohs pour la paz,
fee-lace ah tee, Say-nyour.

Percussion patterns for refrain:

Hand drum   Claves

Tambourine   Gourds

83 Praise and Thanksgiving

♩ = 54

The traditional first stanza of this round has often been sung as a table grace. Marie Post added stanzas 2 and 3 to make a joyful parting song for worship. Stanza 1 invites everyone (present) to give thanks; stanza 2 expands the invitation to include "all people," reminiscent of Psalm 100 (see 10). And stanza 3 is a prayer that we may live thankful lives, sharing as well as singing about the good gifts we have received from God.

The simplicity of the melodic line enables even young children to participate. Sing energetically and with joy, feeling a rhythmic swing with one beat per measure. Preschoolers could easily join in singing the response "All together, joyfully sing," while older children lead them in learning the stanzas. The children will enjoy singing as a three-part round once they feel comfortable with the tune and text. If they have little experience in singing rounds, instrumentalists could play the first two entrances with the children following at the third entrance of the round. Then divide the children into three groups and, if possible, ask a melody instrument to join each group. Guitar, autoharp, or keyboard could serve as accompaniment; the keyboard accompaniment is compatible with both unison and round singing. Create a pattern for Orff instruments simply by repeating the first four measures of the bass clef.

Round

1 Praise and thanks - giv - ing let ev - ery - one bring
2 All peo - ple, join us and sing out God's praise.
3 May we go out from here shar - ing God's love.

un - to our Fa - ther for ev - ery good thing.
For all his bless - ings your hap - py songs raise.
Help us in com - ing days our faith to prove.

All to - geth - er, joy - ful - ly sing!

Words: stanza 1, Alsatian; translated by Edith Lowell Thomas, 1950; stanzas 2-3, Marie J. Post, 1974
Music: Alsatian round; harmonized by Dale Grotenhuis, 1985
St. 2-3 and harm. © 1987, CRC Publications

10 10 8
LOBET UND PREISET
Capo 1

This song would serve well as a hymn of praise for many joyful occasions, particularly a Thanksgiving service. Sing as a call to worship (st. 1-2), a joyful conclusion to the offering, a closing doxology, or even a recessional hymn with the children leading the congregation out. If your congregation knows it well and is used to rounds, sing it entirely as a round; otherwise, sing stanzas 1-2 together and conclude with stanza 3 as a round.

♩ = 112

Shalom 84

Round

Sha - lom, my friends, sha - lom, my friends, sha -

lom, sha - lom! God's peace go with you, God's

peace go with you. Sha - lom, sha - lom!

The original Hebrew words for this song are Shalom, *which means "peace,"*
and chaverim *(pronounced shah-veh-reem), which refers to "good friends."*
Here are the original words:

Shalom, chaverim, shalom, chaverim, shalom, shalom!
Shalom, chaverim, shalom, chaverim, shalom, shalom!

Orff instruments

Bass xylophone   Alto metallophone   Soprano metallophone

Glockenspiel

Words and Music: Israeli folk song; Orff arrangement by Emily R. Brink
Orff arr. © 1994, CRC Publications

Here is another parting round, this time from the Israeli tradition. (See 85 for another shalom song and ideas for use in worship.)

In this song your children will learn two Hebrew words in addition to the two they probably already know—Hallelujah and Amen. Treat the children and the whole congregation to the following "Shalom Dance."

Form two circles, one inside the other, of an equal number of people. Each person faces a partner from the other circle.

Shalom, my friend,
extend right hand; palm up

Shalom, my friend,
extend left hand palm up—
now both hands of each partner
should be extended in a gesture
of welcome or service

Shalom,
put own hands together as if in
prayer; bow head slightly

Shalom!
repeat

God's peace go with you,
shake right hands with part-
ner—hold

God's peace go with you,
repeat with left hands—now
both hands should be grasped
with partner—arms will be
crossed

Shalom,
raise grasped hands above head

Shalom!
lower hands still grasped with
partner

Now the outside circle moves to the right to meet a new partner. Repeat song and movement until the outside circle faces the original partner.

85 Shalom to You

♩ = 63

Here is another shalom song (see also 84), this time of Mexican origin. The text focuses on the desire of God's children to be filled with God's peace (shalom) in all their living. This song, with its Hebrew word and Hispanic melody, is an example of how Christians from many different times and places are united.

The original Mexican folk hymn had one stanza that would be most fitting for a funeral. Elise S. Eslinger was inspired by the original words to write several additional stanzas. The original stanza, based on Romans 14:8, follows.

When we are living,
it is in Christ Jesus.

And when we're dying,
it is in the Lord.

Both in our living
and in our dying,

we belong to God,
we belong to God.

On the first line, "Jesus" is sung on two half notes rather than on a whole note. Traditionally, the last line is repeated.

Repetition in this quiet song will help children learn it easily. Sing each phrase and have the children echo it back to you. Accompany with guitar, autoharp, or keyboard. You may create a second instrumental part by combining the tenor and alto lines; for example, a cello player could begin each of the first three lines with the tenor part, shifting to the alto line in the second measure to the end. Alternatively, play that new line an octave higher by violin or flute to form a quiet descant above the melody.

Sing this parting song following the benediction. Ask the children to come forward and sing it to the congregation, then have the congregation sing it back to them. This song would be appropriate for any service of farewell. Add the original stanza for a funeral service.

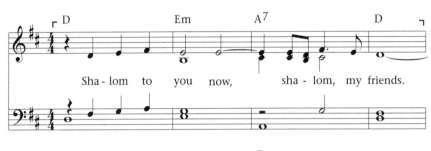

Sha-lom to you now, sha-lom, my friends.

May God's full mer-cies bless you, my friends.

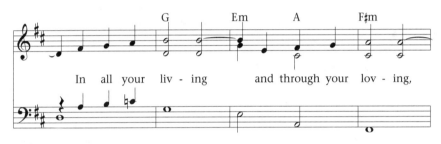

In all your liv-ing and through your lov-ing,

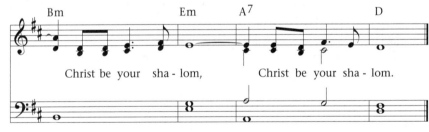

Christ be your sha-lom, Christ be your sha-lom.

Words: Elise S. Eslinger, 1980
Music: Anonymous; harmonized by Carlton R. Young, 1989
Words © 1983, The United Methodist Publishing House. Harm. © 1989, The United Methodist
Publishing House.

SOMOS DEL SENOR
Capo 2

Singing God's Story

86 All Creatures of Our God and King

This text, based on the "Canticle of the Sun," was written by Francis of Assisi in 1225. Francis was born into a rich family, but he dressed in rags and lived a simple life close to nature, dedicated to teaching and helping the poor. He believed that all creation praises God. References to Psalm 145:10 and Psalm 148:3, 7 are found in these two stanzas. (Most hymnals include more stanzas.)

This German melody was first paired with the text in an English hymnal for schoolchildren in 1919. Each musical phrase, except the final "alleluia," is repeated, so there are many possibilities for antiphonal singing. You may divide the group into two parts and have one group sing a phrase with the other singing the repeat, all joining for the final "alleluia"; or have the groups alternate every two phrases; or have both groups sing two phrases together but alternate on "alleluia" and "O praise him," singing the final "alleluia" together again. It is traditional to place a fermata (hold) on the end of the second "alleluia." Also point out the importance of giving the next to the last note three full beats. Sing with strong clear voices, singing the textual phrases smoothly and medium-loudly, and the "alleluia" and "O praise him" phrases slightly detached and louder. Use a keyboard accompaniment and alternate contrasting C instruments (flute, recorder, violin, oboe) on the melody.

♩ = 80

1 All crea-tures of our God and King, lift up your
2 Cool flow-ing wa-ter, pure and clear, make mu-sic

voice with us and sing: al-le-lu-ia, al-le-lu-ia!
for your Lord to hear; al-le-lu-ia, al-le-lu-ia!

O burn-ing sun with gold-en beam, and shin-ing
Fierce fire, so mas-ter-ful and bright, pro-vid-ing

moon with sil-ver gleam, O praise him, O praise him,
us with warmth and light, O praise him, O praise him,

Words: Francis of Assisi, 1225; translated by William H. Draper, 1910
Music: Auserlesen Catholische Geistliche Kirchengesäng, Cologne, 1623

LM with alleluias
LASST UNS ERFREUEN

Sing as a call to worship, as a processional, or as a response to the reading of one of the psalms listed above. Its emphasis on nature makes this song especially appropriate in spring. Have the children sing the main text of the first stanza and the whole congregation join on the refrain parts. Ask your church organist or pianist to play a setting of this hymn for a prelude on a Sunday that you plan to sing it.

al - le - lu - ia, al - le - lu - ia, al - le - lu - ia!

♩ = 88

Alleluia 87

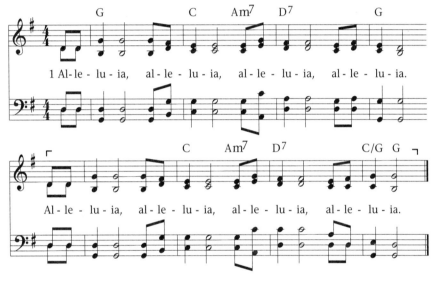

1 Al - le - lu - ia, al - le - lu - ia, al - le - lu - ia, al - le - lu - ia.

Al - le - lu - ia, al - le - lu - ia, al - le - lu - ia, al - le - lu - ia.

2 He's my Savior, alleluia . . . . (4x)
3 He is worthy, alleluia . . . . (4x)
4 I will praise him, alleluia . . . . (4x)

The children should know that "alleluia" (st. 1) means "praise God." Stanzas 2 and 3 give reasons for praise (see Matt. 1:21b; Rev. 4:11; 5:12), and stanza 4 concludes with a personal statement.

This simple melody should be sung simply and meditatively. Emphasize good pronunciation of each syllable, especially a good "ah," with the lower jaw relaxed down, and a clear "loo." On stanzas 2-4 you may wish to add variety by dividing into two groups, group one beginning the phrase and group two responding with "alleluia." Or assign soloists to begin each phrase. Since harmony also adds character to this chorus, try teaching a few older singers the alto part. Accompany lightly on guitar or invite a child to accompany on the autoharp.

Especially with the added stanzas, this meditative chorus can stand independently in any service. After the children have sung, the congregation can respond by repeating stanza 1. Pair with another song in the same key (see Key Index), for example, following the refrain of "O Come, All Ye Faithful" for a beautiful call to worship during the Christmas season.

Words and Music: Jerry Sinclair, 1972

SINCLAIR

Alleluia

Younger children will especially enjoy this song thanking God for life. They may also enjoy listing and then singing about other gifts for which they are thankful. The refrain suggests that we should thank God for specific gifts of love every day.

Children will easily learn both words and music. Ask the children to echo back the phrases you sing. Take care to distinguish the slightly varied patterns in both the stanza and refrain on "giving us life" and "every day," especially the third pattern. Trace the direction of the melody with your hand as you sing.

You may wish to divide the group into two sections. Teach the verse to group one and the refrain to group two. Next, switch groups. Accompaniment with guitar or autoharp would suit the gentle nature of this song. Try for long flowing melodic phrases even though the melody "bounces." Ask the children to imagine that they are steadily pulling a long string out of their mouths as they sing. The individual words are on the string, and each word must be enunciated, yet the notes must be connected.

The children may share this song with the congregation as an expression of thanksgiving at any service. Specific stanzas can be created to fit the given theme of the service.

88 We Thank God

♩ = 69

* Additional stanzas: love, faith, hope, joy, Mom, Dad, and so on.

Words and Music: Kathleen Hart Brumm, 1988

© 1988, in *Sixteen Scripture Songs for Small Singers*, published by Brummhart Publishing Co. Used by permission.

♩ = 54

For the Beauty of the Earth 89

1 For the beau-ty of the earth, for the glo-ry
2 For the joy of hu-man love, broth-er, sis-ter,

of the skies, for the love which from our birth
par-ent, child, friends on earth, and friends a-bove,

o-ver and a-round us lies,
for all gen-tle thoughts and mild. *Refrain* Christ, our Lord, to

you we raise this, our hymn of grate-ful praise.

Words: Folliott S. Pierpont, 1864
Music: Conrad Kocher, 1838; adapted by William H. Monk, 1861; arranged by
Robert Roth, 1989

77 77 77
DIX

When we see anything beauti-ful in nature, we can praise God, who created everything. We can also praise God for giv-ing us families and friends. The author of this hymn lived in the city of Bath, in England. One day, while sitting on a hill overlooking the city, he was moved to praise God for that beautiful view. Two stanzas of his beautiful hymn of praise are included here, each concluding with the refrain of "grateful praise."

This hymn has been a fa-vorite of many Christians for over a hundred years. Discuss how the love of brothers, sis-ters, parents, grandparents, and friends surrounds us, both on earth and in heaven above. To introduce this hymn you may wish to make a collage of pic-tures of things on earth, things in the skies, and people.

The stanzas consist of two identical musical phrases. Sing with flowing legato voices. Take care to sing the refrain as one long line and with more volume. If a breath must be taken, do so after the word "this," so as to keep the flow of words meaningful.

Sing this song of thanksgiv-ing at any time, especially when seasons change or when celebrating the "communion of the saints." Stanza 2 could be used during a service in which the theme is the family.

This is one of a set of songs written by Mrs. Cecil Frances Alexander especially to help children understand the Apostles' Creed. Based on Genesis 1:31, "God saw all that he had made and it was very good," it illustrates the phrase "Maker of heaven and earth." The refrain emphasizes that God created all things by using the word "all" four times.

The old English folk melody should be sung brightly with a light accompaniment of autoharp and recorder or guitar and flute. Make sure the children know the refrain well before teaching the stanzas. Soloists or small groups of children could sing the stanzas with the entire group on the refrain.

Sing this hymn in worship dealing with a creation/ecology theme, Heidelberg Catechism Lord's Day 9, or on Thanksgiving Day.

90 All Things Bright and Beautiful

1 Each lit-tle flower that o-pens, each lit-tle bird that sings—
2 The pur-ple-head-ed moun-tain, the riv-er run-ning by,
3 The cold wind in the win-ter, the pleas-ant sum-mer sun,
4 He gave us eyes to see them, and lips that we might tell

he made their glow-ing col-ors, he made their ti-ny wings.
the sun-set, and the morn-ing that bright-ens up the sky.
the ripe fruits in the gar-den—he made them, ev-ery one.
how great is God Al-might-y, who has made all things well.

Words: Cecil F. Alexander, 1848
Music: The Dancing Master, 1686; harmonized by John Worst, 1974
Harm. © 1994, CRC Publications

76 76 with refrain
ROYAL OAK

Who Made Ocean, Earth, and Sky?

♩ = 63

Gm **D** **Gm** **D** **Gm**

1 Who made o-cean, earth, and sky? God, our lov-ing Fa-ther.
2 Who made lakes and riv-ers blue? God, our lov-ing Fa-ther.

D **E♭** **D** **Gm**

Who made sun and moon on high? God, our lov-ing Fa-ther.
Who made snow and rain and dew? God, our lov-ing Fa-ther.

B♭ **F** **Gm** **D** **Gm**

Who made all the birds that fly? God, our lov-ing Fa-ther.
God made lit-tle chil-dren too; God, our lov-ing Fa-ther.

Descant

The descant may be played by one or two instruments. When using two instruments, alternate every two measures—one playing the question, the other the answer.

Words: Richard Compton, 1921   Capo 3
Music: traditional Finnish melody, arranged by Richard L. Van Oss, 1992

Young children will enjoy this question and answer song. Our loving God made everything that has been created! The questions are like a "catalog" of God's creation. Motions or pictures will help learn the words. Gather one picture for each part of creation mentioned, perhaps placing them into a notebook. Every time the answer is given, insert a big heart in the notebook. As you show the notebook, ask the song's questions, and every time you turn to a heart page, encourage children to join with you on the answer.

Have fun with this little minor melody, concentrating on the "answering phrase" first. As you sing it, show the melody direction with your hands, instructing everyone to do the same. Encourage children to play this answer phrase on a variety of instruments such as piano, flute, tone bells, or handbells. During another session, conduct an "ear check": sing the complete song on "tah," asking which two lines are the same. Assign children to sing the song's questions, using solos and various groups. Be sure to include the delightful descant which can be played on the flute, recorder, or violin. Triangles could also be played on the concluding beats of each line.

Children could offer this song of praise during a worship service with a creation theme or for a baptism service.

God has given us a very beautiful world to live in. He has also given us the responsibility of caring for it. This song celebrates God's creation and reminds us of our need to care for what God has lovingly given us. Posters or charts of scenes from nature will help the children learn the text of each stanza.

The simple and childlike melody is easily accessible to children of all ages. Encourage children to use their clear "head" voice at the beginning of the refrain and to use that sound quality throughout the refrain, blending their "head" tones into the lower register of their voices. Notice that the meter signature designates singing this song with a flow of two beats per measure. The stanzas are formed in two-measure phrases. Don't breathe after the first measure; try singing in two-measure phrases. Since there is little time for a breath after measure 4, it might be better to connect those phrases. On the refrain, sing in groups of four-, two-, and four-measure phrases. Use a simple accompaniment with keyboard, guitar (picked), or autoharp.

Sing in services that focus on God's creation, ecological issues, providence, or thanksgiving. You may wish to pair this song with a reading of Genesis 1 (particularly vv. 27-31) or Psalm 8.

92 Forest Trees

$\quad = 68$

1 For - est trees, what are these? Gifts of God to
2 Clear blue skies, crys - tal streams, sing - ing birds, and
3 Ba - by seals, full - grown whales, o - ceans blue, and
4 Na - ture parks, farm - ing land, air to breathe for

all his chil - dren.
fer - tile val - leys. Just on loan, not our own:
all the fish - es.
all God's chil - dren.

we must care for them. Thank you, Fath - er,

for these gifts en - trust - ed to our keep - ing.

Words: stanzas 1-2, Mary Lu Walker; stanzas 3-4, Bert Polman, 1992
Music: Melody by Mary Lu Walker; arranged by Sean Ivory, 1993

Capo 3

F   Dm   Gm⁷   C⁷

All the good things of the earth, we will care for

F   *Final ending*

them.

♩ = 92

Heleluyan (Alleluia) 93

Round

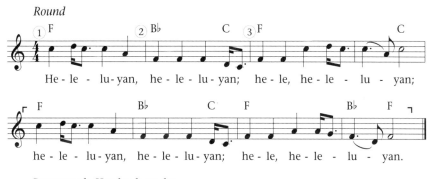

① F   ② B♭   C   ③ F   C

He - le - lu - yan, he - le - lu - yan; he - le, he - le - lu - yan;

F   B♭   C   F   B♭   F

he - le - lu - yan, he - le - lu - yan; he - le, he - le - lu - yan.

Pronounced: Hay-lay-loo-yahn.

Hand drum

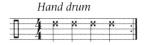

Words and Music: Traditional Muscogee (Creek) Indian; transcription by Charles H. Webb

Music transcription © 1989, The United Methodist Publishing House.

HELELUYAN
Capo 1

This Native American alleluia comes to us in the Muscogee language spoken by the Creek people who lived in the south-eastern part of what is now the United States. The Creek, like the Cherokee, were forced to migrate west to a designated "Indian Territory." This song may have originated before or during that forced march, often called the "trail of tears." Passed from one generation to the next, it has since become the "tribal anthem" of the Muscogee/Creek people. Charles Webb first notated the song in 1987 after hearing it sung on a videotape by a Muscogee United Methodist family in New York.

It is best sung without ac-companiment except for hand drum. Sing with energy, accent-ing each note. When children are familiar with the melody, it may be sung as a round.

Sing in a World Communion service. Consider pairing with "Many and Great" (94), an-other Native American song.

This song has become known as the "Dakota hymn." It was written in the Dakota language by Joseph Rennville, a fur trader who was half Dakota and half French, and translated by Philip Frazier, a Sioux who became a Congregational minister. The text is based on Psalm 104:24-30 and Jeremiah 10:12-13. The first stanza honors God as Creator of the universe; the second is a prayer for God's care and blessing in our lives, and communicates the wonder of a God who not only formed the entire creation but is also interested in our daily living.

The Native American melody comes to us from the Dakota tribe. The tune name, LACQUIPARLE, is the name of the place where Rennville had his trading post and where there was also a mission.

The form of the melody is ABA—the third section is identical to the opening one. Encourage the children to sing the octave leap at the beginning of the second phrase smoothly; they should use their "head" voice on the upper notes. Use a hand drum with the notated pattern to encourage a strong and steady beat. You may also wish to play the bass clef parts on an Orff bass xylophone, with or without the drum accompaniment (C and G could be played throughout). A flute or recorder playing the melody with drum accompaniment would also make an effective introduction to the song.

Sing in worship services that focus on God's creative acts and his providential care in our lives, as a response to a reading of a creation psalm or as a prayer response. Also consider pairing with 93.

94 Many and Great

♩ = 92

1 Many and great, O God, are your works, Maker of earth and sky; your hands have set the heavens with stars; your fingers spread the mountains and plains. You merely spoke and waters were formed; deep seas obey your voice.

2 Grant us communion with you, our God, though you transcend the stars. Come close to us and stay by our side: with you are found the true gifts that last. Bless us with life which never shall end, eternal life with you.

Optional drum pattern

Words: Joseph R. Renville, c. 1846; translated by Philip Frazier, 1929
Music: Traditional Dakota

LACQUIPARLE

This Is My Father's World 95

♩ = 126

1 This is my Fa - ther's world, and to my lis - tening ears all
2 This is my Fa - ther's world: O let us not for - get that
3 This is my Fa - ther's world: he shines in all that's fair; in

na - ture sings and round me rings the mu - sic of the spheres.
though the wrong is great and strong, God is the rul - er yet.
rus - tling grass I hear him pass— he speaks to me every - where.

This is my Fa - ther's world; I rest me in the thought of
He trusts us with his world, to keep it clean and fair— all
This is my Fa - ther's world: why should my heart be sad? The

rocks and trees, of skies and seas—his hand the won - ders wrought.
earth and trees, all skies and seas, all crea - tures ev - ery - where.
Lord is King, let heav - en ring! God reigns; let earth be glad.

Words: Maltbie D. Babcock, 1901; stanza 2 revised by Mary Babcock Crawford, 1972. SMD
Music: English; adapted by Franklin L. Sheppard, 1915 TERRA BEATA
Capo 1

"I'm going out to see my Father's world," Maltbie Davenport Babcock would say as he walked along the Lake Ontario shore. Two stanzas of this song are taken from a poem he wrote, inspired by the scenery. Seventy years later his granddaughter wrote stanza 2, adding concern that we take good care of God's world.

Ask your children to name places they have visited that especially showed the beauty of God's creation. Show a photograph of the world as viewed from space or a poster displaying various scenes from the song. Explain that a sphere is a star or planet, and that long ago people believed planets made music as they revolved in the universe. Ask, "How does nature sing?"

Help your singers to truly enjoy this song by choreographing imaginative hand and arm motions to correlate with the phrases. (For a rhyming game on the line "in the rustling grass I hear him pass," see 98.)

This lively English folk tune has a very wide range of an octave and a fourth. The second and fourth lines are identical. Assign three groups, each to sing a four-measure phrase on "tah," standing to sing as you cue them: ABCB. Ask: Which phrase was repeated, and where? Which phrase was the highest? Encourage good posture, and sing the song lightly and energetically.

This song is appropriate in many worship settings, especially those focusing on creation, providence, and ecology. Sing during a springtime prayer service for crops and for thanksgiving or as a response to a psalm of praise.

Psalm 104 is one of the great creation psalms. After describing many of the wonders that God made, the psalm writer acknowledges that all God's creatures depend on God for their food, their safety, for their life. When God takes away their breath, they return to the dust. Then comes verse 30:

> When you send your Spirit, they are created,
> and you renew the face of the earth.

This refrain, part of a larger song by David Haas in *Gather,* captures the heart of Psalm 104. Only by the Spirit of God can the earth be created, sustained, or renewed.

The melody, with its descending lines, is very simple. Try singing in two-part canon on the repeat. Simple guitar accompaniment would be very appropriate. The keyboard part is challenging; watch the sixteenth notes in measure two—they are over in a flash.

Sing as a prayer response, especially when praying for justice in any part of God's world. Also use as a refrain in responsorial style to the reading of Psalm 104, another creation psalm, or the song "Thank You, God, for Water, Soil, and Air" (97).

96 Send Us Your Spirit

♩ = 116

*Sing in canon on repeat

Words: David Haas
Music: David Haas, arranged by Jeanne Cotter

Thank You, God, for Water, Soil, and Air **97**

Thank you, God, for water, soil, and air,
  large gifts supporting everything that lives.
    Forgive our spoiling and abuse of them.
      Help us renew the face of the earth.
    Refrain (no. 96)

Thank you, God, for minerals and ores—
  the basis of all building, wealth, and speed.
    Forgive our reckless plundering and waste.
      Help us renew the face of the earth.
    Refrain

Thank you, God, for priceless energy,
  stored in each atom, gathered from the sun.
    Forgive our greed and carelessness of power.
      Help us renew the face of the earth.
    Refrain

Thank you, God, for weaving nature's life
  into a seamless robe, a fragile whole.
    Forgive our haste, that tampers unawares.
      Help us renew the face of the earth.
    Refrain

Thank you, God, for making planet earth,
  a home for us and ages yet unborn.
    Help us to share, consider, save, and store.
      Come and renew the face of the earth.
    Refrain

Many creation hymns of earlier times thanked God for the beauty of creation. But we have spoiled and abused God's beautiful creation. Brian Wren writes

"Thank You, God" was written out of a conviction that we need to sing to God about creation from an awareness of the fragility of our environment. I wrote it because I believe that we should sing honestly—that what we sing should be connected with the world we look at when we leave church, the air we breathe and the exhaust fumes we make when we drive.

To introduce the song, display a large picture of planet earth or a few ecological posters with positive and negative images. Ask your children to list parts of creation they are thankful for. Then ask them to list ways we are not treating God's world with love. Notice how each stanza begins with gratitude and concludes with a prayer for forgiveness, asking God to help us renew the earth, a reference to Psalm 104:30. After introducing each stanza, make a list of specific suggestions to help renew (make like new) the face of the earth.

The hymn is presented as poetry to be read in responsorial style, using 96 as a refrain. All the children should read the final bold print line of each stanza (notice the change in the final stanza). For the first three lines, have three readers each on a line. Or, assign the first two lines of thanksgiving to one reader and the third "forgive us" line to another reader.

The children could lead the congregation in this prayer, especially in prayer services for crops and industry, thanksgiving services, or any service focusing on stewardship of earth's resources. Illustrate with appropriate slides or with recordings that feature the sounds of water and wind.

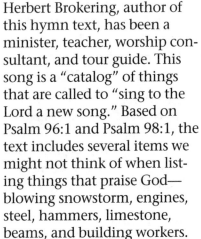

Herbert Brokering, author of this hymn text, has been a minister, teacher, worship consultant, and tour guide. This song is a "catalog" of things that are called to "sing to the Lord a new song." Based on Psalm 96:1 and Psalm 98:1, the text includes several items we might not think of when listing things that praise God—blowing snowstorm, engines, steel, hammers, limestone, beams, and building workers.

Children will enjoy learning and adding to this hymn. Teach the refrains first, using a bright sound, feeling one large beat per measure. The word "sing" should ring out! There are two refrains; one sung twice inside the stanzas and another after each stanza. Note how the melody emphasizes the words "Lord" and "marvelous" by arching them over many notes using a melisma (one syllable sung on a number of tones). Come up with additional stanzas naming even more modern items, such as video games.

Here is another idea for extending this text borrowed from an earlier creation hymn. Brokering wrote these new lines after the first one from "This Is My Father's World" (95):

"In the rustling grass, I hear Him pass,"
In the splashing bass, I hear Him pass,
In the rushing mass, I hear Him pass,
In the angry lass, I hear Him pass,
In the blaring brass, I hear Him pass.
(Uncovered Feelings, Herbert Brokering. Fortress Press, 1969.)

98 Earth and All Stars

$\quad\quad\quad\quad\quad\quad\quad\quad\quad\quad\quad\quad\quad\quad$ ♩ = 132

Words: Herbert Brokering, 1964
Music: David Johnson, 1968; arranged by Emily R. Brink, 1993
© 1968, Augsburg Publishing House. Used by permission of Augsburg Fortress.

457 457 with refrain
EARTH AND ALL STARS

He has done mar - vel - ous things.

I too will praise him with a new song!

Have the children speak these and other lines they come up with, followed each time by singing the refrain "Sing to the Lord a new song."

Sing in any service of praise, especially at the beginning of a school year. The structure invites antiphonal singing. Perhaps groups of children could sing alternate lines in the stanzas with all the children on the short refrain, joined by the congregation on the refrains at the end of each stanza.

5   Classrooms and labs!
    Come, boiling test tubes!
  Sing to the Lord a new song!
    Athlete and band!
    Loud cheering people!
  Sing to the Lord a new song! *Refrain*

6   Knowledge and truth!
    Come, piercing wisdom!
  Sing to the Lord a new song!
    Children of God,
    dying and rising,
  Sing to the Lord a new song! *Refrain*

Illustration: In Genesis 1 and 2 "heavens and earth" are mentioned together several times. God is the Creator of all that is contained in the universe. Along with everything in creation, we are called to praise the Creator. (See also Psalm 96, 98, 148 and other psalms.)

Young children will enjoy this song about Noah and the ark, taken from Genesis 6 and 7. Begin with some questions and let older children look up some of the answers in their Bibles.

- Who built the ark?
- How old was Noah when he built the ark? (*600 years*)
- What kind of wood was used? (*some Bibles say cypress, but the exact kind is not known*)
- How long, wide, and tall was the ark? (*450' x 75' X 45'*)
- How many animals entered the ark?

Sing this melody in a lilting manner, giving the half note the main beat. Begin with the refrain; have a leader (or one group) sing the questions, with the others on the response. The tune will come easily for your singers because it uses natural intervals for young voices.

Have fun learning the stanzas by using simple motions:

Stanza 1
built . . . bark
　fist makes pounding motion on other hand

long, wide, tall
　hands show length, width, height

large, small
　hold hand high, then lower

99 Who Built the Ark?

♩= 69

Who built the ark? No-ah! No-ah! Who built the ark? Broth-er No-ah built the ark.

1 Now old man No-ah built the ark, built it out of a hick-o-ry bark. He
2 Then in came the an-i-mals, two by two, hi-po-pot-a-mus and kan-ga-roo. Then
3 Then in came the an-i-mals, more and more, some through the win-dow and some through the door. And

Words and Music: traditional American; adapted by Patricia Nederveld, arranged by Emily R. Brink, 1992

built it long and wide and tall, with
in came the an-i-mals, can't you see, the
then the wind be-gan to blow, the

plen-ty of room for the large and small.
great big cats and bum-ble bees.
rain start-ed fall-ing, it's time to go.

Stanza 2

two by two
*one hand, then the other, show
two fingers*

hippopotamus
hold both hands in a circle

kangaroo
hold hands "bent"

animals
repeat "two by two" motion

big cats
hold hand high

bumblebees
hold two fingers apart

Stanza 3

more and more
"two by two" motion

window, door
*hold one hand above other,
then farther apart*

wind . . . blow, rain
swing arms and move fingers

time to go
wave

Invite children to accompany this song. On the refrain "questions" and on the stanzas, use all the Orff instruments you have, playing simple patterns using F and C. On the refrain "answers," play the melody pitches on xylophone or tone bells.

The children could contribute this song in a service dealing with Noah or for a baptism service. Also sing in a special praise time of children's songs.

Illustration: After the flood Noah sent out the dove from the ark. "When the dove returned to him in the evening, there in its beak was a freshly plucked olive leaf! Then Noah knew that the water had receded from the earth" (Gen. 8:11). The dove with the olive branch is a symbol of God's faithfulness and the restoration of peace between God and creation. It is also a symbol of the Holy Spirit.

This is a sung response to specific Scripture readings about Abraham. Emily Brink, editor of *Songs for LiFE* and of the 1987 *Psalter Hymnal,* composed the music for this text, which was written by her sister Helen Walter. An entire children's drama incorporating this song can be found in *Reformed Worship* 27 (March, 1993).

Invite two older children to read the Scripture, one for the opening lines, the other for the voice of God. (Scripture references are printed at the bottom of the first song page.)

After each of the three sections of Scripture, sing a stanza. Stanza 1 speaks of our journey of faith. Like Abraham, who followed where God called him, we are all on a journey of faith. Stanza 2 continues the story of Abraham. Point out that stanza 3 is Sarah's song of joy when she finally has a baby. Ask the children if they know the name of that baby, and see if anyone knows what Isaac means (*laughter*). This stanza invites all God's children to laugh with joy that God always keeps his promises. We too can celebrate the miracle of being counted as one of Sarah's children.

The melody, "unashamedly imitative of an Israeli folk song," is in two sections, each involving some repetition. In the A section, the first line is repeated a step higher in the second line. The B phrases are slightly longer. To teach this song, ask the children to echo you line by line. Accompany with keyboard *or* guitar/autoharp, but do not use keyboard *with* them since the chords are a bit different. On stanza 3, add rhythm instruments.

100 We Are on Our Way

♩ = 112

1 We are on our way__ to the prom - ised__ land.
2 A - bra - ham went for a walk with God, who was his friend.
3 I nev - er thought it pos - si - ble, not in a thou - sand years.

We are on our way__ to the prom - ised__ land.
God said, "Look up at all the stars— you can - not see their end.
But God per - formed a mir - a - cle and took a - way my fears.

Our God will lead and guide__ us, he will
And can you count the grains of sand on the
He took a - way my bit - ter - ness and

walk a - long be - side__ us, our God will lead and
shore or in a des - ert land? So ma - ny shall your
now I laugh and sing for joy, so dance with me and

Words: Helen Walter, 1989; readings from Genesis 12:1-2; 15:5; 17:19; 21:1-2
Music: Emily R. Brink, 1992
© 1993, CRC Publications

guide_____ us as we go to the prom - ised land.
chil - dren be— so ma - ny you can - not count."
sing with me; sing a new song of praise and joy.

Consider singing with Scripture readings in congregational worship when the theme of the service is the life of Abraham. Or sing stanzas 1 and 3 without the readings. Stanza 1 could be sung by itself as a song of encouragement; stanza 3, after a testimony of gratitude for answered prayer and deliverance after a time of trouble.

Reader:

The Lord said to Abraham,
"Leave your country, your people,
    and your father's household.
Go to the land I will show you.
I will make you into a great nation,
and I will bless you." *Sing stanza 1*

The Lord took Abraham outside and said,
"Look up at the heavens and count the stars—
if indeed you can count them."
Then he said to him,
"So shall your children be." *Sing stanza 2*

The Lord said to Abraham,
"Your wife Sarah will bear you a son,
    and you will call him Isaac.
I will establish my covenant with him
    as an everlasting covenant."
The Lord did for Sarah what he had promised.
Sarah became pregnant
    and bore a son to Abraham in his old age,
at the very time God had promised him. *Sing stanza 3*

Joseph's story is a thrilling tale of kidnapping, slavery, imprisonment, and a sudden rags-to-riches switch. But the theme of Joseph's story and of this song is God's providential care. Joseph was part of God's plan "to save his own." This narrative song includes the kidnapping of Joseph (st. 1), the years of feast and famine and the salvation of Joseph's family (st. 2-4), based on Genesis 37, 41-47. The final stanza summarizes God's work and calls for our praise.

The large amount of text may be difficult for the youngest children to master, but older children will learn it easily. You may want to teach the younger children stanzas 1 and 4, which summarize the story in childlike language. If you have time, teach the stanzas in sequence, using stanza 5 as the unifying stanza for each week.

The melody has the story-telling quality of a folk song. The F-natural in the last line lends an "ancient world" feel to the entire melody. Sing simply, with a rhythmic flow of two beats per measure. Use either the keyboard or strummed guitar for accompaniment. All of the open fifth chords of the bass clef part could also be played on a bass xylophone. For an even simpler Orff pattern, repeat the first two bass clef measures throughout.

Sing at any service where the focus is on God's providential care or on the story of Joseph.

101 Song of Joseph

♩ = 80

1 Young Joseph's father liked him best, which made his brothers mad. They sent him off to Egypt-land, so lonely and so sad.

2 But God watched over Joseph there, and with his powerful hand, he caused the crops to fill the fields. Now Joseph ruled the land.

3 But then a famine struck the earth, and all the fields were dry. All Joseph's brothers came to him, for food that they could buy.

4 God had a plan to save his own, the people that he loved. Now Joseph's family joined him there and praised our God above.

5 God can turn evil into good, and right he makes from wrong. O praise his name forevermore and fill each day with song.

Words: Bonnie Bratt Meyer, 1983
Music: Emily R. Brink, 1994
© 1983, 1994, CRC Publications

Capo 3

Moses 102

♩ = 92

1 Mo - ses, go, sleep - ing on the Nile.
2 Mo - ses, go; God is call - ing you.
3 Mo - ses, go, though the jour - ney's hard;

Mo - ses, go; in a lit - tle while
Mo - ses, go; here's what you must do.
Mo - ses, go; you can trust your Lord.

hear the prin - cess com - ing. She'll take you home.
Lead____ all God's peo - ple out of that land.
See the Red Sea part - ing; walk right on through.

God is watch - ing o - ver. You're not a - lone.
Lead them home to Ca - naan, prom - ised land.
God is with his peo - ple; God is with you.

Words: Carol Greene
Music: Hungarian folk song, arranged by Charlotte Mitchell
© 1975, Concordia Publishing House. Used by permission.

This song recounts highlights of the story of Moses that children love best, beginning with the rescue of baby Moses and ending with God leading Moses and the Israelites "right on through" the Red Sea. Children can celebrate that God takes care of his people and of them too: "God is with his people; God is with you" (st. 3).

"Moses, go" is repeated six times. Children love this repetition because they know what is coming, and they find it easy to learn. Carol Greene has concisely condensed three Old Testament stories about Moses and God's people into a meter for children of all ages to learn. Begin by speaking the text rhythmically so that the children can feel it before they learn the melody.

This delightful Hungarian folk song is easy to teach. Point out that the first two phrase lines are identical. Phrases three and four begin the same; phrase three comes up at the end, while phrase four returns down to the home tone. Make sure the children feel the rest in measures 2, 4, 6, 8, 12, and 16. The simple harmonic arrangement lends itself to Orff instruments (alto, tenor, or bass xylophone could read the chord symbols), autoharp, and rhythm instruments, playing on beat one of each measure. Make sure the instruments do not cover up the voices.

Sing in any service where the Scripture and sermon deal with Moses. Also consider singing at a baptism service or as a response to the reading of the Ten Commandments.

Children love to hear the story of Moses, Pharaoh, the Israelites, and the Red Sea (Ex. 3-14). Bring a big stick to class and pretend it is Moses' staff. Briefly narrate the story by speaking stanzas 1-4. Every time you raise the "staff," instruct children to extend both arms and boldly join you in speaking Moses' words. Be dramatic and imaginative, encouraging children to participate with gestures and movement. Conclude your narrative with the applicatory prayer of stanza 5. Explain to your children that long ago, slaves used to sing this African-American spiritual as they worked in the fields and dreamed about freedom.

This is a typical call-and-response song. Teach children to sing "let my people go," just as they spoke it in the narrative. As you sing the stanzas in this style, children will soon be eager to sing the refrain. Add "offbeat" clapping on the refrain on beats 2 and 4. Challenge older singers to clap patterns, such as a half note followed by two quarter notes, and combine different sounds, such as foot stomping, finger snapping, or thigh patting. Try solos or small groups on the narrative part, with all joining on the responses. Have one group sing an echo on the first two measures of the refrain. For a simple Orff accompaniment, see the pattern below.

Sing, call-and-response style, in a service that deals with the exodus or redemption and freedom in Christ. Or sing in a litany for an Easter Vigil service. Consider pairing with "Love Is Never Ending" (204), which is in the same key.

103 When Israel Was in Egypt's Land

$\quad$ = 60

1 When Israel was in Egypt's land,
2 The Lord told Moses what to do, Let my people go,
3 As Israel stood by the waterside,

oppressed so hard they could not stand,
to lead the Hebrew children through, Let my people go.
at God's command it did divide,

Refrain

Go down, Moses, way down in Egypt's land,

tell old Pharaoh: Let my people go.

4 When they had reached the other shore, Let my people go,
  they let the song of triumph soar, Let my people go. *Refrain*

5 Lord, help us all from bondage flee, Let my people go,
  and let us all in Christ be free, Let my people go. *Refrain*

Words and Music: African-American spiritual; arranged by Emily R. Brink, 1993 $\quad$ GO DOWN, MOSES
Arr. © 1994, CRC Publications

Orff accompaniment

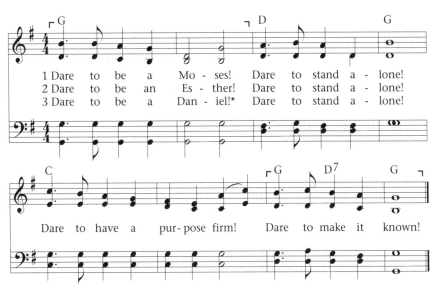

Dare to Be a Daniel! 104

♩ = 80

1 Dare to be a Mo - ses! Dare to stand a - lone!
2 Dare to be an Es - ther! Dare to stand a - lone!
3 Dare to be a Dan - iel!* Dare to stand a - lone!

Dare to have a pur-pose firm! Dare to make it known!

* *Additional Bible names:*
  Noah, Joseph, Rahab, Hannah, David, Mary, Peter, Stephen

Words: stanzas 1-2, traditional; stanza 3, Philip P. Bliss, 1873
Music: Philip P. Bliss, 1873

What child or adult doesn't enjoy listening to the "hero" tales of Scripture? This short chorus celebrates the commitment of God's people throughout salvation history—people who obeyed God and dared to do what was right, even when they were the only ones. And it calls us to that same courage and commitment. Ask the children if they know any "heroes" for God or if they can think of ways to be a "hero" for God.

This melody, known to many adults from their Sunday school experiences, may not be familiar to the children today. It is simple and easily learned by the echo method, singing in two-measure phrases. Repeat the sequence singing four-measure units, then sing the whole song. Explain to the children that having a "purpose firm" means setting a goal and working to fulfill it.

Sing as a call to commitment in a service focusing on one of these heroes of faith.

Illustration: The burning bush and sandals refer to God's call to Moses in Exodus 3:1-5. Moses saw flames coming from a bush, but the bush did not burn. Then the Lord spoke from the flames and told Moses to take off his sandals, since he was standing on holy ground. God also appeared in flames or fire on other occasions, as in the "pillar of fire" described in Exodus 13:21.

This triumphant text is based on the beginning of the Song of Moses and Miriam in Exodus 15. It celebrates the Lord's victory over the Egyptians after the Israelites crossed the Red Sea. Jewish tradition calls for singing the Song of Moses each Sabbath evening to remember the Exodus. Both stanzas were written anonymously in the mid-twentieth century.

The lively Israeli folk tune has three four-measure phrases, each repeated before the next begins. Using the echo method, sing short units (even one or two measures at a time), tracing the shape of the melody with your hand. Have the children echo without breaking the rhythm, going back and forth until the four-measure phrases are learned. Because the first phrase of this song moves quickly and is quite "wordy," younger children initially will feel more comfortable singing the final two phrases of the song. Once they know it well, you may wish to have the children sing in canon—two to four voices, depending on the size and singing experience of your group. Use many joyful noises for accompaniment, including guitar, piano, violin, tambourine, hand drum, and hand clapping, in any combination. For starters, do a vigorous hand clap at the two places with eighth rests in the final phrases: "The Lord is God and (clap) I will praise him." Encourage a tempo that provides rhythmic drive while maintaining good diction. Children will especially enjoy learning the circle dance (below).

Sing in worship services that focus on the theme of the Exo-

105 I Will Sing unto the Lord

♩ = 108

Words: from the Song of Moses and Miriam, Exodus 15:1-2
Music: Israeli folk song; harmonized by Emily R. Brink, 1992
Harm. © 1994, CRC Publications

TZENA

strength and song, has now be-come my vic-to-ry. The

Lord is God, and I will praise him, our cov-enant God, and

I will ex - alt him. The Lord is God, and

I will praise him, our cov-enant God, and I will ex-alt him!

Another stanza to sing during the Easter season:

I will sing unto the Lord,
for he has triumphed gloriously:
the grave is empty. Won't you come and see? *Repeat*

The Lord, my God, my strength and song,
has now become my victory. *Repeat*

The Lord is God, and I will praise him,
our covenant God, and I will exalt him. *Repeat*

dus, or in any service during the Easter season, especially for an Easter Vigil service. The Easter stanza could be used as a frame surrounding "Christ the Lord Is Risen Today" (172).

Circle Dance

I will sing unto the Lord, for he has triumphed gloriously, the horse and the rider thrown into the sea.
children join hands and circle to the right

I will sing unto the Lord, for he has triumphed gloriously, the horse and the rider thrown into the sea.
hands still joined, children circle to the left

The Lord, my God, my strength and song,
each child claps hands and twirls around once

has now become my victory.
each child claps hands and twirls around again

The Lord is God, and I will praise him,
children join hands and walk in to meet others in center of circle with arms lifted

our covenant God, and I will exalt him.
children walk back out to form circle again, then drop hands and hop around on right foot with right arm lifted

The Lord is God, and I will praise him,
children join hands and walk in to meet others in center of circle with arms lifted

our covenant God, and I will exalt him!
children walk back out to form circle again, then drop hands, clap, and lift both arms in praise

The text of this African-American spiritual is based on the story of the fall of Jericho. The Lord commanded Joshua,

March around the city once with all the armed men. Do this for six days. Have seven priests carry trumpets of rams' horns in front of the ark. On the seventh day, march around the city seven times, with the priests blowing the trumpets. When you hear them sound a long blast on the trumpets, have all the people give a loud shout; then the wall of the city will collapse and the people will go up, every man straight in (Josh. 6:3-5).

This dramatic story begs to be acted out. Imagine with the children the strange procession around the city for six days with trumpets blaring but the people not making a sound. Although they must have wondered what good it would do, the people obeyed the Lord, and on the seventh day, when Joshua said "Now!" they all gave a great shout. The rest is history.

It doesn't take too much imagination to understand the appeal this song had for African-American slaves. God often uses the weakest means or the most helpless situation to show his power and saving grace. This spiritual exists in many slightly different versions because each generation passed it on orally to succeeding generations.

The strong and rhythmic melody should be sung with confidence and lots of energy. The syncopations on the words "Jericho," "tumbling," and "men of" are a bit tricky. Teach the three "Jericho" measures first, clapping steadily on beats 1 and 3 and making sure "cho" is sung before the clap. Chil-

106 Joshua Fought the Battle of Jericho

Words and Music: African-American spiritual; arranged by Emily R. Brink, 1992
Arr. © 1994, CRC Publications

Capo 5

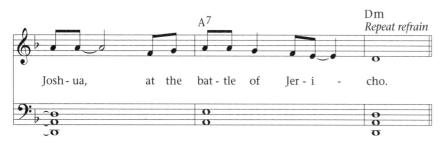

Josh - ua, at the bat - tle of Jer - i - cho.

2 Up to the walls of Jericho
   he marched with sword in hand.
   "Go blow those ram's horns," Joshua cried,
   "for the battle is in God's hands."

3 Then the horns began to bellow,
   the trumpets began to sound,
   and Joshua commanded the children to shout,
   and the walls came tumbling down.

dren will enjoy singing the refrain. You may ask an older child or group to sing the stanzas, with all joining on the refrain. Stanzas 2 and 3 might best be sung by a soloist, at least at first, since there are differing numbers of syllables among the three stanzas.

Accompany with keyboard, guitar, or autoharp. The lower Orff xylophones could play following the notated block chords or simply by following the chord symbols. Add a vocal ostinato part to the stanzas by singing the initial three notes of the refrain ("Joshua fought") at the beginning of every measure in the stanza. For a grand finale, the children could give a loud shout on the very last beat (beat 3 of the final "down").

Sing in a worship service that has as its theme the fall of Jericho. Or sing any time a group of children's songs are sung as an offering of praise.

Illustration: A "musical" instrument a bit like a trumpet, the ram's horn could produce only a few notes. It was used to lead people in a religious or military procession or to inspire fear in the enemy by its loud sound. The ram's horn (*shophar*) is still used in Jewish festivals to announce the New Year and the Day of Atonement.

This triumphant song of praise from Brazil is based on the Song of Deborah in Judges 5. Deborah was the leader in Israel at the time and a prophet of the Lord. God told her how the Israelites were to fight an important battle and when God gave them the victory, she sang a victory song. This song is a celebration that "our God is good and has chosen those who are humble." You may wish to ask the children how God has shown his goodness and given them strength in their lives.

The Brazilian Norah Buyers composed the words and music under the pen name of Luiza Cruz. Written in Portuguese, the native language of Brazil, it has since become popular in other countries as well. Here it is translated into both English and Spanish, except for the first line, which is left in Spanish. Sing both syllables of "canta" with the same "ah" vowel. Explain to the children that "canta" is the Spanish word for "Sing."

Children will enjoy the rhythmic energy so characteristic of much Hispanic music. Their singing should reflect joy and celebration. The little pattern for castanets is only a start. Add enthusiastic accompaniment with keyboard, guitar, hand clapping, tambourine,

107 ¡Canta, Débora, Canta!

♩ = 60

"Canta" is the Spanish word for "sing."

Words and Music: Luiza Cruz, 1973; English translation by Gertrude C. Suppe, 1987; Spanish translation by Raquel Gutiérrez-Achon, 1987; based on Judges 5.

DEBORA

cho - sen those who are hum - ble. For our God is good!
co - ge a los hu - mil - des. Por - que bue - no es Dios,

God is good and will strength-en___ the peo - ple with might!
bue - no es Dios. Él los for - ta - le - ce con su po - der.

and various other rhythm instruments. If available, it would be fun to add a string bass or bass guitar on the bass line. Perhaps have a solo voice sing the stanzas, with all children singing on the initial line and the refrain. Using a lighter accompaniment on the verse and adding more instruments on the refrain would make the praise exclamation more pronounced. Have a trumpet or violin play the descant.

Sing in worship services where God's deliverance of his people is retold and celebrated. The children could sing the verses, with the congregation joining them on the refrain.

Castanets

Descant for refrain

We don't know how old Samuel was when his mother, Hannah, brought him to the temple. He may have been only four or five, since Hannah kept him at home only until he was weaned. And although we don't know how long Samuel had lived at the temple when God called him, we do know he was still a boy. 1 Samuel 3:1-10 is the basis for this song by Betty Carr Pulkingham. Each stanza is a dialogue between God, Samuel, and Eli, with commentary from a narrator.

The first three stanzas and the first half of the fourth stanza reflect the Scripture story; the last two lines of the fourth stanza extend God's call for children to "come to him" (see Matt. 19:14, where Jesus says, "Let the little children come to me, and do not hinder them, for the kingdom of heaven belongs to such as these").

The melody carries the story of the song in a simple and childlike manner. Notice that the melody placed with the calling of Samuel matches the "sing-song" call children use when calling their friends to play. Sing this repetitive melody as a story, with different groups acting out the different characters. The repetition in the biblical account is found here too; stanzas 1 and 2 are identical.

The number of syllables don't always match the number of notes; in this case the boundaries of the written rhythm can be "bent" to fit the words so that a sense of conversation is conveyed. In lines 3 and 4 of stanza 1 the original melody had a low B pickup at the beginning, making an octave jump and landing on the

108 Samuel

♩ = 69

Words and Music: Betty Carr Pulkingham

Capo 1

2 Samuel, Samuel, God is a callin' to you, Samuel. *(repeat)*
   Here am I. Here am I, for you were a callin' to me, Father Eli. *(repeat)*
   I called you not, I called you not. Go and lie down upon your cot. *(repeat)*
   He lay right down. He lay right down on his cot upon the ground. *(repeat)*

3 Samuel, Samuel, God is a callin' to you, Samuel. *(repeat)*
   Here am I, here am I, for you were a callin' to me, Father Eli. *(repeat)*
   Go lie down and it shall be, if the Lord is really calling thee,
       say to him, "Lord, speak to me, for thy servant heareth, heareth thee."
   He lay right down, he lay right down on his cot upon the ground. *(repeat)*

4 Samuel, Samuel, God is still a callin' to you, Samuel. *(repeat)*
   Lord, speak to me, speak to me, for thy servant heareth thee. *(repeat)*
   Come to me, come to me. Children, children, will you come to me? *(repeat)*
   Come to me, come to me. God is a callin' to his children. Come to me. *(repeat)*

high B on the second word. It is easier to mention that here than it would have been to notate it. However, the rhythm of the fourth line should be strictly observed: children will need to sustain the first note for its whole value (five beats) before moving to the end of the stanza. The accompaniment will be very helpful (and should be bouncing, especially on that measure). In conducting that long note, draw your hand through the air all five beats to encourage sustained singing.

Divide the children into two groups, with older children on Eli's part and the younger children on Samuel's part. Once children are well acquainted with the song, assign individual children to sing the different parts of the narrative; two additional children can mime the actions and reactions of Samuel and Eli through the song.

Sing in worship services in which Scripture and sermon focus on Samuel or in any service where God's call to obedient service is the theme.

Illustration: The jar with oil points to the Old Testament practice of anointing priests, kings, and sometimes prophets. The anointing symbolized being set apart for special service to God. Samuel anointed David as king (1 Sam. 16:13). Jesus' "title" is "Messiah," or "Christ," both of which mean "anointed one." In some Christian traditions, oil is still used for anointing, especially for healing (James 5:14).

♩ = 92

109 Only a Boy Named David

This traditional song for young children is based on the story of David and Goliath in 1 Samuel 17. Make sure the children have heard this story before learning the song. Because of the repetition in the text, children will learn quickly. The motions are fun for young children and they also help them to remember the words.

Teach this enjoyable song by the echo method, singing phrase by phrase with the motions from the very start. Have a recorder play the melody accompanied by piano or autoharp. You may want to have the children hold the note on the word "air" in the last line, as if the stone is travelling through the air, before singing the last phrase up to tempo.

Sing in children's programs or in services dealing with the story of David and Goliath.

On- ly a boy named Da- vid, on - ly a lit - tle sling,

on - ly a boy named Da- vid, but he could pray and sing.

On- ly a boy named Da- vid, on - ly a rip - pling brook,

on - ly a boy named Da- vid, but five lit - tle stones he took. And

one lit - tle stone went in the sling, and the sling went round and

Words and Music: Arthur Arnott, 1931; based on 1 Samuel 17:49

Capo 1

Motions:

(a) *Hand held out, palm down, as if measuring.*   (e) *Hold up five fingers.*
(b) *Circle hand above head.*   (f) *Hold up one finger.*
(c) *Hands folded.*   (g) *Shoot arm forward.*
(d) *Wiggle fingers, moving arm left to right.*   (h) *Fall down or clap.*

Teaching this story-song about Elijah will certainly add variety to your repertoire! Learn the words by sections or scenes, noticing how every two lines rhyme. Each scene clearly tells a story. Try using as a drama: pantomime each scene as it is sung, or enact each scene before or after that section is sung (see outline below). Use your imagination and write a separate little script using the relevant Bible passages and possibly even a narrator. Introduce each scene with a title sign, for example, stanzas 1-3 could be called "Elijah Interferes."

Notice that stanza 13 summarizes the story with a fitting commentary, including the meaning of Elijah's name. It would be a fitting introduction or conclusion for any of the scenes. Andrew Kuyvenhoven calls Elijah "the reformer of the Old Covenant church." Indeed, Elijah was so important that when John the Baptizer was to be born, the angel told his father that John would "go on before the Lord in the spirit and power of Elijah . . . to make ready a people prepared for the Lord" (Luke 1:17).

Assign different groups to each scene, with everyone responding on stanza 13. Scene 4 (st. 11-13) will require your creativity and everyone's imagination as you pantomime or dramatize. Do you want to add more color and spice? Include props, costumes, and even backdrops! Here is an outline with list of characters:

110 Elijah

♩ = 100

1 E-li-jah planned to in-ter-fere
2 E-li-jah to a wi-dow said,
3 E-li-jah prayed to save from death

with A-hab's i-dols and ca-reer. "No dew, no rain!"
"Give me some wa-ter and some bread. Your flour, your oil,
the wi-dow's son, who lost his breath. "He lives, he lives!"

the pro-phet said, as drought u-pon the land was spread.
will not run out un-til the rain will end the drought."
the pro-phet said, as sad-ness turned to joy in-stead.

Elijah at Mount Carmel

4   Elijah bravely set a test
    to see which god would be the best:
    "Who will it be that sends the fire?
    Which god can answer your desire?"

5   Elijah dared to make some fun
    when all the dancing had begun:
    "Your god is gone, or thinking deep.
    Shout loudly, for he is asleep!"

Words: Bert Polman, 1994; based on 1 Kings 17-18, 2 Kings 2
Music: S. C. Molefe
Words © 1994, CRC Publications

LM
ASITHI AMEN

Scene 1: Elijah Interferes (1 Kings 17): Elijah, King Ahab, widow, widow's son

Scene 2: Elijah at Mount Carmel (1 Kings 18:16-40): Elijah, Ahab, followers of Baal, followers of God

Scene 3: Elijah at Mount Horeb (1 Kings 19): Elijah, Jezebel, Elisha

Scene 4: Elijah's Ascension (2 Kings 2:1-12): Elijah, Elisha

6   Elijah took his sacrifice
    and poured the water on it thrice.
    He prayed, "Give us a sign to tell
    that you are Lord of Israel!"

7   Elijah saw the fire descend
    and heard the people's shout ascend.
    He said to them, "If God is Lord,
    seize all who disobey his word!"

Elijah at Mount Horeb

8   Elijah ran to save his life
    from Jezebel, King Ahab's wife,
    and prayed to God with sigh and moan,
    "I've had enough! I'm all alone!"

9   Elijah hid himself in fear
    as storm and quake and fire appeared.
    But when the wind as whisper blew,
    God spoke: "I have more work for you."

10 Elijah followed God's command
    to find new leaders for the land.
    "Elisha, come," the prophet spoke,
    "You must succeed me; here's my cloak."

Elijah's Ascension

11 Elijah traveled through the land
    and crossed the Jordan on dry sand.
    Then he went up to heaven's height
    in whirling wind, with fire alight.

12 Elisha knew God heard his prayer,
    that he would be Elijah's heir,
    when he could see his master rise
    on fiery chariot to the skies.

13 Elijah's deeds to us proclaim
    the fitting meaning of his name:
    "The Lord's my God! The Lord's my God!"
    Tell of God's glory all abroad.

Children will quickly learn this South African melody. The second phrase is the same as the first, only higher. The third phrase has inner repetition, and the final phrase returns to the rhythm of the first.

Syncopation makes this melody fun! Play a little clapping echo game and challenge children to echo your rhythm patterns. Begin with the "no dew no rain" pattern, and then expand to complete phrases. Ask the children which phrase uses a different rhythm.

Choose a child to sing the "Elijah" solo. Help by playing that single note as each scene begins. Someone could also speak that name in a stage whisper. Encourage older children to learn this easy alto part, a third below the melody. Sing with energy and enthusiasm.

Include this song and drama in a service that emphasizes following God and proclaiming his glory. Adopt the first two lines of this song as the theme for a special service with missions emphasis, and let the children joyously proclaim it with this song and drama. If you repeat stanza 13 throughout the piece, encourage the congregation to sing along as the drama progresses. Or ask your minister to preach a series of sermons on Elijah and use this song as an introduction or conclusion to the series. Children may also enjoy learning the original South African words to this song, which was

sung when Desmond Tutu became Archbishop of Capetown:

Solo: Ma-si-thi
All: A-men. Siakudumisa. (repeat) (see-ah-koo-doo-mee-sah)
Amen bawo. Amen bawo. (bah-woe)
Amen Siakudumisa.

Amen. We praise your name, O Lord!

Jonah's song is recorded in Jonah 2. Verse 1 sets the scene: "From inside the fish, Jonah prayed to the Lord his God." Then comes Jonah's song, followed by verse 10, "And the Lord commanded the fish, and it vomited Jonah onto dry land." The first two stanzas of this song tell of Jonah's failure and how God reached out to save him from drowning. The final stanza is Jonah's response of praise and thanks for God's grace and salvation. Children have fears of drowning and other terrible accidents; they can well relate to the terror Jonah felt. But this is a song of confidence and trust that the Lord will save.

The melody has the character of an Israeli folk song, moving usually in stepwise motion with a comfortable range for children's voices. The melody is constructed in four four-measure phrases. The first repeats exactly with its own little refrain. The second also has a built-in refrain and some musical repetition. The syncopated beginning of every phrase creates a lot of energy; almost like Jonah's gasping for breath! The second measure also begins with the same syncopated catching of breath. Encourage the children to sustain the longer notes and take good breaths at all those syncopated eighth rests.

For accompaniment, include guitar/autoharp and/or keyboard. A violin (or flute, recorder or xylophone) could create a descant by transposing

111 Jonah's Song

♩ = 116

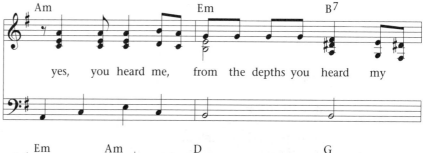
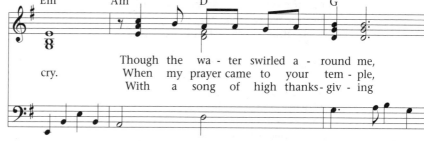

Words: Edith Bajema, 1993
Music: Vicki Williams, 1994
© 1994, CRC Publications

the lowest part of the treble clef line up an octave. Children will also enjoy clapping and playing a variety of rhythm instruments.

In addition to singing in a service about Jonah, sing as a response of thanksgiving following the assurance of pardon in the service of confession, for baptism, or during the Easter season (see notes below on the illustration). There are also a number of circumstances in the life of a congregation when this song could be sung as a joyful testimony of gratitude: when someone is restored to the fellowship of the church after a time of doubt or rebellion, when health is restored after serious illness, or when someone is spared serious injury in an accident.

Illustration: The picture of the boat and the fish reminds us of Jonah, who was thrown overboard, "but the Lord provided a great fish to swallow Jonah, and Jonah was inside the fish three days and nights." In Matthew 12:40, Jesus compares his burial with Jonah being in the belly of the fish.

Young children will enjoy this motion song about the miraculous catch of fish (John 21:1-6). The story takes place after Jesus' resurrection. At first the disciples didn't know it was Jesus who called out to them to throw their net on the other side. But after "the nets were filled with great big fishes" (153—they counted them!), the disciple whom Jesus loved recognized him: "It is the Lord!" Peter jumped right out of the boat to meet Jesus, and they had breakfast together. This was the third time Jesus appeared to his disciples after he rose from the dead.

There are only two chords in the simple arrangement of this traditional children's folk tune. In addition to autoharp or guitar, children could play Orff instruments in a simple pattern like this:

Lines 1 and 3: Play quarter notes back and forth on F and the C above

Line 2: Play quarter notes back and forth on low C and the C above

Line 4: Combine one measure from line 2 and one from line 1

Invite young children to sing this song in congregational worship during the Easter season, right after an older child reads the passage from John 21.

112 Peter and James and John

♩ = 72

2 (casting out, pulling in)   (hands upturned)
   They fished all night, but they caught nothing, (3x) . . .

3 (arms swinging)
   Along came Jesus walkin' on the seashore, (3x) . . .

4 (two-armed, overhand throw)
   He said, "Throw your nets over on the other side, (3x) . . .

5 (spread arms high and wide)
   The nets were filled with great big fishes, (3x) . . .

Words and Music: traditional, based on John 21:1-8; arranged by Mimi Farra, 1979

Jesus Called the Twelve Disciples 113

♩ = 63

Je - sus called the twelve dis - ci - ples: Pe - ter and An - drew,
James and John. He called Phil - ip and Bar - tho - lo - mew; six so
far, we're half - way done! Thom - as, Mat - thew, James, and
Thad - daeus, Si - mon, Ju - das; fi - nal - ly, we have twelve. But
our King Je - sus al - so is call - ing you and me.

This text is a delightful vehicle for children (or adults!) to memorize the names of Jesus' twelve disciples. Frank DeVries, the author of this text, is an educator, obviously looking for a way to make these names easy to remember. The names follow the order in Matthew 10:1-4. Point out the two most difficult names—Bartholomew and Thaddeus—to the children before speaking the entire text in rhythm.

The tune is an easy one for children to learn (the beginning is reminiscent of the well-known children's song for learning the alphabet). Point out that of the four phrases in the song, three are almost exactly the same. The third phrase is completely different from the others (A A' B A''). Accompany with autoharp or guitar.

Young children could offer this song as a call to discipleship after a sermon, especially during the Sundays after the Epiphany when the focus is on Jesus' ministry and his invitation to follow him.

Words and Music: Frank DeVries, 1982
© 1982, CRC Publications

87 87 D
JESUS CALLS

How does Jesus build his church? He calls common, ordinary people and gradually builds their faith through daily experiences. As their faith increases, God uses them to build his church and kingdom. Jesus' disciple Peter was one of these ordinary people. He started out as an uneducated fisherman and became a great preacher and leader of the early church. Each stanza relates one episode of Peter's life; stanza 8 is a response to any of the other stanzas, or to the complete song.

Here are some ideas for teaching the song. Ask children to identify anything in the room that reminds them of each stanza. Make sure you have scattered around a variety of visuals, pictures, and symbols, such as a small play boat, cross, heart, fishing net, fishing pole, church, little play people, play animals and creatures, and anything else you can find that might be helpful. Set up a little scene using imaginative props, and carry on the conversation and action of each stanza using paper bag puppets of Jesus and Peter. Or check your local Christian bookstore for a flannelgraph set on the story of Peter and use that to illustrate each stanza. Perhaps some children might enjoy miming or acting out each scene. Bible references follow:

- Matthew 4:18-19: Jesus calls Peter
- Luke 9:18-20: Peter's confession
- Matthew 14:29-31: Jesus and Peter walk on water
- Matthew 26:69-74: Peter disowns Jesus
- John 21:15-19: Jesus again calls Peter

114 Jesus Called to Peter

♩ = 112

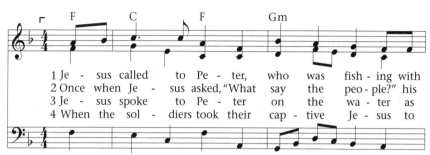

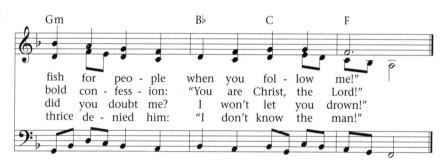

Words: Bert Polman, 1994
Music: Melody by Wim ter Burg, 1971; harmony by Henry Hageman, 1994; descant by Emily R. Brink, 1994

Words, harmony, and descant © 1994, CRC Publications. Melody © 1971, Wim ter Burg. Used by permission.

10 6 10 5
OF ALL THE PEOPLE
Capo 5

- Acts 2:22-36: Peter preaches

- Acts 10:9-35: Peter's vision

5 After Jesus asked, "You love me, Peter?"
   He said, "You know I do."
   "Then go feed my sheep," responded Jesus,
   "Follow me anew."

6 Gifted by the Holy Spirit, Peter
   proclaimed aloud the word:
   "Jesus, who was crucified, has risen;
   he is Christ, the Lord!"

7 Peter's vision held all kinds of creatures
   and some he would not eat;
   but the Lord taught Peter, "All the nations
   make my church complete!"

8 Thank you, Lord, for using Peter's story
   to guide us in our search
   for the ways in which we may experience
   how you build your church.

The melody is in two long phrases, with the first half the same each time. As you sing it for them, ask the children to identify where the pattern is repeated in the song, and point out the similarities of the two main phrases. Trace the melody direction with your hand. Emphasize the dotted-note rhythm by "echo-clapping" the rhythm pattern of the first six notes. Include a flute playing the descant, and use it not only with several stanzas, but also as a peaceful introduction and conclusion. Or play the descant on the piano.

Check the preaching schedule in your congregation to find out if one of these incidents in the life of Peter will be the focus of a service. Then learn the relevant stanza, along with the first and possibly the last stanza. Stanzas 1, 2, and 5 would make an appropriate combination for a service with a mission theme.

Descant

Illustration: The net and fish illustrate Jesus' call to fishermen Peter and Andrew to become fishers of people (Matt. 4:19). In the Christian tradition, the fish continues to be a symbol for Peter. It has also been a symbol for Jesus. The early Christians used it as a secret code during times of persecution—the letters of the Greek word for fish, *ichthus,* stand for "Jesus Christ, Son of God, Savior."

The best way to teach the words of this favorite children's Bible-story song is simply to sing the story with the motions. The traditional version has only one stanza. Later, a second was added by Herman Proper, a Sunday school teacher in Surrey, British Columbia, to complete the story (Luke 19:1-9). Use the suggested motions on stanza 1. Then, since most children are unfamiliar with it, spend a little more time on the second stanza. Since young children love to do motions, you may repeat some of the motions used from stanza 1 on stanza 2, and even add a few new ones.

Sing the first phrase on "la" for your children, showing the direction of the melody with your hands. Ask your group if anyone knows a song using that melody, and encourage everyone to sing it on "la" with you, again showing the melody's direction. Do this two more times to illustrate how the same phrase is just repeated, and then applaud everyone for already singing three-quarters of the song. Conclude with the same routine on the final phrase, also repeating it.

Then add the words. Make sure your children do not clip off the ending phrase notes. Hold them for two beats, allowing a half beat for a breath. Encourage a strong voice on the spoken part (but no shouting).

Sing unaccompanied or with very light accompaniment. Older children could accompany on autoharp, perhaps others who can read music could play the bass on Orff instruments.

Include this song in worship in a praise time that includes favorite children's songs.

115 Zaccheus

$\quad$ = 66

1 Zac-chae-us was a wee lit-tle man, a wee lit-tle man was he. He climbed up in a syc-a-more tree, for the Lord he want-ed to see. And as the Sav-ior passed that way, he looked up in the

Words: stanza 1, traditional; stanza 2, Herman Proper, 1980
Music: traditional; arranged by N. R. Schaper
St. 2 © 1994, CRC Publications

Capo 1

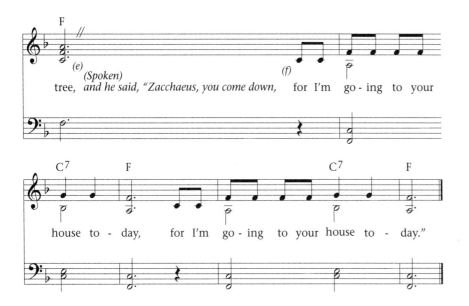

tree, *and he said, "Zacchaeus, you come down,* for I'm go - ing to your

house to - day, for I'm go - ing to your house to - day."

2 Zacchaeus knew that he'd done wrong,
   and sorry for his sins was he.
   "Lord, to the poor I'll give one half
   of all my goods," said he.
   "And if I've cheated anyone,
   four times will I repay."
     And Jesus said,
     "Salvation has come to you!
   I have come to seek and save.
   I have come to seek and save."

Motions for stanza 1
   (a) Hands in front, right palm raised above left palm.
   (b) Alternate hands in climbing motion.
   (c) Shade eyes with right hand and look down.
   (d) Shade eyes with right hand and look up.
   (e) Speak these words while looking up and beckoning with hand.
   (f) Clap hands on accented beat.

This song tells the story of Peter healing a crippled beggar (Acts 3:1-8). Explain to the children that "alms" means anything given to help the poor. In this story, Peter helps the man with something much better than "silver and gold." The lame man—now the walking man—expresses his joy and thanks by "walking and jumping and praising God."

Be sure you have memorized this song with the motions before teaching the children. First teach the words with motions, speaking in the given rhythmic pattern. Then add the music. Younger children may enjoy acting out this song as it is sung. Choose a Peter, John, and lame beggar. As the children sing, the characters can make the story come to life. The final phrase appropriately concludes with the repetition of Peter's words. Accompany with keyboard, guitar or autoharp. On the "walking and jumping" section, play in a more accented style to demonstrate the text.

In a worship service, children could sing as a response to the reading of Acts 3:1-8. Or sing as a response to a testimony of healing.

116 Silver and Gold Have I None

♩ = 60

Words and Music: anonymous, based on Acts 3:1-8; arranged by Betty Pulkingham, 1974

Actions:

(a) fold hands, as in prayer
(b) hold out palms
(c) hold out empty hands, shake head
(d) extend hand
(e) point upward
(f) sweep hands upward
(g) march (in place)
(h) jump up
(i) raise arms

This song is based on the conversation of the angel and Mary Magdalene following Christ's resurrection (John 20:11-18). Both text and music of this traditional African-American spiritual were adapted by June Armstrong Fischer for use in the Children and Worship program. The story is profoundly simple, one that any child can understand.

The melody is also accessible to children, though the syncopation may be a challenge. As you learn this yourself before teaching it, tap constant eighth notes while singing until the syncopated patterns feel natural and comfortable. Sing in two broad and relaxed beats per measure to convey a spirit of compassion and hope. A simple guitar accompaniment would be effective; unaccompanied singing would also serve the text and the history of the song well—slaves sang this song in the fields as they worked without instrumental accompaniment. If the children are able to sing in parts, some could sing the tenor line, either transposed up an octave for a descant part or as written for a low "alto" part.

Sing this spiritual at an Easter service or in services that focus on the resurrection of Jesus Christ and the comfort and hope that it brings.

117 O Mary, Don't You Weep

♩ = 100

Words and Music: African-American spiritual; adapted by June Fischer Armstrong, 1991

Capo 3

O Ma - ry, don't you weep; don't you mourn.

He's not dead. He has ris - en. O Ma - ry, don't you weep.

Illustration: When Jesus rose, his burial clothes were laid aside. The stylized tombstone and cloth point to the absence of Jesus' body. The rays of light suggest the dazzling light of the angel, "like lightning," who came to roll away the stone from the tomb (Matt. 28:3).

Each of the four stanzas of this song retells an important event in Paul's life:

Stanza 1: Saul's conversion on the road to Damascus (Acts 9:1-15)

Stanza 2: The calling of Paul and Barnabas to mission work (Acts 13:1-3)

Stanza 3: Paul and Silas in jail; the Philippian jailer (Acts 16:25-34)

Stanza 4: The shipwreck on the way to Rome (Acts 27:13-25)

The refrain calls all Christians to be like Paul in sharing the gospel with all people.

Bert Polman, chair of the committee that prepared *Songs for LiFE,* wrote this and "Jesus Called to Peter" (114) for this section of the hymnal. Make sure children understand the difference between pray and "prey" (sneak up on) in stanza 1.

Most adults will recognize the tune ST. CATHERINE, which traditionally has been associated with the hymn "Faith of Our Fathers."

The first and third phrases are identical, and the second and forth are similar (A B A B'). Sing with smooth, flowing lines; do not overly stress the first beats of the measures.

To teach the song, help the children to see what each stanza describes. Cut out enough squares of four different pieces of colored construction paper for each child present. Pass out the slips of paper, one per child. Try not to have children with the same color sit next to each

118 Paul, Preacher of the Word

♩ = 126

1 Da - mas - cus bound, Saul meant to prey
2 At An - ti - och, the Christ - ians prayed
3 When Paul and Si - las sang in jail,
4 En route to Rome, on Paul's last trip;

on an - y fol - lowers of the Way.
and sought the Ho - ly Spir - it's aid.
an earth - quake caused their chains to fail.
a storm wrecked hav - oc on the ship.

In stunned sur - prise he heard the Lord:
"Call Paul and Barn - a - bas," they heard.
Then from his su - i - cide de - terred,
Then Paul spoke up: "I serve the Lord;

"I've cho - sen you to preach my word!"
"Set them a - part to speak God's word."
the jail - er heard their sav - ing word.
he'll save us by his might - y word!"

Words: Bert Polman, 1994
Music: Henri F. Hemy, 1864; arranged by Bert Polman, 1994
Words and arr. © 1994, CRC Publications

88 88 88
ST. CATHERINE

Refrain

O Lord, help us to speak like Paul
and share with all your gos - pel's call.

other. Hold up one color, and teach one phrase to all the children holding that color. Continue with the remaining three colors and phrases. Next, instruct the children to trade cards with their neighbor and learn a new phrase. Continue in this way until everyone has learned the whole song. Finally, teach the refrain to all. Chords for accompaniment by a guitar or autoharp are provided.

Sing in a service whose theme is missions. Have the children sing one stanza, joined by the congregation on the others. Or sing as a parting hymn at the close of a worship service as a reminder of our mission.

Illustration: Although we often think of Paul as the traveling preacher, his great legacy is the letters he wrote to the early churches. Through those letters, Paul is still preaching today. Children will enjoy learning about ancient writing tools such as parchment and papyrus scrolls and reed quills.

Darkness and light are important symbols for Advent and Christmas. The first line of this hymn is based on the promise of the Messiah in Isaiah 9:2, "The people walking in darkness have seen a great light." When people asked Jesus if he was the Messiah, he responded by referring to another prophecy in Isaiah—the blind would see, the lame walk, and the deaf hear (35:5-6). The part about the lame walking must have meant a lot to composer Dosia Carlson, who had polio as a child.

This hymn lends itself well to responsorial singing. Divide the children into two groups, each singing alternating two-measure phrases. The prayerful response of "Come, come, come, Jesus Christ" can easily be sung and signed by younger children. Picture each of the key words in the remaining text as a memory aid: darkness, blindness; sickness, poverty; trouble, arguments. The last four measures should be sung by the entire group; only the final word is different in each stanza: love, hope, peace.

The primarily stepwise movement of the melody is not difficult for children to learn—it flows easily with two beats each measure. When first teaching this song you may wish to concentrate on the final four-measure phrase and the responses of "Come, Lord Jesus." Keep the accompaniment simple and sustained, preferably with organ or piano. The guitar/autoharp part is best not played with the keyboard part.

Sing during Advent, perhaps choosing different stanzas for different weeks according to the theme. Also sing anytime during a healing service.

119 People in Darkness Are Looking for Light

♩ = 52

1 Peo-ple in dark-ness are look-ing for light. Come, come,
2 Peo-ple with sick-ness are pray-ing for health. Come, come,
3 Peo-ple in trou-ble would like to be free. Come, come,

come, Je-sus Christ. Peo-ple with blind-ness are long-ing for sight.
come, Je-sus Christ. Peo-ple in pov-er-ty want to have wealth.
come, Je-sus Christ. Peo-ple with ar-gu-ments want to a-gree.

Come, Lord Je-sus Christ. These days of ad-ven-ture when
Come, Lord Je-sus Christ. These days of ad-ven-ture when
Come, Lord Je-sus Christ. These days of ad-ven-ture when

all peo-ple wait are days for the ad-vent of love.
all peo-ple wait are days for the ad-vent of hope.
all peo-ple wait are days for the ad-vent of peace.

Notice the "play on words" in this song: Days of <u>advent</u> are days of <u>adventure</u>.

Words and Music: Dosia Carlson, 1983
© 1983, Dosia Carlson. Used by permission.

Capo 2

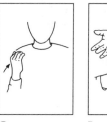
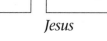

Come   *Jesus*

♩ = 69

Psalm 72 120

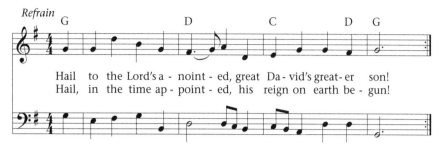

Refrain

G D C D G

Hail to the Lord's a - noint - ed, great Da - vid's great- er son!
Hail, in the time ap - point - ed, his reign on earth be - gun!

Endow the king with your justice, O God,
    the royal son with your righteousness.
He will judge your people in righteousness,
    your afflicted ones with justice.
He will save the children of the needy;
    he will crush the oppressor. *Refrain*

He will rule from sea to sea
    and from the River to the ends of the earth.
The kings of Tarshish and of distant shores
    will bring tribute to him;
    the kings of Sheba and Seba will present him gifts.
All kings will bow down to him
    and all nations will serve him. *Refrain*

For he will deliver the needy who cry out,
    the afflicted who have no one to help.
He will take pity on the weak and the needy
    and save the needy from death.
He will rescue them from oppression and violence,
    for precious is their blood in his sight. *Refrain*

May his name endure forever;
    may it continue as long as the sun.
All nations will be blessed through him,
    and they will call him blessed. *Refrain*

Orff instruments
Bass xylophone *Glockenspiel*

Words: from Psalm 72 (NIV); refrain by James Montgomery, 1822
Music: German

Psalm 72 is a royal psalm that points to Jesus as the eternal king who would bring justice and deliverance to the needy and oppressed. This King will do everything right!

The refrain is taken from the first two lines of James Montgomery's setting of Psalm 72, found in many hymnals. Ask an older child or children to read the psalm text, alternating with everyone singing the refrain. The refrain should both introduce and conclude the reading.

This refrain (two lines; notice the repeat!) is easily learned by rote. Sing with strength and majesty. For the repeated statements, accompany with Orff instruments, keyboard, guitar, or autoharp. Also consider using handbells, choir chimes, or piano for the Orff instrumentation; then play the bass xylophone part an octave lower than written.

In worship, this psalm could be one of the Scripture readings during Advent or Epiphany or for any service where the focus is on the reign of Christ. You may wish to combine it with "Jesus Shall Reign," a hymn based on Psalm 72.

For an Orff introduction, the bass xylophone begins with one statement of its pattern and is joined by the glockenspiel, also playing its pattern once. The children then join in the refrain. This introductory pattern can begin each of the repetitions of the singing of the refrain. Following the final refrain the pattern could be reversed with the glockenspiel and xylophone playing together and then the xylophone concluding with its pattern alone. (If you use handbells, remember that a xylophone has a short, percussive sound that on handbells could be achieved with a pluck or *martellato*; the glockenspiel's sound decays over a longer period of time and handbells could either be damped after the note value has been completed or rung free.) The instrumental parts should not be played with the keyboard accompaniment. For another kind of introduction and a postlude (but not while children are singing), ask trumpeters to play the refrain in royal fanfare style.

This hymn was originally written in German for a feast day in honor of John the Baptist. The words are based on Isaiah 40:1-5, which points to the coming of the Christ. Stanza 1 comes from Isaiah 40:1-2, stanza 2 from verses 3-4, and stanza 3 from verses 4-5. It is a call to make everything ready for the Lord.

The tune, one of the most beloved melodies from the Genevan Psalter of 1551, was originally composed for Psalm 42. Some children may notice that there is no time signature at the beginning. This is because not all measures have the same amount of beats in them. The best way for children to learn the rhythm of this hymn is by hearing it first. Sing a phrase (measure) and have children echo back. Children who would like to play this piece on an instrument will find it easiest to count two beats for each half note, one beat for each quarter note, and four beats on the whole notes. Sing at a "comfortable" speed. One of the C instruments (violin, flute, recorder, oboe) could play the melody on the treble clef line, with a cello playing the bass clef line. Try adding finger cymbals or triangle on the first beat of each measure. Four-part accompaniment can be found in many hymnals under the tune names FREU DICH SEHR or GENEVAN 42.

In congregational worship, have the children sing one stanza, with the congregation

121 Comfort, Comfort Now My People

♩ = 72

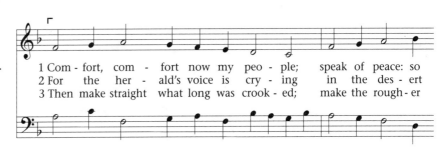

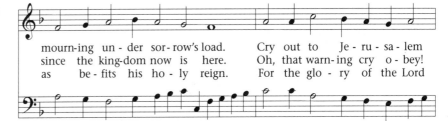

Words: Isaiah 40:1-5; versified by Johannes Olearius, 1671; translated by Catherine
    Winkworth, 1863
Music: Louis Bourgeois, 1551; arranged by Norma de Waal Malefyt, 1992
Arr. © 1994, CRC Publications

87 87 77 88
GENEVAN 42

joining on the others. Or have a soloist (or small group) sing stanza 1, the entire group sing stanza 2, and a soloist on the first half of stanza 3, with the entire group singing the last half. Another possibility is for two equal groups to sing antiphonally, the first group taking lines 1 and 3, and the second group lines 2 and 4.

Sing during Advent as a call to worship or before a prayer of confession. Or sing at services emphasizing the second coming, repentance, profession of faith, missions, or commitment. Ask your organist to play a prelude on this tune when the children are learning it.

sins I cov - er and her war - fare now is o - ver.
rise to meet him and the hills bow down to greet him.
see the to - ken that God's word is nev - er bro - ken.

Come, Thou Long-Expected Jesus 122

♩ = 108

F   C   F   Bb   C   F

1 Come, thou long - ex - pec - ted Je - sus, born to set thy peo - ple free;
2 Is - rael's strength and con - so - la - tion, hope of all the earth thou art:
3 Born thy peo - ple to de - liv - er, born a child and yet a king,
4 By thine own e - ter - nal Spir - it rule in all our hearts a - lone;

Dm   A   Dm   C   F   C   F

from our fears and sins re - lease us, let us find our rest in thee.
dear de - sire of ev - ery na - tion, joy of ev - ery long - ing heart.
born to reign in us for - ev - er, now thy gra - cious king - dom bring.
by thine all - suf - fi - cient mer - it raise us to thy glo - rious throne.

Words: Charles Wesley, 1744
Music: *Psalmodia Sacra*, 1715; adapted by Henry Gauntlett, 1861; arranged by
Robert Roth, 1989
Arr. © 1989, Robert Roth. Used by permission.

87 87
STUTTGART
Capo 5

This hymn, written by Charles Wesley when he was thirty-seven years old, is one of over 6,500 hymns he wrote (for more on Wesley, see 19). Although it is a Christmas hymn, we use it more during Advent because the words in stanzas 1 and 2 sound so much like those of the Old Testament prophets who wrote of the coming of the Messiah. Stanzas 3 and 4 speak not only of Jesus' birth but also look toward his second coming. It teaches us that Jesus is King of all, and ends with the prayer that he will be the only ruler of our lives and hearts.

Sing with strong unison voices. Choose either guitar (autoharp) or keyboard accompaniment. Solo instruments could play along on the melody. A good descant for C instrument (oboe, flute, recorder, violin) can be found in *Psalter Hymnal* 329. This would need to be transposed for B-flat trumpet or clarinet.

Sing this hymn for worship during Advent. Stanzas 1-2 could be a call to worship and stanzas 3-4 a response to the benediction. Or sing the entire song just before a prayer of confession. Also sing at Christmas, in carol services, and services with the second coming as the theme.

This beloved Advent hymn, written hundreds of years ago, helps us to prepare for the celebration of Christ's birth. Each stanza begins with an "O," expressing intense longing for the Messiah, followed by one of the names in the Bible for the Messiah. Each is part of a set of prayers called "O antiphons" (an antiphon is similar to a refrain).

Three "O antiphons" are included here:

- *Stanza 1:* Immanuel (God with us)
- *Stanza 2:* Branch of Jesse's stem (part of the royal family of David)
- *Stanza 3:* Bright and Morning Star (Christ is the light of the world)

You may want to explain several words to the children: "ransom" refers to the Israelites' waiting for Jesus to set them free; "captive" means they were prisoners; "exile" means living in a country that is not your own, which could make you lonesome. God sends away ("dispel") shadows with his light as the sun disperses shadows in a child's bedroom. Children may enjoy adding other ways we wish God would come—as Healer, Peacemaker, King.

Introduce the song by explaining the background of the "O antiphons": During Advent we look forward to the birth of Jesus. In the Old Testament we read of all the ways people thought Jesus would come. How would you want Jesus to come? After Jesus did come, people collected some of the ideas from the old Testament and added some of their own, creating prayers called "O an-

123 O Come, O Come, Immanuel

1 O come, O come, Im-man-u-el, and ran-som cap-tive Is-ra-el that mourns in lone-ly ex-ile here un-til the Son of God ap-pear.
2 O come, O Branch of Jes-se's stem, un-to your own and res-cue them! From depths of hell your peo-ple save, and give them vic-tory o'er the grave.
3 O come, O Bright and Morn-ing Star, and bring us com-fort from a-far! Dis-pel the sha-dows of the night and turn our dark-ness in-to light.

Refrain

Re-joice! Re-joice! Im-man-u-el

Words: Latin, 12th century; composite translation
Music: Processionale, 15th century; adapted by Thomas Helmore, 1854; arranged by Richard Proulx, 1975; adapted by Robert Roth, 1989
Accompaniment © 1975, G.I.A. Publications, Inc. Used by permission.

LM with refrain
VENI IMMANUEL

Duet accompaniment (right hand only)
or alternative accompaniment (both hands)

Illustration: The tree refers to the line, "O come, O Branch of Jesse's stem"—which in turn is a reference to Isaiah 11:1. King David's father, Jesse, is the tree stem from which both David and Jesus sprout as branches.

tiphons." Encourage the children to feel the same anticipation of Jesus' birth.

Teach the refrain first (you may wish to teach only the refrain to the youngest children). The chant style of the melody should allow the quarter notes to flow in a natural speech rhythm, not in strict metronomic beats. Its flexible rhythm takes on the accents and stresses of each word. Read through the verses and say them together, emphasizing the accented syllables. Teach the phrases by echo method, tracing the shape of the melody with your hand movements. To help the children feel as well as sing the continuous movement of the line, "paint" the melody through the air with a scarf.

Sing unaccompanied, or with very simple guitar/autoharp chords. For keyboard (piano and/or organ) accompaniment, consider playing both parts on stanza 1, only the main (lower) part on stanza 2, and only the higher second part on stanza 3, with the bright high notes for the "Bright and Morning Star." Both parts could be played on all the refrains.

Include in any Advent service. Consider singing stanza 1 as a processional, with a group of children coming in single file, bent over, each tied to the other in long purple ribbon "chains" to symbolize the "lonely exile." On the refrain, have them release the chains and twirl, swinging the ribbons now as streamers.

John the Baptizer quoted these words from Isaiah when he was preaching in the desert (Matt. 3:3). And when he saw his cousin Jesus coming to be baptized, John announced that this was the Lord the people were looking for. All of us are also called to "prepare the way of the Lord" in our living and talking, in our work and play. We want to be ready because when Jesus does come back, "all people will see the salvation of our God."

These profoundly simple words are set to a very simple melody by Jacques Berthier, composer for the community of Taizé in Southern France (see 13 for more on the music of Taizé).

Teach this song by echo method, one phrase at a time. When the children know it well, introduce the canon to the older children; the younger children could sing the second pattern as an ostinato, repeating throughout. Play the given chord pattern two times on keyboard or guitar as an introduction before bringing the voices in. After singing through once in unison, begin in canon, and/or add the descant on flute, violin, or even bells. A few Orff patterns are given below; create others by repeating any two-measure fragment of melody, descant, or the accompaniment.

During Advent, the children could sing this song in unison as a processional. After they reach the front, the adult choir and/or congregation could join, either in unison or in canon.

124 Prepare the Way of the Lord

♩. = 69

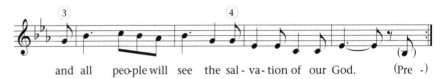

Pre-pare the way of the Lord. Pre-pare the way of the Lord, and all peo-ple will see the sal-va-tion of our God. (Pre -)

Descants

(second time)

Accompaniment

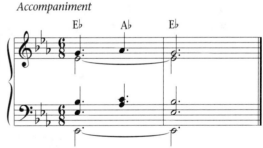

For a piano duet, one person plays the melody an octave higher while the other person plays this pattern four times.

Eb Ab Eb

Bass xylophone *Alto metalaphone* *Soprano glockenspiel*

Words: Isaiah 40:3; 52:10
Music: Jacques Berthier and the Community of Taizé, 1984
© 1984, Les Presses de Taizé. Used by permission of G.I.A. Publications, Chicago, IL.

Capo 1

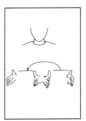 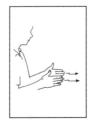 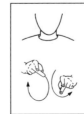 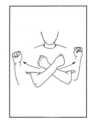 

Prepare *Way* *People* *Salvation* *God*

Song of Mary 125

♩ = 60

1 My spir - it glo - ri - fies the Lord, in
2 All gen - er - a - tions from now on shall
3 His mer - cy shall ex - tend to those who
4 He brought down rul - ers from their thrones, but
5 He helped his ser - vant Is - ra - el, re -

God my Sav - ior I re - joice, for he be - held my
call me blest and spread my fame, for he has done great
fear the Lord from age to age; he has re - vealed his
lift - ed those of low de - gree. He filled the hun - gry
mem - bering to be mer - ci - ful, keep - ing his word to

hum - ble state and in his love made me his choice.
things for me— might - y and ho - ly is his name.
might - y arm, scat - tering the proud in all their rage.
with good things, but emp - ty sent the rich a - way.
A - bra - ham and to his seed for - ev - er - more.

Orff instrument pattern
Alto xylophone

Words: Luke 1:46-55; versified by Dewey Westra, 1931; revised for *Psalter Hymnal,* 1987   LM
Music: Trier manuscript, 15th century; adapted by Michael Praetorius, 1609; arranged   PUER NOBIS
 by Emily R. Brink, 1994

The song of Mary, recorded in Luke 1:46-55, is one of the most loved in all of Scripture. Some churches with daily services sing it every day! Mary's song, called the Magnificat (see also 13 and 14), is a canticle, that is, a Scripture song that is not a psalm. It has the characteristics of a psalm of thanksgiving, praising God for his mighty acts of salvation, for his mercy to the poor and hungry and humble, and for his faithfulness.

It is set to a very old Christmas tune called PUER NOBIS, which means "a boy to us [is born]." The octave range and gentle, joyful character is well suited to children's voices. Encourage the children to sing long phrases (breathing at punctuation marks) and to use their "head voices" on the upper notes. Notice the possibility of performing in canon; the bass line picks up the melody at the end of the first line and continues it to the end of the stanza. The last two measures of the melody would need to be added to complete the stanza in round. That canon part could be sung or played by an instrument, perhaps a cello, or a flute an octave higher. The instrumental part can be used both as an accompaniment and as an introductory pattern.

Sing during Advent and Christmas as an opening hymn of praise or after the assurance of pardon or on any occasion of thanksgiving for God's grace.

Stanza 1 of this song is a paraphrase of Luke 12:35-40, stanza 2 of Romans 13:11-14. Like "Prepare the Way of the Lord" (124), it urges us to be ready to meet the Lord. We need to be alert and prepared because we know that Christ will return, but we do not know when. In order to be ready, we may have to make some changes in our lives.

Teach the song by the echo method, clapping as indicated right from the start. Sing with bright clean rhythmic precision. The "alleluia" phrases could be more lyrical, contrasting with the other more percussive phrases. Make sure you sing the syncopation crisply on "coming."

For the Orff patterns, play the soprano line with soprano glockenspiel, the alto line with alto glockenspiel or xylophone, and the lower open fifth lines with bass xylophone. When Orff instruments are used, do not use the piano.

In congregational worship, children could this song as a response to the call to confession or as a charge to the congregation just before the benediction. Sing during Advent, on Ascension Day, or any time the focus of the service is the second coming of the Lord.

126 Stay Awake, Be Ready

♩ = 120

Orff instrument patterns

[Play 3 times]

[Play 3 times]

Words and Music: Christopher Walker, 1988

Capo 3

♩ = 120

Look Up! 127

1 Look up! Look up! Look up! See the light of the pro-phets.* Look

up! Look up! Look up! See the light of the pro-phets.*

Refrain

For the word of the Lord is a light, shin-ing in the dark-ness

un-til the Day dawns, and the Morn-ing Star a - ris-es in your hearts.

*2 angels   3 star   4 Jesus

Alto metallophone
Stanzas (play 4x)   *Refrain*

Words and Music: June Fischer Armstrong, based on 2 Peter 1:19
© 1991, CRC Publications.

Capo 5

June Fischer Armstrong wrote this song, based on 2 Peter 1:19, for the Children and Worship program used in many churches. The emphasis is on light— the light of God's Word and the light of Jesus, who is the Morning Star. The light of the prophets, angels, and star all show the way to Jesus, the Light of the world.

Teach the melody to children by singing a phrase and letting them echo back. Show them that the first line is identical to the second. Sing with strong voices at an even tempo. Accompany this song with the suggested Orff instruments and recorder or with autoharp or guitar.

To "act out" this song, divide the children into three groups and give each child a flashlight. Sing the three "look up" units in turn. The first group looks up and turns on their flashlights when singing the first "Look up!"; the second group looks up and turns on their flashlights while singing the second "Look up!"; the third group on the third time. All three groups sing on the "See the light . . ." phrase. Keep flashlights on for the refrain but point them outward. Gradually raise them up on the last phrase "and the Morning Star arises in your hearts." The use of flashlights would be most effective in a darkened room. Or have the children use these motions without the flashlights.

Sing as an Introit during the Advent, Christmas, or Epiphany seasons. Or sing as preparation for Scripture reading. With a few word changes (see st. 2-4) it could possibly be sung with the lighting of the Advent wreath each week in Advent, depending on the theme chosen for the candles.

Bert Witvoet, Canadian writer and editor, composed this song for his congregation to sing when lighting Advent candles each week during Advent. The stanzas progress from the Old Testament prophets to Bethlehem, the shepherds, the angels, and finally, "Christmas day!"

Sing each stanza for the children, instructing them to echo the last line. Ask some questions about the words:

- *Stanza 1:* Who came to Israel? What did they do?

- *Stanza 2:* Where was Christ's birth? What was the miracle?

- *Stanza 3:* Who saw the light? What did the angel say?

- *Stanza 4:* Who sang at midnight? What did they sing?

- *Stanza 5:* What day is celebrated? Why sing?

As you sing the song, trace the direction of the melodic lines with hand motions. Children can also follow the direction with their hands.

In congregational worship, sing the appropriate stanza(s) each week during Advent along with the lighting of Advent candles. On Christmas Day, sing all five stanzas.

128 The Prophets Came to Israel

♩ = 60

1 The proph-ets came to Is - ra - el to tell them
2 In Beth - le - hem in a cat - tle stall a mir - a -
3 The shep- herds watched their flocks of sheep when light broke

what to do. They point-ed to the birth of Christ, and
cle we find: that such a low - ly place should hold the
from the sky. They heard a daz-zling an - gel say, "A

what they said came true, and what they said came true.
Sav - ior of man - kind, the Sav - ior of man - kind!
child is born near - by, a child is born near - by."

4 The angels sang a midnight song,
their eyes were filled with joy:
"the Son of God has come to earth
to be a little boy,
to be a little boy."

5 It's Christmas day! We celebrate
the coming of a king.
He came to set his children free,
and that is why we sing,
and that is why we sing.

Words and Music: Bert Witvoet, 1980; harmonized by Bert Polman, 1981
© 1987, Bert Witvoet

CM with repeat
FIVE CANDLES
Capo 5

♩ = 96

Away in a Manger 129

Words: American carol, 1885
Music: William J. Kirkpatrick, 1895

11 11 11 11
CRADLE SONG
Capo 5

No one knows who wrote the words to this delightful and familiar Christmas song. It has been sung and loved by children and adults alike since it first appeared in 1885. The first stanza and the beginning of the second present a childlike view of the nativity. Explain to the children that "lowing" means mooing. The ending of stanza 2 is a bedtime prayer for Jesus to watch over us during the night until morning is "nigh" or near. Stanza 3 is a prayer for Jesus to watch over us forever and make us ready to live with him in heaven.

The melody is one of several that have been used with the text. Point out that it consists of two phrases that are repeated, with a slight change at the end (ABAB').

Use light accompaniment on piano, autoharp, or guitar, with recorder, flute, or violin on the melody. Children should sing this as a gentle lullaby, not too fast, with sweet light voices. Young children will enjoy adding motions to the first stanza—rocking a baby, laying head in hands as if sleeping, wiggling fingers above their heads for twinkling stars, and again rocking a baby.

Sing at an evening service during the Christmas season, such as Christmas Eve, or as part of a children's program. Or sing stanza 3 any time during the year as a prayer or prayer response.

Tom Colvin wrote this contemporary Christmas carol in Malawi, Africa, when he was a missionary there. He learned that in Africa, a child's name is often chosen according to the parents' hopes for the child or the events associated with the child's birth. This text follows that pattern. The refrain refers to the event of Jesus' birth, while stanzas 1-4 reflect on naming the child, who Jesus is, and why he came to earth (Matt. 1:21, 23.) Stanza 5 concludes with a response of praise and service. Explain to the children that "boy-child" is the same as baby boy, and "Jesu" (*Yay-zoo*) is Jesus. Even the youngest children can learn the refrain.

The melody is based on a traditional Malawian dance tune. It should be sung with no pauses or breaks between refrain and stanzas. Have a soloist sing the question in stanza 1 with the group responding in stanzas 2-5. Children can sing the refrain and the congregation the stanzas, or you can explore other possibilities: all children on the refrains; stanza 1, solo; stanzas 2-4, small groups; stanza 5 and final refrain, children with congregation.

Enjoy attempting an African sound on the refrains with different gentle and light percussion patterns on drums, wood blocks, or tambourines. For an instrumental prelude/introduction, have one instrument (flute, recorder, violin) play the melody. The bass clef part could be played by cello or transposed up two octaves to form a flute or violin descant.

Sing during the Christmas season, especially in a "carols (or hymns) from many lands" service.

130 That Boy-Child of Mary

♩ = 63

1 What shall we call him, child of the manger?
2 His name is Jesu, God ever with us,
3 He came to save us, he came to help us,

What name is given in Bethlehem?
God given for us in Bethlehem.
born here among us in Bethlehem.

Repeat refrain

4 One with the Father, he is our Savior,
    heaven-sent helper of Bethlehem. *Refrain*

5 Gladly we praise him, love and adore him,
    give ourselves to him of Bethlehem. *Refrain*

Words: Tom Colvin, 1967
Music: Malawian; adapted by Tom Colvin, 1967; arranged by Norma de Waal Malefyt, 1992

BLANTYRE
Capo 5

♩ = 69

Go, Tell It on the Mountain 131

Refrain

Go, tell it on the moun-tain, o-ver the hills and ev-ery-where;

go, tell it on the moun-tain that Je-sus Christ is born.

1 While shep-herds kept their watch-ing o'er
2 The shep-herds feared and trem-bled when
3 Down in a low-ly sta-ble the

si-lent flocks by night, be-hold, through-out the
lo! a-bove the earth rang out the an-gel
hum-ble Christ was born, and God sent us sal-

Repeat refrain

heav-ens there shone a ho-ly light.
cho-rus that hailed our Sav-ior's birth.
va-tion that bless-ed Christ-mas morn.

This African-American spiritual tells the story of Jesus' birth as found in Luke 2:8-20. A long time ago people used to shout good news from the tops of hills and mountains (see Isa. 42:11). The refrain of this song reminds Christians to tell everyone the good news of Jesus' birth.

The dotted notes and syncopation of the refrain (typical of African-American spirituals) suggest that it should be sung joyfully, with strong voices. Clapping on the refrain would also be appropriate. The stanzas may be sung more smoothly. Perhaps soloists could sing the verses with everyone joining on the refrain. Or have a small group whisper repeatedly (in rhythm) "Go, tell it on the mountain" during one or all of the stanzas.

Sing at carol services, church school programs, and on Christmas Day. The end of the refrain could be altered to "that Jesus lives again!" or "that Jesus Christ is Lord!" for Easter, mission services, and other occasions.

Words and Music: African-American spiritual; arranged by Emily R. Brink, 1991
Arr. © 1994, CRC Publications

76 76 with refrain
GO TELL IT
Capo 5

The word "gospel" means "good news!" This joyful Christmas song announces the very good news that Jesus is born! Ask the children who announced the news when Jesus was born long ago, and assign someone to read Luke 2:10-12.

The text was written by the well-known children's composer Natalie Sleeth, a delightful, upbeat, creative musician with a buoyant spirit who loved the magic of language. Sleeth's beautiful texts are reflections of her positive outlook and deep faith (for more on Sleeth, see 175).

Since the text uses repetition and follows a distinct pattern, it is easy to learn. Use song charts for stanzas 1, 2, and 4, drawing simple symbols and pictures for each phrase (see ideas next page). As you look at the pictures on your charts, help children see the sequence of the responses, noticing what words in each stanza rhyme. When they know those words, insert the contrasting stanza 3. Use a different color for your song chart and ask what new words begin it. Teach one melody at a time, contrasting the two: bright and rhythmic, smooth and inviting. Help children imagine they are a "walking newspaper." Use the analogy of the town crier who used to walk through the streets announcing important news.

Stanza 4 offers several possibilities. The original anthem goes through the four stanzas without the descant, then, after an interlude, everything repeats with a descant. In this adaptation, the vocal descant could be played by an instrument. Or, teach all the children the descant. Sing it first without the main melody, then re-

132 Good News

♩ = 60

1 Good news! Good news! News of great joy! For
2 Good news! Good news! Joy-ful-ly sing! For

un-to us in Beth-le-hem is born now a boy!
un-to us in Beth-le-hem is cra-dled a King!

3 Come, come, be of good cheer! Christ, our

Descant

News! News! Joy-ful-ly sing! For

Sav-ior, is here! 4 Good news! Good news! Wel-come the morn! For

Words and Music: Natalie Sleeth, adapted from the anthem "Good News"
© 1980, Hinshaw Music, Inc. Used by permission.

Capo 5

Beth - le - hem's man - ger now cra-dles a King! For there in
Bb   Am   C7   F   Bb

un-to us in Beth-le-hem Lord Je-sus is born! For un-to us

a sta - ble Lord Je - sus, our Sav- ior, is born!
Am   Gm   C7   F

in Beth - le- hem Lord Je - sus is born!

Instrumental descant

peat, dividing the group into a two-part choir. Notice that the song concludes with a little coda; the last line repeats, but is stretched out just a little bit.

You may wish to add a triangle to the main beats of the first melody. As a final polishing touch include a flute or violin playing the instrumental descant and a small group of children singing the final counter-melody. Introduce the song with the first two lines, played by the piano and/or flute.

Begin your Christmas worship with your children singing this joyful announcement!

This traditional eighteenth-century French carol tells the Christmas story (Luke 2:8-20). In stanza 1, shepherds tell about hearing the angels. The Latin refrain—pronounced *GLOW-ree-ah EEN eck-SHELL-sees DEH-oh*—quotes the angels' song in Luke 2:14a, "Glory to God in the highest." In stanza 2 bystanders are asking the shepherds why they are so happy, what they saw, and what good news they heard. Stanza 3 is the shepherds' reply.

The music is a traditional eighteenth-century French "noel" or Christmas tune. Children often name it as a favorite, probably because the refrain is so much fun to sing. One possibility for singing is to divide children into three groups: shepherds, bystanders, and angels. Shepherds sing stanzas 1 and 3, bystanders stanza 2, and angels the refrain: the first time with the shepherds, the second time alone, and the last time with everyone. If possible, place the angels group in a balcony or at the opposite end of the church from the others. The repetition in the refrain calls for a contrast in dynamics. The first half could be sung softer and the second half louder, suggesting additional angels joining the group, or the other way around, suggesting an echo. Make sure every note in the descending groups of eighth notes in the refrain is sung clearly without "sliding."

Use a light piano or organ accompaniment. Try adding a triangle or handbell tuned to A playing two beats per measure during selected stanzas. Glockenspiel on the melody of the refrain makes a nice addition.

Sing at Christmas time when the angels and shepherds are emphasized or in a children's program where carols from different countries are sung. The refrain makes a nice introit or response to the Scripture lesson or an assurance of pardon.

133 Angels We Have Heard on High

1 An - gels we have heard on high, sing - ing sweet - ly through the night,
2 Shep - herds, why this ju - bi - lee? Why these songs of hap - py cheer?
3 Come to Beth - le - hem and see him whose birth the an - gels sing;

and the moun - tains in re - ply, ech - o - ing their brave de - light.
What great bright - ness did you see? What glad tid - ings did you hear?
come, a - dore on bend - ed knee Christ the Lord, the new - born King.

Refrain

Glo - ri - a

in ex - cel - sis De - o. Glo - ri - a

in ex - cel - sis De - o.

Words and Music: French carol, translated by James Chadwick

77 77 with refrain
GLORIA
Capo 5

Gloria, Gloria 134

♩ = 60

Glo - ri - a, glo - ri - a, in ex - cel - sis De - o!

Glo - ri - a, glo - ri - a, al - le - lu - ia, al - le - lu - ia!

Dm   Gm   C   F

For a piano duet, one person plays only the melody while another person plays this pattern four times:

Orff instrument patterns may be created by repeating any of the four patterns of the melody or accompaniment.

Flute descants

Words: Luke 2:14; Taizé Community, 1978
Music: Jacques Berthier, b. 1923

Capo 5

Here is another "Gloria" song based on Luke 2:14a (see 133). "Gloria in excelsis Deo" is Latin for "Glory to God in the highest." These words are combined with the Hebrew word "Alleluia!" meaning "Praise the Lord!" Although especially appropriate for Christmas, this simple round may be sung at any time of the year.

Sing through once all together, then follow immediately with the four-part round, each part singing the melody two times. Orff instrument patterns make a lovely accompaniment. Here are three possibilities for creating Orff patterns from the song which could be repeated throughout:

- first two measures, treble clef
- first two measures, bass clef
- last two measures, treble clef

Experiment, using different combinations of patterns. These patterns may also be played on keyboard or handbells. The piano duet part may be played with handbells (playing the bass clef up an octave). A flute could double the melody or play one (or a combination) of the descants.

Sing this beautiful round in almost any part of a worship service. Try singing from the back of the church (balcony, narthex) to begin the service. Or sing as a response to prayer, Scripture, the sermon, or the benediction. Consider singing directly after 133, without a break.

135 Sheep Fast Asleep
Hitsuji Wa

♩ = 100

1 Sheep fast a-sleep, there on a hill, grass for their bed;
2 Star in the sky, shin-ing so bright, si-lent and pure,
3 Glo-ry to God! Glo-ry on high! Sing you "No-el!"

all is still. Cold win-ter night, the frost ap-pears;
won-drous light! What tid-ings brings it Is-ra-el?
Day is nigh! All you who dwell on earth be-low,

shep-herds keep watch by their fire. Soft there a sound,
Can we new hope in it find? Good news it brings!
peace be to you, and good-will. Come, let us go

far, far a-way. Is it the stream? Winds at play? Nay, friend, it
"Fear not, I pray! Born is God's Son, born to-day! God's gift of
to Beth-le-hem; fol-low the star, seek-ing him. Let us a-

Words: Japanese hymn by Genzo Miwa, 1907; translated by John Moss, 1957
Music: Chugoro Torii, 1941

87 87 87 86
KORIN

This gentle Japanese Christmas carol combines the story of the shepherds (st. 1), the star (st. 2), and the angels (st. 3). It concludes with an invitation: "Come, let us go to Bethlehem; follow the star, seeking him." Show children where Japan is located on a map to show that God's people all over the world celebrate the birth of Jesus!

The text paints word pictures, asks questions, and answers them, rather like a conversation. You may wish to ask an older child to narrate the text lines that set the scene and ask questions, and have the whole group read the answers. Explain the meaning of such words as "nay" (no), "spheres" (planets and stars), "Immanuel" (God is with us), and "Noel" (Merry Christmas).

The music reflects the gentleness of the text. The tune is constructed in two eight-measure sections that are exactly alike except for the ending. The initial phrases are made up of short one-measure units. Sing them one at a time with the children echoing. Sing stanza 1 quietly to reflect the pastoral scene of "sheep fast asleep." Wonder with the children what it must have been like for the shepherds to hear the angels singing. Unlike most Western carols, these angels sing softly at first, and the shepherds wonder what they are hearing. Continue to sing quietly on stanza 2 (about the star, "silent and pure"). Begin stanza 3 brightly, building to a climax in the first half but then quieting to conclude with peaceful adoration.

For accompaniment, use soft keyboard or guitar/autoharp. On stanza 2, add finger cymbals on the fourth beat every two measures. Introduce the song with a flute duet on the treble clef parts playing up one octave; have them play again on stanza 3.

Sing as a quiet call to worship or as a response to Scripture for a Christmas Eve candlelight service, Christmas Day worship, the two Sundays following Christmas, or for a program of "carols from many lands."

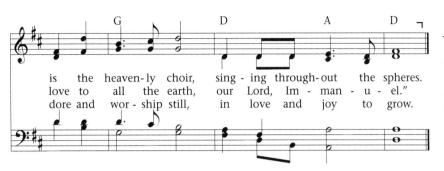

is the heaven-ly choir, sing - ing through-out the spheres.
love to all the earth, our Lord, Im - man - u - el."
dore and wor - ship still, in love and joy to grow.

♩ = 66

He Came Down 136

1 He came down that we may have love*; he
came down that we may have love*; he came down that we may
have love.* Hal - le - lu - jah for - ev - er - more. *(Why did he come?)*

* 2 joy 3 peace 4 hope

Words: traditional
Music: from the Cameroons

John Bell, of the Iona Community in Scotland, tells of first hearing this folk song at a conference in Germany in 1986. A group of Presbyterians from the Camaroons in Western Africa sang it, and, in characteristic African style, they danced while they sang. They moved in a circle, "using their hands to beckon Christ, as it were, from heaven to earth." At the end of each stanza, the cantor would call out, "Why did he come?" and they would move into the next stanza. John Bell quickly wrote down what he heard and later published it in *Many and Great* (G.I.A.).

The song is accessible to children of all ages. Be the cantor yourself as you encourage the children, or have a child with a strong leading voice sing the question. The only challenge in learning this song is the quarter note triplet pattern. Practice before introducing it: first, clapping half notes, count out measure 1, alternately saying "1-2, 1-2-3," dividing the beats as evenly as possible. Next, still clapping, sing the first measure on "ta." Finally, still clapping, sing the text. Add a simple descant by having a flute, clarinet, oboe, or recorder play the tenor line an octave higher than notated.

Sing as a praise chorus in any worship service. Or sing as a theme song for Advent—begin the first week with the first stanza and add a new stanza each succeeding Sunday, perhaps during the lighting of the Advent candles.

This familiar carol is a paraphrase of Psalm 98 by Isaac Watts, "the father of the English hymn" (1674-1748). Until this time, churches in the Reformed tradition only sang psalms. Watts wanted to sing about Christ in New Testament language, so he started rewriting the psalms, thereby creating the English hymn. He composed over six hundred hymns and psalm versifications.

One of the most famous is this bright and festive Christmas song. The words are set to ANTIOCH, a tune by the American composer Lowell Mason. Mason helped start music education in schools in the United States.

Since children may already know this melody, see if they can identify it by tracing the melodic direction of the first two phrases with hand motions, making no allowance for note values. Point out that the first eight notes outline a descending major scale—all steps and no skips—and then climbs back up. Now trace the phrase shapes again, adding rhythmic value to your hand motions. This festive text commands a solid accompaniment. Some older children who read music may be able to sing the echo part on the third and fourth lines; have them sing that bass line up an octave.

Sing at Christmas time, at Ascension, and at other times of year when celebrating the reign of Christ.

137 Joy to the World!

♩ = 96

1 Joy to the world! The Lord is come: let earth receive her King. Let every heart prepare him room, and heaven and nature sing, and heaven and nature sing, and heaven, and heaven and nature sing.

2 Joy to the earth! The Savior reigns: let all their songs employ, while fields and floods, rocks, hills, and plains repeat the sounding joy, repeat the sounding joy, repeat, repeat the sounding joy.

3 He rules the world with truth and grace, and makes the nations prove the glories of his righteousness and wonders of his love, and wonders of his love, and wonders, wonders of his love.

Words: Isaac Watts, 1719; based on Psalm 98
Music: Lowell Mason, 1848

CM with repeats
ANTIOCH

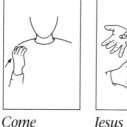

Come   *Jesus*

♩ = 66

Come, Lord Jesus 138

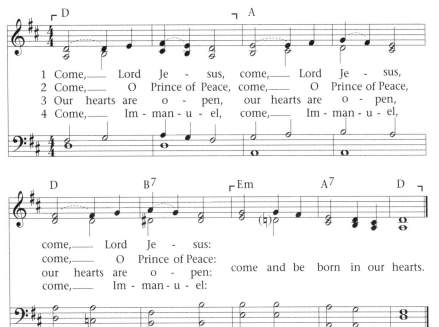

1 Come,___ Lord Je - sus, come,___ Lord Je - sus,
2 Come,___ O Prince of Peace, come,___ O Prince of Peace,
3 Our hearts are o - pen, our hearts are o - pen,
4 Come,___ Im - man - u - el, come,___ Im - man - u - el,

come,___ Lord Je - sus:
come,___ O Prince of Peace:
our hearts are o - pen: come and be born in our hearts.
come,___ Im - man - u - el:

Words and Music: Carey Landry

This meditative prayer song asks Jesus to come and "be born in our hearts." Each stanza ends with that prayer, perhaps inspired by Nicodemus's question to Jesus about being born a second time. Jesus told him that he needed to be born of water and the Spirit in order to see the kingdom of God (John 3). Nicodemus had a hard time understanding that; perhaps it takes a more childlike faith to understand that Jesus needs to come in each of our hearts.

The text is similar to "O Come, O Come, Immanuel" in its use of names associated with Jesus: Prince of Peace (Isa. 9:6) and Immanuel (Isa. 7:14 and Matt. 1:23). "Immanuel" means "God with us." The melody matches the repetitive text; the first melodic phrase is repeated twice, up a step each time, and it ends with a quiet descent (AAAB). Accompany with guitar or quiet keyboard.

During Advent, consider singing different stanzas each week that are related to the Scripture passages. Or sing as a prayer response any time.

Illustration: Joseph is often in the background of our Christmas celebrations. This picture of the "holy family" recognizes the role of Joseph's faithfulness and support in the story of the birth of Jesus.

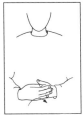
Born

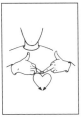
Hearts

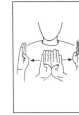
Prince of Peace

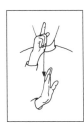
Open

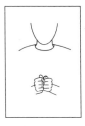
Immanuel (God

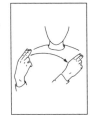
with   *us)*

This beautiful carol from the Huron people of Canada is the first known Canadian hymn and is perhaps the earliest hymn in all of North America. The text was written in the Huron language by Father Jean de Brebeuf, a Jesuit missionary to the Huron and Iroquois peoples of Canada 350 years ago. Its rich imagery suggests a folk tale passed down from generation to generation. The words of the stanzas are a native Canadian interpretation of Jesus' birth; the refrain is the song of the angels.

In 1642, Father Brebeuf wrote,

The (Indians) have a particular devotion for the night that was enlightened by the birth of the Son of God. There was not one who refused to fast on the day that preceded it. They built a small chapel of cedar and fir branches in honor of the manger of the infant Jesus. They wished to perform some penance to prepare themselves for better receiving Him into their hearts on that holy day, and even those who were at a distance of more than two days' journey met at a given place to sing hymns in honor of the new-born child. (The International Book of Christmas Carols, Walton Music Corporation)

Encourage the children to let their imaginations take them back a time long ago, before VCRs, before automobiles, before electricity. One miraculous night something extraordinary happened. Read the words of the carol and talk about how different peoples view Jesus' birth. Some hymnals include the Huron words "mighty Gitchi Manitou" in place of

139 Huron Carol

♩ = 72

1 'Twas in the moon of win-ter-time, when all the
2 With-in a lodge of bro-ken bark the ten-der
3 The ear-liest moon of win-ter-time is not so
4 O chil-dren of the for-est free, the an-gel

birds had fled, that God the Lord of all the earth sent
babe was found; a rag-ged robe of rab-bit skin en-
round and fair as was the ring of glo-ry on the
song is true; the ho-ly Child of earth and heaven is

an-gel choirs in-stead; be-fore their light the
wrapped his beau-ty round; but as the hun-ter
help-less in-fant there. The chiefs from far be-
born to-day for you. Come kneel be-fore the

stars grew dim, and won-dering hun-ters heard the hymn:
braves drew nigh, the an-gel song rang loud and high:
fore him knelt with gifts of fox and bea-ver pelt.
ra-diant boy, who brings you beau-ty, peace, and joy.

Words: Jean de Brebeuf (Huron), c. 1643; translated by Jesse Edgar Middleton, 1926
Music: French Canadian

86 86 86 with refrain
JESOUS AHATONHIA

Refrain

Je - sus your King is born, Je - sus is

born, in ex - cel - sis glo - ri - a.

Drum pattern:

"God the Lord of all the earth" in stanza 1.

The tune of the stanzas suggest a clear flowing line of music. The form of the song is AAB with refrain. Teach the refrain first, so that all of the children can respond to the story as you sing the stanzas. Next, supply a chart with the words or pictures of the stanzas printed on it. Have the children look for the common theme of each verse, then teach the stanzas by the echo method.

You may choose to have individual voices sing each stanza, with the whole group on the refrain. Perhaps a recorder could play the melody line with the singing of each verse.

Sing at Christmas services and in services celebrating songs from around the world.

Illustration: Although the "swaddling clothes" mentioned in older translations may not be very clear to children, the picture shows this common way of dressing a baby. Luke 2 dramatically highlights the combination of heavenly significance and ordinary humanness. The baby Jesus is pictured here with arms open wide, perhaps lying on hay, perhaps surrounded by light.

This simple chorus from Venezuela is just the refrain of a longer carol found in the *United Methodist Hymnal* (1990). It was written by George Lockwood, a missionary for a time to Costa Rica. Lockwood became interested in making many Hispanic songs from Latin and South America available to North American Christians.

Point to Venezuela on a map, and explain to the children that on Christmas, Christians everywhere honor Christ the Lord in all kinds of languages. Begin by assigning the children to speak the "child so lovely" phrase. Then speak the complete song, alternating their part with your responses. Ask,

• Who is the child so lovely?

• Who (in the Bible story) could sing this song? *(Mary and Joseph, shepherds and wise men)*

Young children will quickly learn this gentle lullaby. As you sing it for them, trace the melody direction with your hand, including a simple gesture on each rest such as holding hands out, palms up. Practice the triplets by tapping the given fingertip rhythm, thinking "galloping, running." Let someone mark the main beats on the claves, add a wood block on every first beat, and play the bass rhythm lightly on bongos. Maracas can play the same rhythm as the fingertips. Accompanying duets on woodwinds would also sound pretty. Keep a gentle rhythm.

140 Child So Lovely
Niño Lindo

♩ = 80

Fingertips on palm:

Words: Venezuelan; translated by George Lockwood, 1987
Music: Venezuelan melody; arranged by Emily R. Brink, 1993

CARACAS

Sing this meaningful profession of faith following the reading or dramatization of the Christmas story. It can be repeated a number of times using various solos (characters) singing the first part, with children and finally the complete congregation responding with the (repeated) refrain. Or sing the first section by itself as a repeated response in a litany.

♩ = 104

Little Baby Jesus 141

1 Lit-tle ba-by Je - sus, born in Beth-le - hem, lit - tle ba-by
2 Lit-tle ba-by Je - sus, born in Beth-le - hem, lit - tle ba-by
3 Lit-tle ba-by Je - sus, born in a sta-ble bare, lit - tle ba-by
4 Lit-tle ba-by Je - sus, born in Beth-le - hem, lit - tle ba-by

Je-sus, born in Beth-le - hem; lit-tle ba-by Je - sus,
Je-sus, born in Beth-le - hem; lit-tle ba-by Je - sus,
Je-sus, ly-ing in a man-ger there; lit-tle ba-by Je - sus,
Je-sus, born in Beth-le - hem; lit-tle ba-by Je - sus,

born to be the Sav-ior of the world for you and me.
born to die; for you and me he came to suf-fer and die.
King to be the Mas-ter of the earth, the sky, and sea.
do come in; come right in-to my heart and save me from sin!

Lit - tle ba-by Je - sus, born in Beth-le - hem.

Words and Music: Blaine H. Allen

Capo 3

This is one of the few Christmas texts combining Jesus' birth with his suffering and death, as well as his kingship. The focus is on what Jesus gave up to save us from our sins. The repetition of the phrase "Little baby Jesus, born in Bethlehem" makes this song easy for children to learn quickly. (The third stanza breaks this pattern of repetition; you may choose to omit it for very young children.)

The melody has the quality of an African-American spiritual although it was composed in the 1960s by Blaine H. Allen. The minor key fits the text in emphasizing Jesus' suffering when he took on our human nature. Sing with feeling—not too fast. Begin each stanza medium-softly, building in volume with each phrase until the last phrase, which should end medium-softly again. To introduce the first stanza, use a single instrument (recorder, oboe, flute, organ solo stop) playing the melody. Add guitar or autoharp accompaniment on the second stanza and organ or piano on the third stanza. Sing the last stanza unaccompanied, if possible, or accompanied by the same solo instrument used on the introduction and first stanza.

Sing as a call to confession or as a response to the prayer of confession during Advent/Christmas/Epiphany.

When you love someone, you like to give that person presents to show your love. And everyone loves to get presents. God gives us many gifts; everything we have, really. At Christmas we especially remember his best gift to us: his very own Son! Ask the children what gifts we can give to show our love for God. What would please God most? This text, written in 1872 as the last stanza to the Christmas poem "In the Bleak Midwinter," addresses that question.

Slowly speak the words line by line, encouraging children to "think" the text. Notice the change in word order in the last line, which is not a question.

Gustav Holst composed this melody for this poem, combined for the first time in *The English Hymnal* of 1906. It has two main phrases; only the last two notes of the first and second are different, and the second is identical to the fourth except for a pickup note (A A' B A'). The phrases are short, allowing children to get good breath support when singing. Sing with smooth legato lines with two beats per measure.

Sing during Christmas/Epiphany as the offertory, prayer response, or conclusion to the service. For a longer offertory, consider combining with "Take My Life" (74).

142 What Can I Give Him

♩ = 60

What can I give him, poor as I am?

If I were a shep-herd, I would bring a lamb.

If I were a wise man, I would do my part. Yet

what I can I give him— give him my heart.

Words: Christina G. Rossetti, 1872; from "In the Bleak Midwinter"
Music: Gustav Holst, 1906

Capo 5

As with Gladness Men of Old 143

♩ = 66

1 As with glad-ness men of old did the guid-ing
2 As with joy-ful steps they sped to that low-ly
3 As they of-fered gifts most rare at that cra-dle

star be-hold, as with joy they hailed its light,
in-fant bed, there to bend the knee be-fore
plain and bare, so may we with ho-ly joy,

lead-ing on-ward, beam-ing bright; so, most gra-cious
Christ, whom heaven and earth a-dore; so may we with
pure and free from sin's al-loy, all our cost-liest

Lord, may we ev-er-more your splen-dor see.
will-ing feet ev-er seek your mer-cy seat.
trea-sures bring, Christ, to you, our heav-enly King.

Words: William C. Dix, 1860
Music: Conrad Kocher, 1838; adapted by William H. Monk, 1861; arranged by
Robert Roth, 1989

Arr. © 1989, Robert Roth

77 77 77
DIX

This Epiphany hymn was inspired by the story of the three wise men in Matthew 2:1-12. Each stanza uses the wise men as a model for the Christian life. Just as the wise men saw the light of the star, we must look to Jesus as our guide (st. 1). Just as the wise men went to worship the Christ, we must also willingly come to worship him (st. 2). And just as the wise men offered their best gifts to Christ, so must we.

Explain that an "alloy" (st. 3) is a compound of two metals. Being "free from sin's alloy" means to rid ourselves of the sin that is so much a part of our lives.

The traditional hymn tune is also used with "For the Beauty of the Earth" (89). It has three long phrases. Point out that the first two are the same and the last phrase is different (AAB). Have children try to take a breath only at the end of each long phrase to preserve the continuity of the text musically. A faster tempo helps convey the joy of the text, as well as making it easier to sing with only three breaths per stanza. Accompany with piano, organ, guitar, or autoharp. Have a C instrument (flute, recorder, oboe, violin) play the melody (or on the descant in *Psalter Hymnal* 358).

Use this hymn on Epiphany Sunday or as part of a service of lessons and carols where the story of the three wise men is read.

This song covers several events in the life of Jesus and of his disciples.

- *Stanza 1:* Jesus calls the first disciples (Matt. 4:18-22).

- *Stanza 2:* They follow Jesus as he healed the sick and fed the hungry.

- *Stanza 3:* Together with people around "the whole wide world," we too follow Jesus.

The first three phrases begin with the same notes, with an interesting melodic structure. Although written in the key of G, the pitch F remains natural (not G-major), but the pitch B also remains natural (not G-minor either). Think minor key on the first line and final two notes, and think a bright major key on "Come leave your nets and follow." The Orff accompaniments will help children learn the pitches. These delightful "walking" patterns, symbolizing following Christ, repeat the same harmonic progression in each phrase. If you do not have all of the instruments suggested here, be creative, even asking children to play two of the patterns on piano. Learn the patterns simultaneously as the children are learning the words. Give several children an opportunity to play one of the instruments throughout the weeks that it takes to learn the song. When everyone knows it, sing as a round.

Sing during the Epiphany season when the focus is on the ministry of Christ or on the mission of the church; also in connection with profession of faith or a commissioning service.

144 When Jesus Saw the Fishermen

1 When Jesus saw the fishermen in boats upon the sea,
2 They followed where he healed the sick and gave the hungry bread.
3 And now his friends are everywhere; the circle once so small

he called to them, "Come, leave your nets and follow, follow me."
And others joined them as they went, wherever Jesus led.
extends around the whole wide world, for Jesus calls us all.

Orff instrument patterns:

Bass xylophone   *Bass metallophone*

Alto xylophone   *Alto metallophone*

Soprano glockenspiel

Words: Edith Agnew, 1953
Music: Richard L. Van Oss, 1992

CM
ST. STEPHEN

♩ = 100

Jesus Said to All the People 145

1 Je-sus said to all the peo-ple as they crowd-ed close to
2 Je-sus said to all the peo-ple as he taught them how to

hear, "God loves you as I love you; God is
pray, "God loves you as I love you; God

with you ev-ery - where." Je-sus showed that God
knows the prayers you pray." Je-sus taught that God

loves me; God is with me ev - ery - where.
loves me; God knows the prayers I pray.

Everyone loves a good story. Children like to sit close when their mom or dad tells them a story. And when Jesus told stories, the people often "crowded close to him" to hear. As Jesus listened to people and healed those who were sick, he showed them how much he loved them and how much God loved them. Although Jesus lives in heaven now, God is as close to us as Jesus was to the people who came to hear him. God loves us and hears us when we pray to him.

The gentle Swedish folk tune is a good match for this comforting song about the love of God. The first two phrases are similar melodically, and the second and third phrases are identical rhythmically. Several times the word "God" covers two notes; take care to sing those notes cleanly, without scooping or sliding. Accompany lightly with guitar, autoharp, or keyboard.

Sing during the Epiphany season when dealing with the teaching ministry of Christ. Sing before or after prayer, as a sermon response, or any time in a baptism service. Consider pairing this song with "Praise God's Name" (47) or "What a Friend We Have in Jesus" (52).

Words: Ann Evans
Music: Swedish folk tune
Arr. © 1972, Graded Press. Used by permission of Abingdon Press.

877 777
JESUS, LAT DIN
Capo 5

This narrative song tells the parable of the good Samaritan (Luke 10:29-37). Each half of the stanzas tells another part of the story of a "certain" character. The refrain ends with the summary of the second table of the law: "love your neighbor as yourself," which is the heart of the story. Ask the children what neighbors Jesus had in mind. Who are our neighbors?

Don't be tempted to "pass by" this song! Although the musical structure, with four different phrases (ABCD), offers little repetition until the refrain, and the narrative character of the stanzas is quite irregular, making it easier for a soloist than a group, you will find it coming back to you throughout the day after singing it a couple of times.

Introduce this song by having a soloist simply "tell" the story in song. Invite a good story-teller or a minstrel from your congregation who could sing and perhaps accompany herself or himself on guitar, to come and teach this song. The children should join on the refrain, which offers the most repetition and is easiest to learn. Simply sing the refrain phrases one at a time with the children echoing.

Consider dramatizing the stanzas. Ask four children to play the parts of the injured Samaritan lying down (the children may want to add the robber!) and the three who "passed by"—the dignified priest, the wealthy Levite, and the Samaritan foreigner who "lent a helping hand." You may want to come up with simple props or signs identifying the characters.

Or teach by rote in the following manner. Write out the

146 The Good Samaritan

♩ = 76

1 A cer-tain travel-er on his way was robbed and left to
2 A cer-tain Le-vite came that way, a man of wealth and

die. Help-less by— the road he lay, and no one—
pride. "I'm much too bus-y to stop," said he and passed on the

heard his cry. A— cer-tain priest came— down that way,
oth-er side. But a cer-tain man from Sa-mar-i-a,

a man most dig-ni — fied. "I will not get in-volved," said he
a strang-er in the land, took pi-ty on the in-jured man

Words and Music: Mary Lu Walker, arranged by H. Myron Braun

and passed on the oth- er side.
and lent a— help- ing hand.

Refrain

Don't pass your neigh- bor

by, my friend; don't pass your neigh - bor by.

Love your neigh- bor as your-self; don't pass your neigh- bor by.

words to the song on white posterboard, using a different color marker to print out the words for each pair of phrases—A, B and C, D—of each stanza (four colors in all). Write the refrain with a black marker. Cut enough squares of four corresponding colors of construction paper (4" x 4") for each child (or group) to have one. Pass out the paper and teach each section of the song to that color group. All sing the refrain. Then have the children trade colored squares and sing it again. Keep trading until the children have sung the song enough times to learn it. Collect all the cards and sing all the sections together.

Sing during Epiphany or for a service featuring a call to mission, either nearby or far away. You may want to accompany the song with slides of various "neighbors." Consider pairing with "Let Me Be Your Servant, Jesus" (244).

Illustration: Two people on a lonely road suggests the threat and danger faced by the man who "fell into the hands of robbers" (Luke 10:30).

147 Four Good Friends

♩ = 60

This is one of many children's songs written by Canadian schoolteacher Frank De Vries. The first four stanzas tell the story of Jesus healing the paralyzed man (Mark 2:3-12); the fifth reminds us that Jesus still heals the hurts and troubles of those who believe in him.

For variety, have "four good friends" sing the first stanza, accompanied by sand blocks; a soloist on stanza 2, with triangle playing on the last beat of each phrase; a soloist on stanza 3 (give the first syllable of "stretcher" a full beat), accompanied by wood blocks or sticks playing a steady beat; the entire group on stanza 4, with finger cymbals on the last beat of each phrase; and the entire group on stanza 5, accompanied by autoharp.

You may wish to add these motions: Have the children form a circle around the "four good friends" and soloists. On stanza 1, the circle moves clockwise with children gradually crouching down. On stanza 2, the circle stops and the children bow their heads, staying in a crouched position. On stanza 3, the circle moves counter-clockwise as the children gradually stand up straight again. Change direction for stanza 4 (clockwise). On the first and third phrases of stanza 5, children raise heads and arms up, then bow heads and lower arms to a position straight out in front of them (palms up) on phrases two and four.

Sing after a prayer of confession in a service with a theme of faith or forgiveness or in a healing service.

1 Four good friends made a hole in the roof,
four good friends made a hole in the roof,
four good friends made a hole in the roof and
lowered their friend before Jesus.

2 "Well, my child, I forgive you your sins" (3x)
   are the words that were spoken by Jesus.

3 "Get off your stretcher and walk, O my son," (3x)
   and he walked, as was told him by Jesus.

4 At that miracle they all were amazed, (3x)
   and they sang many praises to Jesus.

5 Jesus still does his healing today; (3x)
   bring your hurts and your troubles to Jesus.

Words and Music: Frank De Vries, 1983; based on Mark 2:3-12
© 1983, CRC Publications

Jesus' Hands Were Kind Hands 148

♩ = 69

1 Je - sus' hands were kind hands, do - ing good to all,
2 Take my hands, Lord Je - sus, let them work for you;

heal - ing pain and sick - ness, bless - ing chil - dren small,
make them strong and gen - tle, kind in all I do.

wash - ing ti - red feet and sav - ing those who fall;
Let me watch you, Je - sus, till I'm gen - tle too,

Je - sus' hands were kind hands, do - ing good to all.
till my hands are kind hands, quick to work for you.

Words: Margaret Cropper, c. 1926
Music: traditional French melody
Words © Stephan Hopkinson

11 11 11 11
AU CLAIR DE LA LUNE

Although the first line doesn't always reveal much about a hymn, this one does. The first stanza of this simple and gentle song tells us about the compassionate hands of Jesus. "Hands" are meant both literally and symbolically, as in "lending a hand" or giving a "helping hand." The second is a prayer that our hands too may be kind and "strong and gentle." The combination of "strong and gentle" is particularly refreshing.

The melody is the traditional French tune AU CLAIR DE LA LUNE (by the light of the moon). The simplicity and familiarity of the tune match the text well. Point out to children that lines 1, 2, and 4 are identical (AABA).

Sing as an offertory or response to Scripture or sermon in any service focusing on the ministry of Christ and our call to follow Christ. Consider also for a footwashing service on Maundy Thursday.

This song is a "catalog" of many of Christ's healing miracles, interspersed with prayers that the Lord would also "heal us today." Scripture references include the following: Luke 4:31-41 (st. 1); Mark 2:3-12 (st. 2); Mark 5:22-24, 35-43 (st. 3); Mark 10:46-52 (st. 4); Matthew 11:4-6 (st. 5); Mark 6:6-13 (st. 6). The final stanza reminds us that we still experience sickness and suffering today. Each stanza is a call and response between leader and group, moving back and forth between reminders of the healing power of Jesus and prayers for his healing power today.

Everyone can learn the refrains and final stanza. Choose a soloist or group to be the leader for the entire song or choose one soloist per stanza. The latter choice allows for quicker learning and gives more children an opportunity to sing by themselves. Work on careful enunciation of the words. Accompany lightly with guitar, autoharp, or keyboard, with a gentle swing on one beat per measure. Because of the amount of repetition, keep the beat going between stanzas; simply count one extra measure for a good breath and keep going. Don't be tempted to cut down on the number of stanzas; the prayer grows in fervor through repetition.

Sing as a prayer for healing during any Epiphany or healing service, with the congregation joining on the last stanza. Perhaps you could organize a visit to a nursing home and have the children sing it, inviting all to join on the inner refrains.

149 When Jesus the Healer

♩ = 60

5 The lepers were healed and the demons cast out. Heal us, heal us today!
   A bent woman straightened to laugh and to shout. Heal us, Lord Jesus.

6 The twelve were commissioned and sent out in twos, Heal us, heal us today!
   to make the sick whole and to spread the good news. Heal us, Lord Jesus.

7 There's still so much sickness and suffering today. Heal us, heal us today!
   We gather together for healing and pray: Heal us, Lord Jesus.

Words and Music: Peter D. Smith, 1979

11 6 11 5
HEALER
Capo 5

This Is My Commandment 150

♩ = 60

Round

This is my com-mand-ment, that you love one an-oth-er that your joy may be full. This is my com-mand-ment, that you love one an-oth-er that your joy may be full, that your joy may be full, that your joy may be full.

Other verses may be added, for example:

This is my commandment, that you trust one another . . . .
. . . serve one another . . . .
. . . lay down your lives . . . .

The first stanza of this Scripture chorus is taken directly from John 15:11-12. It is placed in this section of the hymnal as an example of the teaching ministry of Christ. Several additional stanzas are suggested, and the children could add others, each ending with "that your joy may be full."

The simple melody has only two phrases (AABA), the second of which is really a repeated extension of the first. Teach this by echo method, two measures at a time. You may want to divide the children into two groups, alternating first on the repeated four-measure phrase in the A section, then alternating on the two-measure phrases in the B section, and finally singing together on the final statement of A. Encourage children to sing with smooth sustained voices on the B section. When they know it well, the song could also be sung as a round. A guitar or autoharp provides adequate accompaniment. Or accompany by repeating the first measure of the bass clef throughout on Orff instruments.

Sing in the service of confession following the reading of the Ten Commandments or as a charge to the congregation before the benediction.

Words: John 15:11-12
Music: anonymous, arranged by Richard L. Van Oss, 1992
Arr. © 1994, CRC Publications

Capo 1

151 If You Love Me

♩ = 63

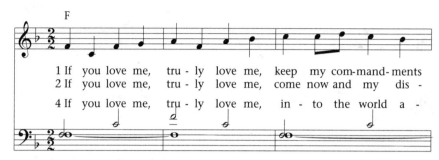

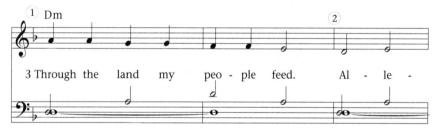

"Find something worth singing and singing about" was the motto of composer Natalie Sleeth (for more on Sleeth, see 175). She certainly achieved that goal in this delightful anthem based on Jesus' words to his disciples in John 14:15.

The song has two sections. The A section, in major, is bright and bouncing, with much repetition of text on the three different stanzas. The contrasting B section (st. 3) has smooth stepwise lines in a minor key. Sing each phrase, helping children by tracing the direction of the melody with hand motions.

This song can easily be turned into a two-part anthem, the way Natalie Sleeth originally composed it. Group one sings stanza 1, and just as it reaches the last note (and holds it!), group two starts stanza 2. When they reach their last note, group one overlaps again to start stanza 3. This time, group two follows in canon after two measures, and the two-part canon continues to the end. Keep a strong half note pulse. Add the Orff instruments (or handbells) to produce a beautiful anthem. For this two-part arrangement, the Orff instruments should play the first pattern four, not five, times.

In worship, sing at the end of the service of confession or as a "sending out" song just before the benediction.

Words and Music: Natalie Sleeth, based on the anthem "If You Love Me" found in the collection *Laudamus*

♩ = 58

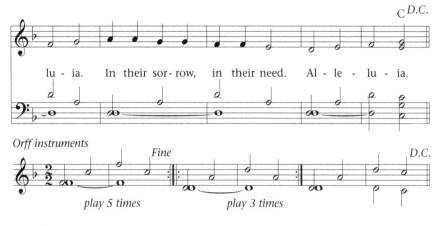

lu - ia.   In their sor - row,   in their need.   Al - le - lu - ia.

Orff instruments

Fine   *D.C.*

play 5 times   play 3 times

I Am the Light of the World 152

I   am the   light of the world,   I   am the   light of the world.   Who-
will nev- er   walk in   the dark,   will nev- er   walk in   the dark,   but

ev - er   fol - lows me   have   the   light of   life.

Orff instruments

Maracas

Words: John 8:12
Music: June Fischer Armstrong, 1991
© 1991, CRC Publications

Capo 1

All children can relate to the fear of darkness. Turn off all the lights and light a candle. Ask the children, "Who is the light of the world?" Learning this song will help children memorize John 8:12, a verse that includes a wonderful promise.

The melody has a very simple structure. The two notes of the first phrase are simply repeated at a lower level. The melody ends the first time by going back up; the second time it settles on F. Use hand motions or even your entire body posture to show the melodic shape as you sing, first stretching straight and tall, then "shrinking" a little, and finally standing normal. Have a child play steady eighth notes on the maracas part. All the children could pat their thighs with alternate hands on that eighth-note pattern as well. Add a triangle or finger cymbal each time on the word "light." Accompany lightly on guitar, autoharp, or keyboard.

Sing before or after a Scripture reading or after the assurance of pardon. It is also appropriate for "sending forth" the congregation at the close of worship.

This is the first of three "king-dom" songs based on Jesus' Sermon on the Mount, which teaches us how to live in the kingdom of God. It is based on the Beatitudes (Matt. 5:3-12). Explain that "blest" and "blessed" are really the same word; both come from the word "blessing" (see also the notes on the illustration).

Begin with the joyful refrain, which almost dances in its triple meter. As you sing, swing your arms or even step back and forth from left to right to feel two beats per measure. Encourage children to take good breaths in order to soar on the long notes (wait with the "s" sound on rejoice; connect it to "and"). Adding a triangle or finger cymbals on the second beat of the long notes (on "-joice" and "glad") will help children keep the beat and add sparkle to the accompaniment.

Like the refrain, the stanzas are constructed in two sections that begin the same and end differently. Since each section begins with a new Beatitude, you may want to use soloists or divide the children into two groups and sing the stanzas antiphonally, with all joining on

153 Blest Are They

♩ = 63

Words: David Haas, based on Matthew 5:3-12
Music: David Haas; arranged by Norma de Waal Malefyt, 1991
© 1985, G.I.A. Publications, Inc. Used by permission.

the refrain. You can help your children sing the interval leaps by showing melody direction with your hand, instructing them to imitate, and noticing how often the melody returns to the same note (D).

Since the stanzas are written in prose style, with different numbers of syllables, the text drives the melodic decisions. For example, at the end of the second measure, the word "spirit" moves from A to D; but at the same spot in stanza 2, the one-syllable word "ones" goes directly to (the small dotted quarter note) D. In measure three, "mercy" in stanza 3 is sung on two notes, not three; that is why there are two stems on some notes. These changes encourage singers to follow the text, but they are not difficult to learn.

Sing as a response of encouragement anytime. Consider pairing with "Seek Ye First the Kingdom" (155), another "kingdom" song.

Illustration: Children will be able to identify the outstretched arms of Jesus with the minister pronouncing a blessing in church. In this context, the blessing means "God's presence and goodness will be with you." The outstretched arms suggest resting a hand on a person's head in blessing.

154 Bring Forth the Kingdom

♩ = 66

The second of three "kingdom" songs based on the Sermon on the Mount, this is based on Jesus' teaching about salt and light (Matt. 5:13-16). Be sure to explain why Christians are called to be "the salt of the earth," "a light on a hill," and "a seed of the Word." In ancient times salt was even more important than it is today—it was used not only to make things taste better but also to keep food from spoiling. The refrain provides a good summary: we need to pray for peace, work for justice, and hope that God will indeed "bring forth the kingdom of mercy."

Keep this song moving with light and clear voices. Use piano or guitar with flute or recorder to keep the accompaniment light also. Orff instruments could be used along with the other instruments or by themselves. You may wish to have a soloist or small group sing the first and third phrases of each stanza and the entire group sing the second and fourth phrases as well as the refrain. For an antiphonal effect, separate the soloist or small group from the large group.

Sing as a response to the reading of the law or as a closing. Or sing in any service where the theme is missions or Christian life.

1 You are salt for the earth, O peo-ple: salt for the king-dom of God!
2 You are a light on a hill, O peo-ple: light for the cit-y of God!
3 You are a seed of the Word, O peo-ple: live for the king-dom of God!

share the fla-vor of life, O peo-ple: life in the king-dom of God!
shine so ho-ly and bright, O peo-ple: shine for the king-dom of God!
seeds of mer-cy and seeds of jus-tice, grow in the king-dom of God!

Refrain

Bring forth the king-dom of mer-cy; pray for the king-dom of peace;

work for the king-dom of jus-tice; hope for the cit-y of God!

Words and Music: Marty Haugen; based on Matt. 5:13-16
© 1986, G.I.A. Publications. Used by permission.

Alto xylophone

[*play to end*]

Glockenspiel

[*play to end*]

Descant for refrain

♩ = 88

Seek Ye First the Kingdom 155

1 Seek ye____ first the king - dom of God and his right-eous -
2 Ask and it shall be giv-en un-to you; seek and you shall
3 We do not live by bread____ a - lone, but by ev - ery

ness, and all these things shall be add-ed un-to you.
find; knock and the door shall be o-pened un-to you.
word that pro - ceeds from the mouth____ of____ God.

Refrain

Al - le - lu, al - le - lu - ia. Al - le -

lu - ia, al - le - lu - ia, lu - ia!

Words: Matthew 6:33; 7:7; 4:4; adapted by Karen Lafferty, 1972
Music: Karen Lafferty, 1972; arranged by Robert Roth, 1989

LAFFERTY

Here is the third and best known of three "kingdom" songs based on the Sermon on the Mount (see also 153, 154). In that sermon, Jesus teaches his people—and us—how to live in the kingdom of God. Karen Lafferty composed this melody and the first stanza after being encouraged and challenged by a Bible study on Matthew 6:33. Stanza 2 is also taken from the Sermon on the Mount (Matt. 7:7). Stanza 3 is based on Jesus' reply to Satan during his first temptation in the wilderness (Matt. 4:4).

The refrain is notated for two-part singing. The "Alleluia" descant is so much a part of this song that it may be learned by all the children. They will already know the main melody from the stanzas. Encourage good breaths and light sustained singing on the held notes. Options include singing in unison on the refrain with accompaniment on the main melody, or combining the "alleluia" descant while some of the children sing stanza 2 or 3. If possible, have your children form a two-part choir on this familiar Scripture chorus. Accompany with guitar, autoharp, or keyboard; also consider adding instruments on the descant part.

In congregational worship, sing before the reading of Scripture, before prayer, as a response to the sermon, or at the close of the service.

After traveling to Israel and hearing this Israeli folk tune, Willard Jabusch wrote this song for a parish folk-music ensemble. The refrain and stanza 1 are based on Psalm 24:7-8 (see 157). It beautifully combines the Old Testament promise with the fulfillment in Christ. Stanzas 2-4 joyfully recount the life, death, and resurrection of Jesus.

The tune begins with a syncopated pattern that is repeated throughout. The melodic phrases are all variations of the first two measures, so children will learn it quickly. Since the song begins with the refrain, be sure the stanzas do not stop the rhythm; keep the beat going in "perpetual rhythm" throughout. Encourage hand clapping and gradually add a variety of rhythm instruments.

You may wish to drop the clapping and extra instruments on the stanzas to concentrate on the text. Divide the first stanza, with a soloist asking the question and all responding. Sing stanza 3 softly, then return to more exuberant singing on stanza 4. Save the little descant until the very end, dividing into two parts. Or have everyone sing that descant, which simply goes up the scale.

Accompany with guitar or autoharp. For an even simpler autoharp accompaniment, children could play an E-minor chord throughout the refrain and a G chord throughout the stanzas.

Sing during Advent, Epiphany, or on Palm Sunday as an opening hymn or even a processional.

156 The King of Glory Comes

♩ = 104

*Sing small notes as a little descant on the final refrain.

Words: Willard F. Jabusch, 1966
Music: Israeli, arranged by John Ferguson, 1973, in *The Hymnal of the United Church of Christ*

12 12 with refrain
PROMISED ONE

Orff instruments for refrain

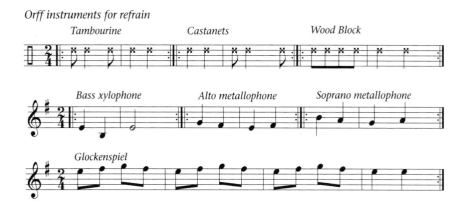

Tambourine   Castanets   Wood Block

Bass xylophone   Alto metallophone   Soprano metallophone

Glockenspiel

Lift Up Your Heads 157

Lift up your heads, O you gates:
  be lifted up, you ancient doors,
    that the King of glory may come in.
     Refrain (no. 156)

Who is this King of glory?
  The Lord strong and mighty,
    the Lord mighty in battle.
     Refrain

Lift up your heads, O you gates;
  Lift them up, you ancient doors,
    that the King of glory may come in.
     Refrain

Who is he, this King of glory?
  The Lord Almighty—
    he is the King of glory.
     Refrain

For a variation on 156, ask two children to read the section of Psalm 24 that is the source of "The King of Glory Comes." Choose two solo readers to stand on opposite sides of the platform, balcony, or room. They should speak like heralds, announcing the coming of the king! One "announcer" reads the first two sections; the other the last two. On the second and fourth sections, have all the children (gathered between the two announcers) ask the question and the announcers give the answer. At the beginning and again after each section, sing the refrain of "The King of Glory Comes" (156).

Words: Psalm 24:7-10 (NIV)

This Mexican Palm Sunday hymn celebrates the entry of Jesus into Jerusalem as recorded in Matthew 21:8-9, with parallels in Mark 11:8-10, Luke 19:36-38, and John 12:12-13. The first stanza recounts the triumphal entry, the second calls us to praise and follow Christ with our "hosannas" also today. The refrain concludes with a burst of "hosannas," an exclamation of high praise. Even the youngest child will enjoy singing this exuberant refrain.

The melody on the stanzas (in contrast to the refrain) is very simply constructed with only four notes in a repeated pattern to carry the narrative text. The refrain also involves repetition, but then adds its own "refrain"—the burst of "Hosannas." Watch out for the syncopation written on the ends of each line of the stanza; these last words should be sung "off the beat," not placed squarely on beat 3 of the measure.

This is a wonderful song to begin teaching part-singing to the children—the soprano and alto lines move in parallel thirds with one another throughout the stanzas. Children should be able to handle

158 Filled with Excitement / Mantos y Palmos

♩ = 60

Words: Rubén Ruiz Avila, 1972; translated by Gertrude C. Suppe, 1979, 1987
Music: Rubén Ruiz Avila, 1972; arranged by Alvin Schutmaat

10 10 10 11
with refrain
HOSANNA

Refrain

From ev-ery cor-ner a thou-sand voic-es sing_____
Mien-tras mil vo-ces re-sue-nan por do-quier; ho-

prais-es to him who comes in the name of God. With one great
san-na al que vie-ne en el nom-bre del Se-ñor. Con un a-

shout of___ ac-cla-ma-tion loud tri-um-phant___ song breaks forth:_____
lien-to de gran ex-cla-ma-ción pro-rrum-pen con voz triun-fal:_____

"Ho - san-na! Ho - san-na to the
"¡Ho - san-na! ¡Ho - san-na al Rey!

King! Ho - san-na! Ho - san-na to the King!"
¡Ho - san-na! ¡Ho - san-na al Rey!"

that movement easily. They will enjoy "signing" the "Hosanna" section of the refrain while they sing in unison.

Sing with a brisk tempo to convey praise and excitement. You may wish to enhance the accompaniment of keyboard, guitar, or a combination of both with the use of various rhythm instruments (which could play a repeated quarter/two eighths pattern). Or add trumpet on the "Hosanna" section.

Sing on Palm/Passion Sunday, perhaps as a frame for the Palm Sunday hymn, "All Glory, Laud, and Honor," when both are sung in the same key. Precede the singing of the traditional hymn with the first stanza and conclude it with the second. Have the congregation join the children on the "Hosanna" section.

Hosanna
(Praise)

This is a delightfully fresh and unusual treatment of Jesus' entry into Jerusalem on Palm Sunday (Matt. 21; Mark 11; Luke 19; John 12). Children will love the "clip-clop" accompaniment that pictures "Jesus, sitting on a donkey's back."

This song reflects the mixed emotions of Palm Sunday, a day when the people rejoice but Jesus weeps. It is in more than one meter and more than one "key"—not exactly in F-major! Some of the accidentals and leaps are quite unexpected. Watch out for the pitches on "donkey" in line two, and the move from G to G-flat in line three. Keyboard accompaniment is essential. Also consider adding a melody instrument. With good accompaniment, children will be able to learn quickly.

Understanding the structure of the melody will help you teach this song. The first two measures are repeated exactly, except the final two notes are repeated up an octave. Then (at the meter change) the melody starts descending the scale from C to F, weaving around F on the refrain. Teach by echo method. Because of the repetition in the stanzas, you may wish to provide charts with the first word for each phrase.

Children may sing the entire song on Palm Sunday or invite the congregation to join on the refrain the final stanza (after hearing it twice).

159 Trotting, Trotting Through Jerusalem

♩ = 66

1 Trot - ting, trot - ting through Je - ru - sa - lem, Je - sus, sit - ting on a don - key's back; child - ren wav - ing

Refrain

branch - es, sing - ing, "Hap - py is he who comes in the name of the Lord!"

Final ending

Words and Music: Eric Reid, 1936-1970

© 1969, 1972, Galliard, Ltd. Used by permission of Stainer & Bell, Ltd., London, England.

Capo 5

2 Many people in Jerusalem
  thought he should have come on a mighty horse
  leading all the Jews to battle— *Refrain*

3 Many people in Jerusalem
  were amazed to see such a quiet man
  trotting, trotting on a donkey— *Refrain*

4 Trotting, trotting through Jerusalem,
  Jesus, sitting on a donkey's back;
  let us join the children, singing, *Refrain*

Illustration: Palm leaves are associated especially with Jesus' triumphal entry into Jerusalem. On that day people took (and probably waved) palm branches as a token of joy and victory (John 12:13). In our annual commemoration of Palm Sunday we may also have a procession into the sanctuary, waving palm branches. (Churches that observe Ash Wednesday often burn the palm leaves of the previous year to provide ashes.)

160 Hosanna! Hosanna!

♩. = 80

This engaging Palm Sunday song, based on the narrative of Jesus' triumphal entry found in all four Gospels, is easy for children to learn. The simplest of the Palm Sunday songs in this section, it has much repetition in both text and melody. So even the youngest child will be able to join in singing "Hosanna!" Imagine with the children what it was like to be a part of that parade.

To capture the spirit of a parade and the strength of the proclamation, use a sturdy accompaniment on keyboard or solid strummed chords on guitar or autoharp.

Sing during Advent or on Palm Sunday. On Palm Sunday, consider combining with "All Glory, Laud, and Honor" (161). Precede and conclude that hymn with the children singing "Hosanna!" Children will enjoy having a "palm parade" around the sanctuary while the congregation sings "All Glory, Laud, and Honor."

Words and Music: Helen Kemp

Capo 1

Hosanna
(Praise)

All Glory, Laud, and Honor 161

♩ = 58

1 All glo - ry, laud, and hon - or to you, Re - deem - er, King,
2 The com - pa - ny of an - gels is prais - ing you on high;
3 To you be - fore your pas - sion they sang their hymns of praise;

to whom the lips of chil - dren made sweet ho - san - nas ring.
and we with all cre - a - tion in cho - rus make re - ply.
to you, now high ex - alt - ed, our mel - o - dy we raise.

You are the King of Is - ra - el and Da - vid's roy - al Son,
The peo - ple of the He - brews with palms be - fore you went;
As you re - ceived their prais - es, ac - cept the prayers we bring,

now in the Lord's name com - ing, the King and Bless - ed One.
our praise and prayer and an - thems be - fore you we pre - sent.
for you de - light in good - ness, O good and gra - cious King!

This text is more than a thousand years old! Theodolph of Orleans (760-821) wrote it around 820 while imprisoned by order of King Louis I. Legend suggests that King Louis passed beneath his prison window during a Palm Sunday procession and heard him singing this hymn. The king was so moved that he freed Theodolph and commanded that this hymn should be sung on all subsequent Palm Sundays. *The Singing Bishop* by Hal Hopson is a musical based on this hymn and legend.

You may need to explain that "laud" means praise and "Hosanna" is a Hebrew word expressing praise and prayer to God. The phrase "before your passion" in stanza 3 refers to the time preceding Jesus' death—the greatest display of his love for us.

Sing on Palm Sunday or as an excellent opening hymn of praise any time of year. On Palm Sunday, sing during a processional of children waving palm branches.

Words: Theodulph of Orleans, c. 820; translated by John M. Neale, 1851
Music: Melchior Teschner, 1615; harmonized by William H. Monk, 1861

76 76 D
ST. THEODULPH
Capo 3

162 Hosanna, Son of David!

♩ = 108

This Palm Sunday "Hosanna" song comes from the classical period and sounds very much like Haydn. The text comes from the words shouted by the Jerusalem crowd when Jesus made his triumphal entry (Matt. 21:9).

Not only does this music sound like a miniature classical anthem, its bright dotted rhythms and chord outlines sound very much like an instrumental melody. Emphasize clean, crisp, dotted rhythms (not triplets, which might be a tempting but "lazy" way to sing it!). Explain that "hosanna" is a Hebrew expression of praise, meaning "save." On the word "David," accent the first syllable and bounce lightly off the second.

The repetition in the melody will help children learn. Counting by four-measure units, the musical phrases can be summarized as follows: AB, AB', C, AB', C, AB'. The text in the AB' sections is repeated as well. The C section is written for two-part choir. If the children have never sung in harmony, this simple two-part section is an excellent place to begin. After everyone has learned the main melody, challenge some of the singers to take big breaths and simply hold D for over two measures before rejoining the main melody. Challenge the children to sing lightly and brightly, as if they were skipping along.

Accompany lightly on keyboard. Consider having two violins and cello (or bassoon) play as a prelude.

Words and Music: G. J. Vogler (1749-1814), based on Matthew 21:9; translated by
    J. Irving Erickson (1914-1992)

Oh, How He Loves You and Me 163

1 Oh, how he loves you and me. Oh, how he
loves you and me. He gave his life— what
more could he give? Oh, how he loves you;
oh, how he loves me; oh, how he loves you and me!

2 Je - sus to Cal - vary did go, love for all
peo - ple to show; what he did there brought
hope from de - spair.

Words and Music: Kurt Kaiser

This simple praise chorus expresses amazement and gratitude for God's rich love for us—a love so lavish that God chose us to be his children and redeemed us by sending Jesus to die for us.

The repetition of text in stanza 1 on successively higher pitches, and then again in the refrain, helps express that sense of overwhelming amazement. The remainder of the text points to the love of God as expressed in Christ's sacrifice. Children will easily learn the melody but will need to be encouraged to use their "head voices" on the higher notes because the song begins quite low in their vocal range. Encourage them to breathe deeply at the beginning of phrases so that the longer notes at the ends of the phrases can be sustained for their full value. Let the melody flow easily with one beat per measure. An accompaniment provided by either guitar or keyboard would be fine, though probably not both. You may wish to repeat the first stanza at the conclusion of the song as an added exclamation.

Sing as a testimony to God's love in any worship service, particularly during Lent. Or sing as a prayer response after the assurance of pardon or during the distribution of the elements in a Lord's Supper service.

The text and music for this Lenten song were composed by Natalie Sleeth (for more on Sleeth, see 175). Originally designed as an anthem for children, it is presented here in a more standard hymn format. The four stanzas tell God's sovereign plan for salvation through Christ's death and resurrection (1 Peter 1:19-21). The words "destined," "decreed," and "ordained" all speak to God's sovereignty. Best suited for older children, the richness of theological language and the quantity of text is probably beyond younger children's comprehension.

The music is gentle and flowing in character. Encourage children to sing legato (smoothly), with an understanding of the four-measure phrase structure. The melody moves predominately stepwise with much repetition of a descending pattern. Children will be able to learn it very easily, but memorizing the text will take some time! The keyboard accompaniment presented here is well suited to the nature of the melody and the text. A "picked" guitar accompaniment patterned after the style of the keyboard accompaniment would also be very effective.

Sing in any Lenten service, an Easter service, or a service where the theme is God's plan for our salvation. Consider pairing with "O Perfect Life of Love" to the tune SOUTHWELL, also in E-minor, as part of a service of confession.

164 Part of the Plan

♩. = 69

Words and Music: Natalie Sleeth, based on the anthem "Part of the Plan"
© 1976, Hinshaw Music, Inc. Used by permission.

by his death the world would know the glo - ry of his ris - ing!

Illustration: The "tree" in this song is another word for the cross. Death on a cross was tortuous and degrading. It was used by the Romans for slaves and the worst of criminals. One of the great marvels of the gospel is that Jesus' horrendous death was the means for our deliverance and glorification. A universal symbol for the death of Jesus and our salvation, the cross is also a general symbol of Christian faith. The crown of thorns was part of the humiliation and pain of Jesus' death (Matt. 27:29).

John 3:14-17, part of Jesus' nighttime conversation with Nicodemus, forms the basis of this song. The first stanza refers to the Old Testament story of the Israelites being bitten by snakes (serpents). God told Moses to raise a serpent up high, and if people would look at it, they would be saved (Num. 21:8-9). The second stanza (which is the same as the fourth) is one of the first that a child memorizes.

The English folk tune fits this text well. Teach by the echo method, singing in canon style right from the start. In other words, sing only the quarter-note patterns, and rather than holding the long notes, have the children repeat immediately (as in the bass clef part). Then work on holding the long notes. Encourage the children to "drink in" (breathe deeply) before they start a phrase so they will be able to sustain the long notes.

The structure of the melody makes it a natural for two-part canon, even for groups that have not sung in parts before. You may wish to have the second part sung by a small group or played by an instrument. To create a more extended anthem, use the accompaniment in Hal Hopson's arrangement of "The Gift of Love."

In worship, have the congregation and children alternate singing stanzas while using some of the options presented above. Sing during a celebration of the Lord's Supper as a response to the preached Word, as a congregational confession of faith, or any time during the season of Lent.

165 As Moses Raised the Serpent Up

Words: John 3:14-17; versified by Marie J. Post, 1985
Music: English folk tune; arranged by Hal Hopson, 1972

LM
GIFT OF LOVE

Lent / Suffering and Death of Christ

♩ = 63

When I Survey the Wondrous Cross 166

1 When I sur-vey the won-drous cross
2 For-bid it, Lord, that I should boast
3 See, from his head, his hands, his feet,
4 Were the whole realm of na-ture mine,

on which the Prince of glo-ry died,
save in the death of Christ, my God!
sor-row and love flow min-gled down.
that were a pres-ent far too small.

my rich-est gain I count but loss,
All the vain things that charm me most,
Did e'er such love and sor-row meet,
Love so a-maz-ing, so di-vine,

and pour con-tempt on all my pride.
I sac-ri-fice them through his blood.
or thorns com-pose so rich a crown?
de-mands my soul, my life, my all.

Words: Isaac Watts, 1707
Music: Lowell Mason, 1824

LM
HAMBURG
Capo 5

Written by Isaac Watts, this has become one of the most loved Lenten hymns in the English language. The first stanza is based on Philippians 3:7-8 ("Whatever was to my profit I now consider loss for the sake of Christ"), and the second on Galatians 6:14 ("May I never boast except in the cross of our Lord Jesus Christ"). The text flows in ascending order of intensity, reaching a climax on the last stanza. Christ's redemptive death moves us to offer him no less than our "soul," our "life," our "all."

The melody contains just five different tones and the third line is the same as the first, so children will easily learn it. This simplicity allows the intensity of the words to shine through. Accompany with keyboard, guitar, or autoharp.

"When I Survey the Wondrous Cross" was written as a communion hymn. Sing also as a response to the assurance of pardon, especially during Lent, or in a service of adult baptism or profession of faith. Because of the level of language and concepts, this song is best sung along with the congregation rather than by children alone.

167 Were You There

♩ = 104

Were we there when Jesus was crucified? Of course not. But this African-American spiritual helps us wonder what it was like. Ask the children about the word "tremble." Do they ever tremble? Explain that "tree" in stanza 2 refers to the cross. As in most folk music, variations on the text are possible; on stanza 4, consider changing the third line to: "sometimes I feel like shoutin' 'glory, glory, glory!'"

The repetition of text and melodic lines make this spiritual very easy to learn. Teach by the echo method, having children repeat each phrase (or phrase segment) back to you. On the middle section, make sure the children open their mouths wide in a well-shaped "O" on the long "Oh." "Walk out" the four beats of the whole note, enabling children to feel the moving energy. Notice that there is no meter signature, so that the "tremble" notes don't have to be held quite as long. This music should not sound "metronomic"; the final counts on phrase endings should feel natural, not counted. But do emphasize that the last "Lord" is a long note; encourage children to hold it for a whole beat (not all six beats). Ask different children to sing the opening lines of the various stanzas as solos, with everyone coming in at "Oh." You may introduce and accompany with flute and quiet keyboard or guitar/autoharp accompaniment.

Include this spiritual in a Good Friday, Paschal Vigil, or Easter service. Each stanza can be sung as a response to appropriate Scripture.

1 Were you there when they cru-ci-fied my Lord? Were you there when they cru-ci-fied my Lord? Oh, some-times it caus-es me to trem-ble, trem-ble, trem-ble. Were you there when they cru-ci-fied my Lord?

2 Were you there when they nailed him to the tree? . . .
3 Were you there when they laid him in the tomb? . . .
4 Were you there when God raised him from the tomb? . . .

Words and Music: African-American spiritual

10 10 14 10
WERE YOU THERE
Capo 1

♩ = 84

Jesus, Remember Me 168

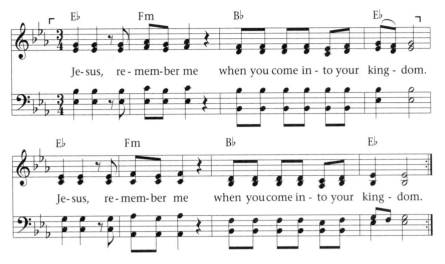

Je-sus, re-mem-ber me when you come in-to your king-dom.

Je-sus, re-mem-ber me when you come in-to your king-dom.

Descant 1 *(begins two beats early)*

(Je - sus . . . .)

(second time)

Descant 2

(second time)

When Jesus was crucified, one of the criminals who was hanging on a cross nearby said, "Jesus, remember me when you come into your kingdom." Jesus answered, "I tell you the truth, today you will be with me in paradise" (Luke 23:42-43). This short, repetitive chant comes from the Taizé community (for more on Taizé music, see 13).

Like much Taizé music, this is meant to be repeated until we no longer focus on the notes or on the specific words. This allows us the freedom to add our personal meditation, both asking Jesus and remembering that Jesus has promised to remember us also when he prays to his Father.

The music is simply two related phrases. Begin singing and ask the children to join in when they feel comfortable. After they know the melody, add instrumental descants if possible—flute, oboe, recorder, violin, or viola.

Sing during Holy Week, or as a prayer response whenever we remember the atoning sacrifice of Christ. The children could begin, with the congregation joining after one or two times, followed by the addition of the descants.

Words: Luke 23:42
Music: Jacques Berthier, 1978

© 1978, 1980, 1981, Les Presses de Taize. Used by permission of G.I.A. Publications.
All rights reserved.

JESUS, REMEMBER ME
Capo 1

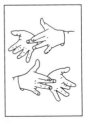

Jesus   *Remember*   *Me*   *Kingdom (1)*   *(2)*

Note: Children should sign "kingdom" at the beginning of the phrase "when you come into your kingdom."

This anonymous folk hymn, probably written by an American, first appeared in print in 1811. It is a meditation on the love of Jesus (st. 1, see Gal. 3:13), so great that he laid aside his crown to save us when we "were sinking down" (st. 2). Stanzas 3 and 4 are expressions of praise and gratitude that we will be singing with millions forever! Explain that "Lamb" (st. 3) refers to Jesus (see illustration, 44), and that "I AM" is a name for God.

Begin by reading each line of text through without repeats to see how two lines of text are expanded into five lines. The music also involves much repetition; the first two lines are repeated in lines four and five. Hum the first two lines, tracing the direction of the line with your hand. Ask the children wondering questions about the text: I wonder how it feels to give up a crown. . . . how Jesus felt when he left the glory of heaven and came to a sinful earth. . . . how it felt to give up power and then become weak.

Autoharp accompaniment would be very effective. Play either the notated chords or create an even simpler pattern, for example, by repeating the first two measures, using just two chords throughout.

Sing during Lent, but also at other times during the service of confession, when preaching on Jonah (st. 2), as a doxology (st. 3), or for a funeral (especially st. 4). For a service of confession, the children could call the congregation to confession by singing stanza 1, joined by everyone on stanzas 2-4 as a response of gratitude after the assurance of pardon.

169 What Wondrous Love Is This

$\downarrow = 66$

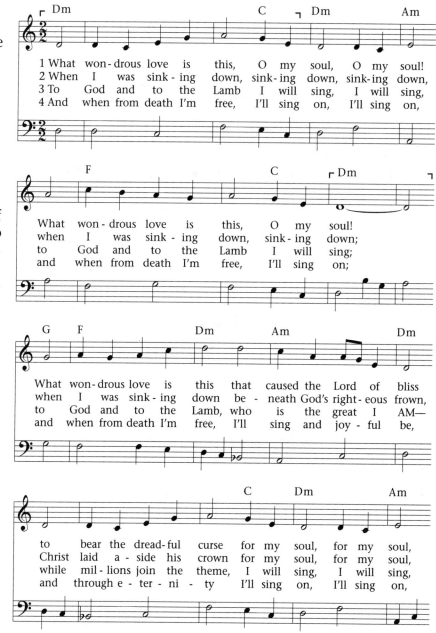

1 What wondrous love is this, O my soul, O my soul!
2 When I was sinking down, sinking down, sinking down,
3 To God and to the Lamb I will sing, I will sing,
4 And when from death I'm free, I'll sing on, I'll sing on,

What wondrous love is this, O my soul!
when I was sinking down, sinking down;
to God and to the Lamb I will sing;
and when from death I'm free, I'll sing on;

What wondrous love is this that caused the Lord of bliss
when I was sinking down beneath God's righteous frown,
to God and to the Lamb, who is the great I AM—
and when from death I'm free, I'll sing and joyful be,

to bear the dreadful curse for my soul, for my soul,
Christ laid aside his crown for my soul, for my soul,
while millions join the theme, I will sing, I will sing,
and through eternity I'll sing on, I'll sing on,

Words: S. Mead's *A General Selection*, 1811
Music: W. Walker's *Southern Harmony*, 1835; harmonized by
Richard L. Van Oss, 1992
Harm. © 1994, CRC Publications

12 9 12 12 9
WONDROUS LOVE
Capo 5

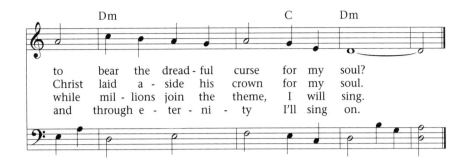

to   bear the dread - ful   curse   for my   soul?
Christ laid a - side his   crown   for my   soul.
while mil - lions join the   theme,   I   will sing.
and   through e - ter - ni - ty   I'll sing on.

♩ = 100

Worthy Is Christ
Digno Es Jesús 170

1 Wor - thy is Christ,   wor - thy is Christ;
2 He   gave his life,   he   died for me;
1 Dig - no es Je - sús,   dig - no es Je - sús;
2 Su   vi - da dio,   por mí   mu - rió;

to   him be praise and glo - ry: wor - thy is   the Lord.
de   re - ci - bir la glo - ria, dig - no es Je - sús.

Words and Music: traditional Spanish

DIGNO ES JESUS
Capo 5

Although we don't know who wrote this Spanish folk hymn, the author surely knew about the songs in Revelation 5. The apostle John has a vision of heaven in which he hears two songs praising Christ Jesus that begin with "Worthy." You may wish to have older children look up those song texts in Revelation 5.

Teach the melody by singing the short two-measure phrases, having the children repeat in echo fashion. Trace the melody direction with your hand, taking care to negotiate the octave leap in the second phrase. On the refrain, sing the dotted rhythms smoothly. Sing meditatively, not too fast. After children know it well, they may even wish to add stanzas, such as "He rose again, he lives for me." Accompany with guitar and keyboard.

This song makes an excellent doxology, especially during Lent and Easter. Sing as a prayer response or a response to Scripture reading. Consider pairing with "Alabaré" (193), another Spanish song based on Revelation 5. Children will enjoy singing the Spanish, especially during worship emphasizing missions or all-nations heritage.

As the title suggests, this hymn was composed for a processional. It was written for a festival service in Westminster Cathedral in England. In many churches, a processional begins with someone holding a large cross high. That person is called a "crucifer," or "cross bearer," which is also the name of this tune (see lower right corner of song page). This powerful hymn calls us all to take up our cross and follow Jesus, telling everyone in the world the good news of Jesus.

You may teach the refrain independently and sing as a response or short doxology. Consider signing or using the motions below to help teach and enrich the singing of the refrain. Choose one or two stanzas to learn for participation in congregational worship. Stanza 2 especially offers opportunities to talk about Christ's love, sealed to us in our baptism. Mention that "brow" means forehead and encourage the children to make a cross sign on their forehead. Challenge them to be witnesses for Christ's love. Sing very majestically, with keyboard and perhaps trumpet accompaniment. The stanzas lead right back into the refrain without interruption.

Sing as a processional or recessional during Lent or Easter. Also sing for baptism, profession of faith, or in any service emphasizing missions. During congregational singing, have the children sing stanza 2.

Words George W. Kitchin, 1887; revised by Michael R. Newbolt, 1916
Music: Sydney H. Nicholson, 1916; arranged by Robert Roth
© 1974, Hope Publishing Co. All rights reserved. Used by permission.

10 10 with refrain
CRUCIFER

Lift high the cross, (*slowly raise arms out and up at sides, forming a cross over the top of the head*)

the love of Christ (*bring crossed arms down over the heart, palms facing chest*)

proclaim (*quickly stretch hands and arms straight out and forward*)

till all the world (*raise hands over head, fully extending arms, fingertips touching to form a circle*)

adore (*repeat 2*)

his sacred name. (*fully extend arms up, forming a large "V," with palms facing in*)

♩ = 63 **Christ the Lord Is Risen Today** **172**

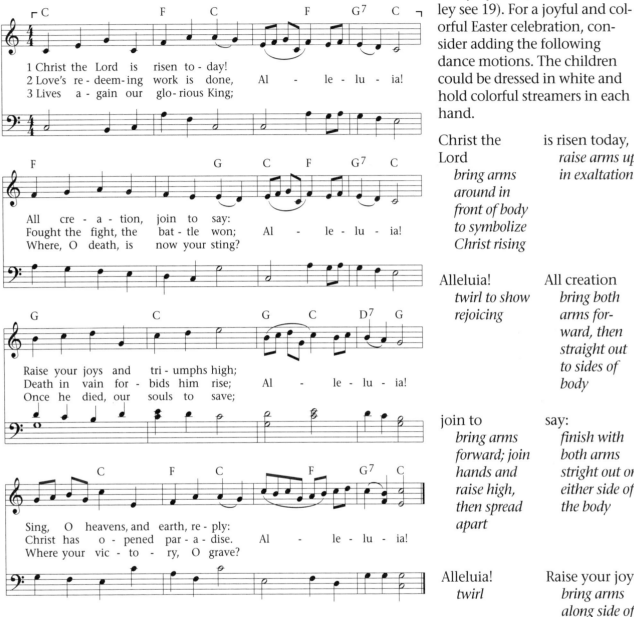

1 Christ the Lord is risen to-day!
2 Love's re-deem-ing work is done, Al - le - lu - ia!
3 Lives a-gain our glo-rious King;

All cre-a-tion, join to say:
Fought the fight, the bat-tle won; Al - le - lu - ia!
Where, O death, is now your sting?

Raise your joys and tri-umphs high;
Death in vain for-bids him rise; Al - le - lu - ia!
Once he died, our souls to save;

Sing, O heavens, and earth, re-ply:
Christ has o-pened par-a-dise. Al - le - lu - ia!
Where your vic-to-ry, O grave?

Words: Charles Wesley, 1739
Music: Lyra Davidica, 1708; arranged by Emily R. Brink, 1993
Arr. © 1994, CRC Publications

77 77 with alleluias
EASTER HYMN

This Easter hymn is one of the best known of Charles Wesley's many hymns (for more on Wesley see 19). For a joyful and colorful Easter celebration, consider adding the following dance motions. The children could be dressed in white and hold colorful streamers in each hand.

Christ the Lord
bring arms around in front of body to symbolize Christ rising

is risen today,
raise arms up in exaltation

Alleluia!
twirl to show rejoicing

All creation
bring both arms forward, then straight out to sides of body

join to
bring arms forward; join hands and raise high, then spread apart

say:
finish with both arms stright out on either side of the body

Alleluia!
twirl

Raise your joys
bring arms along side of body with hands cupped

and triumphs high;
bring arms down, swooping around quickly, and up again— clenching fists in triumph

Alleluia!
twirl

Sing, O heavens
start with hands over mouth and bring arms out—as if to show song flowing up from the mouth

and earth, reply:
same as last step—symbolizing reply

Alleluia!
twirl

Donald Fishel based this well-known song on passages from the letters of Paul (Rom. 4:24-25; Rom. 6:6; 1 Cor. 15; Gal. 2:20). The stanzas tell of our new life in Christ; the refrain calls us to give thanks and praise to God for this new life.

The melody is simple and easily learned. Sing a phrase at a time and have the children echo back. Once children know it, they should sing without any pauses between refrain and stanzas. They should try to sing each phrase completely in one breath. Each stanza may be sung alone or in conjunction with any of the other stanzas in any order. Accompany lightly with piano, guitar, or autoharp, with flute or recorder on the melody or descant. Try varying the accompaniment on the stanzas—possibly having no accompaniment on one or more. You may also divide the children into two groups and have them sing the phrases of the stanzas and refrain antiphonally, joining together for the final refrain.

Sing at Easter, but also at other times such as baptism, profession of faith, and mission services. Sing stanzas 3 and 4 as a response to the prayer of confession, stanzas 1 and 5 as a call to worship, and stanza 2 as a closing. Sing the refrain as a response to the Scripture reading, sermon, or at the offering.

173 Alleluia, Alleluia! Give Thanks

Words and Music: Donald Fishel, 1971; arranged by Emily R. Brink, 1993; descant by Roy Hopp, 1993

CHURCH STREET
Capo 5

Descant

♩ = 66

He's Alive! 174

Round

The Lord is ris-en from the dead. The Lord is ris-en,

as he said. He's a-live! He's a-live! He's a-live!

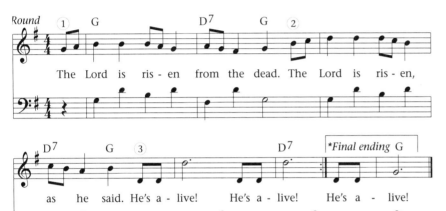

After group ③ is finished, everyone sings the final ending together.

Orff instruments

Bass xylophone   *Alto xylophone*

Alto glockenspiel   *Soprano glockenspiel*

Words and Music: Tom Fettke; arranged by Richard L. Van Oss, 1992

When Jesus rose from the dead, an angel announced to the women who came to the tomb: "He is risen!" (Matt. 28:6, Luke 24:6-7). This song announces that good news.

The text and melody are accessible to children of all ages; older children will enjoy singing as a three-part round. The third part of the round, with its octave leaps paired with the text "He's alive!" provides a natural exclamation point to the piece. Encourage children to use their "head voices" while singing this refrain—try to have them sing with a clear, bell-like quality.

The simple keyboard accompaniment is very effective. Children will enjoy playing Orff instruments as well. Any of the Orff parts could also be played on recorders.

Have the children sing this "announcement" in connection with the reading of the Easter story from Matthew or Luke. Also consider singing as a children's "prelude" to congregational singing of another Easter hymn in the key of G.

Natalie Sleeth was a prolific composer of songs for children and youth (several are included in this hymnal). Sleeth initially took up the challenge of writing interesting songs for children after her daughter complained of singing boring children's anthems in church school. Although she had multiple sclerosis, Sleeth's life was filled with joy because she knew God was watching over her. Just before she died in 1992, she wrote this parable for her grandchildren.

Once upon a time—long, long ago—everything was dark and had no shape or form. And God looked around and said: "I want to make a world," and so the world was made. God made day and night and earth and sky and land and sea and trees and mountains and all sorts of creatures that could walk or run or swim or fly. But something was missing, and God sat down on a cloud to think. "I know what my world needs!" God said, "People!" So God created a man and a woman and gave them the power to make more people, and through the years the world became a busy place with all sorts of men and women and children everywhere! And God said: "I will give each of my people special gifts, and I will help them use these gifts to make the world the best place it can be!" And God looked down and smiled and said: "That's good! That's good!"

Now one of the people on God's earth was a child named Natalie,

175 This Is the Day

♩ = 63

Words and Music: Natalie Sleeth, adapted from the anthem "This Is the Day"
© 1976, Hinshaw Music, Inc. Used by permission.

Capo 5

and God gave her the gift of music. As she grew, she learned to use this gift in many ways, and she gave thanks that she could share it with others. And Natalie had family—a husband and children and grandchildren, too, and each one was special, and she loved them all. And God looked down and saw Natalie and smiled and said: "That's good! That's good!"

But one day Natalie began to realize that she was getting older and that her body was beginning to wear out. And she talked to God about it and asked for help. God heard her and said: "My child, when I made the world and filled it with people, I had a plan. I wanted my people to have life for as long as they could, but not forever, because then my world would be too full with no room for anybody. I planned it so that when it was

let us sing! This is the day that the Lord has made! Re-

joice! Re-joice, and be ex-ceed-ing glad! This is the day that the

Lord has made! Re- joice! Re-joice! Hal-le-lu-jah! Re-

joice! Re-joice! Hal-le-lu - jah!

time to leave the earth, my people would come and live with me in heaven, where there is no pain or sickness or sadness or anything bad." And Natalie said softly to God: "Is my time to come and live with you getting near?" And God said: "Yes, but be not afraid, for I will always be with you and take care of you." And Natalie said to God: "But I will miss my family and my friends, and they will miss me!" And God said: "I will comfort them and turn their tears to joy, and they will remember you with happiness and be glad for your life among them."

So slowly Natalie began the journey to heaven, and day by day drew nearer to God. In the distance she could see light and hear music and feel happiness she had never known before. And as she moved toward the gates and into the household of God, she said to herself, with joy in her heart: "That's good! That's good!"

Reprinted by permission from *Choristers Guild LETTERS,* August, 1992.

The title of this joyful Easter stanza comes from Psalm 118:24: "This is the day that the Lord has made; let us rejoice and be glad in it" (see also 3). The song combines the psalm quotation in the refrain with two Easter stanzas celebrating the resurrection of Christ.

Children will enjoy this song's vitality. Like her other songs, it has short phrases and rhythmically moving accompaniments. The repetition makes it easy to learn. Considering the refrain as the A section and the stanzas as the B section, the structure is ABABA, with an added final ending. Begin with the refrain, having the children echo each phrase. Then sing the B sections and coda, with the children singing all the A sections. Another day, teach the B sections by the echo method.

Piano accompaniment should be played lightly and brightly with even eighth-note accompaniment. On the stanzas (B sections), you may wish to add finger cymbals on the first beat of every measure or even a simple descant on the glockenspiel, playing only the note C every third beat.

Sing just the refrain as a call to worship any time. Or sing the entire song for an Easter morning service.

When Thomas first heard the news that Jesus was alive, he didn't believe it. This song, based on John 20:24-28, tells the story of Thomas coming face to face with Jesus following his resurrection. The narrative is presented in the stanzas, each phrase of which is punctuated by an invitation to "Come and see! Come and see." The refrain affirms our faith and trust in Jesus, the risen Lord.

While the text of the stanzas may be too much for younger children to learn, the refrain and response of "Come and see" is accessible to children of all ages, as is the African-American melody.

Teach this song by "call and response." Invite someone to play the role of Thomas and sing the narrative parts of the story, with the children responding with the "Come and see" phrase. Notice the syncopation in the response and encourage children to sing it correctly; don't allow them to "square off" the rhythm. The refrain should be sung with conviction and strength. As children become more familiar with the song, divide them into two groups, one taking the narrative, the other the response, and all joining on the refrain.

Sing the Sunday after Easter or for a service dealing with doubt and faith.

176 Come and See

♩ = 80

1 The night was dark and filled with gloom.
2 Then sud-den-ly the Lord ap-peared (Come and see!
3 Well, Thom-as said, "My God, my Lord!"

Come and see.) to see his friends and calm their fears.
They hid with-in a se-cret room.
Now I be-lieve the liv-ing Word.

(Come and see! Come and see.) To Thom-as he said,
Now Thom-as had not
Go tell the peo-ple

seen the Lord.
"See my hand." (Come and see! Come and see.) It
far and wide,

He
'twas

Words: John Ylvisaker, based on John 20:24-28
Music: African-American spiritual
Words © 1982, John Ylvisaker. Used by permission.

Hispanic music often expresses joy with a syncopated beat. This Puerto Rican Easter chorus is a jubilant statement of faith. It contains the heart of the gospel along with the repeated exclamation, "Glory be to Jesus."

The melody has a two-measure rhythmic pattern. Measure one (and every other measure thereafter) contains the syncopated part. Make sure you know it well yourself before teaching it to the children. One way to learn it is to divide each of the first two measures into eight sixteenth notes. Counting to eight evenly in each measure, clap or tap the pattern in the first measure on 1, 2, 4, and 7, and in the second on 1, 3, and 5. The fourth beat is the tricky one; land on it strongly, jumping ahead of the regular beat (5). Do it slowly at first, then gradually increase the tempo until you can "feel it" on the words "Glory be to Jesus." Teach the rhythm to children by example and "feel" rather than with the counting routine. Accompany with keyboard, guitars, tambourines, castanets, and other rhythm instruments, as well as hand clapping. Sing with enthusiasm. Guitarists, strum with strength! Sing at least twice in a row; after singing it in English, try Spanish!

Sing in any service as a confession of faith or doxology, especially during Eastertide.

177 Oh, How Good Is Christ the Lord
Oh, Qué Bueno Es Jesús

Words and Music: Puerto Rican folk hymn; harmonized by Dale Grotenhuis, 1985   OH QUE BUENO
Harm. © 1987, CRC Publications

He Is Lord 178

♩ = 88

1 He is Lord, he is Lord, he is ris-en from the dead, and he is Lord! Ev-ery knee shall bow, ev-ery tongue con-fess that Je-sus Christ is Lord.

2 He is King, he is King, he will draw all na-tions to him; he is King! And the time shall be when the world shall sing that Je-sus Christ is King.

3 He is Love, he is Love,
he has shown us by his life that he is Love!
All his people sing with one voice of joy
that Jesus Christ is Love.

4 He is Life, he is Life,
he has died to set us free, and he is Life!
And he calls us all to live evermore,
for Jesus Christ is Life.

Words: anonymous, based on Philippians 2:10-11; John 12:32
Music: anonymous, harmonized by Dale Grotenhuis, 1986
Harm. © 1987, CRC Publications

HE IS LORD
Capo 3

No one knows who wrote the first stanza and melody of this song, but it has become such a favorite that more stanzas have been added. Stanza 1 is based on the short profession of faith in Philippians 2:10-11 "that Jesus Christ is Lord." Stanza 2, based on John 12:32, calls us to praise Christ as the King who draws everyone to him. Stanza 3 is based on 1 John 3:16 and points us to Christ as the beginning and model of love. Stanza 4, based on 1 John 5:11, celebrates the gift of life now and forever.

All the children can learn the first and last lines; the middle lines will be more challenging. Picture symbols will help reinforce the theme of each stanza for younger children: a scepter for stanza 1, a crown for stanza 2, a heart for stanza 3, and a butterfly for stanza 4.

Sing with strength and conviction as a confession of faith. Sing with a solid accompaniment of keyboard and/or guitar, not too fast. For guitar, a firm block strum serves the text well on stanzas 1, 2, and 4, while a "picking" pattern would add a gentler dimension to the text of stanza 3. When singing the entire hymn, conclude with a repeat of stanza 1.

Sing this in worship as a profession of faith at any service, particularly during the Easter season and for celebrating the Ascension. Have the children sing during the distribution of the elements at a Lord's Supper service.

179 Clap Your Hands

♩ = 84

The first stanza of this jubilant Bible song, written by Jimmy Owens, is based on Psalm 47:1, 5. It is coupled with "hosanna," a Hebrew exclamation meaning "save" (Ps. 118:25). Later, a second stanza by Bert Polman, chair of this hymnal committee, was added. This stanza has an Ascension emphasis.

Even though it can be sung in a four-part round, children should first sing in unison. After they know it well, sing as a two-part round, bringing in the second group at the circled ③. Gradually divide the round into more parts.

Be sure to accompany this song with clapping! Clap on beats 1 and 3, but on "voice of praise" clap on beats 1, 2, and 3. On the "Hosanna" and "Praise him" measures, raise hands high on beat 1, down on beat 3. Also accompany with keyboard and/or guitar, tambourines, and other rhythm instruments. Create a simple Orff pattern by playing C for the first three measures, then G and C in the fourth measure on half notes. Or play the following pitches every half note: CG/CG/CC/GC. Sing with enthusiasm.

In worship, sing on any festive occasion, especially on Ascension Sunday. Sing as a call to worship (especially st. 1) or as a response to the reading of Psalm 47. After singing once in unison, let the children lead the congregation in the round. Consider pairing with 180, another festive ascension hymn. Sing stanza 1 on Palm Sunday.

Words: stanza 1, Psalm 47:1, paraphrase by Jimmy Owens, 1972; stanza 2, Bert Polman, 1991
Music: Jimmy Owens, 1972; harmonized by Charlotte Larsen, 1991

CLAP YOUR HANDS

♩ = 69

Rejoice, the Lord Is King 180

1 Re - joice, the Lord is King! Your Lord and King a - dore.
2 His king-dom can-not fail; he rules o'er earth and heaven;
3 He sits at God's right hand till all his foes sub - mit,
4 Re - joice in glo - rious hope; for Christ, the Judge, shall come

Re - joice, give thanks and sing and tri - umph ev - er - more.
the keys of death and hell to Christ the Lord are given.
bow down at his com-mand, and fall be - neath his feet.
to gath - er all his saints to their e - ter - nal home.

Lift up your heart, lift up your voice.
Lift up your heart, lift up your voice.
Lift up your heart, lift up your voice.
We soon shall hear the arch - an - gel's voice;

Re - joice, a - gain I say, re - joice!
Re - joice, a - gain I say, re - joice!
Re - joice, a - gain I say, re - joice!
the trump of God shall sound, re - joice!

Words: Charles Wesley, 1744
Music: John Darwall, 1770; harmonized by Charlotte Larsen, 1992
Harm. © 1994, CRC Publications

66 66 88
DARWALL'S 148th

On Ascension Day we rejoice that Jesus went back to his Father in glory, having perfectly completed his work on earth. God has exalted him to the highest place, and now Jesus rules over all creation as our King.

Like most of Charles Wesley's hymns, this text is rich and filled with scriptural allusions (see also 19, 122, 172). Teach the last two lines first as a spoken response to your narration of stanzas 1-3; later teach the different response to stanza 4.

As you sing this triumphant melody, trace the direction of the lines with your hand, and ask the children to do the same. Notice the dramatic opening leaps and the final ascending scale. Sing joyfully, at a lively tempo. Accompany with strong keyboard and trumpet.

This great hymn of praise is fitting anytime. Sing as a call to worship or opening hymn, especially for Ascension Day. The children may call the congregation to worship by singing stanza 1, with all joining on stanzas 2-4. If possible, add a trumpet on the melody for the last three stanzas.

When Jesus ascended into heaven, there was a great victory celebration. The angels sang to honor King Jesus (st. 1) because Jesus rose from the grave (st. 2) and now rules in power and majesty from "pole to pole" (st. 3). This hymn invites us to join in that celebration. The "crown" idea comes from Revelation 19:12: "On his head are many crowns." When Jesus ascended into heaven, he was crowned King of kings.

Although you may need to explain several words to the children, they will readily understand the melody's spirit of exuberant praise. In spite of having very little repetition, the melody is very accessible to children. Sing a phrase at a time, tracing the direction of the melody with your hand. The melody is divided into two halves, each with two short and then one long phrase. The first phrase sounds like a trumpet fanfare, which is very fitting for a king! Encourage children to take good breaths before singing the long phrases. To teach the text, prepare all of stanza 1 on a chalkboard or overhead. Sing a phrase at a time, with the children echo-

181 Crown Him with Many Crowns

♩ = 60

Words: Stanzas 1, 3, Matthew Bridges, 1851; stanza 2, Godfrey Thring, 1874
Music: George J. Elvey, 1868; descant Hal H. Hopson, 1979
Descant © 1979, G.I.A. Publications. All rights reserved.

SMD
DIADEMATA

ing. Erase one word (not necessarily the key word) from each phrase and sing the song together again. Continue until all of the words are erased.

Accompany with strong keyboard and consider adding trumpet for a regal sound. When the children are secure on the melody, invite some older children or a trumpeter to add the descant.

Sing as an opening hymn or doxology for Ascension Day or for any service celebrating the victorious rule of Christ. Sing also as a confident prayer for peace (st. 3).

Illustration: The crown is a universal symbol of honor—usually the honor of royalty. In the Bible, Jesus is called King of kings (Rev. 19:16), and he wears a crown (14:14 and 19:12). The monogram under the cross consists of the Greek letters χ (*Chi*, pronounced ki, as in kite) and ρ (*Rho*, pronounced row). These are the first two letters of "Christ" in Greek and have become a standard abbreviation and monogram.

This simple song speaks of the Spirit's work in our hearts. The text's repetition makes it accessible to even the youngest children. They will learn the song quickly by extracting the key words from each stanza.

The song has the characteristic of "perpetual motion": the ends of the stanzas lead right back into the refrain without stopping the rhythm. All the children could sing the entire song, or different soloists or groups could sing the stanzas.

To introduce the song, softly sound a wind chime for four measures, then accompany with keyboard, guitar, or autoharp. Or try handbells if your church has them. Have the lowest F available play on the first beat. Have all the handbells of the C-major scale (C-C1) play a soft sound randomly during a four-measure introduction, ending with a C to give the pitch. They could then play the pitches of the chord symbols.

Have children sing in congregational worship on Pentecost Sunday, perhaps after the assurance of pardon or before the Scripture reading.

182 On the First Pentecost

♩ = 66

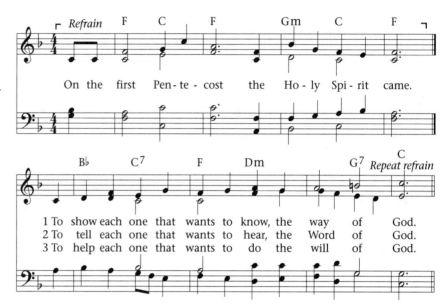

On the first Pen-te-cost the Ho-ly Spi-rit came.

1 To show each one that wants to know, the way of God.
2 To tell each one that wants to hear, the Word of God.
3 To help each one that wants to do the will of God.

Words: Coby Veenstra
Music: Norma de Waal Malefyt, 1992
© 1994, CRC Publications

Capo 5

Illustration: The dove and the flames are biblical references to the Holy Spirit. Matthew 3:16 tells us that "as soon as Jesus was baptized . . . he saw the Spirit of God descending like a dove and lighting on him." Acts 2 tells about the pouring out of the Spirit, when the disciples "saw what seemed to be tongues of fire that separated and came to rest on each of them" (v. 3). Pentecost banners often portray bright red flames.

♩ = 72

O Holy Spirit, Breathe on Me 183

1 O Ho-ly Spir-it, breathe on me,
2 O Ho-ly Spir-it, fill my life,
3 O Ho-ly Spir-it, make me new,
4 O Ho-ly Spir-it, wind of God,

O Ho-ly Spir-it, breathe on me,
O Ho-ly Spir-it, fill my life,
O Ho-ly Spir-it, make me new,
O Ho-ly Spir-it, wind of God,

and wash a-way my sin, fill me with love with-in:
take all my pride from me, give me hu-mil-i-ty:
make Je-sus real to me, give me his pu-ri-ty:
give me your power to-day, to live in you al-ways:

Final ending

O Ho-ly Spir-it, breathe on me.

Words and Music: Norman Warren, 1980; arranged by Emily R. Brink, 1994   Capo 5

This prayer song lists many ways the Holy Spirit works in our lives. Children may be interested to know that "spirit" and "breath" are very much alike. We cannot see the Holy Spirit; neither can we see the breath or "wind of God" (st. 4). But we know that Jesus sent the Holy Spirit to help us live Christ-like lives.

The opening line is a little refrain for all the stanzas. Explain to the children that "humility" means to think of others as more important than themselves, and "purity" means to be clean, without sin.

Teach children to begin each stanza without a pause. The melody has some distinctive leaps that will be challenging for children to master. Encourage them to use their head voices on the upper notes of the second and third phrases. The rhythm of this melody—which is identical in the first two lines—unifies the music. This gentle prayer is served well by a simple keyboard accompaniment. Or accompany with guitar, following the chords as printed. Perhaps older children or a soloist could sing the initial three phrases, with the younger children or all children responding with the final phrase.

Sing at a Pentecost service or as a prayer for a profession of faith or ordination service. You may wish to pair this twentieth-century hymn with the historic "Spirit Divine, Inspire Our Prayer" (185).

During an evangelistic crusade in 1926, Daniel Iverson listened to a sermon on the Holy Spirit. Moved by that sermon, he sat down at the piano and composed the first stanza and tune of this song. The first stanza has only two lines of text. Much later, Michael Baughen added the second stanza. Notice how the first stanza reflects an individual focus (renewal of the individual heart); the second emphasizes corporate worship (the unity of believers).

The melody is very simple. The first and last lines are identical (except for the final note) and the second is similar to the first. Sing this prayer quietly but firmly, with accompaniment on piano or guitar. To emphasize the elements of personal and corporate worship, have the children sing stanza 1 with their hands at their sides, then join hands to express fellowship on stanza 2.

Sing during the season of Pentecost, after profession of faith, in a service of ordination, or in a service of dedication for those entering Christian missions. Also sing as a frame around congregational prayer, singing stanza 1 before the prayer and stanza 2 at the conclusion. Have the children sing stanza 1 and the whole congregation stanza 2.

184. Spirit of the Living God

♩ = 104

1 Spir-it of the liv-ing God, fall a-fresh on me;
2 Spir-it of the liv-ing God, move a-mong us all;

Spir-it of the liv-ing God, fall a-fresh on me.
make us one in heart and mind, make us one in love;

Melt me, mold me, fill me, use me.
hum-ble, car-ing, self-less, shar-ing.

Spir-it of the liv-ing God, fall a-fresh on me.
Spir-it of the liv-ing God, fill our lives with love.

Words: stanza 1, Daniel Iverson, 1926: stanza 2, Michael Baughen, 1982
Music: Daniel Iverson, 1926

IVERSON
Capo 1

Spirit Divine, Inspire Our Prayer 185

♩ = 72

1 Spir - it di - vine, in - spire our prayer and make our
2 Come as the light; re - veal our need, our hid - den
3 Come as the fire and cleanse our hearts with pu - ri -
4 Come as the dove and spread your wings, the wings of

hearts your home; de - scend with all your
fail - ings show, and lead us in those
fy - ing flame; let our whole life an
peace and love, un - til your church on

gra - cious power; come, Ho - ly Spir - it, come!
paths of life where - on the right - eous go.
of - fering be to our Re - deem - er's name.
earth be - low joins with your church a - bove.

Words: Andrew Reed, 1829, alt.
Music: Johann Crüger, 1647; harmonized by Bert Polman, 1994
Harm. © 1994, CRC Publications

CM
GRAFENBERG
Capo 3

This Pentecost song was written for a prayer day in London, England for "the renewal of religion in the British churches." It is a prayer for the Holy Spirit to live in our heart. Explain that "divine" means to be holy or sacred. Stanzas 2, 3, and 4 describe three different forms the Holy Spirit takes—light, fire, and a dove (see illustration, 182).

The melody has four distinct phrases that fit children's voices very well. To help children learn, cut out four different colors of circles, one for each phrase. Divide children into four groups, giving each a colored circle (if the group is small, make enough circles for each child). Teach each group one phrase. After the song has been sung this way once, have children exchange circles. Continue in this manner until everyone knows the entire song. Then collect the circles and ask everyone to sing the phrases as the appropriate color circle is held up.

Sing as a prayer, with keyboard, guitar, or autoharp accompaniment. Since only three chords are given, you may wish to ask a child to accompany on autoharp. Consider asking a flutist to play the alto line an octave higher to form a descant.

In congregational worship, sing as a prayer of confession or as a conclusion to prayers of intercession on Pentecost Sunday or anytime. Have the children sing stanza 1, with the congregation joining on 2-4.

This text was written by Ambrose of Milan, a fourth-century church father who introduced congregational and antiphonal singing into the Western church. Ambrose is remembered for his teaching the doctrine of the Trinity in his songs—a response to the Arian heresy prevalent during his time. Notice how this brief prayer for the Holy Spirit's grace in our lives mentions all three persons of the Trinity. The fullness of grace can be seen in the fruits of the Spirit.

The melody has a flowing, reflective character. Sing with one beat per measure—children should aim to sing phrases, not individual notes. Encourage them to breathe deeply so they can sing each phrase with one breath. A natural crescendo occurs in the ascending pattern of the third and beginning of the fourth phrases. A keyboard accompaniment is most effective. You may add an instrumental (flute) descant by playing either the bass line two octaves higher than written or the alto part one octave higher.

On Pentecost Sunday, consider combining with the speech rhythm songs at 190 (as a processional and call to worship) or 187 (as a parting hymn). But don't just sing on Pentecost Sunday—also sing in any morning service as a call to worship, prayer response, or parting song.

186 Now Holy Spirit, Ever One

♩ = 126

Now Ho- ly Spir- it, ev- er one

with God the Fa- ther and the Son,

pour forth in- to our hearts, we pray,

the full- ness of your grace to- day.

Words: Ambrose of Milan, 4th century; versified in *Hymnal 1982*
Music: William Knapp, 1738; harmonized by Emily R. Brink, 1994
Harm. © 1994, CRC Publications

LM
WAREHAM

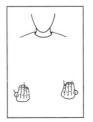

Now

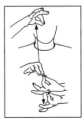

Holy Spirit

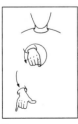

Ever

One

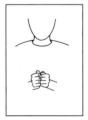

With

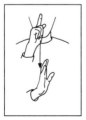

God

Father

♩ = 84

The Spirit of the Lord 187

with hand drum beating quarter notes throughout

p The Spir-it of the Lord fills the world! Al-le-lu-ia!

mf The Spir-it of the Lord fills the world! Al-le-lu-ia!

f The Spir-it of the Lord fills the world! Al-le-lu-ia!

pp (Group 1) Come, Ho-ly Spir-it. Come, Ho-ly Spir-it.

(continue as ostinato, until the beginning of the last line)

(Group 2) Fill the hearts of the faith-ful!

(Group 3) Kin-dle in them the fire of love!

f ... *ff* *a shout* (All) Let the right-eous re-joice be-fore God! Al-le-lu-ia!

Betty Ann Ramseth had a wonderful idea when she put scriptural and liturgical texts to rhythm. For a change of pace, children will enjoy learning a "speech song."

The last thing Jesus told his disciples when he ascended into heaven was, "You will receive power when the Holy Spirit comes on you, and you will be my witnesses . . . to the ends of the earth" (Acts 1:8). This "speech song" celebrates the power of the Spirit to "fill the world!"

To introduce this song, briefly tell the story of Pentecost, holding a hand drum, and start beating it to introduce the first line. As you repeat the first line (louder each time), encourage the children to join you. Then divide them into three groups for the middle section, everyone very softly tapping the beat along with your drum beat. Group 1 continues to sing while groups 2 and 3 sing. Everyone has time to get a good breath before the final unison line.

For variety, add a hand clap on the rests before and after each "alleluia." The final clap should be with arms raised.

The children could offer this as a call to worship or closing of the service. Sing at Pentecost or for any service emphasizing the call to service and mission in the world.

Words: Based on the Introit and Gradual for Pentecost
Music: Betty Ann Ramseth

(continued)

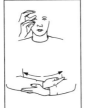

Son

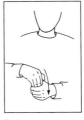
Into

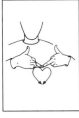
Hearts

Pray

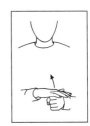
Fullness (fill)

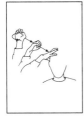
Grace

Today
Sign *Now*
plus *Day*
(above).

Teach your children this delightful Bible song, and they will forever remember the fruit of the Spirit (Gal. 5:22-23). Prepare a "Fruit of the Spirit" tree (see diagram on facing page) with empty branches. Also prepare colored circles with hanging loops labeled with the fruits of the Spirit. Explain that the trunk stands for God (Father, Son, and Holy Spirit) and the branches represent Christians. The tree needs fruit: Christian characteristics produced by the Spirit. While learning the song, have the children hang the fruit. In groups of three, speak the list of characteristics together, noticing how the words are grouped according to number of syllables. Sing with a relaxed lilt as an expression of "joy."

Sing during the Pentecost season, or for any worship service that stresses Christian character, as a response after the assurance of pardon. Consider pairing with 182.

This African-American spiritual, with its short, repetitive phrases in text and music, will be quickly learned and enjoyed by children of all ages. They may also enjoy adding stanzas, a practice that is consistent with this song tradition.

Sing with energy and enthusiasm. Accompany with keyboard, guitar, or autoharp. Add clapping and rhythm instruments on half notes to give rhythmic appeal and accentuate the syncopation at the beginning of the last phrase. This makes a good warm-up song!

Sing alone or in combination (with, for example, 2, 12, or 187) at Pentecost or during any time of joyful singing.

188 The Fruit of the Spirit

♩ = 104

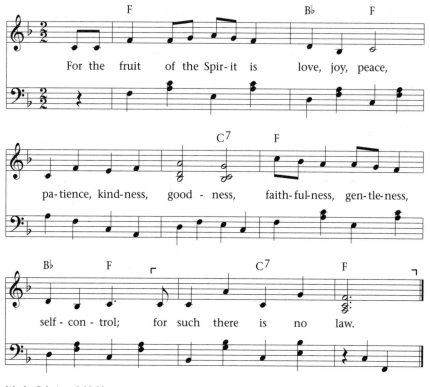

Words: Galatians 5:22-23
Music: Brian C. Casebow
© Brian C. Casebow. Used by permission.

Capo 1

189 I'm Gonna Sing

♩ = 72

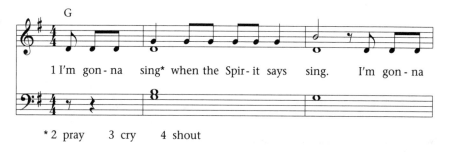

* 2 pray   3 cry   4 shout

Words and Music: African-American spiritual

sing when the Spir-it says sing. I'm gon-na sing when the

Spir-it says sing, and o-bey the Spir-it of the Lord.

♩ = 100

Walk! Walk! 190

Group 1
p

Walk! Walk!

Group 2
mf

Walk by the Spir - it!

Group 3
f

Let us live by the Spir-it in love, joy, peace, and pa-tience,

kind-ness, good-ness, faith-ful-ness, gen-tle-ness, and self-con-trol.

Like 188, "Walk! Walk!" lists the fruit of the Spirit, and like 187, it involves three speaking groups. The first two groups should be smaller than the third, since they provide an accompaniment to Group 3.

For a processional, one child leads the choir in, single-file, establishing the beat with a wood-block. Group 1 follows, speaking four measures before group 2 begins to speak. Group 3 begins four measures later and can repeat its passage as groups 1 and 2 quietly accompany. Then group 2 drops out, and finally group 1.

Words: Galatians 5:22-23,25
Music: Betty Ann Ramseth, 1970

Reprinted from *That I May Speak,* © 1970, Augsburg Publishing House. Used by permission of Augsburg Fortress.

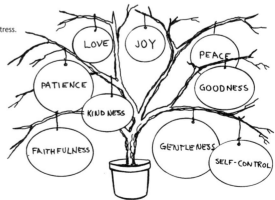

This hymn is a prayer for the coming of the Holy Spirit to the church today. The text conveys energy and strength ("challenge," "vigor," "might") as well as gentleness and peace ("murmur," "healing"). Note the opening word of each stanza (and each phrase) and ask the children:

- *Stanza 1:* What is the Holy Spirit like? (Like . . .)

- *Stanza 2:* To whom does the Holy Spirit come? (To . . .)

- *Stanza 3:* How and why does the Spirit come? (With . . .)

Although the text is most suited to older children and adults, all children can easily sing the closing refrain.

Carl Daw wrote the text especially for this tune. Counting by four-measure phrases, the second is the same as the first, but one step higher. Each phrase starts out alike, but the second half keeps climbing up an entire octave, preparing for the refrain, which then weaves down again to the opening note. The octave climb follows a G-minor scale; children will need to hear it sung or played a few times to be able to sing it accurately. The rhythmic delay on the initial "come" of the last phrase is a bit surprising to our ears. It effectively conveys our sense of expectation and longing for the coming of the Spirit. The composer recommends antiphonal singing, with the first group on the first four-measure phrase,

191 Like the Murmur of the Dove's Song

♩ = 88

1 Like the mur - mur of the dove's song, like the
2 To the mem - bers of Christ's bod - y, to the
3 With the heal - ing of di - vi - sion, with the

chal - lenge of her flight, like the vig - or of the
branch-es of the Vine, to the church in faith as -
cease - less voice of prayer, with the power to love and

wind's rush, like the new flame's ea - ger might:
sem - bled, to her midst as gift and sign:
wit - ness, with the peace be - yond com - pare:

Come, Ho - ly Spir - it, come.
Come, Ho - ly Spir - it, come.
Come, Ho - ly Spir - it, come.

Words: Carl P. Daw, Jr., 1981
Music: Peter Cutts, 1968

87 87 6
BRIDEGROOM
Capo 3

the second on the next, and all singing the refrain. Playing the bass/tenor line two octaves higher than written on a flute provides a haunting descant. This song lends itself well to liturgical dance; the final phrase could also be signed.

Sing on Pentecost or as a prayer for the power of the Spirit any time.

♩ = 66

There's a Spirit in the Air 192

Descant

Praise the love! Praise the

1 There's a spir - it in the air, tell - ing Chris - tians
2 Lose your shy - ness, find your tongue, tell the world what
3 When be - liev - ers break the bread, when a hun - gry

love! Al - le - lu - ia!

ev - ery - where: "Praise the love that Christ re - vealed,
God has done: God in Christ has come to stay.
child is fed, praise the love that Christ re - vealed,

Al - le - lu - ia!

liv - ing, work - ing in our world."
Live to - mor - row's life to - day!
liv - ing, work - ing in our world.

4 When a stranger's not alone,
where the homeless find a home,
praise the love that Christ revealed,
living, working in our world.

5 May the Spirit fill our praise,
guide our thoughts and change our ways.
God in Christ has come to stay.
Live tomorrow's life today!

Words: Brian Wren, 1969, revised 1987
Music: John W. Wilson, 1967

77 77
LAUDS

Brian Wren wrote this joyful hymn of encouragement for Pentecost. It encourages believers to praise Christ (st. 1), witness (st. 2), and serve others (st. 3, 4). Note that the "spirit in the air" (small s) in stanza 1 is a result of the work of the Holy Spirit (capital S) in stanza 5, which is a concluding prayer.

Stanzas 1, 3, and 4 each end with the same phrase; stanzas 2 and 5 end with another. Teach your children these two refrain lines first, emphasizing that we must not put off praising, living, and working as Christians for another day. Make a simple symbol for each phrase (such as a heart and a smiling face) and display it as you repeat the refrain. Speak the entire song, asking children to respond with the correct phrase when they see its symbol. (Encourage "soft" r's on "world.")

The music builds to a climax with longer and higher notes on the last phrase. Note also that there is no meter signature: the last phrase breaks the pattern on that delightful musical climax. Echo the melody in two-measure phrases, encouraging children to sing with good posture and good breathing. Be sure to hold out the vowels. Again, teach the last two phrases first, so even young children will be able to sing along. Use different soloists or small groups to begin each stanza. Since the descant is more difficult, it should be played by flute or violin or sung by experienced singers (perhaps from the adult choir). Sing with a lilting swing.

Sing to open or close worship, especially during Pentecost season or for a Lord's Supper service. Also sing as a children's anthem, perhaps with the "Walk! Walk!" processional (190). Or choose one or two stanzas for the children to sing, with the congregation joining on the rest.

193 Alabaré

♩ = 108

In his vision of heaven, the apostle John saw angels and saints singing songs of praise to the Lamb (Rev. 5:11-14). This bilingual song describes what John saw. The English text was written by Bert Polman as another versification based on the same text; it is not a precise translation of the Spanish. In English, the refrain means: "I will bring praise to my Lord."

The melody's short phrases, parallel thirds, and rhythmic style are in the style of a Hispanic folk song. Make use of the little echo phrases in the refrain: sing the "alabaré" and have the children echo. If your children sing well together, try singing in parts on the second half of the refrain. The lower part simply repeats the first half. Perhaps soloists or older groups could sing the stanzas, which are more challenging because of the tempo and the amount of text.

Accompany with keyboard and, if possible, also with guitar; hand clapping or other light percussion (tambourine) may be added on the refrain (but not on the stanzas). Sing with joyful exuberance!

Sing as a doxology or praise song any time, especially during the seasons of Easter or Ascension. Hispanic choruses are often combined in medley; consider combining with "There's No God as Great" (240) and "Worthy Is Christ" (170).

Words: Spanish words by Manuel José Alonso; English words by Bert Polman, 1986; based on Revelation 5:11-14
Music: José Pagán

11 10 10 10 with refrain
ALABARE

heard the song they sing to praise the Lamb.
praise the Lamb who gave his life for us:
peat the cho- rus, prais- ing God in song:

Thou- sands are pray- ing, mil - lions are sing- ing; a -
pow - er and glo- ry, wis - dom and hon - or be
bless - ing and hon- or, glo - ry and pow- er be

F   *Repeat refrain*

loud they raise their voice to praise the Lamb.
to the Lamb who gave his life for us.
to the Lord for - ev - er - more, A - men!

Spanish words:

1 Juan vio el número   de los redimidos,   y todos alababan al Señor.
  Unos oraban,   otros cantaban,   y todos alababan al Señor.

2 Todos unidos   alegres cantemos   gloria y alabanzas al Señor.
  Gloria al Padre,   gloria al Hijo,   y gloria al Espíritu de amor.

3 Somos tus hijos,   Dios Padre eterno,   Tú nos has creado por amor.
  Te adoramus,   te benedecimos,   y todos cantamos en tu honor.

Singer and composer Andraé Crouch, an African-American leader in contemporary gospel music, has composed over 300 gospel songs. Many have become standards in gospel music. In writing this song, Crouch must have had the last two chapters of the Bible in mind: Revelation 21:4 promises that in the new creation there will be "no more death or mourning or crying or pain," and in Revelation 22:20, Jesus promises, "I am coming soon." The simple repetition of these promises makes this joyful song of encouragement easy for children to learn.

The melody features the strong beat and syncopation characteristic of gospel music. Set up a rhythmic pattern of alternating patschen (thigh taps) and clapping on every quarter note, beginning with the patsch. As the children continue this pattern, sing the first line without accompaniment. The children repeat. Continue phrase by phrase, keeping the patschen-clap pattern going. Note that the second half of each line is identical, and the entire third line is the same as the first. The final phrase breaks the pattern on the "Hallelujah"; invite children to "sign" or raise hands on that line.

Add electric bass guitar, electric guitar, and various percussion instruments to keyboard accompaniment for a joyful "gospel" sound. In addition, keep clapping on beats 2 and 4.

In congregational worship, sing any time as a song of encouragement, especially during Easter and Ascension.

194 Soon and Very Soon

♩ = 66

1 Soon and ver - y soon we are going to see the King;

soon and ver - y soon we are going to see the King;

soon and ver - y soon we are going to see the King.

Hal - le - lu - jah! Hal - le - lu - jah! We're going to see the King.

2 No more dying there . . . .
3 No more crying there . . . .

Words and Music: Andraé Crouch, 1978; music adapted by William Farley Smith, 1987

VERY SOON
Capo 3

For All the Saints 195

♩ = 60

1 For all the saints who from their la-bors rest,
2 May all your sol-diers, faith-ful, true, and bold,
3 O blest com-mu-nion, fel-low-ship di-vine!

who to the world by faith their Lord con-fessed,
fight as the saints who no-bly fought of old,
We feeb-ly strug-gle, they in glo-ry shine;

your name, O Je-sus, be for-ev-er blest.
and win with them the vic-tor's crown of gold.
yet all are one with-in your great de-sign.

Al-le-lu-ia, al-le-lu-ia!

Words: William W. How, 1864
Music: Ralph Vaughan Williams, 1906
Used by permission of Oxford University Press, London.

10 10 10 with alleluias
SINE NOMINE

Who are the saints? All those who live and die in the Lord. This classic hymn helps us remember that Christians are not only people living on earth today but also those who are now living with Jesus. The first stanza thanks God for those who have gone before us and are now in heaven; they "rest from their labor" (Rev. 14:13). Stanza 2 speaks of Christians as present-day soldiers who carry on as the saints of old once did. And stanza 3 helps us understand what the Apostles' Creed means by "the communion of the saints."

Although the text is best suited for older children, all children can join on the alleluias. To help children memorize the text, make a chart with key words from each stanza suggested by the children:

For All the Saints		
1. For	*saints*	*rest,*
		confessed,
name	*Jesus*	*blest.*
A		
2. May	*soldiers*	*bold,*
fight	*saints*	*old,*
and win		*gold.*
A		
3. O blest		*divine!*
We feebly		*shine,*
Yet all		*design.*
A		

The tune SINE NOMINE means "no name"! English composer Vaughan Williams (a double last name) has composed one of the finest tunes of the twentieth century. It comes with a firm "walking" bass line; all the quarter notes give the piece a feeling of marching forward. Another unusual musical highlight is the solo bass note sounded before the voices enter. There is no repetition in the melody, so it will take some effort to learn. Use firm keyboard accompaniment, and add a flute or violin to support the melody.

Sing in congregational worship for All Saints Day (first Sunday in November), at a funeral service, or any time we remember the "communion of the saints." Choose one or two stanzas for the children to sing, and have the congregation sing the others (most hymnals have additional stanzas).

Children will have less trouble than adults imagining mountains singing and trees clapping their hands. Written by Steffi Karen Rubin, this Scripture chorus is based on Isaiah 55:12-13, one of the most delightful pictures in the Bible. A second stanza that helps provide the context was added by Bert Polman, chairperson of this hymnal committee.

Not only God's people will be saved, but so will creation! No more thorns ("briars and nettles"), no more pollution, no more war, no more sin anywhere. When God makes the new heaven and new earth, creation itself will share our joy. Creation is groaning now (Rom. 8:22), but when God redeems his creation, everything will be made new, even the trees of the field. We rejoice because we know God keeps his promises.

The joyful text is paired with the syncopated rhythms of a Jewish folk melody, composed by Stuart Dauermann of the "Jews for Jesus" organization. Explain that much of the melody moves before or after the beat, including the very first note.

Sing stanza 1 with the refrain, including the clapping as indicated. Slow down the tempo a bit and learn it a step at a time. Sing stanza 1 again, asking a few questions to help children learn:

- What will we feel as we go out and are led?

- What three things from creation are mentioned?

- What kind of shouts will there be?

196 The Trees of the Field

♩ = 112

Words: Isaiah 55:12-13; st. 1 by Steffi Karen Rubin, 1975; st. 2 by Bert Polman, 1985
Music: Stuart Dauermann, 1975

And all the trees of the field will clap their hands,

(clap, clap) the trees of the field will clap their hands,

the trees of the field will clap their hands

while you go out with joy.

- What will the trees do?
- Can trees really clap their hands? (Psalm 47 speaks of nations clapping hands, and Psalm 98 even has rivers clapping hands!)

Direct the main beats with your hand, using an up-and-down motion (not too fast). Ask the children to direct the beats also. Then have the pianist play the melody, and help everyone notice how many notes are played off their beats. Repeat the exercise, this time adding humming. Finally, add the words. Soon everyone will be ready to add the claps and start increasing the tempo.

Another time learn the words for stanza 2, using the method above and asking appropriate questions. Make sure everyone understands that fruitful trees and bushes will replace thorny, bare ones, and that through everything, God is always faithful.

Accompany with keyboard, guitars, tambourines, and vigorous hand clapping.

Sing for any festive and joyous occasion. Also sing as a response for any part of the service that speaks about God's salvation or as a joyful "sending forth" of God's people.

Illustration: In the Bible the tree often stands for abundant life or life with the Lord (see Ps. 1). It is also a picture of abundant growth "in the last days"—a sign of God's permanent presence with his people. In the passage from Isaiah on which this song is based, and in others, trees and other "things" are given human characteristics: trees clap and mountains sing.

197 Swing Low, Sweet Chariot

♩ = 50

This African-American spiritual can be traced back to slaves on the tobacco plantations of the Carolinas. As they worked, these people sang songs that expressed their longing for a better home. This song is based on the story of God sending a fiery chariot to take Elijah to heaven (2 Kings 2:7-12; see also 110, st. 11-12).

Ask children what Bible story the slaves were remembering in this song. Tell them to listen for the name of a river and ask them what they know about the Jordan. Crossing the Jordan River has always been a symbol of passing from death to new life, just as the Israelites crossed from the desert into the land God promised them.

The melody has syncopated rhythms, repeated patterns, and a call-and-response structure—all characteristic of African-American spirituals. Even the youngest children can sing the repeated response beginning "coming." They will soon understand that the melody direction is altered every other time, especially if you illustrate the melody with a cardboard chariot moving up or down or staying the same. Try clapping the quarter note all the way through, noticing that some notes move after the beat and others on the beat. Be sure to hold the first "home" for two beats, and begin the second "swing" on the first beat. Have

Words and Music: African-American spiritual

SWING LOW
Capo 5

Alto metalaphone   Glockenspiel   Soprano xylophone

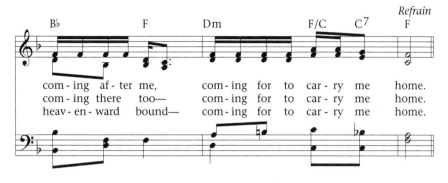

com-ing af-ter me, com-ing for to car-ry me home.
com-ing there too— com-ing for to car-ry me home.
heav-en-ward bound— com-ing for to car-ry me home.

all the children sing the complete refrain and all the "coming" phrases, and invite soloists or groups of older children to sing the stanzas, perhaps a different group on each stanza.

Accompany with keyboard, autoharp, or guitar. Or, since the melody is pentatonic (only five tones), consider Orff instruments. A couple of simple patterns are given below; the second is based on the fragment "carry me home." Or develop other patterns, using pitches from the melody.

Consider pairing with "All Night, All Day" (199), another pentatonic song. The refrains in particular fit very well when sung simultaneously. Begin by singing "Swing Low, Sweet Chariot," and assign a group to sing "All Night, All Day" during the concluding refrain. Continue the medley by singing the stanza(s) of "All Night, All Day" and again conclude with the two combined refrains. You may add more variety by including ostinato patterns and a variety of soloists. Sing with a gentle, lilting, flexible rhythm.

In worship sing as a conclusion to a sermon on heaven or the new creation. Let the children lead a praise time by singing a group of songs, and include the congregation on refrains and responses.

Illustration: "Swing Low, Sweet Chariot" combines two images: crossing the Jordan river into the promised land is an image for crossing from death to new life; the chariot and horses of fire that take Elijah to heaven (1 Kings 2:11) are symbols of power and authority.

Living in God's World

This simple African-American spiritual is a wonderful profession of faith! The world, and everything in it, belongs to God. And since God loves the world, God will take care of it, and us, and even the "little tiny baby."

Five stanzas are suggested here, but others may be added, such as "He's got the wind and the rain. . . . " Just as the text is not "static," neither is the melody. You may know a slightly different version of the tune, as is common in folk music. No one version is "right."

Even the youngest children will enjoy the simple repetitive structure of this spiritual. Sing with a light accompaniment on guitar or piano. Add motions corresponding to the text of each stanza. Try some solo singing on individual stanzas, with all joining in on the final line. Clapping off the beat (on beats 2 and 4) will give rhythmic appeal and also accentuate the syncopations characteristic of African-American music. You may wish to give each child a small marble to hold. Encourage them to keep the marble in their pocket all week as a reminder that God cares for the world and for them, no matter what they are doing.

In congregational worship, sing as a hymn of assurance when focusing on God's rule and providence or on family life.

198 He's Got the Whole World

♩ = 112

2 He's got the little tiny baby in his hands. (3x)
  He's got the whole world in his hands.

3 He's got you and me, brother, in his hands. . . .

4 He's got you and me, sister, in his hands. . . .

5 He's got everybody here in his hands. . . .

Words and Music: African-American spiritual

WHOLE WORLD

All Night, All Day 199

♩ = 56

Refrain

All night, all day, an-gels watch-ing o-ver me, my Lord.

All night, all day, an-gels watch-ing o-ver me.

1 Now I lay me down to sleep.
2 Lord, stay with me through the night.
An-gels watch-ing o-ver me, my Lord.

Pray the Lord my soul to keep.
Wake me with the morn-ing light.
An-gels watch-ing o-ver me.

Repeat refrain

The words to the first stanza of this African-American spiritual are based on a traditional children's bedtime prayer. You may want to begin by asking children how many of them start their own bedtime prayers with these words. Point out that this song speaks of God's great love for all his children. God watches over us not only when we are awake but also when we are asleep.

The music and words suggest a quiet mood. Encourage children to make their voices sound soft, smooth, and beautiful. This song could be accompanied very nicely on the autoharp. Younger children may enjoy taking turns quietly strumming the autoharp while you or an older child press the chord buttons. Another child may keep a steady beat by playing an F on a tuned bell (handbell, glockenspiel, etc.).

Try splitting the children into two groups (or soloist and one group). The first group (or soloist) sings the first half of each line. The second group sings "Angels watching over me (my Lord)."

Sing the refrain as response to the benediction in congregational worship.

Words and Music: African-American spiritual

Capo 3

This simple round is based on the opening words of one of the best-known and most loved psalms in the Bible (Ps. 23:1-2). Many children will already know the story of the Good Shepherd who takes care of his sheep.

Introduce the text by showing your children a shepherd's staff or a picture of sheep (see illustration at 202). Ask some "wondering" questions: I wonder who the shepherd is . . . Why does he lead by "still waters"? How can we "walk with him always"?

The song is divided into two sections, with the first beginning and ending the entire song (ABA). Teach the entire song to the whole group, having the children echo every two measures. Note that the second half of each line is repeated. After they know the melody, divide children into two groups and try singing as a two-part round. This is an excellent song for introducing two-part harmony.

Accompany with keyboard, inviting a child to play the duet part either on the piano or on an Orff instrument. Since only two chords are involved, children could also accompany on the autoharp. Add finger cymbals (or triangle) after every "always" (on the second beat of every half note).

In worship, sing as a song of commitment in a New Year's service, for profession of faith, or as a response to God's will for our lives. Have the children sing it once through, then invite the congregation to join in the round.

200 The Lord Is My Shepherd

♩ = 108

Alternative words: "I'll follow him," or "I'll live for him"

Second piano part, for playing as a duet:

Repeat through the entire song.
May also be played on Orff instruments.

Words: Psalm 23:1-2
Music: folk melody; arranged by Charlotte Larsen, 1992
Arr. © 1994, CRC Publications

Capo 3

♩ = 112

The Lord, My Shepherd 201

1 The Lord, my shep-herd, rules my life and
2 The Lord re-vives my fail-ing strength, he
3 Though in a val-ley dark as death, no

gives me all I need; he leads me by re-
makes my joy com-plete; and in right paths, for
e-vil makes me fear; your shep-herd's staff pro-

fresh-ing streams; in pas-tures green I feed.
his name's sake, he guides my fal-tering feet.
tects my way, for you are with me there.

4 While all my enemies look on,
   you spread a royal feast;
   you fill my cup, anoint my head,
   and treat me as your guest.

5 Your goodness and your gracious love
   pursue me all my days;
   your house, O Lord, shall be my home—
   your name, my endless praise.

Duet accompaniment

Words: Psalm 23; versified by Christopher M. Idle, 1977
Music: Jessie Seymour Irvine, 1872; arranged by Richard L. Van Oss, 1991

CM
CRIMOND
Capo 3

Psalm 23, a profession of joyful trust in the Lord as the good Shepherd-King, is one of the first Psalms a child learns (see illustration at 202). The previous song included just the first two verses; this text covers the entire psalm. You may wish to teach the five stanzas over a period of several weeks, even an entire season.

Older children may look for the name of the tune in the lower right-hand corner of the song page. CRIMOND is named for a town in Scotland. The melody became popular after it was used at the wedding of Queen Elizabeth and Prince Philip in 1947. Encourage children to sing with their head voices, taking good breaths to be able to sing the rather long phrases each on a breath. Accompany with keyboard and possibly also with guitar. The addition of the second bass part as part of a duet accompaniment will provide a lot of charm. A child with a background in piano could play the initial part, with an older child or adult adding the rhythmic bass line. The left hand of the initial accompaniment could be played gently by a clarinet, oboe, or flute an octave higher than written as a descant (in that case, it should not be played by a keyboard instrument below).

This Psalm serves as an expression of trust appropriate for many different points during a worship service. Have the children sing the first stanza, with the congregation joining on the other stanzas. Consider singing as response at the sacraments of baptism and the Lord's Supper.

202 This Is How We Know

♩ = 60

When you teach this Bible song to your children, not only will you give them a favorite song but also Bible verse engraved on their memory for life. (See 57 for more on Scripture songs by Frank Hernandez.)

Ask an older child to look up 1 John 3:16 in the Bible and read it aloud. Also read a passage from the Gospel of John: "I am the good shepherd. The good shepherd lays down his life for his sheep" (John 10:11). Wonder with the children what it means that Jesus "laid down his life for us."

Sing phrase by phrase with the children on the echo part. The echo is built right into the structure—except for the two ending phrases, when everyone sings together. The strength of the melody lies in its stepwise motion and its matching of one word to every note. Trace the direction of the melody with your hands and encourage the children also to follow the up-and-down motions of the phrases. Have the keyboard accompaniment reach up and play both sung parts at first. (The original keyboard accompaniment was much more involved and the echo part was played an octave higher than the children sang.)

When everyone knows it well, switch roles and ask the children to lead, with only keyboard on the echo part. Point out the slight overlaps between the main and echo parts. Make sure children hold their notes

Words: 1 John 3:16 (NIV)
Music: Frank Hernandez, 1990; arranged by Norma de Waal Malefyt, 1992
© 1990, Birdwing Music (Admin. by The Sparrow Corp.). All rights reserved. Used by permission.

the full value. Then have all the children sing the main part and invite a flute, recorder, or violin player to play the echo part. Put an eighth rest at the end of the first ending, ensuring a good entrance on beat 1 for the repeat.

This song requires clear entrances and cutoffs. Everyone should focus their eyes on you! After your group can sing the complete song using the piano accompaniment, add the second echo part, sung by a small group of older singers. Be sure to explain that on both endings one echo is deleted and the concluding phrase is sung in unison. Remember to give the echo clear cues for entrances.

Teach your singers to crescendo as the song builds through the first ending. Keep a steady, walking tempo. Remind everyone to stay attentive until the last piano chord has finished sounding.

In worship, sing as part of an assurance of pardon or as a concluding meditation for a service centered on Christ's love and redemption, especially for Lent or for a Lord's Supper service.

As a fun exercise, teach the melody using the scale numbers, echoing each little phrase, and using the rhythm of the main part:

1 2 3 4 5
6 5 4 3 2
1 2 3 4 5
3 4 3 2
6 7 5
3 2 3 1
1 2
6 5
7 8 *first ending*
3 2 1 *second ending*

Illustration: In both the Old and New Testament the Lord is portrayed as a shepherd. Psalm 23 is the best-known passage using the image of the shepherd protecting and guiding his flock. In John 10:11, Jesus applies this Old Testament image to himself: "I am the good shepherd." And Hebrews 13:20 calls him "our Lord Jesus, that great Shepherd of the sheep." God's people are, of course, the sheep who are to obey and follow the shepherd.

David A. Hoekema composed this text and the tune for the baptism of his daughter Janna, for whom he named the tune. Hoekema says,

One morning in June while I walked the half mile up the hill from my home to my office, a spirited little tune hummed its way into my mind, and at the same time some words and ideas that I had toyed with took clearer shape in relation to the tune. During the next week or so, I added the harmony and refined the text. I believe that this hymn was a gift given to me to celebrate my daughter's baptism.

Of all baptism hymns, this one most powerfully places baptism in the context of God's covenant with his people. The stories of Noah and the flood, of Abraham and Sarah, and then of Christ, all lead to God's covenant promise in the refrain: "I am your God; you are my people." Stanza 4 brings the story up-to-date, "to us and our children," and ends with our response of faith. Scripture passages corresponding to the stanzas are as follows:

- *Stanza 1:* Genesis 7; 9:13-15; 1 Peter 3:18-22

- *Stanza 2:* Genesis 15:5; 17:1-8; 21:1-7

- *Stanza 3:* Hebrews 8

- *Stanza 4:* Acts 2:38-39

Sing this strong tune with energy. The chromatic descending lines (beginning the last measure of the first page) can be tricky to sing correctly; be sure of yourself and/or rely on instrumental reinforcement as you teach it to the children.

The hymn has an abundance of unrhymed text, but its narrative character of will help the

203 You Are Our God; We Are Your People

♩ = 104

1 It rained on the earth for-ty days, for-ty nights,
2 God told A-bra-ham, "I will give you a land,
3 And when Je-sus Christ came to live on the earth,
4 To us and our chil-dren the pro-mise is made,

and all of the world was de-stroyed. The ark No-ah
a peo-ple as man-y as the stars." Though child-less and
God's pro-mise to us was ful-filled. His life and his
if we will but trust in his word. In bap-tism

built at the call-ing of God saved God's cho-sen
old, he and Sar-ah be-lieved and trust-ed the
death were a new cov-e-nant, as-sur-ance of
join-ing the peo-ple of God, we live in the

ones from the flood. God gave to No-ah the
word of the Lord. God gave them I-saac, a
love full and free. God gave his Son, his
pow-er of his grace. God gives us life, and we

Words and Music: David A. Hoekema, 1978
© 1985, CRC Publications

JANNA

rain - bow sign: "Such a flood I will not send a -
son, at last, and___ this is the cov - enant he
on - ly Son; to___ all who re - ceive him he
give him thanks: "To___ you be our praise ev - er -

gain— I am your God; you are my peo - ple."
made: "I am your God; you are my peo - ple."
says: "I am your God; you are my peo - ple."
more! You are our God; we are your peo - ple."

older children learn it. The singability of the melody and the joy with which children have responded to its folklike character makes learning well worth the effort. Younger children can certainly learn the concluding phrases (the final one is also the title of the song) as a statement of trust.

Accompany with keyboard at a tempo which does not sound too light; sing at a pace which permits the text to come through clearly. For variety, older children or adults could sing the text of each stanza as solos or in groups, with all children responding on the affirmation, "I am your God, you are my people."

Sing for baptism services in connection with preaching on covenant history. Hoekema says it is also fitting to sing after a week of rain!

Illustration: The rainbow is a very important sign in Genesis 9:12-17. God makes a solemn promise to Noah, the earth, and all living creatures that he will never again destroy the earth with a flood. This solemn promise is a covenant between God and his people. Today God continues to keep that covenant—always with a sign. We speak of baptism as a "sign" and seal of God's covenant promise. The rainbow reappears in Ezekiel 1:26-28 and in Revelation 4:3 and 10:1 as a sign of divine power and majesty.

Of all the psalms in the Bible, Psalm 136 is most obviously a liturgical psalm written for song leader (one of the Levites) and choir. The leader sweeps through all of history—creation, the Exodus, establishment in the Promised Land—each statement calling forth a refrain from the choir: "His love endures forever."

This setting by Marty Haugen is based on the Exodus part of the psalm. Haugen followed the same responsorial structure: each line of the narrative is set off by the exclamation that God's love is never-ending. Ask children to give examples of God's love in their lives; intersperse their examples with the response lines of this song. Haugen's tune is reminiscent of Israeli folk music and fits well with the storytelling style of the text. The melody can be easily learned by all. Choose some older students to sing the narrative part either as a group or individually. Younger children can sing the refrain lines. The music should be sung without a break at the end of the stanzas; just keep the beat going and start right on the next stanza.

Guitar accompaniment would be ideal for this song, particularly on the response lines. The narrative could be unaccompanied or accompanied lightly with a simple strum where chord changes are marked. Sing at a tempo that reflects a spirit of joy and thanks.

Sing in worship services remembering God's covenant, when the Exodus story is the theme of the service, or as a response of thanks following the assurance of pardon. Consider pairing with "When Israel Was in Egypt's Land" (103), which is in the same key.

204 Love Is Never Ending

♩ = 60

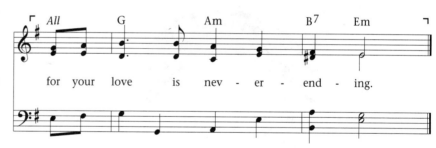

Words: Based on Psalm 136; versified by Marty Haugen
Music: Marty Haugen

Psalm 91 205

♩ = 96

Refrain

The Lord will raise you up on ea - gles' wings,

bear you on the breath of dawn, make you to shine like the

sun, and hold you in the palm of his hand.

Those who go to God Most High for safety
   will be protected by the Almighty.
I will say to the Lord, "You are my place of safety and protection.
   You are my God and I trust you." *Refrain*

God will save you from hidden traps
   and from deadly diseases.
He will cover you with his feathers,
   and under his wings you can hide.
His truth will be your shield and protection. *Refrain*

The Lord is your protection;
   you have made God Most High your place of safety.
Nothing bad will happen to you;
   no disaster will come to your home.
He has put his angels in charge of you
   to watch over you wherever you go. *Refrain*

Words: from Psalm 91 (New Century Version); refrain by Michael Joncas, 1979   ON EAGLES' WINGS
Music: Michael Joncas, 1979; harmonized by Norma de Waal Malefyt, 1992
© 1979, 1989, New Dawn Music. All rights reserved.

Psalm 91 is a psalm of trust and confidence that God will take care of us. The refrain is based on verse 4, where God is described as a bird that protects his young by tucking them under his feathers. Exodus 19:4 speaks of God carrying his people "on eagle's wings." And Deuteronomy 32:11 portrays God as an eagle who "stirs up its nest and hovers over its young, that spreads its wings to catch them and carries them on its pinions." Tell the children how eaglets learn to fly: they are prodded from the safety of their nest to fly off a steep cliff. The mother eagle flies under them to catch them on her wings because their first attempts at flight are not very successful. She carries them higher, then releases them so they can try to soar again. The mother eagle is always there to protect, encourage, and teach her young. And we need the protection, encouragement, and insight that only God can provide. Our children need to feel the "hug" of God expressed in this song: it is a promise that provides security for their living.

Children will enjoy singing the refrain. Pictures of an eagle, a sunrise, a "noonday" sun, and an open hand will help the children to remember the four ideas in the refrain. Sing at a tempo that reflects a secure and unhurried sense of trust and confidence. Provide accompaniment with either a gently strummed guitar or a keyboard.

Sing the refrain as indicated while an older child reads the given text from Psalm 91. Or sing the refrain only as a response of trust in any service or at the conclusion of a service, following the benediction.

206 It Makes No Difference

♩ = 60

We all want to belong, to be accepted. This song reassures us that it makes no difference who we are (st. 1), where we live (st. 2), or how we look (st. 3). God loves us and hears us when we pray (Gal. 3:28). But some things *do* make a difference— "how we treat our neighbors and our friends" (st. 4).

Short stanzas and a simple structure make this song accessible to even the youngest children. For variety, ask different soloists or groups to sing the stanzas with everyone joining on the refrain. Accompany with keyboard, guitar, or autoharp. Note the optional endings given in the score; they create a pleasant variation in the accompaniment. With autoharp or guitar, invite someone to play the bass clef part; a cello player could play it as written, or a flute or violin could transpose up two octaves to form a descant.

Sing as a call to prayer in any service where the theme is our responsibility to our neighbor.

1 It makes no dif - ference who we are, what
2 It makes no dif - ference where we live, in
3 It makes no dif - ference how we look, what
4 It makes a dif - ference how we treat our

lan - guage we may speak;
ci - ty, town, or farm;
col - or is our skin;
neigh - bors and our friends;

Refrain God loves us all and

hears our prayers— he knows our needs and cares.

Optional endings

1-3 (cares.) / 4

Words: Doris Clare Demaree; adapted by Bert Polman, 1993
Music: Sean E. Ivory, 1993

CM
FULTON

♩ = 60

God Is So Good 207

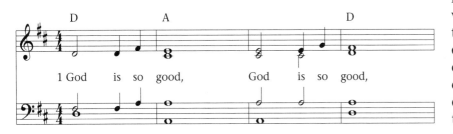

D   A   D

1 God is so good, God is so good,

G   D/A   A⁷   D

God is so good, he's so good to me.

2 He cares for me . . . .
3 God answers prayer . . . .
4 I praise his name . . . .

Descant

Stanza 1 in different languages:

Korean: Cho-u-shin Ha-na-nim, Cho-u-shin Ha-na-nim,
cham cho-u-shin, na ui Ha-na-nim.

Spanish: Dios es muy bue-no, Dios es muy bue-no,
Dios es muy bue-no, es muy bue-no pa-ra mi.

Swahili: Mungu yu M-we-ma, Mungu yu M-we-ma,
Mungu yu M-we-ma, Yu m-we-ma Kwan-gu.

Words and Music: traditional; descant by Susan Nipp

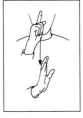
God

Good

Me

Children may respond to the many wonderful things God has done for them with this very simple profession of faith, trust, and love. It is simple enough to learn quickly, and children will enjoy adding their own stanzas. Perhaps they could even create stanzas for different times of year, for example, "He died for me . . . " (Lent) and "He rose again . . . " (Easter).

The limited range of the melody makes it an ideal song for very young voices. And the repetitive text lends itself well to signing, which young children also enjoy. Encourage children to sing any time, without accompaniment.

When children know the song, consider "dressing it up" a bit for singing in a worship service. For example, the descant could be played on handbells, Orff instruments, choir chimes, or flute. Or older children could play the descant on recorders or sing it on an "ah" vowel or with text, while the younger children sing the melody. Compose an additional, somewhat easier, descant by singing or playing the tenor line an octave higher than written. You may wish to write this out to avoid confusion for the children. Sing gently, with a quiet sense of trust.

Sing as an introduction or response to prayer or as a response to another song in the key of D (see key index). Repeat the first stanza as a closing refrain to the entire song.

208 Psalm 27

♩= 100

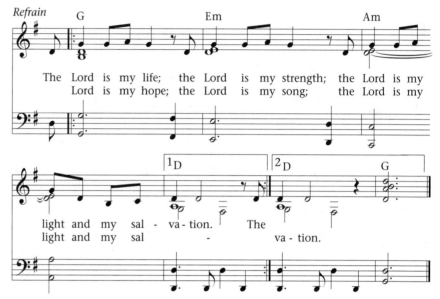

Refrain

The Lord is my life; the Lord is my strength; the Lord is my
Lord is my hope; the Lord is my song; the Lord is my

light and my sal - va - tion. The
light and my sal - va - tion.

The Lord is my light and my salvation;
  whom shall I fear?
The Lord is the stronghold of my life;
  of whom shall I be afraid? *Refrain*

One thing I asked of the Lord,
  that will I seek after:
to live in the house of the Lord
  all the days of my life,
to behold the beauty of the Lord,
  and to inquire in his temple.
For he will hide me in his shelter
  in the day of trouble;
he will conceal me under the cover of his tent;
  he will set me high on a rock. *Refrain*

Now my head is lifted up
  above my enemies all around me,
and I will offer in his tent
  sacrifices with shouts of joy;
I will sing and make melody to the Lord. *Refrain*

This joyful declaration of confidence in the Lord is the theme of Psalm 27. Sometimes we are afraid, but we know God will take care of us. With God for us, who can be against us? Tell the children that this song is a testimony of God's constant care.

Each short little phrase begins "The Lord is my . . . " and ends with a different word each time. Sing with firm confidence. Signing motions will help strengthen the ends of each of those little phrases. You may want to divide your children into two groups. The first two groups take turns on the first two phrases and then sing together on the "light and salvation."

Choose an older child to read the words from Psalm 27, all the children beginning with the refrain and repeating as indicated. The reader should portray the same confidence and strength as in the refrain. For accompaniment, use keyboard and/or guitar. Take delight in the final "splash" chord at the end (but don't bang it; be light, not heavy). Pianists may want to play that chord up an octave (especially the last time). Or invite Orff or bell players to peal out just that last chord each time.

Sing as the opening of worship, as a response, or as part of the Scripture reading of the day. Invite the congregation to join the children on the last statement of the refrain.

Words: from Psalm 27 (NIV); refrain by Michael Joncas, b. 1951
Music: Michael Joncas

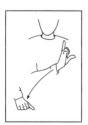

Lord

Life

Strength
(strong)

Light

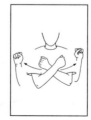

Salvation

Hope

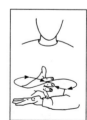

Song

♩ = 112

Amazing Grace 209

1 A - maz - ing grace— how sweet the sound— that
2 'Twas grace that taught my heart to fear, and
3 The Lord has prom - ised good to me, his

saved a wretch like me! I once was lost but
grace my fears re - lieved; how pre - cious did that
word my hope se - cures; he will my shield and

now am found, was blind but now I see.
grace ap - pear the hour I first be - lieved!
por - tion be as long as life en - dures.

4 Through many dangers, toils, and snares
   I have already come;
   'tis grace hath brought me safe thus far,
   and grace will lead me home.

5 When we've been there ten thousand years,
   bright shining as the sun,
   we've no less days to sing God's praise
   than when we'd first begun.

Words: stanzas 1-4, John Newton, 1779; stanza 5, *A Collection of Sacred Ballads*, 1790
Music: Virginia Harmony, 1831; arranged by Emily R. Brink, 1992
Arr. © 1994, CRC Publications

CM
NEW BRITAIN

Children will enjoy learning the story of this English hymn author. John Newton's mother died when he was only six; at eleven he joined his father at sea. After a short stint in the British Navy, he joined a slave trading ship that brought slaves from Africa. By that time Newton hated his life more and more. A turning point came when he prayed during a fierce storm that almost sank his ship. Gradually Newton's life changed. He became acquainted with Charles Wesley (see 19) and other Christians, and decided that he could no longer deal in the slave trade. Newton studied to become a minister and began preaching against slavery. This is the most famous of the many hymns Newton wrote.

The text of is drawn from several Scripture passages, including 1 Chronicles 17:16-17; Ephesians 1:3-14; John 9:25; and Psalm 142:5. Near the end of his life Newton said, "There are two things I'll never forget: that I was a sinner, and that Jesus Christ is a great Savior!" This hymn is Newton's spiritual autobiography, but the truth it affirms—that we are saved by grace alone—is one we can all confess with joy and gratitude.

One reason this song is so well-known in North America is the folk hymn tune from Appalachia with which the text is paired. Because the melody is pentatonic (only five pitches) it offers many possibilities for singing in canon or improvising accompaniments. For a two-part canon, the second part begins two measures after the first. Accompany with open-fifth block chords (G D) on a lower Orff instrument played every two measures or with random ringing of the pentatonic pitches in the melody (D E G A B) on tone chimes or bells.

Sing in worship as a response to God's forgiveness, as an assurance of pardon, or as a confession of faith. Invite the children to sing one stanza, perhaps stanza 3, by themselves.

Georg Neumark, the German author of this hymn, was a teacher who lived during the Thirty Years War. Neumark experienced many hardships—he was robbed, and for a time he couldn't find a job. When he finally got a position as a tutor, he was so relieved and grateful to God that he wrote these words. Ever since, Christians have sung this hymn of encouragement.

Though the text will be challenging to young singers, it is quite accessible to older children. Explain that "discerning" (st. 2) means understanding and "unswerving" (st. 3) means without weakening. The key word of the whole song is "trust."

Neumark also wrote the tune, composed in the typical "bar" form of German chorale tunes: the first section is repeated, and the third, though different, ends the same as the first two (AAB). The repetition and stepwise motion make the melody very accessible. Teach by the echo method, singing by four-measure phrases and tracing the direction of the melody with your hands. The triple meter will require good breaths and sustained notes. Let children's voices soar on

210 If You But Trust in God to Guide You

♩ = 120

1 If you but trust in God to guide you
2 On - ly be still and wait his plea - sure
3 Sing, pray, and keep his ways un - swerv - ing,

and place your con - fi - dence in him, you'll find him
in cheer - ful hope with heart con - tent. He fills your
of - fer your ser - vice faith - ful - ly, and trust his

al - ways there be - side you to give you hope and
needs to full - est mea - sure with what dis - cern - ing
word; though un - de - serv - ing, you'll find his prom - ise

strength with - in; for those who trust God's change - less
love has sent; doubt not our in - most wants are
true to be. God nev - er will for - sake in

Words: Georg Neumark, 1641
Music: Georg Neumark, 1657; arranged by Emily R. Brink, 1993
Arr. © 1994, CRC Publications

98 98 88
WER NUR DEN LIEBEN GOTT
Capo 3

love build on the rock that will not move.
known to him who chose us for his own.
need the soul that trusts in him in - deed.

Descant

the third section; encourage good posture, good breathing, and a clear, bright, sound. Accompany with keyboard, and when the children are confident, add the descant, played by a young flutist or violinist. Be sure to give good cues for the descant player after their measure of rest.

In worship, sing as a response of trust, hope, and confidence in God's faithfulness. Also sing for New Year's Day, profession of faith, or a commissioning service.

Illustration: The lamp and open Bible illustrate Psalm 119:105: "Your word is a lamp unto my feet and a light for my path" (see 57, which is a setting of this song). Psalm 119 sings the praises of God's Word and God's law, that is, God's loving will for his people. God's Word is compared to a light that shines ahead of us as we travel the road of life. That light shows us where we should go and helps us avoid dangers.

This is one of several songs in this hymnal written by Natalie Sleeth (for more on Sleeth, see 175).

Sing briskly, with confidence. Sing stanzas 1 and 4 medium-loudly. Stanza 2 should start out softly and build in volume until stanza 3, which should be sung very strongly. Because the song has two endings and a repeat, children may need help following along at first. Point out that it is written in the form AABAA. Notice that stanza 3 has a different melody than the others. Stanza 5 is actually a repeat of stanza 1, but a descant may be added. You may want to teach the descant to all the children, and then divide the group in two for a two-part choral ending. For a more elaborate arrangement, purchase a copy of the anthem for the pianist; children can sing from this setting. Try adding tambourine on stanzas 1 and 4. Choose flute or recorder to play the melody on selected stanzas.

Sing in worship services before or after a prayer or as a choral response to the benediction. Or sing at services that include the reception of new members, baptism, profession of faith, or commitment to following God's will. It is also appropriate for funeral or memorial services.

211 Everywhere I Go

Words and Music: Natalie Sleeth, 1975; arranged by Charlotte Larsen, 1992
Words and melody © 1975, Choristers Guild.

3 He is with me day by day; he will be my strength and stay; from his path I will not stray but fol-low in his way.

D.C. al Fine

Descant for instrument or voices on stanza 5

Ev - ery - where God is there, tend - ing all with lov - ing care, He is near me ev - ery - where I go.

Illustration: The sun, moon, stars, and the world portray the wide expanse of God's creation. They also testify to our assurance that God is present everywhere (see especially Ps. 139:7-12). God's presence and nearness is a great comfort to his children.

Proverbs 3:5-6 NKJV is set to music in this short Scripture chorus by Frank Hernandez (for more on Hernandez, see 57). This proverb gives wise advice to all those who want to follow Jesus. Children will understand what it means to follow the leader. The Lord will lead us if we follow him.

The song includes three instructions for living. Using motions will help children remember them. For the first, place hands over heart. Explain that the second phrase, "lean not on your own understanding," means something like: "Don't think you know it all!" Place hands on head. On the third phrase, cup hands around mouth; to "acknowledge" the Lord means to speak up and say whom you are trusting.

This flowing melody helps create the spirit of quiet confidence at the heart of the text. Children will be tempted to sing in one-measure phrases, so encourage them to take good breaths and sing through the long notes, breathing only at the rests. Sing very smoothly, ending on a firm long note.

In worship sing as a response or introduction to any Scripture reading, for profession of faith, for the beginning of the church school year, or at the close of worship as a fitting reminder for daily living.

212 Trust in the Lord

♩ = 100

Trust in the Lord with all your heart and lean not on your own un-der-stand-ing. In all your ways ac-know-ledge him, and he shall di-rect your paths.

Words: Proverbs 3:5-6 (NKJV)
Music: Frank Hernandez, 1990; arranged by Norma de Waal Malefyt, 1992

Trust and Obey 213

♩ = 120

When we walk with the Lord in the light of his
While we do his good will he a - bides with us

Word, what a glo - ry he sheds on our way!
still, and with all who will

trust and o - bey. Trust and o - bey, for there's

no oth - er way to be hap - py in

Je - sus but to trust and o - bey.

Words: John H. Sammis, 1887
Music: Daniel B. Towner, 1887

669 D with refrain
TRUST AND OBEY
Capo 3

In 1887, Rev. John Sammis, a Presbyterian minister, heard of a young man who, when he became a Christian, testified, "I am not quite sure, but I am going to trust and I am going to obey." Inspired by these words, Rev. Sammis wrote this hymn, based on 1 John 5:2-3 and Proverbs 16:20. Only the first stanza is included here.

All children know the consequences of not obeying their parents; they get into trouble! Children need to trust wise parents that obedience is really the only way that things go well. Only when we trust and obey the Lord will we be "happy in Jesus."

The melody is by Daniel Towner, composer of over 2,000 gospel songs, and long-time music instructor at Moody Bible Institute. Echo the tune with your children, line by line. Work on breathing at the punctuation markings, trying to sing through the other long notes. On the refrain, however, the children will need an extra breath; add one after "Jesus," adding an extra beat in order to do so. But don't slow it down; just one extra quarter note will be enough.

Accompany with keyboard, guitar, or autoharp. For a simple piano duet, create a bass line out of the chord symbols. In other words, for the first three beats play a low F, then move down to C and right back up to F, and so on.

In worship, sing before or after Scripture or sermon, especially on any occasion of commitment and dedication. If available, have your congregation sing other stanzas, with the children joining on the chorus.

This spiritual may be African-American or it may be a "white" spiritual from the rural Appalachian culture. Point out to the children that our lives can be described as a journey or walk. Ask them to tell about some of the trials and troubles they see around them. This song asks Jesus to be with us even in our troubles. It expresses our faith that God is walking with us.

The tune is somber and rather plaintive in character. A "walking" tempo should hold steady, but the melody should feel free over the basic beat. Encourage children to use their "head" voices on the third phrase of the song and to use them in the lower tones as well. The syncopation at the end of the third line is repeated exactly in the last line; make sure you know it well before trying to teach the children.

When sung as a prayer, sing in a simple, humble manner. Accompany quietly with guitar, autoharp, or keyboard. As an affirmation of faith, sing more strongly. If your older children are very confident, try singing as a two-part round, with the second group coming in after one measure. The pentatonic melody and the rhythm, which moves back and forth every measure between shorter and longer notes, make this a good candidate for singing in canon.

Sing in worship as part of the service of confession, as part of a prayer, and in services where the focus is on the comfort we have in Jesus.

214 I Want Jesus to Walk with Me

♩ = 80

Words and Music: African-American spiritual

WALK WITH ME

Those Who Wait upon the Lord 215

♩ = 88

D   A   D

1 Those who wait up-on the Lord shall re-new their strength,
2 Those who love the God of life shall re-new their strength,
3 Those who live a life of love shall re-new their strength,

Em   A   D

they shall mount up on wings as ea-gles;

G   A   Bm

they shall run and not be wea-ry, they shall walk and not faint.

Em   A⁷   D   G   D

Help us, Lord; help us, Lord, in your way.

4 Those who offer gifts of praise . . . .
5 Those who grow in his wisdom . . . .
6 Those who seek first his kingdom . . . .
7 Those who wait upon the Lord . . . .

Words and Music: Stuart Hamblen, based on Isaiah 40:31; arranged by
    Emily R. Brink, 1993

TEACH ME LORD
Capo 2

Introduce this comforting song, based on Isaiah 40:31, by asking the children what they know about eagles. Eagles, which have always been known for their sharp vision and powerful wings, are mentioned in several Scripture passages (see 205). This song lists several ways that we can become strong again after we have been weak and tired. Children could add to the many stanzas offered here. The song is both a confident expression of faith and a prayer for strength to live God's way.

Since only one line changes for each stanza, it is very easy to learn. In later sessions teach the additional stanzas about activities we should be involved in as we wait upon (trust) the Lord.

This tune will soon become one of your children's favorites. Trace the melody direction with your hand motions. Sing smoothly, with firm confidence.

Include this delightful song in any service (even early Advent) that emphasizes hope in the Lord. Sing as a response to God's will for living, a response of assurance following the reading of Isaiah 40:28-31, or as closing words of encouragement. Choose solos or small groups to sing additional relevant stanzas, with everyone responding on the final line. Include the congregation on the final repeat of stanza 1. Consider pairing with "Psalm 91" (205).

216 Psalm 46

♩= 80

Refrain
Dm / Gm / Dm

God is my rock and my sal - va - tion, the
El Se - ñor es mi fuer - za, mi

Am⁷ / 1 Dm / 2 Dm

strength___ of my life. life.
ro - ca y sal - va - ción. ción.

God is our refuge and strength,
    an ever-present help in trouble.
Therefore we will not fear, though the earth give way
    and the mountains fall into the heart of the sea,
though its waters roar and foam
    and the mountains quake with their surging. *Refrain*

There is a river whose streams make glad the city of God,
    the holy place where the Most High dwells.
God is within her, she will not fall;
    God will help her at break of day.
Nations are in uproar, kingdoms fall;
    he lifts his voice, the earth melts. *Refrain*

Come and see the works of the Lord,
    the desolations he has brought on the earth.
He makes wars cease to the ends of the earth;
    he breaks the bow and shatters the spear,
    he burns the shields with fire.
"Be still and know that I am God;
    I will be exalted among the nations,
    I will be exalted in the earth." *Refrain*

This refrain is part of a song Juan Espinosa wrote based on Psalm 46. That Psalm has wonderful promises in it; one of the most encouraging is that God will make "wars to cease." Children (and adults!) can take comfort from God's promise that all fighting and trouble will one day be over.

The refrain is very vigorous—and rather low for children's voices. Don't push their voices on the lower notes. The repeat sign indicates that the best way to sing this is to begin in English and then repeat in Spanish. Children will enjoy singing in two languages; a guide to pronunciation is given below. If they also sign it, they will be communicating in three languages!

The most typical instrument for accompanying music in this style is the guitar. For an introduction, have the guitar play the first measure vigorously two times before the children enter.

When children know the refrain, add the entire psalm. Choose a good reader from among the older children. Or choose three readers, one for each section of the psalm text. Begin with the refrain and sing again after each section of the psalm.

Sing and read this psalm of trust and encouragement in any service, particularly when praying for peace in the world.

El Señor *(el Say -NYOUR)*

es mi fuerza *(es mee foo-AIR-zah)*

mi ro-ca y salvacion *(mee ROW-kah‿ee sahl-VAH-see‿own)*

Words: Psalm 46 (NIV)
Music: Refrain by Juan A. Espinosa, 1978

Capo 5

God

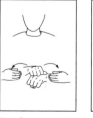
Rock

Salvation

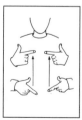
Strength

Life

Protect Me, God: I Trust in You 217

♩ = 96

1 Pro - tect me, God: I trust in you. I tell you now,
2 Your peo - ple are a cho - sen race, and I de - light
3 Lord God, you are my food and drink; my work for you
4 Thank you, my Lord, for warn - ing me; by night and day

"You are my Lord; on you my hap - pi - ness de - pends."
in faith - ful friends, but pa - gan ways I will not share.
is joy in - deed; glad is the her - i - tage that's mine.
you guide my thoughts. With you be - fore me, I stand firm.

Pro - tect me, God: I trust in you.

Flute or Violin Descant

Cello or Piano

Words: Psalm 16; versified by Michael Saward, 1970
Music: M. Christian T. Strover, 1973; arranged by Charlotte Larson, 1992; descant by Emily R. Brink, 1991

888 with refrain
MEPHIBOSHETH
Capo 3

Several years ago in England, a number of Anglican clergy and musicians looked for new ways to make the psalms come alive for this generation. Using fresh language from translations and varied musical styles, the group compiled an influential collection called *Psalm Praise*. This setting of Psalm 16:1-8 is one of the best of the collection. The refrain is a simple, trusting prayer for protection; the stanzas are a confession of delight, trust, and confidence in the Lord.

Christian Strover called his tune MEPHIBOSHETH. He explains, "Mephibosheth, a son of Saul, was lame in both feet. He was welcomed by David and lived in his house and was fed at his table. The prayer of the song is appropriately illustrated in David's care and provision."

The phrases of the melody are short, so teaching by the echo method will be effective. All children can sing the refrain; teach the stanzas to the older children. The only tricky part in the melody is the group of triplets; make sure you do not rush the beginning of the next measure. First instruct children to hum the melody, accompanied only by a single melodic line. Clap or tap a strong half-note pulse, and the tricky rhythms should fall into place. Create a beautiful anthem, including young instrumentalists playing the descant for several stanzas and also as the introduction.

Sing this prayer for safekeeping as part of a Lord's Supper service, for a profession of faith, or at the conclusion of a service.

218 When I Am Afraid

♩= 60

All children know what it is to be afraid. Ask them to give examples of what frightens them and what they do when they are afraid. Then introduce this song by Frank Hernandez (see 57), based on Psalm 56:3-4a. When David wrote this psalm, his enemies were after him and he was very afraid. Tell the children that when we are afraid like David was, we too can sing this song. David knew that God would take care of him.

The song is constructed in two parts, with the first part repeated at the beginning and then again at the end (AABA). Begin with the first section, singing along with the signing motions.

Save the second section for another time. If you are short on time or have very young singers, assign the middle section to a group of older children. Accompany with keyboard, guitar, or autoharp. Add a tambourine on the A section, lightly playing on the beats; in section B add a soft hand drum, or even a triangle, on beats 1, 3, and 4. Sing with confidence, knowing that we really can trust in God!

In worship, sing along with the reading of Psalm 56 (in the same style as 216) or with another appropriate psalm. Or sing as a response to a sermon on trusting in God.

Lyrics: When I am a-fraid, I will trust in you, I will trust in you, I will trust in you. When I am a-fraid, I will trust in you, in God, whose word I praise, God, whose word I praise. In God I trust when I am a-

Words: Frank Hernandez; based on Psalm 56:3-4a
Music: Frank Hernandez; arranged by Emily R. Brink, 1994

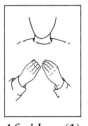
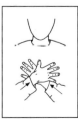
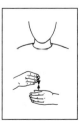

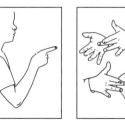
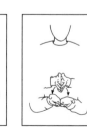

Afraid   (1)   (2) Trust   (1)   (2) You   Word   Book)
                                                          (Jesus'

C   F   G   Am

fraid,   in   God   I   trust,   in

D⁷   G   D   G   D.C.

God, whose word I praise.

♩. = 80

Our Help 219

Speech rhythm

Our help,   our help,   our help   comes from the   Lord,

the   Ma - ker   of   heav - en   and   earth.

Our help,   our help,   our help   comes from the   Lord.

Ostinato accompaniment:

Our   help,

Words: Psalm 121:2; Psalm 124:8
Music: Richard L. Van Oss, 1992
© 1994, CRC Publications

John Calvin began worship services with these words from Psalm 124:8 (and Ps. 121:8). Many churches in the Reformed tradition still continue this practice. This declaration of dependence upon God even has a name, "votum," though no one seems to know where it comes from.

This speech choir setting is meant for two or three groups. Two small groups could perform the echo ostinato antiphonally or standing together, as the large group speaks the main text. Children can accompany themselves with combinations of claps and finger snaps, sticks, etc. Assign someone to keep a steady beat on a hand drum. Consider accompanying with Orff instruments playing random pitches on F G A C D (take off all the bars but those). Repeat the entire piece, adding new instruments each time. Start with hand drum and voices alone, then add rhythm instruments, and finally melodic Orff instruments.

In worship, begin the service with the worship leader asking, "Children of God, where does your help come from?" Then the children respond. This piece could be used as an unusual processional: if your church has three aisles, the main group could come down the center, with the antiphonal ostinato groups coming down each side aisle.

Consider pairing with a related song such as "Trust in the Lord," (212) or "When I Am Afraid" (218). Include in a litany, perhaps on the occasion of a church anniversary, dedication, Old Year's Eve, or New Year's Day.

220 Lead Me, Guide Me

♩ = 108

This African-American gospel song was written by Doris Mae Akers. The deeply personal text reflects our desire for God's leading, guidance, and protection. Scripture references for the refrain include Psalm 5:8 and Luke 1:79; for stanza 2, Psalm 23:3.

Improvisation is a trademark of early gospel music. Thus the printed notes are intended (only) as guides for the creativity of singer(s) and accompanist(s). The piano is the ideal accompanying instrument. Feel free to improvise additional chords or triplet figures. Don't worry about the exact rhythm of the dotted eighths and sixteenths; just make them triplets as well.

A relatively slow tempo best suits the devotional character of this hymn. The words of the refrain are most appropriate for children; teach stanza 2 in conjunction with the memorization of Psalm 23.

Children will delight in singing this gospel hymn! Options for singing include having an older child or group singing the stanzas and all children singing the refrain. In worship, the congregation could sing the stanzas, with the children responding on the refrain; or, if the children know the stanzas, the congregation could join them on each refrain.

Sing especially when the focus of worship is on personal testimony and prayer for divine guidance.

Words and Music: Doris M. Akers; arranged by Richard Smallwood, 1981

LEAD ME
Capo 1

1 I am weak and I need your strength and power
2 Help me walk in the paths of right - eous - ness;
3 I am lost if you take your hand from me,

to en - dure with grace___ my weak - est hour.
be my aid when Sa - tan and sin op - press.
I am blind with - out___ your light to see.

Help me through the dark - ness your face to see.
I am trust - ing you___ what - e'er may be.
Lord, for - ev - er may I your ser - vant be.

Lead me, O Lord, lead me.

Repeat refrain

Many Christians have prayed these words by Richard of Chichester, who lived about 800 years ago in England. (The original first line reads "Day by day, dear Lord, of thee three things. . . .") We need to pray daily for God's help to see, to love, and to follow Jesus, our Lord. How can we see Jesus? In a way, we see Jesus in each other because Jesus told us that he would live in us (John 14:20). We try to be like Jesus, and try to see Jesus in others too.

The words of this short prayer will be easy for children to learn. The opening phrase tells what this prayer is about, and then come three parallel rhymed phrases, rounded off by the repetition of "day by day."

The tune may be a bit more difficult, especially the leaps in the second phrase. Trace the direction of the melody with your hands as you sing. Encourage the children to sing with smooth voices. On "clear-ly" and "dearly," stress the first syllable and avoid a hard "landing" on the second.

Encourage children to sing as a daily morning prayer in their personal or family worship time. In corporate worship, sing as a prayer response.

221 Day By Day

♩ = 63

Day by day, dear Lord, for these three things I pray: to see you more clear-ly, to love you more dear-ly, to fol-low you more near-ly day by day.

Words: Richard of Chichester, 1197-1253
Music: D. Austin; harmonized by Richard L. Van Oss, 1992
© D. Austin

Capo 5

Illustration: "Lead Me, Guide Me" (220) and "Day by Day" are about God's leading and our following. From Abraham traveling "to the land that I will show you" to Paul's mission journeys, God has been leading his people and they have followed. The father and daughter is a fitting illustration of God's caring guidance and our trusting response.

♩ = 72

I Belong to God 222

(hands on chest)
You made ev - ery part of me, and I be - long to you. I'll

(point to mouth)
lift my voice to sing for you,

(hands outstretched)
lift my hands to work for you,

(point to eyes)
use my eyes to see your world,

(point to ears)
use my ears to hear your word.

(hands on chest)
You made ev - ery part of me, and I be - long to you.

"Body, mind, spirit, voice . . . it takes the whole person to sing and rejoice," says Helen Kemp, arranger of this song and internationally-recognized authority on training children's voices. This song for young children calls on the whole body to praise God.

The repetition in the melody makes this little confession accessible to even the youngest children. Use the motions to help teach the words. Explain to the children that by their good tone, posture, breathing, and pronunciation, they are using "every part" to praise God!

In congregational worship, have younger children sing this at a baptism service or at any time of offering and dedication. Consider pairing with the "Psalm 139" refrain (228), which could precede and follow this song. Or have the children sing this song before and after the congregational singing of "Take My Life" (sung to the traditional tune in F).

Words and Music: Marie Pooler, altered by Helen Kemp

Capo 5

223 Believe in the Lord

♩ = 112

"What must I do to be saved?" the Philippian jailer asked Paul. He answered, "Believe in the Lord Jesus, and you will be saved" (Acts 16:31). Children will enjoy hearing this story. Although Paul and Silas had been beaten and it was late at night, they were praying and singing hymns to God. Suddenly a violent earthquake shook the prison, and the doors flew open. Paul and Silas could have walked out, but they stayed. The jailer was so impressed that he asked how he could be saved. He washed their wounds and fed them supper. That very night, he and his whole family were baptized.

Frank Hernandez has provided a simple Scripture chorus to help children memorize this concise statement of salvation (for more on Hernandez, see 57). As an introduction, ask one child to ask the jailer's question. The others sing this response.

Sing and have the children echo the first two phrases. Then ask if the phrases are the same or different. Ask the same question after the third and fourth phrases. When the children know the song, sing it twice. On the repeat, divide into two groups, singing every other phrase until joining together on the final phrase. Accompany with keyboard and/or guitar or with flute and guitar.

In congregational worship, sing any time the theme is God's plan of salvation, particularly when the sermon is from this part of Acts or the book of Philippians.

Words: Acts 16:31
Music: Frank Hernandez

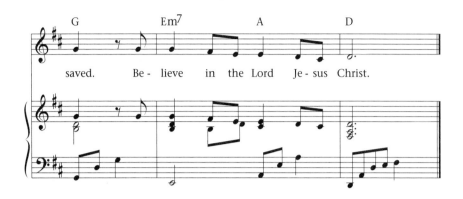

saved.   Be - lieve   in   the   Lord   Je - sus   Christ.

♩ = 100

Be Still 224

Group 1

2/4 "Be   still.   Be   still."

Group 2

"Be   still and   know   that   I   am   God."

After one person begins by announcing "And God said,"
group 1 begins with a hushed articulate command; group 2 adds their
voices; then group 1 continues alone, diminishing toward the end.

Many children know Psalm 46:10 set to the melody at 225. Here is another setting for speech choir by Betty Ann Ramseth.

Teach this Scripture verse to your youngest children, and have them contribute it in congregational worship before the Scripture reading. Add a soft drum beat playing quarter notes to keep the children together. Perform as indicated in two groups or all together as one group. Consider pairing with 225.

Words: Psalm 46:10
Music: Betty Ann Ramseth, 1970

Reprinted from *That I May Speak*, © 1970, Augsburg Publishing House. Reprinted by permission of Augsburg Fortress.

225 Be Still and Know

♩ = 112

This simple Scripture chorus (see also 224) combines parts of three short texts: Psalm 46:10 (st. 1), Exodus 15:26 (st. 2), and perhaps Psalm 31:14 (st. 3). Make sure the children understand that God is speaking in stanzas 1 and 2. In stanza 3, we are telling God that we believe and trust in him.

As the first line suggests, sing with quiet confidence. Make sure the children don't "slide" or "scoop" where one word is sung on two notes. You may want to split the children into two groups for the first stanza. One group whispers "Be still" over and over (with "be" getting one beat and "still" getting two beats and the accent), while the second group sings the song. In worship, sing stanza 1 as a call to worship, before the prayer of confession, or before the Scripture lesson. Also sing as an alternate refrain for Psalm 46 (see 216) or in combination with 224. Sing stanza 2 in a healing service. Sing stanza 3 alone or pair with "When I Am Afraid" (218) as a response of faith near the end of the service.

1 Be still and know that I am God.
2 I am the Lord who heals your life.
3 In you, O Lord, we put our trust.

Be still and know that I am God.
I am the Lord who heals your life.
In you, O Lord, we put our trust.

Be still and know that I am God.
I am the Lord who heals your life.
In you, O Lord, we put our trust.

Words: anonymous, based on Psalm 46:10; Exodus 15:26; Psalm 31:14
Music: anonymous; arranged by Norma de Waal Malefyt, 1992
Arr. © 1994, CRC Publications

888
BE STILL AND KNOW

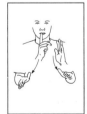

Be still

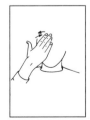
Know

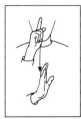
God

I Have Decided to Follow Jesus 226

♩ = 84

1 I have de-cid-ed to fol-low Je-sus, I have de-cid-ed to fol-low Je-sus, I have de-cid-ed to fol-low Je-sus— no turn-ing back, no turn-ing back.

2 The world behind me, the cross before me—(3x)
   no turning back, no turning back.

3 Though none go with me, I still will follow . . . .

4 Will you decide now to follow Jesus? . . .

Words and Music: anonymous

Throughout history, God calls people and they listen and obey. God called Samuel, and he listened and obeyed. Jesus called the disciples to follow him, and they did. Today, God still calls us to listen, follow, and obey. And we need to respond.

This song of commitment to following Jesus may have come from India. It is very appropriate for a new believer, especially one who is making a costly change. Let children know that sometimes when people leave another religion to make a commitment to Christ, other family members throw them out or persecute them. Most North Americans don't face that kind of costly commitment.

But all Christians know that every day we need to follow Jesus. We need to find the courage to do what is right, "though none go with me." The final line of the refrain suggests that the writer of this song made a real "turn" in his or her life—to "repent" means to turn around and go in another direction.

Sing with firm conviction, keeping a steady beat, perhaps clapping on the half notes. Accompany with keyboard, guitar, or autoharp. Or create a second instrumental part by having a cello play the tenor line or having that same line played an octave higher by oboe or violin.

In worship, sing as a response to a call to commitment or following a profession of faith.

227 Standing On the Lord's Side

This text comes from the covenant renewal ceremony at the end of Joshua's life (Josh. 24). Joshua assembled all the tribes of Israel after they had begun living in the promised land. He reminded them how God had protected Abraham, Isaac, and Jacob; how God had brought them out of Egypt; and how God had given them this land. Joshua called the Israelites to fear God and serve him. He told them to "take a stand," to choose between false gods or the true God. "But as for me and my household, we will serve the Lord" (v. 15). Then the people made their promise; three times they said, "We will serve the Lord" (vv. 18, 21, 24).

This call-and-response song employs much repetition of words and music. The leader initiates the question, and all children respond with their answer. Ask several children to be leaders, even those who are shy. Note that their ending notes rise on the first question but fall on the second. Repeat the song with different leaders, and treat the section beginning "I stand, I stand" like a refrain, with everyone singing.

Sing with confidence, expressing your unfailing desire to "stand on the Lord's side." Play the accompaniment with vigor, either on the piano or guitar. As an expression of faith, sing after a spoken profession of faith.

Words and Music: traditional; arranged by Emily R. Brink, 1992
Arr. © 1994, CRC Publications

♩ = 66

Psalm 139 228

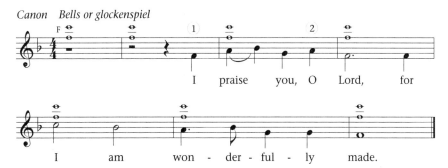

Canon *Bells or glockenspiel*

I praise you, O Lord, for

I am won - der - ful - ly made.

Lord, you have examined me
　and know all about me.
You know when I sit down and when I get up.
　You know my thoughts before I think them.
You know where I go and where I lie down.
　You know thoroughly everything I do.
Lord, even before I say a word, you already know it. *Refrain*

You made my whole being;
　you formed me in my mother's body.
I praise you because you made me in an
　amazing and wonderful way.
What you have done is wonderful.
　I know this very well. *Refrain*

You saw my bones being formed
　as I took shape in my mother's body.
When I was put together there,
　you saw my body as it was formed.
All the days planned for me
　were written in your book
　before I was one day old. *Refrain*

God, your thoughts are precious to me.
　They are so many!
If I could count them,
　they would be more than all the grains of sand. *Refrain*

This responsorial setting of Psalm 139 begins with a refrain of praise for God's creation of human life. Since our society sends mixed signals on the value of life, children need to be assured of God's care for them. This song of faith affirms how God wonderfully and lovingly made us.

Based on verse 14, this quiet and simple refrain introduces and concludes the reading of the psalm text. It is also woven into the text. The clear quality of a handbell or glockenspiel ideally accompanies the refrain. Once the children know the response, encourage them to sing it in a two-part round. For a variation, a flute could also play the second part of the round.

For congregational worship, choose a good reader from among your older children or choose four readers, one for each section of the psalm. Sing any time Psalm 139 would be appropriate. Consider using as a frame for "I Belong to God" (222).

Words: Psalm 139:1-4, 13-18 (NIV); refrain by Randolph Currie
Music: Randolph Currie

229 Psalm 1

♩ = 54

Canon

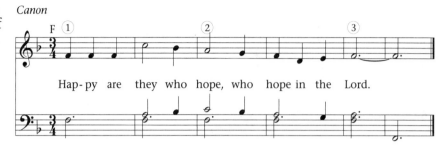

Hap-py are they who hope, who hope in the Lord.

Happy are those
  who do not follow the advice of the wicked,
or take the path that sinners tread,
  or sit in the seat of scoffers;
but their delight is in the law of the Lord
  and on his law they meditate day and night. *Refrain*

They are like trees
  planted by the streams of water,
which yield their fruit in its season,
  and their leaves do not wither.
In all that they do, they prosper. *Refrain*

The wicked are not so,
  but are like chaff that the wind drives away.
Therefore the wicked will not stand in the judgement,
  nor sinners in the congregation of the righteous;
for the Lord watches over the way of the righteous,
  but the way of the wicked will perish. *Refrain*

Orff instrument patterns
Alto metallophone   Soprano xylophone

Psalm 1 sets out two patterns for living: one that involves finding delight in the Lord and one that doesn't. This setting of the psalm is responsorial: a short refrain is sung at the beginning and at intervals throughout the reading or chanting of the entire psalm text. "Responsorial" simply refers to the response structure.

The refrain is very simple: after hearing it once or twice, everyone should be able to join in without the need for printed music. Begin with Orff instruments (or piano, or bells, or any other instruments that would help set the pitch clearly). Play the "alto" pattern twice, then add the "soprano" pattern twice, then have a soloist sing the refrain, followed immediately by the children singing it. Continue to precede each statement of the refrain by having the instruments play their pattern twice together. After a few weeks, if the refrain is going well, repeat the final statement as a two- or three-part round. Children will enjoy that challenge! Select children who are willing to work at reading the psalm well so that word and music, psalm and refrain, form one entire piece.

Sing in worship at the service of confession as a guide for grateful living.

Words: Psalm 1 (NRSV); refrain by Robert J. Thompson
Music: Robert J. Thompson; arranged by Emily R. Brink, 1994

♩ = 84

Rejoice in the Lord Always 230

Round

① F / C⁷ / F
(clap)

Re - joice in the Lord al - ways, and a - gain I say, Re - joice!

② F C⁷ F

Re - joice in the Lord al - ways, and a - gain I say, Re - joice!

③ C⁷ F

Re - joice! Re - joice! And a - gain I say, Re - joice!

④ C⁷ F

Re - joice! Re - joice! And a - gain I say, Re - joice!

Orff instruments

Alto metallophone   Glockenspiel

Words: Philippians 4:4
Music: traditional; arranged by Emily R. Brink, 1993
Arr. © 1994, CRC Publications

REJOICE
Capo 3

Sing this Bible song cheerfully, in keeping with Paul's advice in Philippians 4:4 to rejoice. As the word "again" suggests, the text includes much repetition, making it accessible to very young children. In fact the very first line contains the entire text of the song.

As with many popular folk hymns, different versions of the tune exist. This one features a second line that is higher than the first. After the children know the song, have them listen to the beautiful harmony created when the lines are combined. Invite different melody instruments to join the voice parts on the round, two parts at first, then perhaps expanding if the children know it well. Ask a young musician to accompany on the autoharp since there are only two chords. If you do not have a metallophone, include handbells or the piano lightly, an octave higher. Clap or snap the glockenspiel's rhythm during the last two lines. Sing rhythmically and enthusiastically.

Begin your worship with this joyful song or sing as a response to a declaration of pardon. After the children sing it through once, have them begin the round, joined by the congregation. Also consider singing as a psalm refrain in responsorial style to a joyful psalm, for example, Psalm 126.

After Jesus ascended into heaven, he told his followers to wait in Jerusalem "for the gift my Father promised, which you have heard me speak about." That precious gift came ten days later: the Holy Spirit. This round has two connected themes: the role of the Spirit in our lives, and our response of love for Jesus and "family, friends, and neighbors." The text is unusual in that the two traditional stanzas are unrelated, and two others were contributed by members of this hymnal committee. Altogether, this little Pentecost round neatly contains the summary of the law: to love God above all and our neighbors as ourselves.

The melody is very simple and accessible to children's voices. Accompany with Orff instruments if possible, or have older children play those patterns in different octaves on the piano. Use two keyboards if you have them! Add the accompaniment parts one at a time, the children singing a stanza with each instrument.

When children know the text and melody, introduce the round in two parts at first, with an instrument or older singer(s) on the second part. If your children can sing the four parts, great. If not, keep the children in two parts and let instruments provide third and fourth. For an introduction, begin with the bass xylophone, after two measures add the alto glockenspiel, and two measures later bring in the singers. Wait with the third and fourth patterns until later stanzas. For a little coda, or postlude, reverse the order.

Sing on Pentecost Sunday or any time as the summary of the law, an offertory, or as a final "charge" to the congregation just before the benediction.

231 Jesus, Jesus, Let Us Tell You

♩ = 63

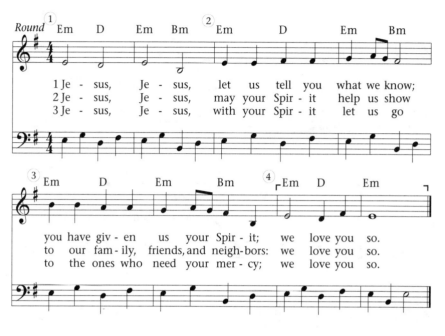

1 Je - sus, Je - sus, let us tell you what we know;
2 Je - sus, Je - sus, may your Spir - it help us show
3 Je - sus, Je - sus, with your Spir - it let us go

you have giv - en us your Spir - it; we love you so.
to our fam - ily, friends, and neigh - bors: we love you so.
to the ones who need your mer - cy; we love you so.

Orff instruments

Another traditional stanza, "The Love Round":

4 Love, love, love, love,
Christians this_is your call:
Love our neighbors as ourselves
for God loves us all.

Words: Stanzas 1 and 4, traditional; stanza 2, Bert Polman; stanza 3, Joanne Hamilton
Music: traditional; arranged by Richard L. Van Oss, 1992

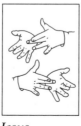

Jesus

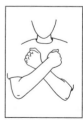

Love

♩ = 84 **Christ, You Are the Fullness** **232**

1 Christ, you are the full-ness of God, first-born of
2 Since we have been raised with you, Lord, help keep our
3 Help us live in peace as true mem-bers of your

ev-ery-thing. For by you__ all things were__
hearts and minds pure and set on things that build your
bod-y. Let your word dwell rich-ly in us

made; you hold them up. You are head of the
rule o'er all the earth. All our life is now
as we teach and sing. Thanks and praise be to

church, which is your bod-y. First-born from the
hid-den with__ you in God. When you come a-
God through you, Lord Je-sus. In what-e'er we

dead, you in all things are su-preme!
gain, we will share your glo-ry.
do let your name re-ceive the praise!

Descant

play 4 times

Orff instrument patterns
Bass xylophone   *Alto metallophone*   *Glockenspiel or bells*

Play pitches softly in random order, not in a row.

Words: Colossians 1:15-18; 3:1-4, 15-17; versified by Bert Polman, 1986
Music: Korean; arranged by Emily R. Brink, 1994
Text © 1987, arr. © 1994, CRC Publications

This hymn of praise to Jesus Christ is based on several passages in Colossians.

- *Stanza 1:* Jesus is truly God; he created everything, and he conquered death (Col. 1:15-18).

- *Stanza 2:* Because Jesus was raised from the dead, we have been raised with him! We serve Jesus as he builds his rule until he comes back again, and then we will live with him (Col. 3:1-4).

- *Stanza 3:* Christ is our leader and the church is his body. We will live together in peace, learning more about God's goodness and singing his praises (Col. 3:15-17).

The text was written for this Korean folk tune. The melody is constructed in four-measure phrases; the second and fourth are repeated (ABCB); the second half of A and C are the same. Even then, the long phrases and triplet rhythms are challenging (though children will love the melody!). The pentatonic (only five pitches) structure offers interesting possibilities for improvising accompaniments. One arrangement possibility is given below. Either flute, recorder, or violin could play the descant.

Sing during services that emphasize Christ's rule over all creation and the worldwide church, especially during the Easter season, on Ascension Day, or Worldwide Communion Sunday. Perhaps have the children's instruments accompany the adult choir, and have the adults and children sing it together.

Introduction: m. 1, gong; m. 2, bass xylophone begins and plays throughout; m. 4, alto metallophone begins and plays throughout; m. 6, flute begins first eight measures of melody, then plays along on st. 1. Gong plays only as indicated on each stanza.

Interlude: four measures; flute drops out; add glockenspiel which now plays to end; sing st. 2.

Interlude: four measures; add flute descant, which continues to end; sing st. 3.

Postlude: instruments continue four more measures; for final note, everyone plays G or D.

The text of this song by Lois Brokering serves as a definition of the title, "Discipleship." It can easily be divided into two sections: the refrain, which asks how we can follow Jesus, and stanzas, which respond to that question in various practical ways. The childlike responses can be learned easily.

The buoyant melody will immediately catch children's attention. Encourage children to sing with a "lilting" rather than "marching" pulse of two beats per measure. A keyboard or guitar will provide adequate accompaniment. The structure invites dividing the children into soloists or groups. For example, each question of the refrain could be sung by a different person. Depending on your particular situation, children could either ask the questions or respond with answers. The refrain both begins and ends the song. If you would prefer to conclude with statements rather than questions, consider substituting the words "This is what it means" for "What does it mean" in each of the final phrases of the refrain. The rhythm of the first note would then become a dotted eighth and a sixteenth. When sung this way, have the entire group of children sing the final refrain.

Sing in any service where the theme is discipleship, as a response in the service of confession, as an offertory, or at the conclusion of the service.

233 Discipleship

♩ = 72

Words and Music: Lois Brokering
© 1990, Herb Associates. Used by permission.

Capo 3

said. I can help my broth - er, see that
wrong. I can sing his prais - es in both

he is fed. I can show my sis - ter
words and song. I'll be friends with oth - ers

kind - ness and care. I can show my
who aren't like me. They be - long to

friends that I know how to share.
Je - sus: we all do, you see.

Repeat refrain

234 Time to Pray

♩= 66

This simple song of prayer and dedication is accessible to all children. Even the youngest can sing the repeated responses in each stanza. The use of signing motions (see index) would also be effective for those responses.

The melody is well suited to young children's voices—its limited range and repetition make it easy to learn. Accompaniment can be played on keyboard, autoharp, or guitar. For a simple alternative accompaniment, create an ostinato pattern one measure long by playing a half note on E-flat followed by two quarter notes on B-flat. This ostinato could be played with handbells or on Orff instruments.

In congregational worship, sing as a call to prayer or as a song of dedication during an offering.

1 Time to pray, time to say, thank you, God, thank you, God,
2 Time to sing, time to bring, praise to God, praise to God,
3 Time to live, time to give all to God, all to God.

for our loved ones far and near, for our friends and
in the night and in the day, ev - ery - thing we
When the need - y seek our door, give un - til we

neigh - bors here. Thank you, God. Thank you, God.
do and say. Praise to God. Praise to God.
have no more. All is God's. All is God's.

Words and Music: Joe Pinson, 1975
© 1975, Joe Pinson

Capo 1

Thank

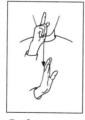

God

Praise

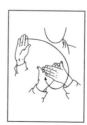

All

For the Fruit of All Creation 235

♩ = 112

1 For the fruit of all cre-a-tion, thanks be to God.
2 In the just re-ward of la-bor, God's will be done.
3 For the har-vests of the Spir-it, thanks be to God.

For his gifts to ev-ery na-tion, thanks be to God.
In the help we give our neigh-bor, God's will be done.
For the good we all in-her-it, thanks be to God.

For the plow-ing, sow-ing, reap-ing, si-lent growth while we are
In our world-wide task of car-ing for the hun-gry and de-
For the won-ders that as-tound us, for the truths that still con-

sleep-ing, fu-ture needs in earth's safe-keep-ing, thanks be to God.
spair-ing, in the har-vests we are shar-ing, God's will be done.
found us, most of all, that love has found us, thanks be to God.

Words: Fred Pratt Green, 1970

Music: Traditional Welsh melody, c. 1784; harmonized by Luther O. Emerson, 1906

84 84 88 84
AR HYD Y NOS
Capo 5

Fred Pratt Green, a minister in England, wrote over 300 hymns, most of them after he retired! Many consider him to be the best English hymn writer since Charles Wesley.

This harvest hymn of thanksgiving to God is about two kinds of harvests. Stanza 1 thanks God for the "fruit of all creation." Stanza 2 reminds us that God has given us these gifts for us to share with others, especially those who are "hungry and despairing." And when we share God's gifts, we can also expect "harvests of the Spirit" (st. 3). Thanks be to God!

The English text is set to a traditional Welsh tune. Counting by four-measure phrases, the structure reveals only two melodic phrases (AABA). Especially effective are the refrains found at the end of each A phrase. Even the youngest children can sing (and perhaps sign) those refrain lines.

When teaching the stanzas, ask some "wondering" questions. How many people helped bring us the food we eat? What does "silent growth" mean? How can we help our neighbors? What spiritual blessings have we received?

Accompany with keyboard, guitar, or autoharp. Consider adding bells or glockenspiel on half notes for the three ascending pitches (D E F) of each "thanks be to God."

Sing in congregational worship for at least three service themes: harvest time, perhaps on Thanksgiving Day (st. 1); dedication and offering for diaconal ministries near and far (st. 2); missions (st. 3).

236 We Are the Church

♩ = 112

Teach this song and you will have taught a significant theology lesson about the nature of the church. "The church is a people!" (st. 1); not a building but a people (note the singular) from "all times and places" (st. 2); who worship God together (st. 3); and then bring the good news to the whole world (st. 4, see Acts 2:1-4).

Teach the refrain first, using the following motions:

I am the church!
point to self

You are the church!
point to partner

We are the church together!
shake partner's hand

All who follow Jesus,
all around the world,
make a circle with arms overhead

yes, we're the church together!
hold hands

The skipping melody of the stanzas is made up of mainly eighth notes. Note that each phrase proceeds along the same path just one step higher in sequence. Keep the rhythm going in "circular" fashion, not stopping the beat until the very end. Younger children may enjoy adding motions as well to the first stanza:

The church is not a building,
hold fists together with knuckles touching

the church is not a steeple,
keep fists together, make a steeple by raising index fingers

the church is not a resting place;
hands on the side of the face in a sleeping position

the church is a people!
motion including all in the room

Words and Music: Richard Avery and Donald Marsh

© 1972, Hope Publishing Co. All rights reserved. Used by permission.

Sing with bright rhythmic energy. Accompany energetically with piano or guitar, and perhaps add some rhythm instruments on the refrains.

Sing in congregational worship at the opening or closing of worship, during Pentecost or any time.

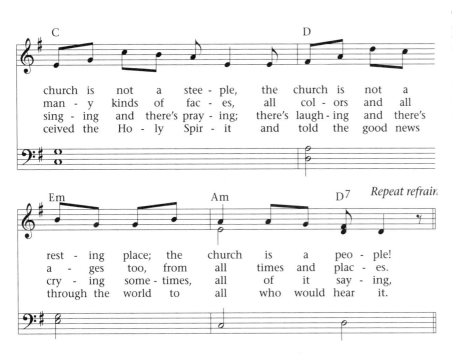

church is not a stee - ple, the church is not a
man - y kinds of fac - es, all col - ors and all
sing - ing and there's pray - ing; there's laugh - ing and there's
ceived the Ho - ly Spir - it and told the good news

Repeat refrain

rest - ing place; the church is a peo - ple!
a - ges too, from all times and plac - es.
cry - ing some - times, all of it say - ing,
through the world to all who would hear it.

♩ = 63

Let Us Love 237

This speech rhythm will serve not only as a refreshing change of pace, but also as a tool for learning 1 John 3:18. Make sure the children understand that we are to love in word or speech, but if our words and speech don't match our actions, than they are not true. Our words and deeds must match.

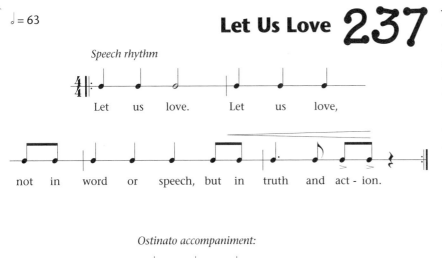

Speech rhythm

Let us love. Let us love,

not in word or speech, but in truth and act - ion.

Ostinato accompaniment:

Let us love.

Words: 1 John 3:18, NRSV
Music: Emily R. Brink, 1992
© 1994, CRC Publications

Speak the first two measures in a warm and loving manner, speaking clearly and holding out the vowel sounds of the first "luhv." Gradually add more energy and volume on the second line, accenting the final syllables. Add a solid clap on the final rest. After the pattern is well-known, add a few voices speak-ing the ostinato. Let someone beat steady half notes on a hand drum or tambourine; begin with a two-measure introduction.

In worship, use this speech rhythm as a response to the reading of the Ten Commandments or 1 John 3:11-24. Or use as a little prelude or postlude to a song that deals with love for our neighbors, such as "Love the Lord" (75), "If You Love Me" (151), "When I Needed a Neighbor" (247), or "Jesu, Jesu, Fill Us with Your Love" (251).

To be part of a family is a very special gift. This song reminds us that in Christ we have all become children of the Lord and are part of God's family. It makes no difference how big we are, or how old, or where we live, or how we look. We need to learn how to live well together as God's family.

This anthem by Natalie Sleeth was originally published in *The Sunday Songbook* in the key of G (for more on Sleeth, see 175). The melody is sectional and repetitive. Counting by four-measure phrases, it has the following pattern: AA'BB'AA'. If teaching this song by rote, use motions or pictures for words that are paired: (young and old, big and little, names and faces). Make different posters for each pair; ask children to hold up the posters to reinforce the order within the song. Young children may find there are too many words for them to grasp at first, but they will enjoy singing the melody and in time will be able to sing the entire song with the older children.

Sing as part of a mission emphasis celebration, for a baptism service, or in any service with a focus on the "holy catholic church."

238 Children of the Lord

♩ = 69

Words and Music: Natalie Sleeth, adapted from the anthem "Children of the Lord"

Capo 3

© 1976, Hinshaw Music, Inc. Used by permission.

This hymn, written in 1987 by Graham Kendrick, was first sung in his home church in London, England. The text expresses his desire for a spiritual awakening across the world that is both communal (us, we, our; see 2 Cor. 3:18) and individual (I, me; see John 12:46). Each stanza deals with some aspect of light (shining, darkness, shadows, brightness). The refrain petitions God to renew our land, our hearts, and the nations with his light. This song has become immensely popular in many countries.

Accompany with keyboard and guitar; sing with full voices. Sing in congregational worship during Epiphany, Easter, or Pentecost as an opening or closing hymn.

The following circle dance was choreographed by the third-grade class of Seymour Christian School in Grand Rapids, Michigan, under the leadership of Tim Quist and Kathy Sneller.

Form circles of five or more children. Dancers should focus their eyes on their hands so the face becomes part of the dance and not a distraction. (This really helps those of us who are self-conscious!) Begin with the refrain. In worship, the whole congregation can join with minor adaptations on the refrain.

Refrain:
raise arms and eyes slowly in a circular fashion until both arms are raised high above head

Shine, Jesus, shine,
fill this land with the Father's glory.
repeat; end with arms reaching high above head

Blaze, Spirit, blaze,
cross hands at wrist, move them gently back and forth to make a flame/dove

set our hearts on fire.
lower flame to heart, turn around slowly until facing center of circle

Flow, river, flow,
join hands, rock right, left, right

flood the nations
hands still joined, take small step, bend and reach to center "let the water rise"

239 Shine, Jesus, Shine

♩ = 112

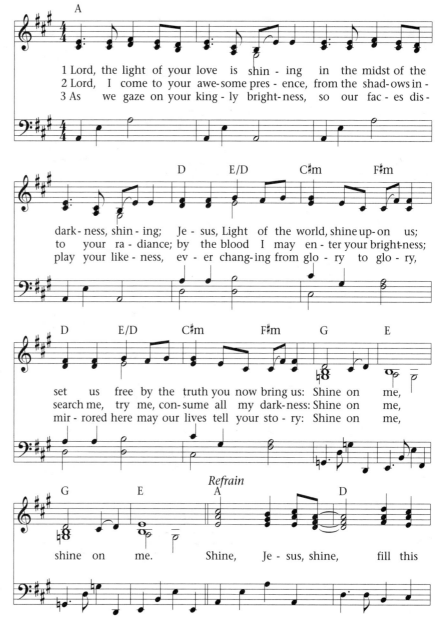

1 Lord, the light of your love is shin-ing in the midst of the
2 Lord, I come to your awe-some pres-ence, from the shad-ows in-
3 As we gaze on your king-ly bright-ness, so our fac-es dis-

dark-ness, shin-ing; Je-sus, Light of the world, shine up-on us;
to your ra-diance; by the blood I may en-ter your bright-ness,
play your like-ness, ev-er chang-ing from glo-ry to glo-ry,

set us free by the truth you now bring us: Shine on me,
search me, try me, con-sume all my dark-ness: Shine on me,
mir-rored here may our lives tell your sto-ry: Shine on me,

Refrain

shine on me. Shine, Je-sus, shine, fill this

Words and Music: Graham Kendrick, 1987

SHINE, JESUS, SHINE
Capo 2

land with the Fa - ther's glo - ry. Blaze, Spir - it, blaze, set our

hearts on fire. Flow, riv - er, flow, flood the

na - tions with grace and mer - cy. Send forth your Word, Lord, and

let there be light!

with grace and mercy.
> *end with arms extended from the side*

Send forth your Word,
> *palms up, bring straight arms to front one at a time—"sign" Bible*

Lord, and let there be light.
> *arms up, look up!*

Stanza 1:

Lord, the light of your love is shining
> *hands high, heads up, "feel the light shining on you"*

in the midst of the darkness shining;
> *put back of left wrist on forehead, lower head, right arm reaches to center to "make darkness," take small step*

Jesus, light of the world, shine upon us;
> *look up, extend arms to side to make the circle big*

set us free by the truth you now bring us:
> *make fists and cross as if tied at wrist, break free on the word "free"*

Shine on me, shine on me.
> *reach arms high, look up, turn to face out for refrain*

Stanza 2:

Lord, I come to your awesome presence,
> *everyone turns to the left and walks slowly in a circle, head bent reverently*

from the shadows into your radiance;
> *on "shadows" stop and turn toward center, reach up, look up but not high this time—the radiance is too great*

by the blood I may enter your brightness,
> *cross arms in front of body, palms facing you, bow head*

search me, try me, consume all my darkness:
> *kneel on one knee; make a motion with hands as if pushing the darkness behind you*

Shine on me, shine on me.
> *raise arms and eyes first, then stand and reach high, turn to face out for refrain*

Stanza 3:

As we gaze on your kingly brightness,
> *arms at side, look up*

so our faces display your likeness,
> *move right hand, palm facing you in front of face, reach up, repeat with left hands, follow with eyes*

ever changing from glory to glory,
> *on the word "glory" bring right hand down in front of you and out to your side, repeat with left hand on the second word "glory"*

mirrored here may our lives tell your story:
> *hold position; with both arms make a giving motion from the chest, arms extended in front of body, palms up*

Shine on me, shine on me.
> *reach arms high, look up, turn to face out for refrain*

240 There's No God as Great / No Hay Dios tan Grande

♩ = 60

Christians all over Central and South America enjoy this infectiously joyful song. Hispanic folk hymns are often sung as medleys, one after the other; this Scripture chorus is itself a medley combining four different passages, each repeated. The first two sections praise God, and the final two sections recognize that God leads the church by the Holy Spirit.

- *Section 1:* What god is so great as our God? (Ps. 77:13).

- *Section 2:* You are the God who performs miracles (Ps. 77:14).

- *Section 3:* "Not by might nor by power, but by my Spirit," says the LORD Almighty (Zech. 4:6; see also Hos. 1:7).

- *Section 4:* You . . . are controlled . . . by the Spirit, if the Spirit of God lives in you (Rom. 8:9).

The melody is sectional and typically Spanish in flavor. Sing phrase by phrase, having the children echo you. Sing with joyful confidence. Note that on the repetitions, the final note is different than on the first ending. Accompany with keyboard, guitar, and a variety of rhythm instruments. For example, shake maracas on eighth notes throughout. Use wood blocks to play a pattern of quarter note and two eighths. Older children who read music may be able to sing harmony as follows: sing the tenor line on the first and

There's no god as great as you, O Lord, O Lord, my God. There's no god who works the might-y won-ders, all the won-ders that you do. Not by our weap-ons, nor by our pow-er, but by your

No hay dios tan gran-de co-mo tú, no lo hay, no lo hay. No hay dios que pue-da ha-cer las o-bras co-mo las que ha-ces tú. No es con es-pa-da, ni con e-jér-ci-to, mas con tu

Words and Music: Spanish; translated for *Psalter Hymnal*, 1987

NO HAY DIOS
Capo 1

Spir - it we are led. Not by our weap - ons, nor by our
San - to Es - pí - ri - tú. No es con es - pa - da, ni con e -

pow - er, but by your Spir - it we are led. The Ho - ly
jér - ci - to, mas con tu San - to Es - pí - ri - tu. Y es - ta i -

Spir - it will move the church, the Ho - ly Spir - it
gle - sia se mo - ve - rá, y es - ta i - gle - sia

will move the church, the Ho - ly Spir - it will move the
se mo - ve - rá, y es - ta i - gle - sia se mo - ve -

church, for by your Spir - it we are led.
rá con tu San - to Es - pí - ri - tu.

third sections, and the alto line on the second and fourth sections. Transpose those same lines up an octave and play as a descant on flute or violin.

Once children know it, try singing part or all in Spanish. In congregational worship, have the children lead the congregation in this profession of faith during the Pentecost season or any time. Consider pairing with other Hispanic songs in F, including "Alabaré" (193) and "Worthy Is Christ" (170).

241 Go into the World

♩ = 66

The book of Matthew ends with what has come to be known as the Great Commission. After Jesus rose from the dead, he told his disciples to come to a mountain where he would meet them, telling them to "make disciples of all nations. . . . And surely, I will be with you always" (Matt. 28:19-20). This song is part of a larger anthem by Natalie Sleeth (for more on Sleeth, see 175).

The text is very simple, with only one new line in every stanza. The music is infectiously rhythmic; be sure to master the syncopation before teaching it to the children. Teach the descant only after the children know the stanzas well. For added interest, have all the children learn the descant part and sing as a new melody on stanza 3, then divide into two groups and sing stanza 3 again in two-part harmony. Accompany lightly and brightly on keyboard. Invite a cellist or string bass player to pluck the bass clef part, and invite a flute or violin player to play the introduction and the melody, especially on stanza 3.

Or you may want to purchase a few copies of the anthem. Keep one for yourself, give one to the pianist, who has a more elaborate accompaniment, and give another copy to an older child or adult who can sing a solo on another section (not included here). That additional text (to different music) is based on John 15:1 and John 8:12:

I am the vine, you are the branches, ever the fruit to bear.

I am the light, you, the reflection everywhere.

Sing in congregational worship for a commissioning service for missionaries or service projects. Or sing at the conclusion of the service, especially during the Easter season and for Ascension Day.

Words and Music: Natalie Sleeth, based on Matthew 28:19-20; adapted from the anthem "Go into the World"

© 1979, Choristers Guild. Used by permission.

♩ = 60 **If You Believe and I Believe** **242**

If you be-lieve and I be-lieve and we to-geth-er pray,

the Ho-ly Spir-it will come down and set God's peo-ple free,

and set God's peo-ple free, and set God's peo-ple free;

the Ho-ly Spir-it will come down and set God's peo-ple free.

Words: from Zimbabwe, based on Matthew 18:19
Music: from Zimbabwe, as adapted from an English song

Matthew 18:19 is the source for this moving song from Zimbabwe: "Again, I tell you that if two of you on earth agree about anything you ask for, it will be done for you by my Father in heaven." Point out Zimbabwe on a map or globe to show the children where this song comes from. Originally this was a freedom song: when the people were fighting for their independence, they sang "Zimbabwe" where this version has "God's people." When we sing it today, we can remember many people who need to be set free from both spiritual and physical bondage.

At first hearing, you may be surprised that this is a Zimbabwean tune. Quite possibly it was originally an English folk song brought to the colonies by English settlers or traders to Southern Rhodesia, then revised by Africans. This song is international, and so is the body of Christ! How did it get into this book? John Bell, a Scottish minister, heard a woman named Tamasari from Zimbabwe sing it. He included it in a little collection of world songs entitled *Sent by the Lord* (see 249).

Two lines contain the text; the rest is repetition. And the music consists of only two phrases (AABA), so the entire song can be learned easily. Sing with keyboard or guitar accompaniment. But perhaps the ideal way, certainly the African way, would be to sing unaccompanied: invite the adult choir to provide harmony to children's voices on the melody.

In worship sing as a prayer response, particularly in prayers of intercession for those who are oppressed.

Although this song is less than twenty years old, it has made a tremendous impact in North America. It challenges us to offer our lives in faithful service to the gospel as missionaries or wherever God has placed us.

Daniel Schutte based this song on the call of Isaiah (Isa. 6:8). In Old Testament times, God called prophets to bring messages to his people. Read the refrain, and ask the children if they know of another prophet whom God called during the night (see 108). Both Samuel and Isaiah were frightened when God called them. But both willingly obeyed God and carried out many difficult assignments. God gave them the strength to follow him. God also calls us to serve and follow him today. This song can move us toward a response of obedience.

Teach the refrain first (see motions on opposite page). All children will be able to learn the refrain easily. The stanzas are more challenging. Since the "I" is God speaking, consider having a soloist on the stanzas. Or have children learn different sections of the text. Obviously, the stanzas consist of repeated sections; two groups could each sing one of the sections, with everyone joining on the final "Whom shall I send?"

To help the children memorize the stanzas, you may want to develop a poster for each stanza with key words and/or pictures and symbols; some ideas are found on the opposite page. Teach the melody by echo method, and trace the melody direction with your hand. Let your children direct this song so they can feel how the rests (for breathing) and dotted rhythms are related to the main beats. Direct first in four, then in two beats per measure. Make sure the long notes are held for their proper values, especially in the refrain, and do not interrupt the final phrase with a breath. Accompany with keyboard and guitar, and sing in a flowing rhythm with a steady beat.

In worship, sing during a special commissioning or "sending forth" service. Also sing as a response to a sermon on commitment.

243 Here I Am, Lord

$\quad \downarrow = 69$

Words: Daniel L. Schutte, 1981; based on Isaiah 6:8
Music: Daniel L. Schutte, 1981; adapted by Carlton R. Young, 1988

77 74 D with refrain
HERE I AM, LORD

Here I am, Lord. Is it I, Lord?

I have heard you call-ing in the night.

I will go, Lord, if you lead me.

I will hold your peo-ple in my heart.

Motions for refrain:
Here I am, Lord.
both arms reach up, palms open

Is it I, Lord?
curved fingertips of both hands rest on chest; look up

I have heard you calling in the night.
both hands to ears, palms out

I will go, Lord,
both arms reach up, palms open

if you lead me.
both arms extended to front

I will hold your people in my heart.
arms cross heart

Here are some ideas for a little drama on the call of Isaiah:

Isaiah: Read Isaiah 6:1-3a

Children: Sing "Holy, Holy, Holy" (66) (Isaiah 6:3b)

Isaiah: Read Isaiah 6:4-7a

Seraph: Read Isaiah 6:7b

Isaiah: Read Isaiah 6:8

Children and congregation sing: "Here I Am, Lord" (children begin with the refrain; congregation sings stanzas)

Every child with younger sisters or brothers will recognize the phrase "Let me do it!" There is something wonderful about children's eagerness to do things for themselves and others. This prayer song exhibits an eager willingness to offer ourselves to Jesus to share in doing his work. The text is easy to learn: each stanza consists of two phrases that begin with the words "let me." Simple motions—pointing to hands and feet, etc.—will help children learn the words. The refrain, with its very short phrases, is also accessible to children of all ages.

Children will delight in singing this cheerful melody. It has enough repetition and stepwise movement to make it easy to learn. Counting by four-measure phrases, the basic form of the song is AA'BA'. The syncopation that begins each phrase in the stanza and the concluding phrase of the refrain provides a rhythmic energy that children will enjoy.

Sing with energy, accompanied by keyboard and strong strummed guitar accompaniment. The children might enjoy adding hand claps (two eighth notes on the "and" of beat 3 and on beat 4). Include rhythm instruments with the clapping to reinforce the rhythmic energy.

Sing as an offertory for a service emphasizing mission and service or the church as a caring community. Also sing in a service that focuses on disability awareness. Consider pairing with "Take My Life" (74), or "The Good Samaritan" (146).

244 Let Me Be Your Servant, Jesus

Words and Music: Judith A. Helms, 1980

♩. = 48

When Did We See You 245

1 "Come now, you bless-ed, eat at my ta-ble,"
2 When did we see you hun-gry or thirs-ty?
3 "When you gave bread to the earth's hun-gry chil-dren,
4 Christ, when we see you out on life's road-ways,

said Je-sus Christ to the right-eous a-bove.
When were you home-less, a strang-er a-lone?
when you gave shel-ter to war's ref-u-gees.
look-ing to us in the fac-es of need,

"When I was hun-gry, thirs-ty, and home-less,
When did we see you sick or in pris-on?
When you re-mem-bered those most for-got-ten,
then may we know you, wel-come and show you

sick and in pris-on, you showed me your love."
What have we done that you call us your own?
you cared for me in the small-est of these."
love that is faith-ful in word and in deed.

Words: Ruth Duck, 1979
Music: Emily R. Brink, 1992
Words © 1979, 1992, G.I.A. Publications, Inc. All rights reserved. Music © 1994, CRC Publications.

Capo 1

This song, a paraphrase of Matthew 25:34-40, is in the form of a conversation between Jesus and his faithful followers when they go to heaven and are invited to sit down at the feast Jesus has prepared for them. Stanza 1 is Jesus' invitation to those who showed their love for him in deeds of kindness to others. In stanza 2 they respond by asking when they saw Jesus hungry or sick or homeless. Stanza 3 is Christ's reply: "When you helped others, you cared for me." Stanza 4 is a prayer of commitment to showing and seeing God's love in all we do.

The melody is gentle and flowing. Encourage children to sing it smoothly. Thinking one beat per measure will encourage a sense of flow. Since there is little repetition in the text, you may want to chart out key words for the children to remember. Each week introduce one stanza and review the stanzas previously learned. When children know the song, assign the roles of Jesus and believers to either individuals or groups of children. You may wish to have a guitar or keyboard accompaniment; a gentle strum on autoharp would also be effective. Create a descant for flute by playing the alto line an octave higher than written. This will reinforce the gentle quality of the melody.

Sing in congregational worship services that focus on living out our commitment to Christ, especially with regard to social justice issues.

Here is another adaptation of an anthem by Natalie Sleeth (for more on Sleeth, see 175). The short verbal phrases are characteristic of her style. Stanzas 1, 2, and 4 ask the question: Who's goin' to . . . obey the Great Commission to spread the good news of Jesus all over the world? The answer comes in the little refrain, "You and I." Stanza 3 tells what that good news is. Children will be eager to sing this lively and energetic song. To teach the text by rote, you may want to make charts for each stanza since there is a lot of text.

The melody includes syncopation in every phrase. Fortunately, the syncopation is identical in every line on the first page and another pattern is identical in every line of the second page. On the first page, be sure to get to the "I" before the beat. Begin singing and have the children join you on each "You and I." Then have them echo each phrase after you. One method of teaching the words is to divide children into three groups; ask one child to be the leader of each group. As leaders stand in front of their groups, they will teach their group their assigned phrase. After singing through the song, the leaders move to a new group. Repeat once more so that all of the groups will have learned all of the phrases. Accompany with keyboard, providing a lively beat.

In congregational worship, sing during any service emphasizing our call to spread the gospel, especially during Epiphany and Pentecost; sing also for Ascension as a response to the Great Commission.

246 You and I

♩ = 72

1 Who's goin' to tell the sto - ry? You and I!
2 Who's goin' to bring the king - dom? You and I!
4 Who's goin' to feed the hun - gry? You and I!

Tell of the Lord's great glo - ry? You and I!
Who's goin' to spread the gos - pel? You and I!
Care for the sick and lone - ly? You and I!

Who's goin' to let the whole world know? Help his dis - ci - ples
Who's goin' to do the kind - ly deed? Com - fort the one in
Who's goin' to let the whole world see peo - ple can live in

grow and mul - ti - ply?
need and help sup - ply?   You and I!
har - mo - ny? Let's try!

Words and Music: Natalie Sleeth, adapted from the anthem "You and I"
© 1976, Hinshaw Music, Inc. Used by permission.

Capo 1

Like 245, this song is based on Jesus' teaching in Matthew 25:35-40. In that song, believers asked Jesus, "When did we see you?" In this song the tables are turned: believers are asked "Were you there when I needed a neighbor?" The "I" is our neighbor, but the connotations are richer. In one sense the "I" is also Christ, who said, "Whatever you did for the least of these, you did for me." Even the "Were you there" resonates with the African-American spiritual by that name (see 167).

The simple text includes much repetition. The melody is composed in the style of a spiritual, with repetition within each stanza. Everyone can sing the refrains; assign different groups or soloists to the stanzas. Children will enjoy adding their own stanzas. (Some may want to change stanza 3 to read, "I was cold, needed clothes. . . .") Always sing the final stanza; note that the question turns into a promise, revealing Jesus as the "I."

Sing with light voices and good breath support in order to negotiate the range of the melody. Accompany with keyboard, autoharp, or guitar. Add a soft hand drum playing the rhythm of "Were you there?" throughout. In the little coda in the accompaniment, add a final statement of "I'll be there," sung as a quiet echo by a few children.

Include in a service emphasizing mission, diaconal ministries, and issues of social justice. Sing as a response to the summary of the Law or at the end of a commissioning service for someone about to travel to a new place of ministry. Consider pairing with "The Good Samaritan" (146).

247 When I Needed a Neighbor

♩ = 96

2 I was hungry and thirsty, were you there? . . .

3 I was cold, I was naked, were you there? . . .

4 When I needed a shelter, were you there? . . .

5 Wherever you travel, I'll be there, I'll be there;
    wherever you travel, I'll be there.
    And the creed and the color and the name won't matter;
    I'll be there.

Words and Music: Sydney Carter, 1965

♩ = 60

The Servant Song 248

D   G   D

1 Will you let me be your ser - vant, let me be as
2 We are pil - grims on a jour - ney; we are travel - ers
3 I will hold the Christ-light for you in the night-time

G   A   G   D   Em   D

Christ to you? Pray that I might have the grace to
on the road. We are here to help each oth - er
of your fear. I will hold my hand out to you,

D   A⁷   D

let you be my ser - vant too.
walk the mile and bear the load.
speak the peace you long to hear.

4 I will weep when you are weeping;
  when you laugh, I'll laugh with you.
  I will share your joy and sorrow
  till we've seen this journey through.

5 Will you let me be your servant,
  let me be as Christ to you?
  Pray that I might have the grace to
  let you be my servant too.

Words and Music: Richard Gillard; arranged by Emily R. Brink, 1992

In many hymns, we bring our prayers and praises directly to God. In this song, we make promises to each other. The text applies the lesson that Jesus taught when he washed the disciples' feet (John 13:1-18). In Mark 10:43-45, Jesus also taught his disciples that "whoever wishes to become great among you must be your servant. . . . For the Son of Man did not come to be served, but to serve."

Stanza 1 recognizes that sometimes it is easier to serve than be served! We all need grace to be good servants to each other. Explain that pilgrims (st. 2) are travelers in strange and new places. Ask the children some wondering questions. How are we all pilgrims? Why are some people afraid? (st. 3). What times do we laugh together? Why should we also cry together? (st. 4). Stanza 5 repeats stanza 1. Choose individuals or small groups to sing stanzas 2-4, with everyone joining on the stanza that "frames" the song.

The melody is very simple, with almost no rhythmic variety until the very end. It should flow in two beats per measure (until the end) rather than sound like a series of quarter notes. The shift of meter should sound like a built-in ritard (slowing down) rather than a speeding up of the rhythm. When singing the word "servant," deemphasize the "r," particularly on the ending phrase. Accompany with keyboard, guitar, or autoharp. Guitar and flute (or violin) together would also be effective: use flute on melody for an introduction and on a descant for stanza 5, created out of the tenor line played one or two octaves higher.

Sing as a conclusion to a sermon on servanthood, a song of encouragement for profession of faith, or a commissioning service for mission or church workers.

Wouldn't it be great if someday missionaries would be sent from Cuba? Even though we have not had much contact with that little country just south of Florida, God has been building his church there. This song indicates that Cuban Christians are ready and willing to be "sent by the Lord." Working for social justice is a task God gives to human beings, not angels. The final lines are a prayer that we carry out this task according to God's will.

The traditional Cuban melody exhibits exuberance and energy in a minor tonality that is characteristic of much Latin American music. The song is in two sections, each repeated (AABB'). Sing with strength and conviction. Repeating the first two lines of text as noted helps to build the conviction; sing the repeat even more energetically. The first two lines are very effective sung in unison; the remainder of the hymn can be sung in two parts. Chldren learning how to sing in parts will be able to master the parallel motion between the alto and soprano lines. The keyboard will provide adequate accompaniment, but the melody would be enhanced with the use of guitar and some rhythm instruments.

Sing in worship as a call to service following the benediction in any service that focuses our attention on missions or social justice.

249 Sent by the Lord

♩ = 100

Sent by the Lord am I; my hands are rea-dy now to make the earth the place in which the king-dom comes. The an-gels can-not change a world of hurt and pain in- to a world of love, of jus-tice and of peace. The task is mine to do, to set it real-ly free. Oh,

Words: Cuban oral tradition; translated by Jorge Maldonado, 1991
Music: traditional Cuban; arranged by Iona Community, 1991

Capo 1

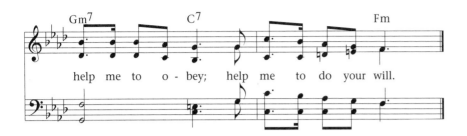

help me to o - bey; help me to do your will.

♩ = 76

On the Poor **250**

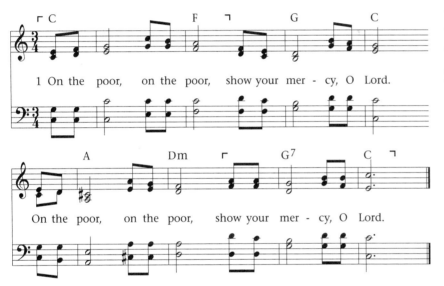

1 On the poor, on the poor, show your mer - cy, O Lord.

On the poor, on the poor, show your mer - cy, O Lord.

2 On the poor, on the poor, show your mercy, O Christ. . . .
3 On the poor, on the poor, show your mercy, O Lord. . . .

Words: adapted traditional liturgical text
Music: from Paraguay
Arr. © 1991, Iona Community. Used by permission of G.I.A. Publications.

66 66
KYRIE GUARANY

On the bottom right corner of the song page, look for the tune name for this song. Both words are significant. "Kyrie" is the first Greek word for a very old prayer of the church that goes all the way back to the psalms: Lord, have mercy. The Guarany are a group of oppressed native South American people scattered all over South America. Many of them live in Paraguay. Their adaptation of the ancient Kyrie has been translated for us to sing.

Notice how the three stanzas parallel the Kyrie (43). Children could add stanzas, for example, "On the sick." You may also include two-syllable words, singing two quarter notes, as in "on the homeless," or "on our cities."

Sing quietly, without hurrying. Allow room for meditation. Consider using this little song as a prayer refrain following the children's spoken prayers. Accompany quietly with keyboard, guitar, or autoharp.

Sing in congregational worship as a response in prayers of intercession for the poor.

The African missionary Thomas Colvin wrote this text in 1963 in the village of Chereponi in northern Ghana. Some new Christians sang a folk tune for him that they thought might be appropriate for a text about Christian love. He wrote this text for the traditional tune, originally a love song, from Ghana. Show the children where Ghana is on a map or globe, and point out that the tune is named after the African village (see the bottom right corner of the song page).

The text is based on two lessons Jesus taught: his answer to the question "Who is my neighbor?" (Luke 10:25-37) in the parable of the Good Samaritan, and his demonstration of servanthood in washing his disciples' feet (John 13:1-20).

Short phrases will make this song easy to teach by the echo method. There is no literal repetition, but each little phrase is repeated at different pitch levels. Invite all the children to sing the refrain; ask soloists or groups to sing the stanzas. Sing rather quietly and lyrically. Accompany with keyboard, guitar, or autoharp. Or use the guitar with cello on the bass clef part (or flute or violin playing the bass clef part an octave higher). Keep the beat going from start to finish; there should be no rhythmic pause between the refrain and stanzas each time.

Sing in worship services where Christian servanthood is the theme; thus, also for mission events and diaconal ministries.

251 Jesu, Jesu, Fill Us with Your Love

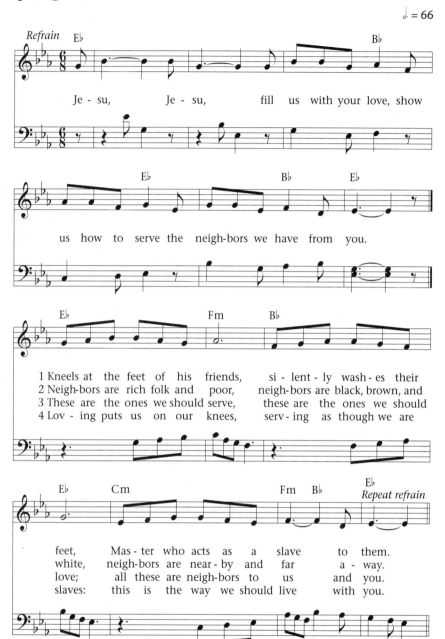

Words and Music: folk song from Ghana, adapted by Tom Colvin; music arranged by Robert Roth

779 with refrain
CHEREPONI
Capo 1

♩ = 84

Send Me, Lord 252

Leader

Send me, Lord.

F   All   C   Dm   C   F   Dm   F

1 Send me, Je - sus, send me, Je - sus, send me,
Je - sus, lead me, Je - sus, lead me,
Je - sus, fill me, Je - sus, fill me,

1,2 | 3

2 Lead me, Lord.
3 Fill me, Lord.

Gm   F   C   1,2 F   C   3 F

Je - sus, send me, Lord.   2 Lead me,
Je - sus, lead me, Lord.   3 Fill me,
Je - sus, fill me,   Lord.

Words and Music: traditional South African
© 1984, Utryck (c/o Walton Music Corp.). Used by permission.

THUMA MINA
Capo 5

This traditional South African hymn is a humble response to God's call to us to serve him wherever he sends us. Stanza 1 is based on Isaiah's response to God's call: "Here am I! Send me" (Isa. 6:8). Other Scripture references that tie into stanzas 2 and 3 are Psalm 31:3b: "For the sake of your name lead and guide me" and Psalm 23:5b: "You anoint my head with oil; my cup overflows." You may also add other stanzas, for example, "use me."

Children will easily learn this short and simple call-and-response song. The first time you introduce this hymn, omit the leader's part. Teach each little phrase by the echo method. When children know it, become the leader yourself, showing how to "dovetail" the response with the ending each time.

Then choose a clear solo voice or a small ensemble for the leader part. The song should not be rushed; allow time for reflection. You may even encourage them to sway every two beats—all going in the same direction! Since much African music is unaccompanied, consider inviting your adult choir to provide a hummed choral accompaniment.

As its position in this book suggests, this song should be sung at the conclusion of a prayer or a service that calls us to commitment. May all these songs help equip us and our children to be willing servants of the Lord.

Send

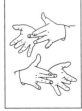

Jesus

Me (only last time in each stanza)

Lord

Lead

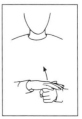

Fill

A Worship Education Curriculum

Worship Education in the Gathering Time

How can we help our children learn to worship God through singing? This Leader's Edition of *Songs for LiFE* presents many creative suggestions for teaching songs to children and making music together. But there is more. The "gathering time" is not just a time for singing, but a time for worship and for learning about worship, a time for preparing to participate in congregational worship.

This larger vision calls for a leader who is both a musician and a worshiper. The traditional term "song leader" does not adequately describe such a person nor does "worship leader" exactly fit, since the gathering time is also a time for education and to prepare to worship God. The time that children traditionally spend together in singing before going to their smaller groups has never really had an appropriate name. We call that time the gathering time. By gathering time we mean a time for children to come together to prepare and learn and develop their understanding and practice of what it means to worship God. Some congregations sing "gathering songs" at the beginning of their worship services.

The resources in this section will help gathering time leaders develop a plan not only for singing together, but also for worshiping together and learning something about what it means to worship God.

The Challenges

One reason there are so few materials to assist church school leaders in the gathering time is all the variables. Every congregation is different. We faced several challenges in developing a curricular approach to worship education.

- Some church schools meet year-round; others begin in September and break for the summer.

- Easter and Pentecost fall on different dates each year, so one calendar plan would not fit for every year.

- Many churches schedule a very short gathering time before the children move to their smaller groups.

- Some smaller congregations combine all children and adults together in one gathering time. Some larger churches schedule separate gathering times for preschool through second grade, and third through sixth grade, for example.

The Unit Plan

Our response to those challenges is to offer a flexible unit plan. Twenty-one units, each from two to four weeks long, provide a structure for choosing songs according to particular themes. Themes include the Elements of Worship, the Christian Year, and Living in God's World (see Contents). Several of the units on the elements of worship are also found in the worship committee manual *Lift Up Your Hearts: Resources for Planning Worship* (CRC Publications, 1995). The correlation is intentional: congregations that use both resources will have a consistent approach to understanding what it means to worship God.

The twenty-one units include seventy-one weeks—more than a calendar year. Some leaders will want to choose a number of units over a two- or even three-year schedule. Some may want to expand units from three or four weeks to five or six weeks, depending on the local calendar and the ability of their singers to learn new songs.

The key is flexibility. Here is one possible three-year curriculum plan following a September-June schedule. The units are listed in the order for that year. Some units would be covered only once in three years, others twice, and some units on the Christian Year would be included every year.

Year 1: Units 1-4, 8-11, 5, 12, 14
Year 2: Units 15-16, 21, 8-9, 18-19, 12-13
Year 3: Units 1, 6-7, 8-10, 19-20, 13-14

Other churches that meet for church school year-round might want to develop a two-year plan. The idea is that over the course of two or three years, children will learn a great variety of songs organized in a well-rounded approach that includes understanding the elements of worship, the Christian Year, and how God desires us to live in his world.

Components of the Units
You may be used to choosing and teaching songs. But in order to use the gathering time for worship education, a new focus is required. Before choosing songs, you should read the unit plans. That will give you the background with which to teach songs in the context of worship education.

Each unit contains the following elements:

Unit Focus
Keep this statement clearly in mind as you choose songs and plan your comments. If a parent should ask a child what they learned about worship today, the child should be able to say something in his or her own words that would come close to this statement.

Unit Goals
Includes three sets of goals:

Faith Nurture (for leader and children)
Faith Knowledge (for children)
Faith Modeling (for leader)

Children and leaders sing together and worship God together. Adults as much as children need to set goals.

Materials
Songs from the hymnal that fit the unit theme are suggested. In addition, you may wish to add songs from your own congregational repertoire. For example, when learning about doxologies (in Unit 7), you may want to spend a bit of time teaching a particular doxology

that your congregation sings. The goal is to relate the worship education in the gathering time to what happens in congregational worship. Often a visual is recommended as an illustration.

Preparing to Lead the Gathering Time
Reading these brief backgrounds will provide, in essence, a minicourse in worship. As in all teaching, those who lead may learn more than the children!

Working with Congregational Worship Leaders
Every unit has suggestions for helping children contribute to congregational worship. Rather than presenting an occasional church school program, the intent here is to involve children in public worship on a regular basis, as often as once a unit or once a month. Their participation could include:

- singing a song, such as a call to worship or an offertory
- singing a stanza of a congregational hymn
- simply joining the congregation on a song that they have learned

Advance communication with the pastor and other worship planners is essential.

Unit Song Suggestions: A Model
At the end of every unit is a suggested list of songs for the unit, following the structure of the sample lesson plan. More information on using this model follows in the article "Developing Lesson Plans."

Developing Lesson Plans

As we stated in the previous article, churches have different calendars and schedules for the church school year and different age groups as well. Because no single set of lesson plans would allow the necessary flexibility, we present one basic model for a twenty-minute weekly lesson plan. A sample lesson plan for Unit 1, Week 1 is provided on page 332. You are encouraged to make copies of the blank lesson plan on page 333 for your own use.

At the end of each unit, a list of songs is suggested as a model. Following this plan provides a systematic way to introduce many songs. The model lesson plan assumes a twenty-minute gathering time. A maximum of eight songs are chosen in several distinct sections. Eight may be too many for groups of children that know few songs. Remember that teaching new songs takes more time, but once the program is "up and running," eight songs may be just right.

Blank Lesson Plan

Keeping records is one important aspect of planning. Also, it is a good idea to keep the focus statement clearly in mind. Writing it down will help.

Gathering Songs (5 minutes)

All songs are listed with their keys. Key relationships are important in setting mood and making connections between songs. The songs in each section of this hymnal are often grouped by key relationships, and the Key Index will help you choose songs in related keys. Sing three songs in this gathering section. Sing them "back-to-back," with little if any speaking in between the songs. When more than three songs are listed, choose three; the fourth song may be introduced, for example, on the second or third week in place of one of the other songs.

Comments (4 minutes)

During this time, the leader greets the children and provides a time for brief interaction and teaching. You may want to use one ancient greeting of the church consistently with the children:

The Lord be with you.
And also with you.

During Eastertide, the following greeting is appropriate:

The Lord is risen.
He is risen indeed.

You may spend part of this time in pointing out some key words and concepts in the songs that relate to the particular unit.

Unit Theme Song (4 minutes)

All twenty-one units include two suggestions for theme songs, which could also be called unit hymns. One year one theme song would be learned; the next time the unit is covered the other song could be chosen. This core list was chosen with care to provide a balance of historic hymns and more recent congregational songs representing many different song traditions. By the time a child is in sixth grade, that child—along with all other children in the congregation—would know these forty-two hymns well. Altogether, these songs represent a core repertoire of congregational songs for children.

Additional Songs (5 minutes)

You may choose three more songs or other activities. Some congregations include, for example, an offering, a report on a particular missionary or service project, or a time for spoken prayer.

Closing Song (2 minutes)

Each lesson ends with a closing song.

Checklist

At the end of each lesson plan, check to determine how much variety you have included. A number of categories are listed to help you plan a balanced list of songs.

Unit Theme Songs: A Core Repertoire

The Elements of Worship

Unit 1   Opening of Worship
- Praise to the Lord, the Almighty
- All People That on Earth Do Dwell

Unit 2   Confessing to God
- Lord, I Want to Be a Christian
- O Christ, the Lamb of God

Unit 3   Listening to God's Story
- Blessed Jesus, at Your Word
- Seek Ye First the Kingdom

Unit 4   Baptism: God Includes Us in His Family
- Baptized in Water
- Jesus Loves Me

Unit 5   The Lord's Supper: God Feeds Us at His Table
- I Come with Joy to Meet My Lord
- Lift Up Your Hearts

Unit 6   Responding to God's Story (1)
- Take My Life
- May the Mind of Christ, My Savior

Unit 7   Responding to God's Story (2)
- Oh, for a Thousand Tongues to Sing
- What a Friend We Have in Jesus

The Christian Year

Unit 8   Advent
- Come, Thou Long-Expected Jesus
- O Come, O Come, Immanuel

Unit 9   Christmas and Epiphany
- Go, Tell It on the Mountain
- Away in a Manger

Unit 10   The Life and Work of Christ
- The King of Glory Comes
- When Jesus the Healer

Unit 11   The Suffering and Death of Christ
- All Glory, Laud, and Honor
- Were You There

Unit 12   Easter: The Resurrection of Christ
- Christ the Lord Is Risen Today
- Alleluia, Alleluia! Give Thanks

Unit 13   Ascension: The Reign of Christ
- Rejoice, the Lord Is King
- He Is Lord

Unit 14   Pentecost: The Work of the Spirit
- Spirit of the Living God
- Spirit Divine, Inspire Our Prayer

Living in God's World

Unit 15   Creation
- All Creatures of Our God and King
- All Things Bright and Beautiful

Unit 16   Providence
- If You But Trust in God to Guide You
- He's Got the Whole World

Unit 17   Redemption
- Amazing Grace
- When Israel Was in Egypt's Land

Unit 18   Mission
- Bring Forth the Kingdom
- Lift High the Cross

Unit 19   Serving Jesus in Our Work and Play
- Let Me Be Your Servant, Jesus
- Jesus' Hands Were Kind Hands

Unit 20   Helping Others Both Near and Far Away
- Jesu, Jesu, Fill Us with Your Love
- Will You Let Me Be Your Servant

Unit 21   Thanksgiving
- Now Thank We All Our God
- For the Beauty of the Earth

Lesson Plan Suggestions

Following are teaching suggestions to illustrate what a complete lesson might look like, one for the first week of each of the three major sections of the unit plans (Units 1, 8, 15). Although the goal of trying to sing eight songs in twenty minutes is a good one, you may decide to choose fewer songs, depending on your children. You will notice from the commentary that speaking is minimal but carefully planned. The children are active most of the time.

Sample One
The Elements of Worship

Unit 1, Week 1
Opening of Worship

You are more than a music leader; you are also a worship leader. Not only will you teach children new songs, you will enable them to draw nearer to their Lord and Savior. Take time before you begin each unit to familiarize yourself with the unit backgrounds. This information will give you confidence and a solid background from which to encourage children to learn and grow in their Christian walk.

There is often a mood of excitement when children gather. They are glad to be together again. Some may be eager to catch up on what their friends have been doing. As children visit for a brief time, ask the pianist to quietly play some of the songs for that day. It's a good idea to spend some time talking with the children—let them know you care about them and what is going on in their lives.

When it is time to begin, stand in front of the children. Use direct eye contact as you encourage children to join you in singing the first three songs. (Ask the pianist to lead from one song to the next in this opening section with no breaks.) The songs are often arranged so that they go from one key up to the next. This will help children sense that we gather to worship our great God with joy and praise!

Establish clearly at the beginning of your time together that when you step to the front of the group and the piano gets louder it is time for the children to stop visiting and to join together in song. Your time together is limited by the clock and you want to make every minute count.

Sing the following gathering songs uninterrupted to set a happy, joyful spirit of entering God's courts with praise.

- I Will Enter His Gates (9)
- Allelu (7)
- In the House of Our God (5)

Continue the momentum with the greeting:

The Lord be with you!
And also with you!

Then tell the children that we have come into God's presence singing songs of praise. We have so much for which we can praise God. He made us and loves us. We are God's children and God is here with us right now!

Let the children know that for the next few weeks they will be learning about what we do in worship. Ask them,

- Did you know there are many people who are not free to gather as a group to worship God? Why? Who says they cannot gather?
- What does worship really mean?

Allow time for a response, but not enough time for children's minds to wander. Continue by explaining that "worship" simply means to praise God as the best, the greatest, the most important, and the only One who is worthy of such adoration.

Then join the children in singing "Praise to the Lord, the Almighty" (sing at least twice to help memorize stanza 1).

After singing this unit theme song, the piano should continue on to the next group of songs, allowing time to let the words speak to the children. Don't be in a hurry. Tell the children that we have come joyfully into God's presence; we have had a brief teaching; and now we want to express our love to God in the next group of songs:

- Alleluia (87)
- Love the Lord (75)
- Father, We Love You (77)

As you prepare to dismiss the children for their group time, remind them that God is worthy to receive all of our worship and that God surrounds each of us with his love every day. Sing "Go Now in Peace" (79), first all together, then divide into two parts and sing again.

The pianist continues to play quietly as the children leave.

Note: If you are using charts or overheads, you will be able to keep the attention of the children focused up front. If you are using the hymnal, you may want to write song numbers on a chalkboard or on a chart and point to them as you proceed. Set guidelines from the beginning: expect everyone in the area in which you are teaching to participate (it is distracting to have adults standing in the back talking or doing something else). Except for that which relates directly to your session, talk should be kept at a minimum.

* * *

Sample 2
The Christian Year

Unit 8, Week 1
Advent

The majority of songs in this unit may be new to you. Perhaps you're convinced you can't possibly learn all these songs! However, this is an opportunity for you and the children to learn some very special songs of the season for a lifetime.

Since the songs are sung for each of the four weeks of this unit, it is most important to have a solid start. Consider inviting a soloist or instrumentalist from your congregation to join you on this first Sunday of Advent. If your approach is positive, the children will also respond positively. Remember that children are often capable of much more than we estimate! So enjoy learning and growing with them.

The first group of songs again sets the tone of coming together and rejoicing!

- People in Darkness Are Looking for Light (119)
- Prepare the Way of the Lord (124)
- O Come, O Come, Immanuel (123)

Keep the momentum flowing and be enthusiastic as you continue with the greeting:

The Lord be with you!
And also with you!

Introduce the idea of the Christian Year by saying something like this: Rejoice! Rejoice! That is what we just sang and that is what we want to do today because we are celebrating the beginning of a new year! No, I did not read my calendar wrong—today is Advent, the first Sunday of the Christian Year. All around us we see lots of signs that the world is getting ready for Christmas. We all like gifts, but we have been given a Gift that is better than any other. That Gift came to us long ago on that first Christmas night when Jesus, our Savior, was born. In the next few weeks we will sing about how Jesus came to earth and how he will come again to take us to our home in heaven.

Then sing the unit theme song "Come, Thou Long-Expected Jesus" (122).

After singing this hymn, the piano should continue on to the next group—setting the mood and letting the words speak to the children. Jesus came as a baby, but he is our Savior.

- Little Baby Jesus (141)
- Send Us Your Spirit (96)
- What Can I Give Him (142)

Remind children of the words they have just sung: give him my heart. Let them know that each one is precious in his sight. He loves each one of us and he is here with us right now. Dismiss them with a blessing such as this: May the words of the next song go with you throughout the next week—and always!

Then sing "Be near me, Lord Jesus," stanza 3 of "Away in a Manger" (129).

The pianist continues to play the last song quietly as the children leave for their small groups.

* * *

Sample 3
Living in God's World

Unit 15, Week 1
Creation

This unit focuses on creation. We worship God, creator of heaven and earth, and are reminded of our responsibility to be stewards of God's gifts to us.

As usual, begin by singing a group of three gathering songs. Let the music and words blend together as the beauty and joy of creation is expressed in song.

- Alleluia, Alleluia! Give Thanks (173)
- All Things Bright and Beautiful (90)
- This Is My Father's World (95)

Continue to express the joy of these songs in your greeting:

The Lord be with you!
And also with you!

Introduce the theme of creation by saying something like this: He is the King of creation!! Flowers, birds, pets, mountains, rivers, sunsets, seasons—he made them all! Sometimes we take it all for granted, don't we? But if we stop for a few minutes and actually think about it, we begin to realize how much he gave us. Our response is to praise God, and so we lift up our voices and sing!

Then sing the unit theme song "All Creatures of Our God and King" (86).

After singing this hymn, you might have someone on a recorder or flute introduce the next song, "Many and Great" (94). This is a traditional Dakota Indian song and lends itself easily to motions.

God has given us so much! We each have a responsibility to take care of what we have and to be good stewards, as this next song expresses. Sing "Forest Trees."

Then have the pianist lead directly into the next song, "Send Us Your Spirit" (96). Sing it two times, the second time in canon. Follow immediately with "Alleluia" (87), including

the stanzas "He is worthy" and "I will praise him."

Encourage children to give their best in singing, and let the music speak for itself. You may choose to do only a few of these songs, but take the time to allow a thoughtful response from the children. As you dismiss children to their small group time, the pianist continues to play "Many and Great" or one of the other songs you have sung together.

Suggestions for Getting Started

1. If possible, organize two groups: preschool through grade 2 and grades 3-6. Alternatively, consider separating the preschool and kindergarten children until after Christmas. Then they can be eased into the larger group after they develop a bit more emotionally, socially, and musically. Try to make the gathering time a positive experience for everyone. Be sure to keep both ends of the age spectrum in mind as you choose music.

2. Invite different parents to come on a rotating basis at least once a month to sit with the children. Leaders of the various grade levels should also sit with and sing with their children. Their presence is an encouragement to the children, and you will appreciate their support as well.

3. Plan to work with congregational leaders in advance to have the children singing for one worship service per unit. If your worship service precedes your church school, extra work is needed to make sure the children come a bit early. Two weeks prior to service participation, send a note home with the children (one per family—the youngest or only child) including service information such as the songs to be sung and when and where children should arrive. Meeting ahead for a few minutes before the service will help the children focus on the purpose for their participation.

4. If the gathering time is held after the service in which children participated, plan a more relaxed session. For example, schedule an older child to bring and play his or her instrument. Those learning to play instruments need to be encouraged. Or divide in-

to teams for listening games (name that song). You may want to spend more time on learning about some aspect of the particular unit you are in.

5. You may choose not to have copies of *Songs for LiFE* in the hands of children each week. Charts or overheads can help to keep their attention focused up front. However, one important goal is to teach children how to use a hymnal. On a regular basis, encourage all those who can read to use the hymnal. They need to learn to "read" the hymnal— to be able to find their way in it, looking for favorite songs, learning new songs, and learning about song authors and composers.

6. Finally, keep good records. Make copies of the "Annual Summary of Units and Unit Theme Songs" (p. 334). This list will be helpful in planning ahead with other worship leaders as well as to keep track of what songs the children have sung in congregational worship.

Keep a record of what you sing each week. One simple method is to start a 3x5 card file for each song. Simply place the title of the song at the top of the card and indicate the dates you used it. Underline those dates in which you sang that song in congregational worship. Or start a computer file, placing the songs in alphabetical order as you go along. In another column, insert the date sung.

Enjoy the Challenge!

This entire approach to leading the gathering time may be very similar to the approach you have used before. Perhaps the main new element is a structure by which you can organize the year. Or maybe the amount of planning required looks like a very time-consuming commitment. Indeed, most teaching follows the two-for-one rule—it takes twice as much time to prepare as to lead. But the rewards are proportional. Leading children in worship is a high calling, and it calls for your best creative efforts. For all the time you spend learning and singing in preparation and with the children, you are storing up for yourself a wonderful treasury of ways to praise God.

Sample Lesson Plan

Date _____Sept. 19_____ Unit __1__ Week __1__ Title _____Opening of Worship_____

Season _____Ordinary_____ Colors/Symbols _____Green_____

Focus Statement: _____In worship, we greet God with praise and adoration._____

_____

Gathering Songs

Key: _____D_____ 1. _____I Will Enter His Gates (9)_____

Key: _____D_____ 2. _____Allelu (7) with Clapping_____

Key: _____F_____ 3. _____In the House of Our God (5)_____

Comments: _____Greeting: The Lord be with you. / And also with you._____

Unit Theme Song

Key: _____F_____ 4. _____Praise to the Lord, the Almighty (27)_____

Additional Songs

Key: _____G_____ 5. _____Alleluia (87)_____

Key: _____D_____ 6. _____Love the Lord (75)_____

Key: _____C_____ 7. _____Father, We Love You (77)_____

Closing Song

Key: _____C_____ 8. _____Go Now in Peace (79)_____

Checklist

___ psalm/hymn/spiritual song _____

___ variety in style, ethnic diversity _____

___ age levels _____

___ movement _____

___ instruments _____

___ song(s) for participation in worship _____

___ key relationships _____

___ what worked well? _____

___ what didn't? _____

Lesson Plan

Date _____ Unit _____ Week _____ Title _____

Season _____ Colors/Symbols _____

Focus Statement: _____

_____

Gathering Songs

Key: _____ 1. _____

Key: _____ 2. _____

Key: _____ 3. _____

Comments: _____

Unit Theme Song

Key: _____ 4. _____

Additional Songs

Key: _____ 5. _____

Key: _____ 6. _____

Key: _____ 7. _____

Closing Song

Key: _____ 8. _____

Checklist

___ psalm/hymn/spiritual song _____

___ variety in style, ethnic diversity _____

___ age levels _____

___ movement _____

___ instruments _____

___ song(s) for participation in worship _____

___ key relationships _____

___ what worked well? _____

___ what didn't? _____

Annual Summary of Units and Unit Theme Songs

Year_____

Unit: _____Dates: _____Weeks: _____

Unit Theme Song: _____

Participation in Congregational Worship: _____

Unit: _____Dates: _____Weeks: _____

Unit Theme Song: _____

Participation in Congregational Worship: _____

Unit: _____Dates: _____Weeks: _____

Unit Theme Song: _____

Participation in Congregational Worship: _____

Unit: _____Dates: _____Weeks: _____

Unit Theme Song: _____

Participation in Congregational Worship: _____

Unit: _____Dates: _____Weeks: _____

Unit Theme Song: _____

Participation in Congregational Worship: _____

Unit: _____Dates: _____Weeks: _____

Unit Theme Song: _____

Participation in Congregational Worship: _____

Unit: _____Dates: _____Weeks: _____

Unit Theme Song: _____

The Elements of Worship

① Opening of Worship

(3 weeks)

Unit Focus
In worship we greet God with praise and adoration.

Unit Goals
Faith Nurture (for leader and children)
- to greet and worship God by singing together
- to praise and adore God for what he has done
- to participate more fully in the beginning of the congregational worship service

Faith Knowledge (for children)
- to tell what worship is
- to describe how the worship service begins
- to sing from memory a hymn for the opening of worship

Faith Modeling (for leader)
- to praise and adore God in song

Materials
1. Songs for the opening of worship, especially from the Gathering and Praise and Thanksgiving sections (1-36)
2. Copies of your church bulletin with notes about how your worship services usually begin

Preparing to Lead the Gathering Time

We often talk about "going to church," meaning we are going to a public meeting that has a special purpose. Anyone may come. God would love it if everyone came. The purpose of this meeting is to worship God and listen to what God has to say. We know that we can talk to God anytime, anywhere. But when we worship as a group in a worship service, something special happens.

God has promised to be present in a special way when we meet to worship as a group. God's family is huge—it includes all the people in the world who meet to worship. Whenever we meet in church, we join together with that big family.

The first word children need to learn is *worship*. Worship simply means to praise and adore God as the best, the greatest, and the most important—the only one worthy of such adoration. If children know that God loves them and takes care of them, they will be motivated to praise and adore God in worship. The essence of worship is not what we know or learn *about* God; it is meeting *with* God—talking, singing, and listening to God and each other. Worship is something we do, not something we attend. Worship is a verb.

Children know what praise is all about. As image-bearers of God, they thrive on praise and give it lavishly. What child has not boasted that her dad or bike or toy is stronger or faster or bigger than her friend's? An important element of praise is telling others how great someone is. Praise expands when we praise someone in front of others. In the same way, we can (and should) praise God directly, but our praise is greater when we tell others how great God is. The psalms are full of testimonial praises: "Sing to him, sing praise to him; tell of all his wonderful acts" (Ps. 105:2). Note how the psalmist connects praise to things God has done, and remember to tell children why we praise God.

Children also know what adoration is about. They give themselves wholeheartedly to someone they love. There is no doubt, no holding back, only implicit trust. Adoration, unlike praise, is not something we tell others about. When we love God for what he has done, we need to tell God directly. Our adoration is rooted in God's love for us, not first of all in our love for God. That is why we can surrender completely.

Now we are ready to talk about the opening of the worship service. This varies from church to church, but some basic similarities exist. Worship often begins with music—an instrumental prelude or a series of praise songs. Often the first spoken words are a **call to worship.** The minister or worship leader recites a verse of Scripture which in effect serves as an invitation to the meeting.

One of the most common calls to worship is taken from Psalm 95:6: "Come, let us bow down in worship, let us kneel before the LORD our Maker" (see 1, "A Psalm for Singing"). Another is from Psalm 96:1: "Sing to the LORD a new song; sing to the LORD, all the earth." Longer passages of Scripture may be read responsively as the call to worship. And often the call to worship is sung by a choir or the congregation. The words used are most appropriately taken from Scripture, since it is God who invites us to worship. The call to worship is sometimes referred to by other names: some churches still use the older term *votum* to refer to the old Reformed practice of starting the service with the words, "Our help is in the name of the Lord . . . " (see 219).

A second part of the beginning of worship is the **greeting.** Just as people say hello to each other when they meet, so God and we greet each other in worship. God's greeting is sometimes called the *salutation.* The greeting, which is often taken from the Bible, may be Paul's greeting used repeatedly in the epistles: "Grace and peace to you from God our Father and the Lord Jesus Christ." The pastor often raises a hand while saying these words, just as we often shake hands when we meet others. The pastor's raised hand is a way of recognizing that God is giving words of blessing. And just as we look at each other when we say hello, we may look at the minister as we hear these words of greeting.

After God greets us, it is our turn to greet God. The best way we can greet God is by singing, so the service also opens with **song.** Group singing is an uncommon activity in today's society—not many people get together to sing

anymore. But God gave everyone a voice and loves to hear us sing.

The call to worship, greetings, and song don't always take place in this order. The call to worship may be in the form of a song. Some congregations open worship with a processional, emphasizing the people's entrance into God's presence. And many churches include greetings between the worship leader and the people, such as this ancient Christian greeting:

Leader: The Lord be with you.
People: **And also with you.**

This would also be an appropriate way for you to greet the children. But rather than using the greeting at the beginning of your time together, begin your session by singing a song or two. Then, once you have the children's attention, greet them and invite their response. If you introduce this greeting, try to use it consistently so the response becomes familiar.

Working with Congregational Worship Leaders

To help the children in your congregation participate in the opening part of the worship service, work together with your pastor or worship leader. Find out which call to worship and greeting will be used during the three Sundays of this unit. Ask that the service begin the same way for each of those three weeks. On the third or fourth Sunday, have the children gather together in front and lead the congregation in song.

If possible, prepare two songs, one a children's song, the other a congregational hymn. The children could sing a simple gathering song as a call to worship, and they could join the congregation for the opening hymn of praise, perhaps singing one stanza by themselves.

Unit Song Suggestions: A Model

Gathering Songs
D   I Will Enter His Gates (9)
Dm I Will Exalt My God, My King (26)
D   Allelu (7)
F   In the House of Our God (5)

Theme Song
F   Praise to the Lord, the Almighty (27)

Additional Songs
G   Alleluia (87)
      Praise the Lord! (23)
D   Love the Lord (75)
C   Father, We Love You (77)
D   Lord, Be Glorified (71)

Closing Song
C   Go Now in Peace (79)

② Confessing to God

(3 weeks)

Unit Focus
In worship we confess our sins and God forgives us.

Unit Goals

Faith Nurture *(for leader and children)*
- to confess our sins to God
- to hear the promise of God's forgiveness
- to respond in thanks and praise

Faith Knowledge *(for children)*
- to tell why we tell God we are sorry for our sins
- to explain why we should obey God's law (because we're thankful!)
- to learn the *Gloria Patri* or another response of praise

Faith Modeling *(for leader)*
- to tell the children your own gratitude for being forgiven by God

Materials
1. Songs from the Confession and Forgiveness sections (37-44)
2. Copies of your church bulletin with notes about the confession, assurance of forgiveness, and responses used in your worship services
3. A cross

Preparing to Lead the Gathering Time

When we meet people we know, one of the first things they ask is "How are you?" And when we meet God in worship, he wants to know the same thing. Unlike many of our hu-man acquaintances, God expects an honest answer. The truth is that we have "sinned and fall short of the glory of God" (Rom. 3:23). So worship properly begins with praise for who God is and then naturally moves on to confession of who we are. This is followed by the good news that in Christ God has forgiven our sins and accepts us as his children. To God's "How are you?" we give a twofold answer: We are sinners estranged from God, but in Christ we are God's redeemed people, called to a life of gratitude and dedication.

In a worship service our response to God's "How are you?" goes by various names. Sometimes it is described as an **Act of Penitence.** Often it is called the **Confession and Assurance** or the **Service of Reconciliation.** These terms emphasize different aspects of the same basic act. *Penitence* means we recognize and are sorry for our sins. The emphasis is on what we are called to do—to face up to our own sinfulness. The phrase *Confession and Assurance* links our action with God's action. It reminds us that the one to whom we confess is not only the Judge of all the earth but also the Merciful One, who loves us and is eager to forgive. Finally, *Reconciliation* highlights the fact that penitence and pardon lead to restored fellowship between God and God's people. That is why the cross is not only a symbol of shame and suffering but also a source of great joy for Christians. It testifies to Christ's work of atonement on our behalf.

Most children should be able to relate the idea of confession and assurance to their own experience. They know what it means to do wrong, to feel sorry, to want to be forgiven, and to make things right again. In worship we come together as one family, the children of God. The liturgical act of confession does not just make us right with God as individuals (though of course it does this as well); it is a solemn reminder of our common family identity. Together we acknowledge our sinfulness; together we hear God's assurance of pardon; together we rededicate ourselves to lives of grateful service and witness. Though it had long been considered only a private act, the sixteenth-century Reformers understood confession as a part of corporate worship.

Ideally, the service of confession and assurance is a dialogue: God speaks, we respond. The first element is usually a **call to confession.** The worship leader may offer a simple invitation to prayer, read an appropriate passage of Scripture, or read God's law (the Ten Commandments or a summary) to remind us of our sinfulness and call us to repentance. The next element is the **prayer of confession.** The prayer can be offered by the worship leader or spoken in unison by the congregation. The confession can also be sung; this is a particularly effective way to involve children. And it can take the form of a litany, a prayer that calls for a repeated congregational response. One of the most widely used litany responses is "Lord, have mercy"—*Kyrie eleison* in Greek. Many churches retain that ancient liturgical response in the language of the early church (see 43).

The prayer of confession sets the stage for the **declaration of pardon or assurance** (sometimes called the *absolution*) offered by the pastor in God's name. Confession can never stand alone; it invites a gracious response. God loves us even when we do wrong, and God forgives us when we are sorry.

As forgiven people, assured of God's mercy, we naturally respond with expressions of praise and dedication. A familiar, time-honored hymn of praise is the *Gloria. Gloria in excelsis,* or "Glory to God in the highest," is an extended song of adoration regularly used in Roman Catholic, Episcopal, and other liturgies. (See also the hymn "All Glory Be to God on High.") The familiar *Gloria Patri* ("Glory Be to the Father") is a more concise form of the hymn. "Gloria, Gloria" (134) is an even shorter and simpler version that can be sung as a round. Frequently used as a response to Scripture, especially the reading of the Psalms, the *Gloria* is often sung in Reformed churches with the recitation of the Apostles' Creed. It is also an appropriate response to the assurance of pardon.

The congregational response of praise may be followed by a statement of rededication or a summary of God's will for his redeemed people. In the Reformed tradition, God's law is often read at this point as a guide for grateful living. Other words of encouragement, usually drawn from Scripture, can fulfill the same purpose.

The service of confession and assurance normally takes place near the beginning of a worship service. It concludes the opening of worship by focusing our thanks and praise on God's forgiveness, and it prepares us to hear God's Word by confirming our identity as a reconciled people.

Working with Congregational Worship Leaders

It should be easy to help children participate actively in this part of worship. Children instinctively understand the idea of penitence and forgiveness, and they love to sing! Once the children have learned a song of confession, ask worship leaders to schedule it regularly for congregational singing. If your congregation commonly uses a song of praise such as the *Gloria Patri,* introduce it to the children during the second or third week of the unit.

Unit Song Suggestions: A Model

Gathering Songs
Dm I Will Exalt My God, My King (26)
F   Praise to the Lord, the Almighty (27)
Dm Sing Alleluia (68)
F   In the House of Our God (5)
F   Praise God's Name (47)

Theme Song
D   Lord, I Want to Be a Christian (40)

Additional Songs
Eb   Jesu, Jesu, Fill Us with Your Love (251)
Em   Jesus, Jesus, Let Us Tell You (231)
D   Lord, Be Glorified (71)
D   God Is So Good (207)
C   Lord, I Pray (37)

Closing Song
Dm Shalom (84)

③ Listening to God's Story

(3 weeks)

Unit Focus
God speaks to us through Scripture and sermon in worship.

Unit Goals

Faith Nurture (for leader and children)
• to hear God speak to us
• to respond with thanks and praise

Faith Knowledge (for children)
• to identify some ways that God speaks to us
• to tell why it's important to listen to God's Word and what it means
• to offer at least one response to God's Word

Faith Modeling (for leader)
• to show love and respect for God's Word

Materials
1. Songs, especially from the Word of God section (56-58)
2. Copies of your church bulletin with notes about the Scripture readings, prayers for illumination, and congregational responses to the readings and/or sermon used in your worship services
3. A Bible

Preparing to Lead the Gathering Time

As we discussed in the last unit, the service of confession and assurance is in the form of a dialogue between God and his people. This pattern of address and response—God to us, we to God—occurs repeatedly throughout a worship service and on many levels. In fact, dialogue is the basic rhythm of all true Christian worship.

It reaches a climax when God's Word is proclaimed. At the beginning of the service we have the privilege of addressing God, knowing that God listens. In this part of the service we have the privilege of hearing Scripture read and proclaimed, knowing that God is speaking to us.

God speaks directly to us! This is the main thing children need to know. God can speak in all sorts of ways—through experiences, friends, and personal study and reflection. But God speaks in a special way when the Word is proclaimed in public worship.

The **service of the Word** has been a central part of worship since the church began, just as it was central to worship in the synagogue in earlier years. Luke 4 tells about a time when Jesus, "as was his custom," went to the synagogue in Nazareth. There he read from the prophets and gave a commentary on the reading. This pattern—Scripture reading followed by sermon—is familiar to every Christian. First we hear the enduring Word of God in the Bible, valid for all people, in all times and places. Then we hear God's living Word proclaimed in the sermon, which applies God's truth to a specific congregation in a specific time and place.

How do we know that God is speaking? In 2 Timothy 3:16, Paul declares that "all Scripture is God-breathed." When the Word is read and proclaimed, the Holy Spirit—the "breath" of God—works within us to help us hear God's voice. This is one of the basic principles of Reformed worship—that the Holy Spirit brings the Word to life in worship. God is not only present; God is working actively among us. True preaching, then, is not a mere human activity but a holy means of communication.

This belief finds expression in a prayer that is often offered just before the reading of Scripture or the sermon. Often called the **prayer**

for illumination, it typically asks for the Spirit's blessing so the Word will be rightly heard and preached.

The "God-breathed" Word, Paul goes on to say in 2 Timothy, "is useful for teaching, rebuking, correcting and training in righteousness." God speaks for a purpose! We listen to God's Word not just because it is a good story or because the person bringing it is an entertaining speaker, but ultimately because this changes us. Although some forms of proclamation are mainly evangelistic—seeking to convince unbelievers of their need for redemption—the primary purpose of proclamation in a worship service is edification. To edify means to erect or build up. The service of the Word is designed to build up the church as the body of Christ so it can do Christ's work more effectively in the world.

The service of the Word usually takes more time than any other part of a worship service, but its structure is quite simple. We have already mentioned the major elements. The first is the prayer for illumination. Ideally this prayer is offered before the Scripture reading and applies to both Scripture and sermon. This prayer is often offered by the person appointed to read the Bible passage; it can also be spoken in unison by the congregation. In some instances it is even sung.

Next comes the **reading of Scripture.** Although Scripture reading is often seen as a task reserved for pastors, any member of the congregation who can read aloud effectively may do so. (The person who reads is called a lector.) The number and types of readings may vary from one congregation to another and from week to week. Often just one passage is chosen—usually the passage on which the sermon is based. This passage may correspond with a theme drawn from a catechism or other confessional statement. Often pastors read and preach about an entire book or section of the Bible over a period of time; this practice is known as *lectio continua.*

In recent years many churches have increased the number of readings used in a worship service. Worship planners might choose one Old Testament and one New Testament reading or a reading from the Old Testament, the gospels, and the epistles. These passages are often drawn from the lectionary, a schedule of readings for each Sunday of the year that is designed to cover a large portion of the Bible in a three-year cycle.

The sermon, also known as a homily, may immediately follow the Bible reading. It may also be separated from the reading, perhaps by a song, to allow the proclamation of Scripture to stand on its own.

Even though the emphasis in this part of the service is on God's message to us, we still have opportunities for **response.** The reading of Scripture, for example, invites a response of acclamation—an expression of praise and joy for the good news revealed. The reader might conclude, for example, by saying, "This is the Word of God" or "This is the gospel of Christ," after which the congregation can respond, "Thanks be to God!" or "Praise be to you, O Christ!" Or the congregation might sing an Alleluia ("Praise the Lord") or other song of praise. Some congregations sing psalms between the readings as a form of response.

The sermon likewise invites response. Often the pastor or a member of the congregation offers a prayer of application or prayer of thanksgiving after the sermon. A period of reflective silence is sometimes appropriate. Spontaneous Amens during the sermon are a familiar feature of worship in some traditions, and a congregational Amen at the end is proper in any tradition.

Working with Congregational Worship Leaders

Many congregations regularly include a children's message in the worship service. If your congregation does this, encourage worship planners to coordinate the children's messages with the unit themes. Or, if the children's messages are tied to the pastor's sermon, try to include songs during the gathering time that reflect that theme. If you do not have a special children's message and if the children in your congregation are present during the sermon, encourage your pastor to make a special effort to address the children in each sermon. If your congregation uses any of the forms of response mentioned in this unit, teach them to the children. You might also teach them a song suitable for use as a prayer for illumination and arrange to have it sung in worship services on subsequent Sundays.

Unit Song Suggestions: A Model

Gathering Songs
Dm   I Will Exalt My God, My King (26)
Dm/D Sing Alleluia (68)
D   Allelu (7)

Theme Song
G   Blessed Jesus, at Your Word (56)

Additional Songs
F   When We Wonder (58)
Eb   Your Word (57)
D   Seek Ye First the Kingdom (155)
Em   Jesus, Jesus, Let Us Tell You (231)

Closing Songs
D   Lord, Be Glorified (71)
D   Shalom to You (85)

④ Baptism: God Includes Us in His Family

(3 weeks)

Unit Focus

Through baptism God assures us that we are members of God's covenant family.

Unit Goals

Faith Nurture (for leader and children)

- to celebrate God's covenant promises
- to thank God for including us in God's family

Faith Knowledge (for children)

- to tell what sacraments are
- to explain why children are baptized
- to tell what the water of baptism means

Faith Modeling (for leader)

- to welcome children as part of God's family

Materials

1. Songs from the Baptism section (59-62)
2. A copy of the form(s) for baptism used in your church with notes about how the sacrament is usually administered
3. Birth and baptismal certificates, a bowl of water, a washcloth and towel
4. The Runaway Bunny by Margaret Wise Brown

Preparing to Lead the Gathering Time

The most obvious way God speaks to us in worship is through the reading and preaching of the Word. But this is not the only way. God also speaks and acts through the **sacraments.** Sacraments (or ordinances, as they are known in some churches) have always been important in Christian worship. In fact, the Re-formers generally insisted on the proper administration of the sacraments as one of the identifying marks of a true church, along with sound preaching and faithful discipline. Most Protestant churches observe two sacraments: baptism and the Lord's Supper. The Eastern Orthodox and Roman Catholic churches, along with a few others, consider other events, such as confession, marriage, and ordination, to be sacraments as well. But all Christians accept baptism and the Lord's Supper as holy actions that Christ himself commanded his church to observe.

The first thing children need to know, of course, is what a sacrament is. The Heidelberg Catechism provides a classic definition: "Sacraments are holy signs and seals for us to see." Sacraments are visible and tangible "pictures" of the promises God makes to us in the Word. At the same time sacraments work to "seal" (confirm, guarantee) those promises, so that we understand them and are assured that they are true. God's Word promises that Christ died to redeem sinners and restore them to God's family. The sacraments confirm that we are members of that family.

While these concepts may seem a bit abstract for young children, the underlying idea is something they can grasp intuitively. Children love to play in the world of make-believe, where a row of kitchen chairs becomes an airplane or the space behind the couch is a cave. As a result, they know all about symbols even if they are unfamiliar with the concept of symbolism. They also know that actions can speak: a parent's hug not only tells them "I love you"; it also lets them experience the fact that this love is true. And that is what sacraments are all about. They are God's way of telling us that he loves us and of showing that this love is real.

Baptism, then, shows that we have been welcomed into God's family, the church. Just as a birth certificate confirms that we belong to our earthly parents, baptism confirms that we belong to our heavenly parent. It assures us that we are children of God and that God will be faithful to his covenant promises. Like the mother rabbit in Margaret Wise Brown's well-known children's story *The Runaway Bunny,* God promises that no matter what we do or where we go, God will love us and be with us. Why do we belong to God? Because in Christ our sins have been forgiven. Just as we use water to wash our bodies, baptism uses water to symbolize the washing away of our sins. (The water symbolizes other things too, such as our dying and rising with Christ, but washing is certainly an important image—and the one children will find easiest to understand.)

God's family is not restricted to adults. Just as children are members of their earthly family before they know who they are, so God reaches out to include us in the circle of his love before we may be aware of it. This belief, rooted in the Old Testament covenant of circumcision, is why Reformed churches have always adhered to the historic Christian practice of infant baptism. Some churches, notably those in the Baptist tradition, believe baptism should be administered only to those old enough to make a conscious commitment to Christ. Though Reformed churches do not accept this position (except, of course, in the case of an adult conversion), they do recognize that baptism remains in a sense incomplete without a commitment as an adult. So when parents present children for baptism, they are asked to reaffirm their own faith and to promise to teach it to their children. And baptized children are expected to affirm their membership in God's family once they are old enough to do so responsibly. Baptism therefore assumes a "growing up" in the faith that leads to a public confirmation or profession of faith.

Because baptism is a sacrament of initiation into the church, it deserves to be celebrated in public worship. Baptism typically occurs quite early in a worship service. Often this may be for practical reasons, but it also makes sense from a liturgical point of view. Since baptism celebrates cleansing from sin, it is appropriate that it occur in the context of confession and assurance.

Specific baptismal practices vary from church to church and denomination to denomination. The basic elements, however, are usually quite similar. Normally the pastor will recite **words of institution**—Christ's command to baptize as recorded in Matthew 28:18-20—as a "warrant" for administering the sacrament. This is usually followed by a statement of the covenant promises confirmed in baptism. God's covenant promises are followed by the covenant promise or commitment of those being baptized (or their parents). Many baptismal forms also include the recitation of the Apostles' Creed, which itself grew out of the baptismal vows of converts in the early church. The sacrament of baptism is always administered with water and in the name of the triune God. Depending on local and denominational traditions, the method may be by sprinkling, pouring, dipping, or immersion. A **prayer of thanksgiving** is usually offered before or after the baptism, and no baptism is complete without a song of celebration and dedication.

Working with Congregational Worship Leaders

It would be ideal if baptism were celebrated in your congregation on one of the Sundays of this unit. Check with the pastor or another worship leader to see if this might be possible, and arrange your schedule accordingly. Teach the children about your congregation's unique baptism traditions. Many churches hang a special banner for each baptismal service. Some congregations even provide small replicas of the banner to those who are baptized. Other congregations use a baptismal candle. Whatever the tradition in your congregation, make sure the children are aware of its use.

In many churches the children are invited to sit or stand around the baptismal font during the sacrament. The pastor then briefly explains what is happening and introduces the newest member of God's family to the children. If your congregation has never done this, you might encourage the pastor to try it. Also arrange to have a baptism song that the children have learned included in the service. If the children have gathered to witness the sacrament up close, they could lead the congregation in singing from the front of the sanctuary.

Unit Song Suggestions: A Model

Gathering Songs
D I Will Enter His Gates (9)
D Allelu (7)
F Alleluia, Alleluia! Give Thanks (173)
F Praise to the Lord, the Almighty (27)

Theme Song
C Baptized in Water (60)

Additional Songs
Bb Children of the Lord (238)
D Seek Ye First the Kingdom (155)
C How Great Is the Love of the Father (59)
D God Is So Good (207)

Closing Songs
C Go Now in Peace (79)
D Lord, Be Glorified (71)
D Shalom to You (85)

⑤ The Lord's Supper: God Feeds Us at His Table

(3 weeks)

Unit Focus
In the Lord's Supper, we are fed and we celebrate God's power and goodness in Jesus.

Unit Goals
Faith Nurture (for leader and children)
- to offer praise and thanksgiving for God's power and goodness
- to remember with gratitude the life, death, and resurrection of Jesus
- to sing expectantly of Christ's return in glory

Faith Knowledge (for children)
- to tell why Christians celebrate the Lord's Supper
- to explain what the bread and wine of communion mean
- to learn at least one hymn used in the Lord's Supper

Faith Modeling (for leader)
- to welcome the children as members of Christ's body

Materials
1. Songs from the following sections: Lord's Supper (63-67), Suffering and Death of Christ (158-171), Resurrection and Ascension of Christ (172-181)
2. A copy of the form(s) for the Lord's Supper used in your church with notes about how the congregation normally participates through responses, prayers, and songs
3. Table setting of communion vessels, some bread and wine (grape juice), a cross

Preparing to Lead the Gathering Time

All children need to know that they are members of a loving family. But they need more than that; they also need instruction, training, and encouragement—and they need to eat. As God's children, we need the assurance, celebrated in baptism, that we are members of God's family. But we also need instruction, training, and encouragement from God's Word. And we need the nourishment that God provides when we gather around the table of the Lord.

The breaking of bread has always been a central feature of Christian worship. Ideally, it forms the second major climax in the worship dialogue, following the reading and preaching of the Word. In practice, no part of the worship service has sparked more disagreement over the years, and none is more complex—or richer in meaning. While children can hardly be expected to grasp things that scholars have spent lifetimes trying to explain, they can become familiar with some of the common names for the sacrament and what each name implies.

Most of us probably know this sacrament best as the **Lord's Supper.** This name calls attention to at least two important facts. One is that the sacrament is basically a *meal:* we do not gather in front of an altar but around a table. The other is that this is the *Lord's* meal. The Lord's Supper reminds us that God came to us as a flesh-and-blood person who ate and drank with his friends. It recalls in particular the meal that Christ shared with his disciples in the upper room before his death and resurrection.

The last supper was not just any meal. It was a Passover meal, a feast celebrating the deliverance of God's chosen people from bondage. By making the Passover bread and wine symbols of his own body and blood, Christ showed the disciples in a new and special way that he had come to deliver all God's people from the bondage of sin. Ever since, following their Lord's command, Christians have shared bread and wine in remembrance of him. "Remembrance" means much more than recalling what Christ did. It is not so much a calling to mind as a taking to heart; it is an act of commitment. Coming to the table is a way of saying that we belong to God, not to ourselves or to anyone else. And God pledges in return that just as surely as bread and wine have life-giving value for our physical bodies, so the body and blood of Christ give us spiritual life, both now and for eternity.

Another familiar term is **Communion.** Services that include the Lord's Supper are often called Communion services. The word "Communion" has a variety of meanings, but at heart it implies being at one with someone, sharing deeply with another person; it's not unlike what children mean by being "best friends." Taking Communion is an act of union with Christ; we are united spiritually with Christ, just as the bread and wine become part of our physical bodies. But Communion not only unites us with Christ; it also unites us with fellow believers. Around the Lord's table we all become "best friends." Communion makes us all brothers and sisters, loving members of God's family.

Early Christians expressed this fellowship in their worship services, especially at the Lord's Supper, with a kiss of peace. The "passing of the peace" is once again emerging in the worship services of many churches. Today it is more likely to involve a handshake than a kiss—though a kiss or hug is hardly out of place within a family.

A third name may be less familiar, though it is as old as the church itself. **Eucharist** is a term derived from a Greek word meaning, simply, *thanksgiving*. If *Lord's Supper* calls attention to what God gives us, and if *Communion* reminds us of our unity with Christ and fellow believers, *Eucharist* suggests that when we celebrate the Lord's Supper, we have something to give

to God. Jesus instituted the supper by offering thanks for bread and wine. When we share bread and wine, we too are called to offer thanks—thanks not just for Christ's death, but also for his life, his resurrection, and his ascension. We even give thanks in anticipation of Christ's future return in glory, for the promise that a place will be set for us at his great banquet table in the new creation.

The Lord's Supper, in short, is not only something to be thankful for; it is in itself an act of thanksgiving. However solemn the event may be, the underlying tone should always be joyful. This sense of joy and wonder is expressed beautifully in the *Sanctus* ("Holy, holy, holy," Isaiah 6:3). That text has been sung during the Eucharist for more than 1,500 years (see 66).

The Lord's Supper normally follows—and in a sense completes—the service of the Word. The close relationship between Word and sacrament is suggested by the story of the disciples on the road to Emmaus after Christ's resurrection (Luke 24:13-35). First, as they are walking, Jesus "preaches" to them, explaining the good news taught in the Scriptures. Afterwards, at the table, the good news takes on flesh and blood as they recognize who is breaking bread with them.

Today churches celebrate the Lord's Supper in a great variety of ways. The celebration may be formal and elaborate or informal and simple. Some churches celebrate every Sunday, others infrequently. Whatever form the celebration takes, however, it probably includes at least four major actions, following the example of Christ in the upper room.

- **Taking.** First, the pastor takes the bread and wine (the *elements*). The elements may have been brought to the table in an offertory procession or they may have been placed on the table before the service.

- **Blessing.** Second, a blessing is offered, giving thanks for God's mighty work of creation and redemption, centered in the gift of God's Son. Usually this includes a prayer of consecration, which sets the elements apart for their special use in the sacrament. Here (or elsewhere in the service) the worship leader reads the words of institution, often quoted from 1 Corinthians 11, where Paul presents what Christ did in the upper room as the "warrant" for the church's celebration today.

- **Breaking.** Third, the pastor breaks the bread and pours the wine.

- **Giving.** Finally, the elements are given to the people. In many churches the people receive the bread and wine while sitting in their seats; in others the people go forward to receive the elements at the table.

These basic actions are often surrounded by prayers, responses, and hymns. The *Sanctus* is often sung as part of the blessing. Another ancient hymn, the *Agnus Dei* ("Lamb of God"), is often sung in connection with the breaking of the bread. Reformed liturgies for the Lord's Supper have traditionally featured a lengthy discourse about the meaning of the sacrament and the proper way to approach it. More recently, many churches have adopted new forms, often based on models from the early church, in which Communion is the climax of an extended prayer of thanksgiving, remembrance, and intercession known as the Eucharistic prayer or the Great Thanksgiving.

Who may sit at the Lord's table? This is a question many churches are wrestling with today. Participation was traditionally limited to adults who had publicly professed their faith. Today many people are coming to believe that children too need the spiritual nourishment of the table. Whatever your church's practice, children should be assured that they belong to God's family and are therefore promised a place at the Lord's table, either now or in the future.

Working with Congregational Worship Leaders

This unit, like the unit on baptism, should ideally be coordinated with the celebration of the sacrament. Be familiar with the specific ways your congregation celebrates the Lord's Supper so you can explain to the children what will happen and why. You might find it helpful to identify the places in your church's liturgy where the actions of taking, blessing, breaking, and giving occur. (Do they occur in the order presented? How are they done?) If you use a form that includes congregational responses, prayers, or hymns, teach the children some of these basic elements so they can join the congregation.

If children do not ordinarily receive communion in your congregation, consider asking the pastor to invite them to sit or stand around the table, much as at baptism, for a brief introduction to the sacrament and perhaps a special blessing. In churches where the people go forward to receive the elements, children may be encouraged to join their parents for a special blessing.

Unit Song Suggestions: A Model

Gathering Songs
Dm Sing Alleluia (68)
D   Oh, How Good Is Christ the Lord (177)
Eb   This Is the Day (3)
F   Alleluia, Alleluia! Give Thanks (173)
F   Rejoice in the Lord Always (230)

Theme Song
F   I Come with Joy to Meet My Lord (64)

Additional Songs
Eb   Children of the Lord (238)
C   As Your Family, Lord, Meet Us Here (65)
Eb   Lord, I Want to Be a Christian (40)
D   Lord, Be Glorified (71)
C   Father, We Love You (77)

Closing Song
F   I Come with Joy to Meet My Lord (64)

Responding to God's Story (1)

(4 weeks)

Unit Focus
We respond to God in worship by dedicating our lips and our lives to God's service.

Unit Goals
Faith Nurture (for leader and children)
- to express faith in God
- to offer gifts of song to God

Faith Knowledge (for children)
- to explain what a creed is
- to tell why we give offerings
- to learn a song of dedication

Faith Modeling (for leader)
- to express your faith to the children
- to demonstrate a spirit of gratitude and generosity

Materials
1. Songs from the Dedication and Offering section (68-77)
2. Copies of your church bulletin with notes about how creeds and other forms of testimony are used in services, and about how and when the offering is taken
3. An offering plate or basket

Preparing to Lead the Gathering Time

Worship is not a spectator sport. God's people do not gather to observe or to have things done on their behalf. As the apostles declared (1 Pet. 2:9) and the Reformers reiterated, the church is a priesthood of all believers.

One of the main responsibilities of Old Testament priests was to offer sacrifices to God. We, the priests of the New Testament era, have the same calling. Romans 12 emphasizes that God wants us to offer "living sacrifices," dedicating ourselves to the cause of God's kingdom rather than to the things of the world. Hebrews 13:15-16 suggests two forms these living sacrifices should take. One is the offering of praise from "lips that confess his name"; the other is "to do good and to share with others." We must offer our lips and our lives, and congregational worship gives us the opportunity to make both of these offerings. The creed calls us to confess God's name, and the offering calls us to share God's gifts with others.

A **creed** is a statement of belief. That sounds simple enough, but it is not something to be taken lightly. When we say "I believe," we are doing more than indicating our agreement with an idea or principle. We are making a serious pledge of allegiance, staking our lives on what is finally and ultimately true. To recite a creed, then, is to take a stand—and therefore the proper posture when speaking or singing a creed is to stand.

The earliest creeds were simple, existential statements arising out of a direct personal experience with Christ. Thomas's exclamation "My Lord and my God!" (John 20:28) and Peter's declaration "You are the Christ, the Son of the living God" (Matt. 16:16) are both creedal statements. The basic creed of the early church was a simple confession: "Jesus is Lord" (Phil. 2:11). When our children sing "Jesus loves me, this I know" they too are giving voice to a simple creed.

Jesus is Lord: that is most important. But even the first Christians found themselves disagreeing about who Christ really was and what he really taught. Over time, therefore, the church began to develop more detailed statements of belief. The best known are the Nicene Creed and the Apostles' Creed, still in use today and little changed in over 1,600 years. We often describe these creeds, along with one or two others, as ecumenical creeds—creeds that the vast majority of Christians in all times, places, and traditions have accepted as authoritative summaries of the faith. While both the Apostles' and Nicene creeds are widely used in worship, the Apostles' Creed is probably more familiar to most people. The popularity of this creed is easy to understand: it is simple, beautiful, and easily memorized.

Unit 4 explained that the Apostles' Creed began as a profession of faith made by converts at the time of their baptism. Its structure reflects the core doctrine of the Trinity: God is Creator, Redeemer, and life-giving Spirit. The Apostles' Creed sums up the New Testament gospel in much the same way that Christ's teaching on the commandments (Matt. 22:37-40) summarizes the Old Testament law.

Over the years, especially during periods of crisis, Christians have developed new statements of belief. The Reformation produced many such statements, including the Belgic Confession and the Westminster Confession. In the 1930s German Protestants approved a confession known as the Barmen Declaration. In 1978 the Reformed Church in America adopted a creed known as "Our Song of Hope," and in 1986 the Christian Reformed Church adopted a contemporary testimony, "Our World Belongs to God." Other denominations have produced similar documents.

These recent confessions have much the same relationship to the ecumenical creeds as a sermon has to Scripture: they seek to apply an unchanging faith to changing present-day situations. They therefore play an important role in worship. They do not, however, command the same universal authority as the traditional creeds. When we recite the Apostles' Creed, we are joining ranks with believers of all ages, many of whom were martyrs for the faith. Strictly speaking, a martyr is a witness, and we too are called to dedicate ourselves as witnesses to God's truth. This is no light task.

The **offering** is no small matter, either, though we often approach it lightly. The offering is an important act of worship—not just a practical way of collecting money to keep the church running. The oldest surviving description of a Christian worship service, written by Justin Martyr more than 1,800 years ago, indicates that offerings were a prominent feature of worship even then. The Reformers too insisted that "remembering the poor" was a vital act of worship.

The word "offering" implies giving freely, presenting something as a token of dedication or devotion. Everything we have is a gift from God, and our offerings are a way of acknowledging God as the giver. Through our offerings we give back some of what God has given us and dedicate it specifically to God's purposes. This is often symbolized by an offertory procession, in which the people present their gifts to God with prayers and songs of gratitude and dedication. In the early church, believers often personally brought their offerings forward. Today, in most churches, deacons or other appointed persons collect the offerings and present them on behalf of the people. The presentation of offerings is a solemn act of dedication by God's people.

Normally we associate the offering with money. But money is not an end in itself. It serves as a symbol of the many other gifts we should return to the Lord. The familiar children's carol "What Can I Give Him" (142) reminds us that the greatest gift we can offer is our "heart"—our deepest devotion. When we offer our heart, all sorts of other things are sure to follow: time, possessions, talents, insights, and concern for others. Some congregations schedule a periodic "offering of letters" in which members write to public officials on behalf of the poor, the hungry, and the oppressed.

Regardless of its form, the offering is a vital part of our response to God. It helps us connect our adoration for God with our life of discipleship. Like the creed, the offering calls us to be martyrs—witnesses to God's truth with our lips and with our lives.

Working with Congregational Worship Leaders

The Apostles' Creed, spoken or sung, is a regular part of worship in many churches. Children should be encouraged to learn it as early as possible so they can join in. A familiar song like "Jesus Loves Me" is also a simple creed, and so it would be appropriate to sing a children's song in place of a traditional creed from time to time in worship.

Children also enjoy participating actively in the offering. If you include an offering as part of church school, encourage the children to present their gifts in an informal offertory procession. This can be noisy and chaotic at times, especially if the group is large, but it's a wonderful experience of the act of giving. (This could also be done in a regular worship service if your congregation is small enough and the atmosphere is sufficiently informal.) If the offertory normally concludes with a song of praise or dedication, make sure the children know it and can sing along.

Unit Song Suggestions: A Model

Gathering Songs
Dm In the Presence of Your People (25)
F   Praise the Lord with the Sound of Trumpet (32)
Dm I Will Exalt My God, My King (26)
     Praise the Lord! (23)
Em   O Sing to the Lord (17)
Dm Sing Alleluia (68)
G   Jesus, Jesus, Praise Him (12)
F   Trust and Obey (213)

Theme Song
C   Take My Life (74)

Additional Songs
D   Seek Ye First the Kingdom (155)
F   Father, I Adore You (28)
Fm   You and I (246)
D   Believe in the Lord (223)
Em   Jesus, Jesus, Let Us Tell You (231)
C   Lord, I Pray (37)

Closing Songs
G   Alleluia (87)
C   Go Now in Peace (79)

Responding to God's Story (2)

(4 weeks)

Unit Focus
God graciously hears our prayers and sends us out with a blessing.

Unit Goals
Faith Nurture (for leader and children)
- to offer God praise and petitions in song
- to hear God's promise of blessing and peace

Faith Knowledge (for children)
- to list the basic elements of prayer
- to recite the Lord's Prayer
- to learn at least one doxology used in worship
- to explain what a benediction is

Faith Modeling (for leader)
- to pray with confidence in word and song
- to offer praise to God and blessings to God's covenant children

Materials
1. Songs from the Prayer (45-55) and Parting (78-85) sections
2. Copies of your church bulletin with notes about how and where prayers and doxologies are used in worship services and about the forms of benediction your pastor customarily uses

Preparing to Lead the Gathering Time

In Unit 6 we noted that one of the ways we respond to God in worship is by acting as priests, offering up living sacrifices of dedication and commitment. As priests we have another responsibility as well: we are called to pray. The

psalms, in fact, clearly connect prayer and sacrifice (Ps. 141:1-2).

In a broad sense, prayer is any form of conscious fellowship with God; hence the apostle Paul can urge believers to "pray continually" (1 Thess. 5:17). In this sense, the entire worship service is a prayer meeting. But usually when we speak of prayer, we have something more specific in mind: our conscious communication with God. Even in this limited sense, prayer is a vital part of our worship dialogue.

Prayer serves many purposes in worship and has a wide variety of forms. Many kinds have been mentioned in previous units: prayers of adoration and acclamation, prayers of confession, prayers of thanksgiving, prayers of invocation, prayers of dedication, and so on. Prayer may be silent or audible, spoken or sung, spontaneous or prepared in advance. Prayers may be offered standing with raised arms (again, see Ps. 141), kneeling, or seated with hands folded and head bowed. Sometimes the pastor or another member of the congregation offers a prayer on behalf of the congregation. At other times, everyone prays in unison or the congregation and leader pray responsively. You may find it helpful to review various orders of worship to identify the roles of different types of prayers in a worship service.

The priestly dimension of prayer is most evident in the **congregational prayer,** sometimes called the prayers of the people. In some churches this is known as the pastoral prayer but congregational prayer is a better term. This prayer "belongs" to the entire congregation even if it is offered by a single person—and there is certainly no compelling reason why this person has to be the pastor.

Another helpful name for the congregational prayer is the **intercessory prayer,** a term that calls attention to this prayer's primary purpose. Whenever we pray, we offer adoration, praise, thanksgiving, confession, and petitions. But in the congregational prayer we address God in a special way as intercessors—go-betweens—for each other and for the world at large. We pray not just for our own congregation and for those we know, but for those in authority, those suffering oppression, the poor, the hungry, the sick, and so on.

In the early church, intercessory prayers were so important that only full members of the church were allowed to participate; all others were dismissed from the service before the prayers began. The prayers themselves often took the form of a litany. The leader would announce a subject for prayer (the *bidding*), the people would pray silently for a time, and then the leader would conclude with a brief summary prayer (a *collect*). Some churches still use this form of prayer for their congregational intercessions.

When the disciples asked Jesus to teach them to pray, he did not lecture them about the principles of effective prayer. Instead, he gave them a model, drawn largely from prayer themes already familiar to devout Jews of the time. The **Lord's Prayer** (48) remains the model prayer for all Christians. It teaches us that what we ask of God must be rooted in praise and blessing ("hallowed be thy name") and must flow out of the most basic of all Christian desires, the desire that God's kingdom come and God's will be done. The Lord's Prayer has a variety of functions in worship. Often—during sacraments, for example—it may be prayed in unison as an expression of our unity in the Lord. It is also used frequently to sum up and draw together all the prayers of the congregation.

One special form of prayer is the **doxology.** A doxology is a "word of praise" for God's glory and goodness. In a sense, doxology is therefore what all worship should be about. Usually, though, we do not talk about doxology in general but about "the Doxology," referring to the familiar hymn "Praise God, from Whom All Blessings Flow" (11). This is often sung as an act of dedication and gratitude after the offering. But doxologies take many forms and they can occur at various points in the service. A *Gloria* (134) or other hymn of praise sung in response

to God's assurance of pardon is a form of doxology. The most familiar version of the Lord's Prayer begins and ends with doxologies—"hallowed be thy name" and "for thine is the kingdom." Certainly there is no better way to end our meeting with God than with a doxology, a last joyful burst of praise and adoration.

If our last word is a doxology, God's last word is typically a **benediction.** A benediction is literally a "good word," an expression of blessing and good will. Just as we tell departing friends to "take care" or "have a safe trip," so God wishes us well as we prepare to leave the service. Like doxologies, benedictions come in many forms. Perhaps the most familiar is the Aaronic blessing found in Numbers 6:24-26: "The LORD bless you and keep you . . . and give you peace" (80). The benediction is usually spoken by the minister with hands raised—an ancient gesture of blessing.

Sometimes the benediction includes a call to mission such as "Go in peace to love and serve the Lord." Like the offering, a benediction of this sort reminds us that our worship must bear fruit in our witness. Having come together as God's children to meet God, we go out with the mandate to promote his rule in the world. Meeting God as part of his family is not only the privilege of a lifetime but also one that involves a lifetime of responsibility!

Working with Congregational Worship Leaders

Singing the doxology is an important way for children to participate fully in worship. Make sure the children are familiar with the songs of doxology that your congregation uses—and make sure they know where to expect them in the service so they can be ready to join in. Ask whether it is possible for the children to occasionally lead the singing of a doxology or teach the congregation a new doxology they have learned.

For children, as for adults, saying the Lord's Prayer together is a good way to take an active part in congregational prayers. A simple prayer song, familiar to the children, can also make

an appropriate beginning or ending to a time
of intercessory prayer.

Unit Song Suggestions: A Model

Gathering Songs
Dm Sing Alleluia (68)
Dm I Will Exalt My God, My King (26)
F   Praise to the Lord, the Almighty (27)
F   Praise the Lord with the Sound of Trum-
     pet (32)
Em O Sing to the Lord (17)
Dm In the Presence of Your People (25)
     Praise the Lord! (23)
F   Praise God's Name (47)
F   In the House of Our God (5)

Theme Song
G   Oh, for a Thousand Tongues to Sing (19)

Additional Songs
D   Love the Lord (75)
Eb   Children of the Lord (238)
D   Seek Ye First the Kingdom (155)
D   Lord, I Want to Be a Christian (40)
C   Father, We Love You (77)
D   Love the Lord (75)
D   God Is So Good (207)
C   As Your Family, Lord, Meet Us Here (65)
D   Lord, Be Glorified (71)

Closing Song
F   May the Lord Bless You (80)

The
Christian
Year

Advent

(4 weeks)

Unit Focus
In Advent we prepare for the coming of Jesus, who came long ago as a baby and is coming back.

Unit Goals
Faith Nurture (for leader and children)
- to remember that Jesus came to earth to be our Savior
- to remember that God's people in all times and places need Jesus
- to feel sure that Jesus is preparing a place for us and will come back to take us to live with him

Faith Knowledge (for children)
- to explain the difference between Advent and Christmas
- to identify the liturgical color of Advent
- to learn an Advent song

Faith Modeling (for leader)
- to share with the children what Christ's coming means to you

Materials
1. Advent songs (119-127)
2. Chart showing the Christian year with the different colors (see Preparing to Lead the Gathering Time); or perhaps a wooden model used in the Children and Worship program
3. Advent wreath

Preparing to Lead the Gathering Time

Advent is the beginning of the Church year, or Christian year, as it is sometimes called. Before talking about Advent, let's take a quick look at the Christian year. The first half of the Church year deals largely with the events of Jesus' life, from his birth through the sending of the Spirit on Pentecost. The second half of the Church year begins after Pentecost and lasts till the next Advent. The first half can be further divided into two "cycles." The Christmas cycle centers around Jesus' birth (Advent, Christmas, and Epiphany). The second cycle centers around Jesus' death and resurrection (Lent, Easter, and Pentecost).

The chart shown here pictures the Christian year as a circle or pie. It indicates the relative length of each part of the year as well as the various colors that are associated with the seasons of the Church year. You may wish to copy the chart onto heavy paper, labeling and coloring each section as indicated. By cutting the pie into sections, the chart becomes a puzzle that children can arrange in the proper order.

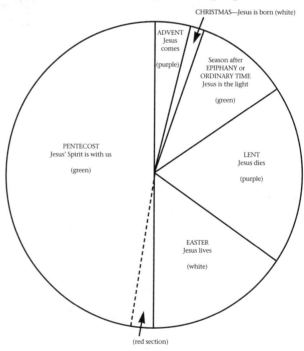

On the four Sundays before Christmas the church begins a new Church year. The first part of this Church year is Advent—a period of four weeks that is used to prepare ourselves for Christmas.

Advent means "coming," or "arrival." During Advent we anticipate and prepare for Jesus' coming. Sometimes the minister may preach about the three "comings" of Jesus. What does this mean?

The first coming that we especially remember is Jesus' birth in Bethlehem. God's Old Testament people had been looking forward to this coming for hundreds of years. "When will our Savior come to rescue us from our enemies and from our sins?" During Advent we will often read passages from the Old Testament that talk about this expectation. And we may hear the stories about Zechariah and Elizabeth, the parents of John the Baptist, and about the angel Gabriel coming to Mary—reminders of Jesus' coming to earth.

But Jesus' coming was not just an event that happened long ago in history books. The second coming that we remember is Jesus coming to live in our hearts and our lives. We know that although Jesus went back to heaven, in a real way he is still with us. Jesus fills our hearts with his Spirit and our lives with his love.

The third coming is an event we look forward to. Some day Jesus will come again. Then all his people from all times and from all over the world will live with him in the new heaven and the new earth. During Advent we anticipate this coming of Jesus, when we will be with him for ever and ever. Until then, we are called to "Prepare the Way of the Lord" (124).

How can we best remember and celebrate Jesus' coming during the Advent season? Besides the minister preaching about expecting Jesus, we also sing about it. We will probably sing "Come, Thou Long-Expected Jesus" (122), and "O Come, O Come, Immanuel" (123)—songs that express the longing of God's people in the Old Testament, and also speak of our longing for Jesus to come again.

During Advent many churches also use an Advent wreath made of evergreen branches to show that Jesus' love for us never dies. The wreath has four purple (or dark blue) candles and one white one. Purple stands for royalty or for suffering. During Advent we remember that Jesus came to suffer and die, and he also is our King. During each of the four Sundays before Christmas, we light one more purple candle. (In some churches one of the candles is pink, which stands for joy.) On Christmas Eve or Christmas Day we light the white candle. This candle stands for Jesus, the light of the world. Some churches also hold a special "candle light" service, where everyone holds a small candle. These candles remind us of the light of Jesus shining in our darkness.

Another way for churches to celebrate Advent is by having a Jesse tree, most often a tree with bare branches. Each Sunday during Advent someone hangs words or pictures or symbols on the branches that remind us of the Old Testament promises about Jesus. For example, words from the prophet Isaiah, such as "Immanuel" (God with us), remind us of the Old Testament promise of a Savior. Pictures of a branch or leaves remind us that Jesus was from the family tree of David.

Working with Congregational Worship Leaders

Advent is one season where children have always been involved in congregational worship. Everyone is attuned to the celebration of the season, resources for observing Christmas are abundant, and most congregations eagerly participate in festivities and traditions.

Coordination in worship planning for this season is especially important. Ideally, one person coordinates all the programs, services, and performances. If such a person is not available, then worship leaders, committee chairpersons, and others involved need to start planning as early as possible, making sure there is good communication between everyone involved.

Unit Song Suggestions: A Model

Gathering Songs
D   People in Darkness Are Looking for Light (119)
Eb Prepare the Way of the Lord (124)
Em O Come, O Come, Immanuel (123)
F   The Prophets Came to Israel (128)

Theme Song
F   Come, Thou Long-Expected Jesus (122)

Additional Songs
Cm Little Baby Jesus (141)
G   He Came Down (136)
D   Come, Lord Jesus (138)
F   What Can I Give Him (142)

Closing Song
F   Away in a Manger (129)

⑨ Christmas and Epiphany

(2 weeks)

Unit Focus
Jesus was born to become the Light of the whole world.

Unit Goals

Faith Nurture (for leader and children)
- to wonder at the mystery that God sent Jesus as a baby
- to be thankful that Jesus came to be our Savior
- to thank God that all people in all places are being drawn to Christ

Faith Knowledge (for children)
- to tell what "epiphany" means
- to describe the colors of Christmas and Epiphany
- to learn a Christmas and Epiphany song

Faith Modeling (for leader)
- to show the children that you, like the wise men, desire to offer your best gifts to Jesus, including voice and heart

Materials
1. Songs from the Christmas section (128-143), others which include the theme of light (127, 152, 208), and possibly some mission songs from the Loving Our Neighbors section (244-252)
2. Boxes wrapped in the colors of Christmas and Epiphany
3. A Christ candle

Preparing to Lead the Gathering Time

Since many church schools schedule a Christmas program and perhaps take a short break over the Christmas holidays, this unit combines Christmas and Epiphany. Undoubtedly, you have been singing Christmas songs during Advent to prepare for the Christmas celebration. Epiphany is a one-day feast on January 6, following the traditional twelve days of Christmas. The weeks that follow are often called the Sundays *after* Epiphany. This short unit provides a natural movement from celebrating the birth of Christ to considering the incarnation: Christ's coming as the light of the world.

First, we celebrate Christmas. On Christmas Eve or on Christmas Day the congregation gathers to tell the story of Jesus' birth again. Just looking at the church sanctuary tells us that this is a joyous occasion. Flowers and plants, a Christmas tree, banners—all of these contribute to a visual feast. The "official" colors for Christmas are white, to show Jesus' purity, or gold, to show that he is King. Lights and candles add to the celebration, and they remind us that Jesus is the Light of the world.

When speaking of the light of Christmas, children will first of all think of the star that led the wise men to Bethlehem. That brings us to the second part of the unit: Epiphany.

On the day of Epiphany we remember the coming of the wise men (or Magi or Kings) from the east. It's appropriate to remember this event apart from the Christmas celebration, since the Magi did not come to Bethlehem until nearly two years after Jesus' birth. Although the focus of Epiphany is on light and joy, we also remember Herod's murder of the infant boys of Bethlehem and Mary and Joseph's flight into Egypt. Jesus' birth was an occasion for joy, but it was also accompanied by grief and suffering.

Epiphany means showing or revealing. God revealed his love to the wise men when they followed the star that led them to Jesus, their Savior. These wise men were not part of the people of Israel. They were unfamiliar with the stories in the Bible. By revealing the news of Jesus' birth to strangers, we learn that God's love, revealed to us in the birth of Jesus, is not just for the people of Israel. It's for all of us.

And the story of God's love should be told all over the world. That's why we also think about missionaries, who tell the story of God's love all over the world, on this day and in the weeks to come.

The liturgical colors for the day of Epiphany, as for Christmas, are white or gold (referring to Jesus). The main symbols are the star, which reminds us of both the star seen by the wise men and of Jesus, "the bright Morning Star" (Rev. 22:16), and light. The wise men were guided by the light of the star and their journey to Jesus brought spiritual light into their lives. Jesus calls himself "the light of the world" (see 152).

This light also applies to God's people. Philippians 2 says we are to shine like stars or lights in a dark world. As we stand and walk in Jesus' light, we reflect that light so that others can find Jesus and escape the darkness in their lives.

Working with Congregational Worship Leaders

Your congregation probably has well-established traditions involving children in Christmas celebrations. Ask your pastor or worship committee if services are planned to celebrate the day of Epiphany using the theme of light, the worldwide church, or missions. Suggest prayers and songs that focus on those themes.

Unit Song Suggestions: A Model

Gathering Songs
F   Look Up! (127)
F   The Prophets Came to Israel (128)
G   He Came Down (136)
F   Good News (132)

Theme Song
F   Go, Tell It on the Mountain (131)

Additional Songs
F   That Boy-Child of Mary (130)
F   Angels We Have Heard on High (133)
F   I Am the Light of the World (152)
F   Gloria, Gloria (134)

Closing Song
Cm Little Baby Jesus (141)

The Life and Work of Christ

(4 weeks)

Unit Focus
We follow Jesus, who teaches us how to live.

Unit Goals
Faith Nurture (for leader and children)
- to rejoice in the love Jesus showed by teaching and healing his people
- to trust that Jesus loves us today
- to want to follow Jesus and be like him

Faith Knowledge (for children)
- to describe some ways in which Jesus helped people—then and now
- to identify the liturgical color for "Ordinary Time," the season after Epiphany

Faith Modeling (for leader)
- to demonstrate your own desire to follow Jesus
- to show concern for people in your congregation

Materials
1. Songs from the Epiphany/Ministry of Christ section (144-157), People of the Bible (99-118, especially 112-116), Walking with God (211-234, especially 221, 226, 233)
2. Chart showing the Christian year

Preparing to Lead the Gathering Time

This unit focuses on the teaching and healing ministry of Christ. The number of weeks for this and the following unit on the suffering and death of Christ may differ from year to year, since Easter is not a set date. You may wish to precede or follow this unit with, for ex-

ample, the unit on Mission (Unit 18). A mission theme would follow naturally out of Epiphany as well as out of the teaching and healing ministry of Christ.

The weeks after Epiphany are called by various names. The name "Ordinary Time" indicates that during this season we do not focus on any particular event or theme in Jesus' life. It is also called "The Epiphany Season" or "The Season after Epiphany." Depending on the date for Easter, this season lasts from six to ten weeks. The liturgical color for this part of the Christian year is green, reminding us of our new life in Christ.

The first Sunday after Epiphany usually focuses on Jesus' baptism. The story of Jesus' baptism helps us understand his ministry. Even though Jesus is not sinful like we are, he came to earth to be like us. Jesus was baptized, just as we are baptized. The Bible teaches that Jesus came in our place.

For this unit we will follow three themes:

1. the call to follow Jesus
2. the teaching of Jesus
3. the miracles of Jesus

Since any one of these themes could provide enough material for the whole unit, you may want to focus on a different one each year.

1. The Call to Follow Jesus
   After Jesus was baptized he chose twelve disciples, his special friends and followers. Later there were many people who followed Jesus, but these twelve went with him on all his travels (see 113, "Jesus Called the Twelve Disciples"). The gospel stories tell how the disciples were chosen in different ways. For example, Simon Peter was called by Jesus from his fishing boat (see 114, "Jesus Called to Peter" and 144, "When Jesus Saw the Fishermen") and Matthew from his tax col-

lecting. But all of them had to leave behind their old life, and all had to give up something that was important to them.

Today Jesus does not come down our streets to call us to follow him in his travels through the country. But he still calls us to follow him. Like the disciples, we must obey Jesus. We must be willing to give up things that are important to us.

2. The Teaching of Jesus

After Jesus had called his disciples, he began to travel through the villages of Palestine, teaching the people along the way (see 145, "Jesus Said to All the People"). At one time he went up on a mountain to teach the crowds. We call his teachings on that day the "Sermon on the Mount" (Matt. 5-7). He said, "Blessed are the merciful, for they shall receive mercy," and "love your enemies." Songs 153-155 and the Lord's Prayer (48) are taken from the Sermon on the Mount. Later Jesus began to tell parables or stories about everyday life with a spiritual meaning. Songs that reflect these teachings include the story of the good Samaritan (146), Jesus as the Light of the world (152), and Jesus as the good Shepherd (200, 201).

In these and many other stories and teachings of Jesus recorded in the gospels, we learn that Jesus loves us and that we should obey him, that he suffered for us, and that one day we will go to heaven to be with Jesus. No wonder this part of the Bible is called "gospel," which means "good news."

3. The Miracles of Jesus

Jesus was not an ordinary teacher—he also performed many miracles during his life on earth. Once, when Jesus and his disciples were in a boat on the Lake of Galilee, a tremendous storm came up, and it looked as if they would all drown. But Jesus commanded the wind and the waves to be quiet and the storm stopped.

Another kind of miracle Jesus did teaches us more about him. Often we read in the gospels that Jesus "was moved with compassion." Jesus had pity on the sick, and he healed them. People with leprosy or epilepsy, those who were blind or paralyzed or

deaf—Jesus made them whole and healthy (see 147-149). Once a paralyzed man was let down by his friends through the roof of a house where Jesus was, and Jesus healed the man and forgave his sins. And when the daughter of Jairus died, Jesus came and brought her back to life.

When we read the gospel stories about Jesus' life, we need to remember this: Jesus did not come just for people who lived hundreds of years ago. He also came for us. God loves us and wants us to obey him. Jesus' teachings and his miracles show us that he is the Son of God, and that he can help us today.

~~~~~~~~~~~~~~~~~~~~

Working with Congregational Worship Leaders

Very likely during these weeks, congregational worship will focus on the teaching or healing ministry of Christ. The children could sing one of the songs mentioned about Jesus' teaching just before the sermon. Or children could participate in brief spoken prayers for the sick, followed by a song about the healing ministry of Christ. A song about following Jesus would be appropriate for the end of the service.

~~~~~~~~~~~~~~~~~~~~

Unit Song Suggestions: A Model

Gathering Songs
C I Have Decided to Follow Jesus (226)
Dm Sing Alleluia (68)
Dm I Will Exalt My God, My King (26)
F I Am the Light of the World (152)

Theme Song
Em The King of Glory Comes (156)

Additional Songs
F When Jesus the Healer (149)
F If You Love Me (151)
Em Jesus, Jesus, Let Us Tell You (231)
D Bring Forth the Kingdom (154)

Closing Song
D Shalom to You (85)

The Suffering and Death of Christ

(4 weeks)

Unit Focus
Jesus suffered and died to save us from our sins.

Unit Goals

Faith Nurture (for leader and children)
• to feel grateful for Jesus' suffering for us
• to feel secure in Jesus' love and forgiveness
• to want to live for Jesus every day

Faith Knowledge (for children)
• to tell what we remember during Lent
• to identify the colors and symbols associated with Lent
• to learn a song for Palm Sunday

Faith Modeling (for leader)
• to express to the children your awareness of your own sin and your gratitude to Jesus for being willing to suffer and die for you

Materials
1. Songs from the Lent/Suffering and Death of Christ section (158-171) and others that deal with the sacrifice of Christ, for example, in the Confession and Forgiveness section (especially 40-44)
2. A cross, standing in a prominent place during each week of the unit
3. A purple cloth

Preparing to Lead the Gathering Time

We began the Christian year with the Christmas cycle. Advent, the time of preparing for Christmas, was followed by Epiphany and a season of Ordinary Time. Now we are ready to begin the Easter cycle. Like Advent, Lent is a time of preparation, this time for Easter, the greatest Christian festival.

During Lent we remember the suffering and death of Christ. The spiritual focus during Lent is on renewal: we rededicate our lives to Christ and to his service. This seasonal dedication does not mean that we fail to follow Christ during the rest of the year; rather, Lent is a time to reaffirm the basic truths of the Christian faith.

The theological implications of Jesus' vicarious suffering and of the atonement are difficult to grasp for adults, and certainly for children as well. But children can understand the basic teaching that Jesus loved us so much that he was willing to suffer and die for us.

Purple is the liturgical color of Lent. Purple is associated with royalty, but during Lent it symbolizes repentance and mourning.

The main symbol associated with Lent is the cross. Other symbols for Lent include ashes for mourning, palm branches for Palm Sunday (sometimes called Passion Sunday), the bread and wine (or wheat and grapes) for the last supper, a basin for foot washing, a rooster (reminding us of Peter's denial), pieces of silver for Judas's betrayal, a crown of thorns, and the lamb for sacrifice.

Lent begins with Ash Wednesday, which is determined by counting back forty days from Easter (excluding Sundays). The number forty reminds us of Jesus' forty days in the wilderness. Another (more recent) way of counting the forty days is to include all the days between Ash Wednesday and Palm Sunday, which begins Holy Week.

On Ash Wednesday, many people attend a church service reminding them of their sins and Jesus' suffering. To show sorrow for their sins, each person receives a dab of ashes on the forehead from the priest or minister. During the following weeks the minister will usually preach about some of the stories of Jesus' last weeks and days. As we remember Jesus' suffering, we also remember our own sins and our need to ask Jesus for forgiveness. Knowing our sin and need for forgiveness makes us thankful that Jesus loved us so much that he was willing to die for us. And remembering that love, we show our love to Jesus.

During Lent Jesus continues to heal the sick, teach the crowds, and invite people to become his disciples. Many people listened to Jesus and became his followers. But others, especially some of the leaders, resisted his teachings and refused to follow him. The longer Jesus taught, the more these people opposed and hated him. Finally, Jesus' enemies put him to death.

Jesus' death was terrible, but we must remember that it was part of God's plan (see 164). Jesus came into the world to heal and to teach, but also to suffer and die for his people. We remember Christ's suffering and death with great sadness, but also with thankful hearts that he died for our sins.

The Bible tells in great detail about the last week of Jesus' earthly ministry, called Holy Week. The week begins with Palm Sunday, an important but complex day to plan. The day includes a wide range of feeling: when the people saw Jesus riding into Jerusalem, they rejoiced and celebrated. Children enjoy singing songs (156-162) and waving palm branches in a procession around the sanctuary. On the other hand, this is the day that Jesus wept. The people soon turned from waving palm branches to waving their fists and shouting "Crucify him!"

On Thursday evening there may be a Maundy Thursday worship service, in which we remember Jesus' last meal with his disciples. The word "Maundy" comes from the Latin word for "mandate" or "commandment." That word is found in John 13:34, when Jesus told his disciples at the Last Supper, "A new command I give you: love one another." There may also be a service on Good Friday to remember Jesus' death on the cross and his burial. Although this is a sad week for Chris-

tians, we know that Easter Sunday is coming—the day when we celebrate Jesus' rising from the grave.

In our observance of Lent it's important to find a balance. Some churches seem to have a morbid fascination with the suffering and cruelty of the cross, while others almost ignore this part of the gospel story. An appropriate balance faces the reality of sin and the need for Jesus' suffering on our behalf, at the same time recognizing an occasion for renewal and dedication.

Working with Congregational Worship Leaders

Encourage your pastor and worship committee to focus on the theme of renewal and dedication. Suggest the repetition of one particular spoken or sung congregational response during these weeks, and teach it to the children. For example, one of the refrains found in 41-44 could be used in the Service of Confession each week during Lent. If the children learn it first, they can teach it to the congregation. For Palm Sunday, the traditional procession of children waving palm branches is an excellent way to involve children in worship.

Unit Song Suggestions: A Model

Gathering Songs
C   Come into His Presence (4)
C   Clap Your Hands (179)
Em Part of the Plan (164)
F   Alleluia, Alleluia! Give Thanks (173)

Theme Song
Bb All Glory, Laud, and Honor (161)

Additional Songs
C   Filled with Excitement (158)
F   When I Survey the Wondrous Cross (166)
F   Worthy Is Christ (170)
G   Alleluia (87)

Closing Song
A   Oh, How He Loves You and Me (163)

 # Easter: The Resurrection of Christ

(3 weeks)

Unit Focus
Jesus arose from the dead, and so will we!

Unit Goals
Faith Nurture (for leader and children)
- to realize that Easter is the most significant day of the Christian year
- to sense that we have new life in Jesus

Faith Knowledge (for children)
- to tell why celebrating Easter is so important to God's people
- to identify the liturgical color of Easter
- to learn an Easter song

Faith Modeling (for leader)
- to demonstrate to the children that in spite of difficulties in your life you live victoriously in Christ

Materials
1. Songs from Easter/Resurrection of Christ section (172-177)
2. A Christ candle

Preparing to Lead the Gathering Time

Easter Sunday is the most important day in the Church year, even more important than Christmas (when we remember Jesus' birth) and Good Friday (when we remember his death). On Easter Sunday we recall that Jesus was stronger than death and evil. He arose from the grave! His victory over death means that we will all be raised from death one day with wonderful new bodies to join Jesus on the new heaven and new earth.

The discovery of Jesus' empty grave was the beginning of an amazing day in the life of his followers, and the beginning of a whole new time in the lives of all of God's people. The women told their story to others, who could hardly believe it. But later that day, and then again in the following weeks, Jesus showed himself to many of his friends. Even those who couldn't believe that Jesus had risen from the dead were convinced when they saw Jesus and shared meals with him. Jesus stayed with his friends for forty day, talking and eating with them. And then Jesus' work on earth was finished, and he went back to his Father in heaven.

The early church designated Sunday as a weekly celebration of Jesus' resurrection. By the second century, the church began to set aside an annual commemoration of the resurrection. An ancient custom is the designation of Easter Sunday as a special day for baptisms. Adults who had converted to the Christian faith were instructed in the faith and walk of the Christian life during Lent, and this instruction was climaxed by their baptism on Easter.

Many languages use a form of the Hebrew *pasch* (Passover) in their designation of Easter (for example, the Dutch *Pasen* and the French *Paques*). The original meaning of "passing over" refers to the Exodus story of the angel of death passing over the houses of the Hebrews; by his resurrection Jesus defeated death once and for all. The English "Easter" may be derived from "east" and a reference to the rising sun. The seven weeks following Easter Sunday are called Eastertide (Easter season) or the Great Fifty Days, climaxed by the Ascension and Pentecost.

White (or gold) is the main color for Easter Sunday and the Easter season. A large white candle (called the paschal or Christ candle) can be lit for every service. Many objects remind us of Christ's victory over death at

Easter—the lily growing from a "dead" bulb, the open tomb, even a fish, which reminds us of Jesus' eating with his disciples after his resurrection.

As with the story of Jesus' suffering and death for our sins, the resurrection story is filled with great theological and spiritual truths. Although the children will not understand all of these truths, they can certainly capture the glorious truth of Jesus' victory and of our sharing in that victory.

Working with Congregational Worship Leaders

After Lent and the sad events of Holy Week we finally come to the day of Jesus' resurrection. Easter Sunday itself is a day of great celebration. But all of the Easter season should continue the theme of joy and celebration of Christ's victory over sin and death. Like Christmas, the Easter season should be a time of singing and rejoicing. Children who play instruments should certainly be encouraged to play along with the hymns. And children can lead the congregation in one or more Easter songs. One response that is appropriate for beginning or ending each service is the echo song "Christ Has Died, Christ Is Risen" (67).

Unit Song Suggestions: A Model

Gathering Songs
Eb This Is the Day (3)
F   This Is the Day (175)
F   Alleluia, Alleluia! Give Thanks (173)

Theme Song
C   Christ the Lord Is Risen Today (172)

Additional Songs
D   Oh, How Good Is Christ the Lord (177)
G   He's Alive! (174)
C   Christ Has Died, Christ Is Risen (67)

Closing Song
F   He Is Lord (178)

Ascension: The Reign of Christ

(3 weeks)

Unit Focus
Jesus ascended to heaven to be our ruler and to prepare a place for us to come and live with him.

Unit Goals
Faith Nurture (for children and adults)
- to be thankful that Jesus is our perfect and just King
- to feel secure that Jesus is taking care of us and his whole creation
- to rejoice that Jesus is preparing a place for us to come and live with him forever

Faith Knowledge (for children)
- to explain where Jesus is today
- to describe what Jesus is doing for us
- to learn a song that celebrates Christ as King

Faith Modeling (for leader)
- to show your own eagerness for the return of Christ, when all will be made right

Materials
1. Ascension songs from the Easter section (178-181); other songs celebrating the kingdom of God (154, 155), the protecting rule of Christ (16, 18, 26), God's care for us (198, 201, 205); also songs from the New Creation section (193-197)
2. A crown

Preparing to Lead the Gathering Time

Forty days after Christ arose from the dead, he ascended into heaven. Forty days after Easter falls on a Thursday, and some churches will have a special service that day to celebrate the ascension of Christ. Other churches will wait until the following Sunday, which is the seventh and final Sunday in the Eastertide season.

This three-week unit is in many ways a continuation of the Easter celebration. But the intent of this separate unit is to focus on the ascension of Christ and prepare the children to help the whole congregation celebrate this great feast day. You may wish to use this unit one year, and the next year follow the Easter unit directly with the unit on Pentecost, preparing the children to join congregational worship on Pentecost Sunday with the songs they have been learning.

No longer is Jesus living in the Middle East in a particular place and time; he is now our King, seated in heaven next to his Father. He is ruling and taking care of us and all creation, and preparing a place for us to come and live with him. But Jesus is no longer here where we can see him. Wouldn't that be better?

Children know about the pain of separation; some children have a hard time when their parents leave them even for an evening. When a pet dies, or worse, when a person we know and love dies, we feel great pain. When Jesus died, the disciples felt that pain. But their sorrow turned to amazement and then joy when he arose again. Why couldn't he just stay with them?

Because God had a different plan. *Q&A: A Summary of Biblical Teachings* (based on the Heidelberg Catechism) lists three different aspects of the ascension; these three could well form the heart of three different weeks for this unit.

First, "What good does it do us that he 'ascended to heaven and is seated at the right hand of God'?" (Q&A 30). When Jesus came to earth to suffer and die, he was separated from his Father; his ascension, therefore, was "going home." Children can certainly understand Jesus' desire to be "home." And from his home with his Father in heaven, Jesus is (1) praying for us, (2) watching over us and the whole world, and (3) sending his Spirit to give us help and protection. If Jesus were still living in one place on earth, he wouldn't be able to take care of the whole world. Now Jesus lives in our hearts through his Spirit.

Second, "How does Christ's return 'to judge the living and the dead' comfort you?" Finally, justice will be done! What should stir our blood and make us very eager for that day is that all those who do bad and evil things will be stopped. They will no longer be able to hurt God's people or God's world. No more crime, no more poverty, no more divorce, no more sickness, no more death, "no more crying there" ("Soon and Very Soon," 194). Advent is one time we look for Christ to come again, but the celebration of the ascension also leads us to anticipate Christ's return. It's a good time to sing songs that look toward the return of Jesus.

Third, "What is our great hope?" Jesus will be in charge, and "we will live with him in the new creation." God's new heaven and new earth will be a perfect and wonderful place. There will be no more competition from the forces of evil. No more pollution, no more smog, no more contamination, no more floods or famines, no more mismanagement of the earth, no more spoiling its beauty. God in Christ is the perfect ruler. What a wonderful hope!

To summarize, celebrating the ascension of Jesus provides "good," "comfort," and "great hope." So don't limit your singing just to the actual ascension of Christ. Celebrate God's protection and care for us on earth. Celebrate God's calling us to be partners in ruling the creation and building his kingdom on earth. Celebrate our responsibility to be God's caretakers. Celebrate God's promise to make all things right. We can look forward to perfect justice and shalom ("Shalom to You," 85).

Working with Congregational Worship Leaders

Work toward a celebrative Ascension Day or Sunday service where the children can participate in the service with singing. Encourage your worship leaders to pray for justice and for the rule of Christ to be extended over all the earth, beginning in your church's neighborhood and in the lives of the congregation's children. And celebrate in prayer and song the evidences of God's shalom in the church's deaconal work and in Christian organizations that work for justice.

Unit Song Suggestions: A Model

Gathering Songs
C   Come into His Presence (4)
C   Clap Your Hands (179)
Dm I Will Exalt My God, My King (26)
F   Alleluia, Alleluia! Give Thanks (173)

Theme Song
C   Rejoice, the Lord Is King (180)

Additional Songs
Em The King of Glory Comes (156)
D   Seek Ye First the Kingdom (155)
F   He Is Lord (178)

Closing Song
G   Song of Hope (82)

Pentecost: The Work of the Spirit

(3 weeks)

Unit Focus
On Pentecost Day we celebrate the pouring out of Jesus' Spirit on his disciples. During the season after Pentecost we see how the Spirit guides the church.

Unit Goals
Faith Nurture (for leader and children)
- to be open to the guidance of the Spirit
- to become involved with the life of the church
- to want to tell the story of Jesus to others

Faith Knowledge (for children)
- to identify some of the symbols and the color for Pentecost
- to tell who the Holy Spirit is and how he helps us
- to learn a song about the work of the Spirit

Faith Modeling (for leader)
- to communicate to the children how the Spirit helps you live a joyful and obedient life

Materials
1. Songs from the Pentecost and the Holy Spirit section (182-192) and from Being the Church (235-243)
2. A banner or picture with a picture of a dove and/or flames

---

Preparing to Lead the Gathering Time

In our journey through the Christian year we have traveled from Jesus' birth, through his life and ministry, his suffering and death, and then his resurrection and ascension to heaven. But there is one more important day in our journey of remembering—Pentecost Day.

You may remember that both the Christmas and Easter cycles began with a time of preparation (Advent and Lent). Both cycles also end with a one-day celebration. The Christmas cycle ends with Epiphany, when we remember the wise men who followed the star to Bethlehem. The Easter cycle ends with Pentecost. On this day the focus is not on following the star to Christ, but on sending out Christ's followers to bring the gospel to people wherever they are.

Going out "to the ends of the earth" takes a lot of courage. And the disciples no longer had Jesus around as their leader. How did the disciples become so strong and courageous? That is the story of Pentecost, which is recorded in Acts 2.

Jesus had promised, "You will receive power when the Holy Spirit comes on you, and you will be my witnesses . . . to the ends of the earth." And on that Pentecost Sunday morning, ten days after Jesus had left his disciples and ascended into heaven, it happened. The Holy Spirit came upon them in a miraculous way. What the disciples heard and saw on that day took away their doubts and fears.

The first thing the disciples heard that Pentecost morning was the sound of a mighty wind—inside their house! And when they went outside, they were able to speak, or at least the people understood them speaking, in all kinds of different languages.

Then the disciples saw something like "tongues of fire" appearing on their heads. Ever since that Pentecost day, flames have become a powerful symbol associated with the Holy Spirit. Red is the color for the day of Pentecost.

Another symbol associated with the Holy Spirit is the dove. You may remember that when Jesus was baptized, "he saw the Spirit of God descending like a dove and lighting on him" (Matt. 3:16). The dove also appears in Scripture much earlier—in the Genesis account of the story of Noah. When the great flood was finally over, a dove returned with an olive branch. Ever since, the dove has become a symbol of peace and hope. See 182 for an illustration of both symbols of the Holy Spirit.

"O Holy Spirit, Breathe on Me" (183) is a prayer for the Holy Spirit to breathe on us; "Spirit Divine, Inspire Our Prayer" (185) is a prayer for the Holy Spirit to come to us "as the fire," to purify and cleanse our hearts, and "as the dove," bringing peace and love.

Those songs reveal something about how we should celebrate Pentecost. The Holy Spirit was not only poured out on Jesus' disciples on that day thousands of years ago. The Spirit fills us too. Jesus promised that he would never leave his followers. We may not hear a loud wind or see flames or speak in different languages, but by faith, we believe Jesus' promise that he sends his Spirit to live in our hearts. Jesus gives the gift of his Spirit to each of his followers. Through that Spirit, we are connected to Christ. We know the Spirit lives in our hearts when we act according to the Spirit— following Jesus in all that we do.

Children (and adults!) can take great comfort in this understanding of the presence of the Spirit. Tell the children that one name for the Holy Spirit is Comforter. And let them know that the Spirit will give them the power to live Christ-like lives. If we live by the Spirit, our lives bring forth good fruit, including love, joy, and peace (Gal. 5:22-23; see also "The Fruit of the Spirit," 188). So take comfort, and take courage!

Many churches celebrate the Trinity on the first Sunday after Pentecost. After that, the church enters a long period called the Season after Pentecost, which lasts until Advent begins again. This period is also called Ordinary Time because there are no special days in the life of Christ to celebrate during that time. The color of Ordinary Time is green, a good color to remind us of our growth in the Spirit and the growth of the church all over the world.

Working with Congregational Worship Leaders

On Pentecost Sunday, the emphasis should be, as in Epiphany, on the global spreading of God's good news and grace. From the beginning of creation, God has been gathering his people. Pentecost is a celebration of the church spreading the good news of Jesus throughout the whole world.

One Pentecost worship event children can appreciate is the reading of the Pentecost story in different languages. Sometimes readers from other countries will dress in national costumes. This reading demonstrates the truth of the "holy catholic (universal) church." The children could well be included by singing a song in a different language (see index on page 423), or by singing any song on the work of the Spirit.

Another good way to involve children is by carrying various national flags in a procession during the service. Again, this procession is a testimony to the worldwide work of the Spirit.

Unit Song Suggestions: A Model

Gathering Songs
F   On the First Pentecost (182)
G   We Are the Church (236)
G   If You Believe and I Believe (242)

Theme Song
Eb Spirit of the Living God (184)

Additional Songs
    Walk! Walk! (190)
F   The Fruit of the Spirit (188)
D   Believe in the Lord (223)

Closing Song
C   Father, We Love You (77)

Living in God's World

Creation

(3 weeks)

Unit Focus
We worship God, creator of heaven and earth.

Unit Goals
Faith Nurture (for leader and children)
- to worship God as the creator of all
- to praise God by singing about the creation
- to affirm our responsibility for creation

Faith Knowledge (for children)
- to tell who created the world and everything in it
- to list the things God created for the heavens and the earth
- to learn a creation song

Faith Modeling (for leader)
- to convey to the children your awe of God the creator through spoken words, song, deeds, and prayer

Materials
1. Songs from the Creation section (86-98); also from the Praise and Thanksgiving (11-36) and New Creation (193-197) sections
2. Photos of family and friends; a potted plant and a household pet (e.g., a hamster); containers with soil and water and a flashlight or candle
3. Posters or pictures to illustrate a creation song such as "All Creatures of Our God and King" (86) or "For the Beauty of the Earth" (89), songs whose stanzas provide obvious suggestions for visuals

Preparing to Lead the Gathering Time

When they are very young, children experience God's creation in a commonsense way: they experience their own bodies; they play with water and dirt; they relate to various people in their family, church, school, and neighborhood; they eat fruit, meat, vegetables, and drink milk, juice, and pop; they encounter a complex world beyond their immediate existence via TV and books. They experience both the beauty and goodness of creation and the ills of creation, which they see in illness, pollution, and waste. As they grow older and learn more about God's creation within and around them, children are able to reflect on these different aspects of creation. They begin to wonder about their own origins and the source of everything in their experience.

There may be a great variety in the faith experience and understanding children bring to church school. Children from Christian homes will likely come to church school with some idea of God as creator and provider. They may know the first verse in the Bible: "In the beginning God created the heavens and the earth," or the first article of the Apostles' Creed: "I believe in God, the Father almighty, creator of heaven and earth." Or they may already know songs such as "Who Made Ocean, Earth, and Sky?" (91) or "All Things Bright and Beautiful" (90). On the other hand, children from non-Christian contexts may think the world exists by chance, or they will explain creation's origins with "that's just how things are."

In introducing the topic of creation, emphasize that God is creator of all, and that God expects us to take good care of the creation. Though God the Father's role in creation is often emphasized, the Bible makes clear that the Son

(John 1:1-3) and Spirit (Ps. 104:30) are full participants in God's creative acts. Though sin has entered the created world, from the very beginning God "saw that it [the creation] was good" and he blessed it with fruitfulness—a blessing that Satan cannot destroy. Church school is not an occasion to explore doctrinal concepts such as creation *ex nihilo* (out of nothing). Instead, your goal is to affirm God as creator and the world as his creation. Following are three suggestions for accomplishing this goal—you could use one for each of the three weeks of this unit (not necessarily in this order).

1. Using a picture of a family (or family with friends), emphasize that God created "me and my family and my friends." All children (even in dysfunctional families) experience some sense of relationship with parents, brothers and sisters, extended family members, and neighborhood friends. Such intimate relationships are a gift from God, who created all human beings. As members of the family of God, we have a responsibility for each other.

2. Using a potted plant and/or a household pet such as a hamster, goldfish, or parakeet, emphasize that God created the plants, flowers, and trees, as well as animals, fish, insects, and birds. God created these forms of life as part of the natural world we live in, and for which we bear responsibility.

3. Using containers of soil and water and a flashlight or lighted candle in a (momentarily) darkened room, emphasize that God created earth, water, and light, the basic elements that constitute the world around us. God created this natural order of nonliving elements and related phenomena, such as seasons, as essential parts of the world. We must live in stewardly harmony with these natural elements.

As well as learning about our responsibility towards the creation, children need to understand that their praise to God is part of a great chorus of praise offered by the entire creation—all heaven and earth—to God. Our human worship is joined by the glorious testimony of heavens and skies (Ps. 19:1), clapping trees (Isa. 55:12; see also "The Trees of the Field," 196), and fearsome sea monsters (Ps. 104:26). All are part of that great chorus of praise of which John prophesied: "To him who sits on the throne and to the Lamb be praise and honor and glory and power, for ever and ever!" (Rev. 5:13).

This leads us to the concept of "heaven" in our focus on God as creator of heaven and earth. "Heaven" is an abstract concept for children. For younger children you may simply say that "heaven" means God's "home" or "throne"; older children may understand that "heaven" also refers to the "sky" (or the cosmos) beyond the earth—which God also created.

Working with Congregational Worship Leaders

As the church calendar is busy from Advent through Epiphany, and from Lent through Pentecost, this unit on creation may well be used during the summer or fall. Discuss with the pastor or other worship leader(s) when and how best to incorporate the creation song the children are learning throughout this unit—perhaps the children can lead the congregation in a stanza during one or more weeks of the unit. You may also wish to display the pictures, posters, or other visuals you have been using in this unit.

Encourage worship leaders to thank God regularly for specific aspects of God's creation: for water, light, seasons, animals, food, family life, friends, expectant mothers (and fathers)—the list can go on. Pray also that we may use God's gifts responsibly and for healing where we have abused the creation's resources or its living creatures. And include periodic notices in the church bulletin to help parents discuss with their children the beauty of nature, the mystery of life, the recycling of materials, the stewardship of water, and other creation issues.

Unit Song Suggestions: A Model

Gathering Songs
F   Alleluia, Alleluia! Give Thanks (173)
G   All Things Bright and Beautiful (90)
Eb   This Is My Father's World (95)

Theme Song
D   All Creatures of Our God and King (86)

Additional Songs
Cm Many and Great (94)
F   Forest Trees (92)
D   Send Us Your Spirit (96)
      Thank You, God, for Water, Soil, and Air
      (97)

Closing Song
G   Alleluia (87)

Providence

(3 weeks)

Unit Focus
We trust God, the almighty provider and ruler.

Unit Goals
Faith Nurture (for leader and children)
- to worship God, who rules and provides for his creation
- to praise God by singing about his providence and rule
- to feel secure, knowing God rules over everything
- to affirm our responsibility for sharing God's gifts

Faith Knowledge (for children)
- to tell what God's "providence" and "rule" mean
- to list ways in which God takes care of us today
- to learn a song about God's care

Faith Modeling (for leader)
- to demonstrate your trust in God to provide and care for you

Materials
1. Songs from the God's Care for Us section (198-210); also from Creation (86-98) and New Creation (193-197)
2. Pictures of "olden days"; pictures of current events or newspaper clippings; and science-fiction drawings of future life

Preparing to Lead the Gathering Time

Though they are here treated separately, ideally the units on creation and providence will become one larger, continuous unit. God's creative acts "in the beginning" are intimately tied to his upholding and governing the world today and throughout history. The God who "created the heavens and the earth" is the same God who "knit me together in my mother's womb" (Ps. 139:13) and who numbers the "very hairs of your head" (Matt. 10:30). Every detail of our life continues to be upheld and ruled by God's mighty hand. Thus creation and providence are intimately linked.

The best way to illustrate this connection for children is to relate creation to their own birth, and providence to the care their parents give them every day, from infancy through the present day. God always creates and provides! The Bible also uses parental imagery to illustrate how intimately God creates and provides (see Deut. 32:18; Job 38:28-29; Isa. 42:14, 46:3-4, 66:9, 13). Hopefully there will be a recent birth in one of the student families (or in your own!) to which you can refer. The children will be able to understand God's providence through the analogy of their parents' love and care for them (even if imperfectly lived).

Because "providence" is an abstract term, you may explain that God's "providence" simply means his *"provide*-ence." Christians emphasize three facets of God's providence and rule, each of which may be stressed during one of the weeks of this unit (in addition to learning a song about God's care for us):

1. The Past. God led the unfolding of his creation from the very beginning and throughout the past. We believe that God created the universe, that God elected those he would redeem in Christ, that God directed the rise and fall of civilizations and rulers, and that God controls our history. To illustrate God's care for people throughout history, you could refer to stories from the Bible—Noah and the flood, Israel at the Red

Sea, Daniel in the lion's den, the birth of Jesus, the birth of the church in Jerusalem at Pentecost, or Paul's missionary journeys. Choose songs that tell about or comment on these stories. Use pictures or drawings of times past to illustrate the teaching that God cares for people throughout history. Photos of great-grandparents and grandparents can also help children recognize God's guiding hand in the lives of their parents and extended families.

2. *The Present.* God actively controls the current affairs of the world. God guides the creation and all creatures, including ourselves. The things that happen in my home and in my neighborhood, or in some Third World country far from home; the decisions made by the leaders of my village or city, or the elders of my church, or the United Nations; the life and death of children, adults, animals, rain forests—all these things are intimately known and directed by God. Children experience current events through television and through photographs in newspapers or magazines. Photographs of current events can help illustrate the idea that God cares for our world today. Songs such as "He's Got the Whole World" (198) or "If You But Trust in God to Guide You" (210) will reinforce the same idea.

3. *The Future.* God holds the future in his hand. Children (and adults!) have much to be afraid of—the threat or reality of war, poverty, illness, family break-up or domestic violence. It is a great comfort for us to confess that God directs human life and the whole world toward the return of Christ and a "new heaven and earth." Though we "see through a glass darkly," we sing with great confidence "Soon and very soon we're going to see the King!" (194). Children and adults alike can feel secure in the knowledge that Jesus the King has our future in his hands.

God's providence is much more than a doctrine. As leader, you will want to show the children that your belief in God's care for you is a source of great comfort in your everyday life. *Q&A: A Summary of Biblical Teachings* (based on

the Heidelberg Catechism) summarizes that comfort in Q&A 23:

What do you understand by God's providence?

That our heavenly Father
takes care of
and rules
    everything in our world.

Working with Congregational Worship Leaders

Ideally used with the unit on creation, this unit on providence may well be used during the summer or fall. Discuss with the pastor or other worship leader(s) when and how best to incorporate the song about God's care the children are learning throughout this unit. You may also wish to display pictures, posters, or other visuals that illustrate God's providing care in our lives. Encourage the worship leaders to thank God regularly for specific aspects of God's providence: for contributions to human culture by discoverers, scientists, artists, rulers; for the work and witness of the saints in the history of the church; for all authorities in family, state, business, school, and church who seek to be agents of God's rule; and for the great comfort we have in knowing for sure that "nothing can separate us from God's love in Christ" (Rom. 8:38-39).

When we pray "your kingdom come" we are praying for the exercise of God's providence, for the rule of his Word and Spirit to prevail, so that "at the name of Jesus every knee should bow . . . and every tongue confess that Jesus Christ is Lord" (Phil. 2:10-11). That confession needs to be portrayed in banners and church school art displays. And, perhaps through bulletin notes, parents should be encouraged to discuss with their children the joys of trusting in God's care for them.

Unit Song Suggestions: A Model

Gathering Songs
G   Lord, Our Lord, Your Glorious Name (15)
G   For the Beauty of the Earth (89)
Em The Trees of the Field (196)
D   He's Got the Whole World (198)

Theme Song
Gm If You But Trust in God to Guide You
     (210)

Additional Songs
G   Everywhere I Go (211)
F   Trust and Obey (213)
F   The Lord Is My Shepherd (200)

Closing Song
D   God Is So Good (207)

Redemption

(3 weeks)

Unit Focus
We worship Jesus, who saves us from sin and death.

Unit Goals
Faith Nurture (for leader and children)
- to thank God for sending Jesus as our Savior
- to receive God's forgiveness for our sin
- to want to live "new" lives in Jesus

Faith Knowledge (for children)
- to tell why we call Jesus our "Savior"
- to recall one story from Scripture about someone Jesus saved
- to learn a "redemption" song

Faith Modeling (for leader)
- to demonstrate in your conversation with the children that you "belong to Jesus Christ" (Q&A 1, in *Q&A: A Summary of Biblical Teachings*)

Materials
1. Songs from various sections, for example, "Amazing Grace" (209), "Oh, for a Thousand Tongues to Sing" (19), "When Israel Was in Egypt's Land" (103), "As Moses Raised the Serpent Up" (165), st. 2
2. Brief biographies of Charles Wesley (see 19) and John Newton (see 209)

Preparing to Lead the Gathering Time

That God freely provides salvation to anyone who believes in Jesus is one of the most basic and comforting confessions of the Christian faith (see John 3:16). Humankind fell into sin (that is, separation from God). And because no creature could restore what God had originally created as good, God sent Jesus, his Son, to be our Savior. Theologians explain salvation in various ways: Christ justifies us (absolves us of guilt); reconciles us (restores our relationship with God, with each other, and with creation); redeems us (pays our punishment for sin); and rescues us (saves us from eternal death).

All these concepts may be summarized in the word "atonement" or "at-one-ment." By paying for our sin, Jesus reunites us with God again. When we were totally helpless and could not save ourselves, God provided a way. Through Jesus' suffering and death for our sins, God adopts us as his children (Rom. 8:14-17).

To illustrate "at-one-ment," ask the children how they feel when they have disobeyed their parents, or told a lie, or blamed someone else for something they did wrong. Usually that makes us want to run and hide. We feel alone, not "at one" with our family or friends. But when we confess what we did wrong and are forgiven, we can experience the joy of "at-one-ment."

Jesus came to bring us to that same relationship of "at-one-ment" with God. We no longer feel dirty and alone, wanting to hide from God. Baptism beautifully illustrates how God washes us clean. Baptism is the sign and seal that our sins are washed away by Christ's blood and Spirit, as surely as water washes away dirt. It involves conversion, cleansing from sin, and renewal by the Holy Spirit (see also unit 4). The Lord's Supper is another illustration of our redemption. Through his crucified body (broken bread) and shed blood (poured wine), Christ paid for our sin, nourishes us to eternal life, and unites us into one family of believers (see also unit 5).

Throughout the history of the church, Christians have expressed in song their love for Jesus, who redeemed them from sin. Following are three Bible stories paired with a hymn about redemption. Choose one of these stories and songs for different years in which this unit is covered. Briefly summarize the Bible story (it is probably already well-known to many of your church school children) and then focus on the hymn and its background. Review the hymn in each of the following weeks of the unit.

1. The Exodus, in which God liberates the people of Israel from captivity in Egypt and brings them to Canaan, the promised land of "milk and honey," is the best-known Old Testament example of a redemption story. Involving the ten plagues, the Passover, and the dramatic crossing of the Red Sea, this story foreshadows the redemption of Jesus as "the Lamb of God who takes away the sin of the world." The struggle between Pharaoh and the Egyptians, on the one hand, and Moses and the Israelites, on the other hand, is powerfully expressed in the spiritual, "When Israel Was in Egypt's Land" (103). This hymn originated among the black slaves in America. Like the Israelites enslaved in Egypt, they yearned for freedom. Both the story of the Exodus and this spiritual express how God intervenes in our lives: when we think everything is hopeless, God provides miraculous deliverance!

2. The apostle Peter, impulsive in his devotion to Christ, is famous for his confession, "You are the Christ" (Matt 16:13-19) and infamous for his three-times denial of Jesus (Matt 26:69-75). But Christ had compassion on Peter—he forgave his sin and commissioned him to become an honored leader, a shepherd of lost sheep, in the early church (John 21:15-23). A parallel story is that of the preacher John Newton, who as a youth "dropped out" of church and became a slave-trading sea captain. Newton was converted to Christianity, and his life began to sail in a different direction. Eventually he became a parish pastor and wrote many hymns, including the well-known autobiographical hymn, "Amazing Grace" (209). Both the apostle Peter and the preacher

Newton experienced the joy of God's forgiveness and the challenge of new ministries.

3. The gospels give us few details about the life of Mary Magdalene. We do know that Jesus healed her of multiple demon possession and that she served him during his earthly ministry (Luke 8:1-3). Most important, she witnessed Christ's crucifixion and resurrection, and she received a special command to bear witness to the risen Lord (Matt 27:56, 61; 28:1-10; John 20:1-18). Her testimony is well-expressed in "Oh, for a Thousand Tongues to Sing" (19), written by Charles Wesley, another great reformer of the Christian church, to commemorate his own conversion to Christ. Mary Magdalene's life story and the detailed stanzas of Wesley's hymn speak (sing!) eloquently of Jesus' power over sin, the joy of forgiveness, and the beginning of a new life with Christ.

Working with Congregational Worship Leaders

This unit on redemption could fit into the church calendar during the Lent or Easter seasons or at some time during the summer or fall. Discuss with the pastor or other worship leader(s) when and how to incorporate the song the children are learning throughout this unit. You may want to display in the church hall pictures of the hymn authors discussed in this unit, and/or print biographical sketches and relevant stanzas in the church bulletin. Encourage worship leaders to thank God for the great heritage of song the church can use today, and for the women and men who contribute to our repertoire of hymns. And pray that the songs we sing may be sincere testimonies from our hearts!

Unit Song Suggestions: A Model

Gathering Songs
G   Jesus, Jesus, Praise Him (12)
D   A Psalm for Singing (1)
G   Oh, for a Thousand Tongues to Sing (19)
F   Praise to the Lord, the Almighty (27)

Theme Song
G   Amazing Grace (209)

Additional Songs
G   Song of Hope (82)
G   Alleluia (87)
F   I Sing a Song to Jesus Christ (31)

Closing Song
Dm   I Want Jesus to Walk with Me (214)

 **Mission**

(4 weeks)

Unit Focus
We worship God, who sends us into the world with the gospel (good news) of Christ.

Unit Goals
Faith Nurture (for leader and children)
- to praise God for giving us our mission here and for calling others to mission in other places/countries
- to thank God for the good news of Christ
- to pray for missionaries at home/abroad
- to affirm our participation in mission in word and deed

Faith Knowledge (for children)
- to tell whom God has called to be missionaries
- to describe some ways in which God's people bring the gospel to others
- to learn a mission song

Faith Modeling (for leader)
- to demonstrate your interest, support, and participation in the missionary enterprise of the church

Materials
1. Songs from the Pentecost and the Holy Spirit section (182-192) and Loving Our Neighbor (241-252) section
2. Posters, photos, slides, video segments of missionary activity in your church's neighborhood and in faraway places; these materials should show children as well as adults; a regional map and a world map or globe
3. Various hats, for example, artist's beret, nurse's cap, hard hat, baseball cap, clown hat, graduation cap, officer's hat, royal crown, etc.

Preparing to Lead the Gathering Time

Ever since Christ commanded his disciples to "go and make disciples . . . baptize . . . teach them" (Matt 28:19-20), God's people have been called to missions. The Holy Spirit continues to reaffirm that "great commission" in two ways: first, all of God's people are called to witness to the gospel of Christ in their everyday lives (the Reformers called this the "office of all believers"), and second, some of God's people are called to specialized ministries as short- or long-term career missionaries. Any of the several "Go ye into all the world" songs (241 ff.) could be learned by the children to affirm the missionary emphasis of this unit.

Unfortunately there is some confusion about the missionary task of Christians, confusion which may have already rubbed off from adults in the church to the children. The three points below are intended to clarify what may be areas of confusion. You may want to cover one each week, using the fourth week to concentrate on learning the song(s) you've chosen.

1. *Who is a missionary?* Some people refer to the work of preachers and missionaries as "full-time" service, thereby implying that those who choose other careers can serve God only "part-time." One way to illustrate this in a way the children will enjoy is for you to bring in as many hats as possible (artist's beret, nurse's cap, hard hat, baseball cap, clown hat, graduation cap, officer's hat, royal crown). Try to bring enough hats for every child to wear one. Let the children have fun identifying each one, then ask, "But which is the missionary's hat?" The answer is, "All of them!" No matter who we are or what we do, children and adults are called to share the good news of Jesus Christ. It is true that some Christians turn

their missionary calling into a long-term professional career, and others take on short-term specialized missionary tasks. But we all share the same calling.

2. *Where does missionary work happen?* Some Christian adults may have given the impression to your church school children that missionary activity takes place primarily in faraway places like Africa, Asia, or South America. It's true that mission work goes on in remote places, but the children need to hear that Christ calls us to be missionaries starting in our own neighborhoods, as well as in faraway places. Jesus says, "You will be my witnesses in Jerusalem, and in all Judea and Samaria, and to the ends of the earth" (Acts 1:8). Mission begins at home! Make sure that the mission illustrations you show (photos, slides, videos, etc.) include children, and that some refer to mission activity in your church's neighborhood. If you have available a regional map and a world map or globe, ask the children to use pins or flags to represent places where mission activity is taking place—including your town, region, state, or province, as well as any foreign countries where missionaries supported by your church are working.

3. *How is missionary work done?* This question can be answered in a variety of ways. Some Christians emphasize evangelism, preaching the gospel, teaching converts, planting new churches, and doing Bible translation—all ways of meeting people's spiritual needs by bringing the Word. Others emphasize social action, relief programs, humanitarian aid, education, and health care. To them, missions consists primarily in bringing the gospel through meeting people's physical needs. In talking with the children about how we do missions, stress the comprehensiveness and the diversity of the church's task. Both are important. Thus, Christian mission agencies each have different emphases and styles of ministries, but all of them share a common task: bringing the gospel of Christ to others. In missions both the preaching of the gospel (see 2 Tim. 4:2) and the deeds of Christian faith (see James 2:14-26) come together in presenting the good news of salvation in Christ.

Working with Congregational Worship Leaders

Congregations vary significantly in their observance of missions. Some have a "mission emphasis week" in conjunction with Pentecost, others favor the period after Christmas/Epiphany and before Lent, and still others choose other times or follow suggestions made by denominational or other mission agencies. Church school leaders may want to plan their mission unit for the same time it is emphasized in congregational worship. Discuss with the pastor or other worship leader(s) when and how to incorporate the mission song the children are learning throughout this unit. Perhaps you could move your display of missions illustrations, photos, or other artifacts that were used for this unit to the sanctuary. Encourage worship leaders to pray regularly for specific missionaries at home and abroad. Also pray that each of us, young or old, may be effective witnesses to the gospel of Christ in our everyday lives. Include periodic notices in the church bulletin to help parents discuss with their children some mission activity in your church's neighborhood or elsewhere. Missions agencies provide helpful prayer guides and calendars to assist you in these efforts.

Unit Song Suggestions: A Model

Gathering Songs
C   Lift High the Cross (171)
Dm People, All, Come Sing and Shout (68)
F   Alleluia, Alleluia! Give Thanks (173)

Theme Song
D   Bring Forth the Kingdom (154)

Additional Songs
A   Shine, Jesus, Shine (239)
Fm Who's Goin' to Tell the Story (246)
Eb Jesu, Jesu, Fill Us with Your Love (251)

Closing Song
G   Song of Hope (82)

Serving Jesus in Our Work and Play

(4 weeks)

Unit Focus
We serve Jesus in our everyday activities.

Unit Goals

Faith Nurture (for leader and children)
- to serve Jesus in our work
- to serve Jesus in our play
- to serve Jesus in our learning
- to serve Jesus in our eating

Faith Knowledge (for children)
- to tell when and where Jesus wants us to serve him
- to suggest ways we can serve Jesus every day
- to learn a "walking with Jesus" song

Faith Modeling (for leader)
- to demonstrate to the children that your whole life is directed toward serving Jesus every day

Materials
1. Songs from the sections Walking with God (211-234) and Being the Church (235-243)
2. Various items to illustrate work, play, learning, and eating: a broom and a dust cloth, a checkers game, sneakers with Velcro tabs and shoes with laces, crackers and milk

Preparing to Lead the Gathering Time

Every part of our life belongs to Jesus. God created us and the rest of creation from the very beginning to serve him. This total claim on our lives is a blessing and a great source of comfort for many Christians. But Satan works in subtle ways to dupe us into thinking that only "spiritual" matters belong to Jesus, and that the rest of life does not need to be centered on Christ. It is easy for us to confess verbally that we want to serve Jesus with our whole life, but living out that confession in our everyday thoughts, words, and deeds is a great challenge.

Children are acute interpreters of how well our deeds as adults accord with our words. A wise parent once explained, "You're worried that your children don't listen to you? You should worry that they're always watching you!" That is equally true in church and in church school. Christian parents and church school leaders should be united in their efforts to demonstrate by their actions and words that all of life has meaning only if centered on Jesus. That task is the focus of this unit and of the songs recommended for it. The following four segments may be used to develop the unit focus. You may want to highlight one for each week of this unit.

1. *We serve Jesus in our work.* Your church school children already know something about work: presumably they have their own chores around the house (just show them a broom and a dust cloth!), and they certainly know adults who work—whether in the home, office, factory, or farm. It is your challenge to help children experience work not just as a chore but as a joyful, meaningful part of life—a way to serve Jesus. Perhaps you could provide a brief testimony from your own life. Do you enjoy cooking tasty meals every day to keep you and your family healthy? Are the daily chores in your household shared by all family members, so that (most of the time!) everyone pitches in to keep your home clean and organized? The children will probably volunteer ways in which they work at home, at school, or in part-time jobs such as delivering newspapers. The bottom line is that all work—the little daily chores

of children as well as the full-time careers of adults—becomes a blessing and takes on a joyful aspect only if it is offered to Christ. When our work is offered to Christ, it becomes a part of our experience of salvation: "It is God who works in you to will and to act according to his good purpose" (Phil. 2:13).

2. *We serve Jesus in our play.* Display the game you brought as a visual reminder of today's theme. Play is a wonderful aspect of human life: make-believe, games, sports, arts, or crafts are just a few ways in which we "play" during our leisure times. Play is done for its own sake, according to its own rules, and thereby brings a rich quality to our lives that work alone does not provide. Adults can get so caught up in work that it becomes difficult for them to play, and sometimes they even turn play into work (think about professional sports!). Most children, however, spontaneously exercise their playfulness in a variety of creative ways. It's difficult to imagine children *not* being playful: only sleeping, eating, and working. "All work and no play makes Jack or Jill a dull child!"

When we understand play as a blessing from God that enriches our lives, we can see that play is as religious as church worship. And like our acts of Sunday worship, we offer our play to Christ. In our prayers and in our play, we thank Jesus for our creativity with toys, our ingenuity with games, and our skill in arts and crafts. For Christians, to play is to have fun for Christ's sake.

3. *We serve Jesus in our learning.* Most of the children in your church school are in kindergarten or in grade school. But children also learn in their own homes, from parents, siblings, or neighbors, and from television too! The learning that takes place in school or church complements that domestic learning. Ask your children to recall how they first learn an alphabet song and later to read, how they first learn to put on sneakers with Velcro tabs and later to tie laces (bring a pair of each kind to your church school), or how they first see different animals in picture books or on television and later see them live in their natural habitat or in a zoo. In each case the children are learning more of God's wonderful world—of the ways in which we relate to nature and how we express ourselves in culture. Although learning can sometimes be frustrating, each step of accomplishment brings a sense of fulfillment and challenge. We may learn different things in church school, day school, and at home, but in all our learning—whatever the setting—we experience more of God's blessings, we understand more about the creation in which we live and serve Jesus, and we walk more closely in God's way of love and obedience.

4. *We serve Jesus in our eating.* We need to eat and drink to stay alive. Children who are starving in developing countries and the reality of food banks in North American cities are grim reminders of our need for food. But our eating and drinking is more than just the chemical processes that take place when we eat food that enables our bodies to stay well. Ask the children what happens when we have a meal: where do we get the food, who fixes it, and who cleans up afterwards? Which foods and drinks are healthy and which are not? (Show the children the crackers and milk you brought.) Do we invite others to share our table with us? What happens when we don't get enough food or drink? Help children understand that the way we eat and drink says a lot about us. When we eat healthy foods, learn to eat modest portions, experience diverse foods from other cultures, and share our resources so that other people may also eat and drink, we are serving Jesus. And we also serve Jesus when we eat and drink at his table, together with all God's people.

Working with Congregational Worship Leaders

This unit may well be used during the Summer or Fall, away from the seasons of Advent/Christmas/Epiphany and Lent/Easter/Pentecost, which have their own specific emphases. Discuss with the pastor or other worship leader(s) when and how to incorporate the "walking with God" song the children are learning throughout this unit. Encourage worship leaders to thank God regularly for our everyday work, play, learning, and food and drink. And pray that all of us children and adults may experience each of these activities as blessed ways in which we may serve Jesus. Organizing a game night for the church would be a fun way to emphasize the idea of serving Jesus in our play!

Unit Song Suggestions: A Model

Gathering Songs
F   Come Bless the Lord (6)
F   If You Love Me (151)
G   Jesus, Jesus, Praise Him (12)

Theme Song
C   Let Me Be Your Servant, Jesus (244)

Additional Songs
F   You and I (246)
Fm   Sent by the Lord (249)
Em   Jesus, Jesus, Let Us Tell You (231)

Closing Song
C   Father, We Love You (77)

⑳ Helping Others Both Near and Far Away

(4 weeks)

Unit Focus
We help others both near and far away.

Unit Goals

Faith Nurture (for leader and children)
- to learn more about other people
- to pray for other people
- to share our gifts with other people

Faith Knowledge (for children)
- to tell why we should be kind and helpful to others
- to suggest some ways we can help other people
- to understand better how we may help other people
- to learn a "service" song

Faith Modeling (for leader)
- to share with the children a way in which you serve Jesus by helping other people

Materials
1. Songs from the section Loving Our Neighbors (244-252)
2. Slides, videos, and artifacts to help learn about the specific community or ministry project that is the focus of this unit

Preparing to Lead the Gathering Time

Note: This unit is especially geared to a community service project, with suggestions that move beyond the regular activities of church school gathering time. Each specific age group may well have small projects they work on together in church school. But in some congregations, perhaps a few times a year, the regular church school schedule is interrupted to allow time for special activities such as producing a drama or musical, listening to a missionary, or participating in a service project. Often such a project involves taking church school offerings to support a particular cause or working in the community on a specific project. For those congregations which make room in their schedules for such activities, this unit offers several ideas.

Helping others is a theme we find throughout the Bible. In Galatians we read that deeds of "love, joy, peace, patience, kindness, goodness, faithfulness, gentleness, and self-control" are evidence of true faith (5:22-23). Jesus himself set the perfect example of helping others by coming to earth as a servant to redeem his people from sin (Phil. 2:6-8), and he taught his disciples the nature of serving others by washing their feet (John 13:1-17).

Serving or helping other people is something we are called to do. It is also a blessing. Jesus said, "It is more blessed to give than to receive." Perhaps you can share a story from your own experience of how your faith was strengthened as you helped someone else. Parents often report how much they are blessed as they raise their children in the fear of the Lord. And children know the good feeling they get when they help someone.

Children and adults can help others in a variety of ways. Presumably your church participates in various ministries and supports several missionaries (perhaps most frequently by contributing part of the church offerings for these causes). Your church school could "adopt" a ministry of its own, perhaps one not already associated with your church. Some church schools rotate through a series of ministry projects in any year. Don't hesitate to get involved with a nearby senior citizens' complex, a special-needs school, or an after-school play center. Here are four suggestions on how your church school children can be more consciously involved in serving Jesus by assisting others in such a ministry project.

1. *Help others by learning more about them.* John Perkins (of the Voice of Calvary Ministries) emphasizes the need for Christians to live among those to whom they minister and thus to experience first-hand the life of that community. Since children don't have the option to relocate on their own, they can experience such a community vicariously by learning more about its people, customs, foods, schools, health care, and specific needs. Videos, slides, maps, and artifacts can be used to "show and tell" these essential aspects of a particular community or project. Whether the project is next door or thousands of miles away, knowing the names of some adults and children in that community and understanding some of their traditions will help your church school children identify more closely with this project. Challenge children to do some studying on their own. Perhaps they could prepare posters with words and pictures describing the community they want to assist, and make a small group presentation to the entire church school.

2. *Help others by praying for them.* A foundation of knowledge about that specific community or project will enable you and your church school children to pray more effectively for that cause. Children (like adults!) need specific details to help them pray. Praying for the poor or the sick in general is abstract. On the other hand, praying for Karl, who is a poor orphan, and thanking God for healing Salina from her malaria, is concrete. Similarly, children need to learn how to pray "Your kingdom come" for specific instances, for example, "May Alma's family accept Jesus," or "Help us raise money for Mr. Craig's hospital to buy medicines." Help children make a prayer list, keeping in mind that such prayers should contain not only petitions but also thanksgiving. Use part of the large group time to pray through a section of your prayer list, or send the children to their smaller groups with specific prayer assignments.

3. *Help others by sharing our gifts with them.* Learning more about the "target" community or ministry project enables children not only to pray more effectively for this cause, but also allows them to make their own contributions. These contributions can take many forms: children can write letters, poems, or draw pictures; collect canned or dry foods, Bible picture books, magazines, and clothing; make up gift parcels with toys, pencils, chalk or crayons, small tools or sewing needles, and soap—the possibilities are almost endless! Encourage children to give the kinds of things they themselves would like to receive, not primarily items donated by parents but items that belong to them that they are willing to give to help others in Jesus' name.

4. *Help others by raising money to assist them.* Gifts of money are also means children can use to help other people. Money is at times rather impersonal, and if it is donated primarily by parents, it may not be a meaningful gift from the children. However, money is certainly a necessity for most ministry projects or communities. Pooling money gifts from various sources enables that community to purchase larger items or items in greater quantities, construct buildings, or pay salaries. The children should understand clearly what their money gifts will be used for. Encourage them to save from their own allowances, or set up a sponsorship program in which children do odd jobs or engage in a marathon singing or athletic event to raise money for a specific cause. The children should "own" this money-raising venture as much as possible, so that it is truly their way of serving their neighbors (whether next door or far away).

Working with Congregational Worship Leaders

This unit on helping others could be used during the summer or fall, away from the church year seasons of Advent/Christmas/Epiphany and Lent/Easter/ Pentecost (which have their own specific emphases), or it could easily fit into a "missions-emphasis" period in your congregation. Discuss with the pastor or other worship leader(s) when and how to incorporate the "service" song the children are learning throughout this unit. Encourage worship leaders to thank God regularly for the specific ways in which this congregation and its church school children are able to assist other people, to pray for those engaged in this specific ministry by name, and to pray that all of us—including the children—may experience the ways in which we help others as rich blessings from God. You may want to print regular notices in the church bulletin to keep everyone up-to-date on the service project. Include the children's prayer list as well.

Unit Song Suggestions: A Model

Gathering Songs
F   Come Bless the Lord (6)
C   Let Me Be Your Servant, Jesus (244)
D   The Servant Song (248)

Theme Song
Eb   Jesu, Jesu, Fill Us with Your Love (251)

Additional Songs
Bb   Discipleship (233)
Fm   Sent by the Lord (249)
      Let Us Love (237)

Closing Song
G   Song of Hope (82)

Thanksgiving

(4 weeks)

Unit Focus
We thank God for his gifts to us.

Unit Goals
Faith Nurture (for leader and children)
- to thank God for daily food and drink
- to thank God for family and friends
- to thank God for his love to us in Christ
- to thank other people for sharing God's gifts with us

Faith Knowledge (for children)
- to list things for which we are thankful
- to suggest ways we can express our thanksgiving to God
- to learn a thanksgiving song

Faith Modeling (for leader)
- to demonstrate to the children that you thank God for his gifts throughout your whole life, in thoughts, words, and deeds

Materials
1. Songs from the Praise and Thanksgiving section (11-36)
2. A thank-you note or card

Preparing to Lead the Gathering Time

Gratitude—an attitude of thankfulness that permeates everything we say or do—is one of the fruits of being a Christian. "Give thanks in all circumstances, for this is God's will for you in Christ Jesus," says Paul in 1 Thess. 5:17. Expressions of thankfulness are found throughout Scripture, for example, Moses and Miri-

am's song in Exodus 15, or the royal thanksgiving in Psalm 118.

Christians often express their gratitude at certain times of the year or in conjunction with certain events. We celebrate a good harvest or a fiftieth wedding anniversary with thanksgiving to God; we offer special prayers of gratitude when we get well after an illness, or when peace is restored between persons or nations. These special times of gratitude help shape our character so that we will be more able to thank God for the little things everyday, and even to be thankful in times of trouble.

But thanksgiving needs to find expression in more than just words: singing, dancing, and deeds of gratitude are all biblical ways of expressing our gratitude. Paul reminds his readers to "sing psalms, hymns and spiritual songs with gratitude in your hearts to God" (Col. 3:16). And throughout Scripture we find the theme that our good deeds express our thankfulness to God. These deeds must be directed towards redressing the hurts and misfortunes of the poor.

Children are familiar with being thankful. Early on they are taught to "say thank you" to those who give them gifts. They see thankfulness expressed by people to each other and to God. As leader, your task is to model a life of gratitude to God and to help children be more conscious of and proactive in their own thanksgiving. In addition to learning a song of thanksgiving, here are some suggestions to help you and your children focus on thanksgiving throughout this four-week unit:

1. *Thank God for daily food and drink.* Jesus taught us to pray, "Give us this day our daily bread." Most of the children in your church school probably get good food and drink every day. Possibly they take that blessing for granted. But television coverage of children dying from hunger in some developing

countries or of food lines in some of our own cities tells the grim story that having enough food is not automatic! Just as God fed the Israelites in the desert with manna, so he blesses us with food and drink. Our thankfulness for these gifts leads us to want to share our food and drink with those in need. You could make a covenant with the children to eat more modest portions of food, to not waste any, and to send food and drink to a local food pantry (perhaps one your church is involved with).

2. *Thank God for family and friends.* All children have a sense of family, even when that family has problems, and all experience friendships. It's certainly appropriate to express our thanks to God in our prayers and songs for giving us friends and family, but there is another way we can show our thanks too. We can tell our family members and friends face to face that we appreciate them: "I thank God that you are part of my life," or "I thank God that you and I can play together." Encourage the children to go home and express their thanks to parents, grandparents, siblings, and friends. And don't forget to explain to the group how important your family and friends are to you and how you express your gratitude to them personally.

3. *Thank God for his love to us in Christ.* From very early on, Christian children learn that "Jesus loves me . . . for the Bible tells me so." God's love to us in Christ is a great cause for giving thanks in our prayers and songs. Since this way of expressing thanks can be rather abstract for children, it's important to stress that another way of showing our thanks to God for loving us is by loving and serving other people. Explain to the children that our words of thanks and praise to God and our grateful deeds are like two sides of the same coin. Let the children suggest ways in which they can live out their gratitude in their family, neighborhood, and church contexts.

4. *Thank other people for sharing God's gifts with us.* God often uses other persons to share his gifts with us. A school teacher, church custodian, corner grocery clerk, or mail deliverer may be the person God is using to help us accomplish a goal, fight temptation, improve our skills, or give us advice. Encourage children to thank God for the important people in their lives by name, and also to thank them face to face. If you've recently had the experience of recognizing God's gift to you in another person, tell the children how you thanked someone for the good things they brought to your life, for the joy you experience in their company, or the godly wisdom you're learning from them.

Working with Congregational Worship Leaders

The obvious time for this thanksgiving unit is the fall, with national day of Thanksgiving. But since our lives are always to be marked by gratitude, this unit could well be scheduled for another time of the year. Discuss with the pastor or other worship leader(s) when and how to incorporate the Thanksgiving song the children are learning throughout this unit. Encourage worship leaders to thank God regularly for the blessings of food and drink, families and friends, teachers, doctors, merchants, and all those who are God's gift to us. Pray that God will enable us to use his gifts and resources as a means of helping other people. If you are using this unit during the Thanksgiving Day service, discuss with your worship leaders how to incorporate a thanksgiving procession in which the children bring forward their gifts of food and clothing for the needy. Include periodic notices in the church bulletin (and not just for Thanksgiving Day) to help parents discuss and enact with their children specific "thanksgiving projects" that focus on helping others—visiting senior citizens, helping out at a sports or games program in a nearby park, and the like.

Unit Song Suggestions: A Model

Gathering Songs
Dm Sing Alleluia (68)
D   I Will Enter His Gates (9)
D   We Will Glorify (18)

Theme Song
Eb   Now Thank We All Our God (33)

Additional Songs
G   We Thank God (88)
G   For the Beauty of the Earth (89)
Bm   Praise the Lord (20)

Closing Song
F   Praise and Thanksgiving (83)

Indexes

Copyright Holders

Each song under copyright, whether text, tune, or arrangement, is so indicated at the bottom of each song page. If you wish to reproduce (or reprint) any copyrighted words or music contained in this book, please contact the copyright holder for permission.

Abingdon Press
201 8th Ave. So.
Nashville, TN 37202
(615) 749–6422

Augsburg Fortress Publishers
426 S Fifth St
Box 1209
Minneapolis MN 55440
(612) 330–3300

D. Austin
Rose Hill School
Alderly
Wooton–Under–Edge, Glos
ENGLAND

A. C. Barham–Gould Estate
c/o D. R. Gould
34 Pollards Dr.
Horsham, West Sussex RH 13 5HH
ENGLAND

Benson Music Group, Inc.
365 Great Circle Rd.
Nashville, TN 37228
(615) 742–6924

Loje Braen
560 Bellview
Winchester, VA 22601

Broadman Press
127 Ninth Avenue North
Nashville, TN 37234
(615) 251–2533

Brummhart Publishing Co.
12 Twinshaven Rd.
Napanoch, NY 12458

AnnaMae Meyer Bush
850 Byerly SE
Grand Rapids, MI 49546
(616) 949–2454

Carl Fischer, Inc.
62 Cooper Sq.
New York, NY 10003
(212) 777–0900

Dosia Carlson
Beatitudes Center D.O.A.R.
555 W. Glendale Ave.
Phoenix, AZ 85021

Gerhard M. Cartford
2279 Commonwealth Ave.
St. Paul, MN 55108

Rev. Brian C. Casebow
25 Fountainhall Rd.
Edinburgh EH9 2LN
SCOTLAND

Choristers Guild
2834 W. Kingsley Road
Garland, TX 75041
(214) 271–1521

Christian Conference of Asia
Attn: Rev. Toshitsugu Arai
Pak Tin Village, Mei Tin Road
Shatin, N.T.
HONG KONG

Concordia Publishing
3558 Jefferson Ave.
St. Louis, MO 62118
(314) 664–7000

The Copyright Company
Maranatha! Music
40 Music Sq. East
Nashville, TN 37203
(615) 244–5588

Covenant Press
5101 N. Francisco Ave.
Chicago, IL 60625
(312) 784–3000

E.C.S. Publishing
138 Ipswich
Boston, MA 02215
(617) 236–1935

Editoria Sinodal
rua Epifanio Fogaca 467
Caixa Postal 11
93001 Sao Leopoldo, R.S.
BRAZIL

Stanley M. Farr
518 Fairmont Rd.
Morgantown, WV 26505

Frederick Harris Music Company
340 Nagel Drive
Buffalo, NY 14225
(800) 387–4013

Dorothy Frisch
6160 Rice Creek Dr.
Fridley, MN 55432

G. I. A. Publications
7404 S. Mason Ave.
Chicago, IL 60638
(708) 496–3800

Hamblen Music Company
26101 Ravenhill Rd.
Canyon Country, CA 91350
(805) 252–3881

Mr. Nobuaki Hanaoka
Japanese United Methodist Church
6929 Franklin Blvd.
Sacramento, CA 95823

Harper Collins Religious
77–85 Fulham Palace Rd.
Hammersmith
London W68JB
ENGLAND

Judith Helms
21 Beverly Drive
Arcata CA 95521

Herb Associates
11641 Palmer Rd.
Bloomington, MN 55437–3437
(612) 888–5281

Hinshaw Music
P. O. Box 470
Chapel Hill, NC 27514
(919) 933–1691

Hope Publishing Company
380 S. Main Pl.
Carol Stream, IL 60188
(800) 323–1049

Stephan Hopkinson
Duke's Watch
2 S. Swithen St.
Winchester, SO23 9JP
ENGLAND

Integrated Copyright Group
Lillenas Publishing Co.
P. O. Box 24149
Nashville, TN 37202
(615) 329–3999

Integrity Music, Inc.
1000 Cody Road
Mobile, AL 36695
(205) 633–9000

Sean Ivory
1138 Hall St SE
Grand Rapids MI 49507

Kevin Mayhew Publishers
Rattlesden
Bury St. Edmunds
Suffolk 1P30 0SZ
ENGLAND

Manna Music, Inc.
P. O. Box 218
Pacific City, OR 97135
(503) 965–6112

Rev. John A. Moss
101 Amherst Rd.
South Hadley, MA 01075

Music Anno Domini
P. O. Box 7465
Grand Rapids, MI 49510
(616) 241–3787

New Dawn Music
P. O. Box 13248
Portland, OR 97213
(800) 243–3296

OCP Publications
5536 NE Hassalo
Portland OR 97213
(800) 243–3296

Oxford University Press
Music Dept.
Walton Street
Oxford OX2 6DP
ENGLAND
Fax 0865–56646

Paulist Press
997 Macarthur Blvd.
Mahway, NJ 07430
(201) 825–7300

Joe Pinson
HCSR
Box 491
Denton, TX 76202

Prism Tree Music
Bob Kilpatrick Ministries
P. O . Box 2383
Fair Oaks, CA 95628
(916) 961–1022

Cary Ratcliff
226 Winstead St.
Rochester, NY 14609

David Ritsema
3955 South Oneida Street
Denver, CO 80237

Robert Roth
330 Morgan St.
Oberlin, OH 44074

Sacred Music Press
The Lorenz Corp.
501 E. 3rd Street
P. O. Box 802
Dayton, OH 45401
(800) 444–1144

G. Schirmer Music
c/o Music Sales Corp.
257 Park Ave. So.
New York, NY 10010

Silliman University
Ms. Elena Maquiso
Ulahingan Research Project
Dumaguete City, 6200
PHILLIPPINES

The Sparrow Corp.
P. O. Box 5010
101 Winners Circle
Brentwood, TN 37024
(615) 371–6800

Stainer & Bell, Ltd.
P. O. Box 110, Victoria House
23 Greneisen Road
Finchley, London N3 1DZ
ENGLAND

Linda Stassen–Benjamin
New Songs Ministries
RR 1, Box 454
Erin TN 37061

Wim ter Burg
c/o G. F. Callenbach B.V.
Postbus 1086
Nijkerk 3860BB
THE NETHERLANDS

Unichappel Music, Inc.
Div. of Hal Leonard Publishing
7777 W. Bluemound Rd.
Milwaukee, WI 53213
(414) 774–3630

United Church Press
700 Prospect Ave. E.
Cleveland, OH 44115
(216) 736–3700

United Methodist Publishing House
201 – 8th Avenue So
Nashville TN 37202
(615) 749–6422

Coby Veenstra
Cricket Music Ministry
P. O. Box 133
Hampton, ON L0B 1J0
CANADA

Walton Music Corp.
170 NE 33rd Street
Ft. Lauderdale, FL 33334

Westminster John Knox Press
100 Witherspoon Street
Louisville, KY 40202
(800) 523–1631

Bert Witvoet
Calvinist Contact
261 Martindale Rd., Unit 4
St. Catharines, ON L2W 1A1
CANADA
(416) 682–8311

WORD Music
3319 West End Ave. Suite 200
Nashville, TN 37203
(615) 385–9673

World Library Publications
3815 N. Willow Rd.
Schiller Park. IL 60176
(708) 678–0621

John Ylvisaker
New Generation Publishing
Box 321
Waverly, IA 50677

Songs Used in the LiFE Curriculum

Note: These songs appear in the order in which they are used in the curriculum.

Preschool and Kindergarten

Year 1

Year 2

Grades 1 and 2

Year 1

Fall

Winter

Spring

Plus

Year 2

Fall

Winter

Spring

Plus

Grades 3 and 4

Year 1

Fall
Seek Ye First the
    Kingdom 155
The Lord Is My
    Shepherd 200
Soon and Very
    Soon 194
Jesus Is a Friend
    of Mine 36
Lord, I Pray 37
Jesu, Jesu, Fill Us with
    Your Love 251
The Good Samaritan   146
The Wise May Bring
    Their Learning 70
Lord, I Want to Be a
    Christian 40

Winter
O Come, O Come,
    Immanuel 123
The Prophets Came
    to Israel 128
Jesu, Jesu, Fill Us with
    Your Love 251
Spirit of the Living
    God 184
Silver and Gold Have I
    None 116
We Are the Church . . 236
Go Now in Peace 79
Lord, I Want to Be a
    Christian 40
The Servant Song . . . 248
Lord, Listen to Your Chil-
    dren Praying 54

Spring
Alleluia, Alleluia! Give
    Thanks 173
He Is Lord 178
We Are the Church . . 236
We Thank You, God . . 38
Children of the Lord . 238
Believe in the Lord . . 223
Go Now in Peace 79
Good News 132
He's Got the Whole
    World 198

Plus
This Is the Day 3
We Thank You, God . . 38
Seek Ye First the
    Kingdom 155
All Creatures of Our
    God and King 86
Amazing Grace 209
Lord, I Pray 37
Love God with All Your
    Soul and Strength . 76

Year 2

Fall
The Lord Is My
    Shepherd 200
My God Is So Great . . . 35
Protect Me, God:
    I Trust in You 217
Lord, Have Mercy
    upon Us 43
God Is So Good 207
We Are the Church . . 236
Hallelujah, Praise
    the Lord 24
Father, I Adore You . . . 28
Psalm 51 41

Winter
Prepare the Way of
    the Lord 124
The Prophets Came
    to Israel 128
We Thank You, God . . 38
Our Help 219
Swing Low, Sweet
    Chariot 197
My God Is So Great . . . 35
Protect Me, God:
    I Trust in You 217
I Will Enter His Gates . . 9
We Are the Church . . 236
Lead Me, Guide Me . . 220

Spring
He's Alive! 174
O Mary, Don't You
    Weep 117
My God Is So Great . . . 35
Jonah's Song 111
Come Bless the Lord . . . 6
He's Got the Whole
    World 198
I Will Exalt My God,
    My King 26
God of Great and
    God of Small 29
Lord, Our Lord, Your
    Glorious Name 15
God Is So Good 207

Plus
Shine, Jesus, Shine . . 239
Trust and Obey 213
Good News 132
In the Presence of
    Your People 25
Here I Am, Lord 243

Grades 5 and 6

Year 1

Fall
Lord, I Want to Be a
    Christian 40
Oh, How Good Is
    Christ the Lord . . . 177
Prepare the Way of
    the Lord 124
You Are Our God; We
    Are Your People . . 203

Winter
Worthy Is Christ/
    Digno Es Jesús . . . 170
I Believe in God 73
There's No God as
    Great/No Hay Dios
    tan Grande 240
He's Got the Whole
    World 198
He Is Lord 178
Were You There 167

Spring
Were You There 167
Oh, How Good Is
    Christ the Lord . . . 177
When Did We
    See You 245
I Believe in God 73
Spirit of the Living
    God 184
Lord, I Want to Be a
    Christian 40
We Are the Church . . 236
Amazing Grace 209

Plus
Blest Are They 153
Many and Great 94
Jesu, Jesu, Fill Us with
    Your Love 251
Bring Forth the
    Kingdom 154
What a Friend We
    Have in Jesus 52
Seek Ye First the
    Kingdom 155
It Makes No
    Difference 206
Lead Me, Guide Me . . 220

Year 2

Fall
Lead Me, Guide Me . . 220
The Lord Is My
    Shepherd 200
Baptized in Water 60
Were You There 167
Worthy Is Christ/
    Digno Es Jesús . . . 170
The Servant Song . . . 248
Father, I Adore You . . . 28
This Is My Father's
    World 95
King of Kings and
    Lord of Lords 16

Winter
Magnify the Lord 13
Song of Mary 125
Love the Lord 75
Jesu, Jesu, Fill Us with
    Your Love 251
How Great Is the
    Love of the Father . 59
Seek Ye First the
    Kingdom 155
King of Kings and
    Lord of Lords 16
Sent by the Lord 249
It Makes No
    Difference 206

Spring
He Is Lord 178
Forest Trees 92
He's Got the Whole
    World 198
Standing in the Need
    of Prayer 46
Lord, Listen to Your Chil-
    dren Praying 54
The Lord's Prayer 48
"Holy, Holy, Holy"/
    "Santo, Santo,
    Santo" 66
Lead Me, Guide Me . . 220

Plus
Love God with All Your
    Soul and Strength . 76
Go Now in Peace 79
Shalom 84
When Jesus the
    Healer 149
In the House of
    Our God 5
The Servant Song . . . 248
Clap Your Hands 179
Take My Life 74
Were You There 167
Worthy Is Christ/
    Digno Es Jesús . . . 170

Songs with Signing Motions

The following songs have signing motions portrayed on the song pages. Not all words in each song have been signed; sometimes only key words are given. These signing motions represent a beginner's introduction to American Sign Language. For a more thorough introduction to American Sign Language, consult the following resources in the order given:

The Joy of Signing, Lottie L. Riekehof. Springfield, MO: Gospel Publishing House, 1978.

Religious Signing, Elaine Costello. New York: Bantam Books, 1986.

American Sign Language Concise Dictionary, Martin L. A. Sternberg. New York: Harper & Row Publishers, Inc., 1990.

Signing Index

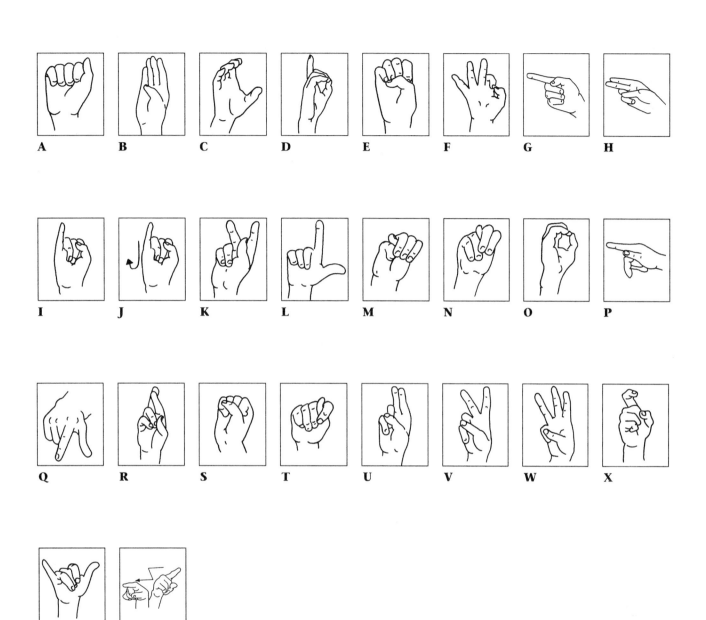

A B C D E F G H

I J K L M N O P

Q R S T U V W X

Y Z

 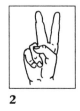   

1 2 3 4 5

Above
Hold right open hand above left open hand, both palms down; move the right in a counterclockwise circle.

Adore
Place the right "A" inside the left curved hand; draw hands up and toward you in a reverent attitude.

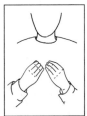 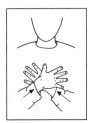

Afraid
(The heart is suddenly covered with fear.) Both hands, fingers together, are placed side by side, palms facing chest. They quickly open and come together over the heart, one on top of the other.

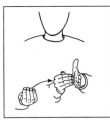

Again
Right curved hand faces up, then turns and moves left so fingertips touch left palm, which is pointing forward with palm facing right.

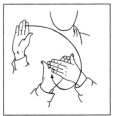

All
Left open hand faces body; with right hand, make a circle going out and around left hand, ending with back of right hand in palm of left. The sweeping movement of the right hand includes everything.

Allelu (See **Alleluia**.)

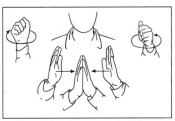

Alleluia
Bring both open hands, palms facing each other and fingertips pointing up, together in front of the chest. Then raise both modified "A" hands near each shoulder, moving them in small circles outward.

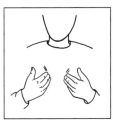

Animals
Place fingertips on chest and rock hands back and forth with the tips still resting on the chest. This represents the breathing motion of an animal.

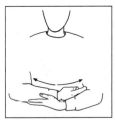

Babe, Baby
Place right hand in the crook of left arm and left upturned hand under right arm; then rock.

Before
Open hands face body; the right is drawn away from the left toward the right shoulder.

Behold
Beginning with the fingertips of the right "V" hand, palm down, pointing at the eyes, twist the right wrist to point the fingers outward alongside the left "V" hand, fingers pointing forward and both palms facing down.

Believe
Touch forehead with index finger and clasp hands, as in holding on to the thought.

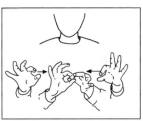

Belong
(Joining together.) Both hands, held in the modified "five" position, palms out, move toward each other. Thumbs and index fingers of both hands then connect.

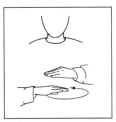

Below
Hold right open hand under left open hand, both palms down; move the right in a counterclockwise circle.

Beside (See **With**.)

Be Still (See **Silence**.)

Bible (Sign **Jesus** plus **Book**.)

Birth (See **Born**.)

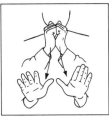

Bless
Place both "A" hands in front of mouth, palm to palm; bring hands forward slightly, open them and bring them down.

Book
Begin with palms of both open hands closed together in front of chest. Then open like a book, with palms of both open hands facing upward, keeping fingers together.

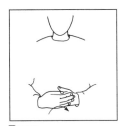

Born
(The baby is brought forth from the womb.) Both cupped hands, palms

facing the body, are placed at the stomach or lower chest, one on top of the other. Both hands are moved out and away from the body in unison, describing a small arc.

Christ
Place the right "C" at left shoulder and then at right waist. Indicates the stole worn by royalty.

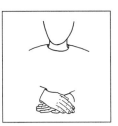

Clean
Right open palm is placed on left open palm and is passed across it. (This symbolizes that all the dirt is rubbed off.)

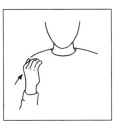

Come
The upright hand beckons.

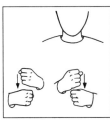

Create
Place right "S" (palm facing left) on left "S" (palm facing right). Turn them so palms face you and strike them together again. Repeat several times.

Creatures (Sign **People** plus **Animals**.)

Dark, Darkest
Open hands, palms facing you and pointing up, are crossed in front of face.

Day
Left arm, held horizontally, palm down, represents the horizon. Right arm, with index finger pointing out, palm up, is moved in a short arc from right to left.

Death (See **Died**.)

Destiny
Raised arm palm facing left, moves forward in a large semicircle. *Note:* The larger and more slowly the sign is made, the greater the distance in the future is meant.

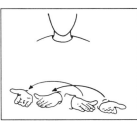

Died
(Turning over on one's side.) Open hands, fingers pointing ahead, are held side by side, with right palm down and left palm up. The two hands reverse their relative positions as they move from left to right.

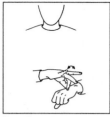

Earth

Place thumb and middle finger of right hand on the back of left hand near the wrist and rock the right back and forth.

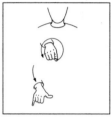

Ever

The right index finger, pointing forward, traces a clockwise circle. The downturned "Y" hand then moves forward either in a straight line or in a slight downward curve.

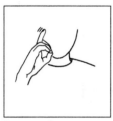

Everywhere

The right "D" hand, with palm out and index finger slightly curved, moves a short distance back and forth, from left to right.

Face

Using index finger, trace a circle in front of the face.

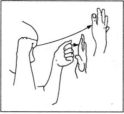

Father

This sign indicates the first person of the Trinity. With right "A" hand at the forehead, palm left, and left "A" hand forward of the forehead, palm right, move both hands upward and outward toward the left while opening into "five" hands, palms facing out.

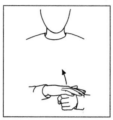

Fill

Downturned open right hand wipes across index finger edge of the left "S" hand, whose palm faces right. Movement of the right hand is toward the body.

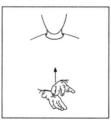

Find

Thumb and index fingers of outstretched right hand grasp imaginary object on upturned left palm. Right hand then moves straight up.

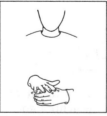

Flow

(Overflow, running over) Place right "and" hand against left palm; move right hand up to the index-finger edge and then over the side, fingers wiggling.

Forevermore (See **Ever**.)

Found (See **Find**.)

Fullness (See **Fill**.)

Future (See **Destiny**.)

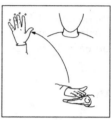

Glorify

Beginning with right open palm across upturned left open palm, bring right hand upward toward right shoulder, opening into a "five" hand and wiggling fingers as hand moves.

Glory (See **Glorify**.)

Go

When giving a command, the index fingers are swung down and forward, one behind the other.

God

Point the "G" hand forward, draw it up and back down, opening the palm, which is facing left. Hand is raised heavenward and then down in a reverent motion.

Good
(Tasting something, approving it, and offering it forward.) The fingertips of the right "five" hand are placed at the lips. The right hand then moves out and into a palm-up position on the upturned left palm.

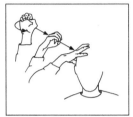

Grace
Begin with right thumb touching fingertips, palm facing forward above the right shoulder. Then twist the wrist inward, spreading fingers while moving down to the right side of the head.

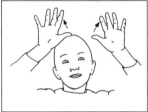

Great
The "five" hands, palms out and arms raised rather high, are positioned somewhat above the line of vision. Arms move abruptly forward and up once or twice. An expression of pleasure or surprise is usually assumed.

Hallelujah (See **Alleluia**.)

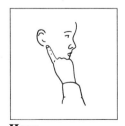

Hear
Place tip of index finger at ear.

Heart
Use extended middle fingers of both hands, palms toward the body, to trace the outline of a heart on the left side of the chest. The middle finger is considered the "feeling finger" in American Sign Language.

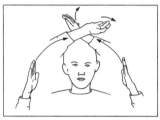

Heaven, Heavenly host
Move both hands up toward each other over the head, palms facing each side of the head. As hands meet at the top of the head, pass right hand in front of left while twisting both wrists outward, ending with both palms angled forward and upward, the right in front of the left, at angles.

Holy Ghost (See **Spirit**.)

Holy Spirit (See **Spirit**.)

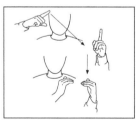

Hope
With right extended index finger near right side of forehead and left extended index finger forward of left shoulder, palms facing each other, bring right finger down toward the left, changing into bent hands facing each other near left shoulder.

I (See **Me**.)

Immanuel
(Sign **God**, **With**, and **Us**, which is the translated meaning from the Hebrew.)

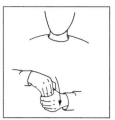

Into
Place tips of the right hand into the left "O" hand, pushing the right hand through and forward.

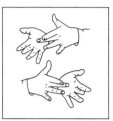

Jesus
Place tip of middle finger of right open hand into left palm and reverse (indicating nailprints).

Keep
(Slow, careful movement.) The "K" hands are crossed, right above left, little finger edges down. Move hands up and down a short distance.

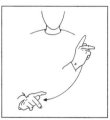

King
This initialized sign follows the shape of the sash worn by royalty. Refers both to Old Testament monarchs and to Christ's designation as King of the Jews. Move the right "K" hand, palm left, from the left shoulder down to the right hip.

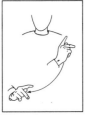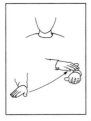

Kingdom
First, sign **King**; then the hand opens and moves upward in an arc to circle over the downturned left hand, indicating an area of land.

Know
The right fingers pat the forehead several times.

Lamb
Hands mime shearing wool from sheep. With left upturned hand extended, repeatedly sweep right "K" hand, palm up, inside of left arm.

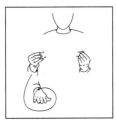

Land
Rub fingertips of both hands with thumb as if feeling soil; make a counterclockwise circle with right open hand, palm down.

Lead
Grasp tip of the left open hand with right fingertips and thumb and pull forward.

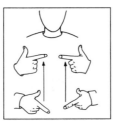

Life
Sign symbolizes vitality. Bring both "L" hands, palms toward body and index fingers pointing toward each other, upward from waist to chest.

Lift
To take up. Both hands, palms down in the "five" position, are at chest level. With a grasping upward movement, both close into the "S" positions before the face.

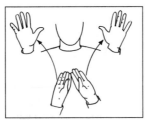

Light
Both "and" hands point forward, index tips touching; open fingers as hands are moved upward and to the sides, ending in a "five" position, palms facing forward.

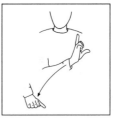

Lord
Touch thumb of right "L" hand, palm facing left and index finger pointing outward at an angle, to left shoulder. Swing right hand outward and upward in a large arc, ending above right side of head with palm facing out and index finger pointing up.

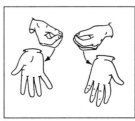

Lost
Both hands in the "and" position, fingernails touching and palms facing up, are dropped and opened.

Love
A natural sign for holding someone or something very dear near the heart. Cross arms of both "A" hands at wrists, palms toward body, across the chest.

Make (See **Create**.)

Me
Point right index finger at yourself.

Mercy

(God's mercy toward humankind.) With bent middle fingers of both "five" hands pointing toward right side of the head, palms facing down, stroke the air toward the head repeatedly.

Mind

Tap forehead with curved index finger, indicating the location of the mind.

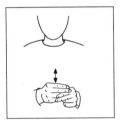

Name

Place middle finger of right "H" across index finger of left "H," to form an X; do two times.

Neighbor

Sign "near" (back of right bent hand approaches inside of left bent hand, both palms facing the body); add the "person" ending (both open hands facing each other are brought down in front of the body).

Never-ending (See **Ever.**)

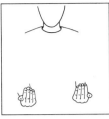

Now

Place both bent hands before you at waist level, palms up. Drop hands slightly. This indicates time that is immediately before you.

Open

Place both open hands side by side; draw hands apart so that the palms now face each other.

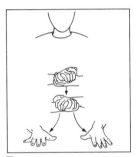

Peace

Clasp hands together, both ways, then open and separate, assuming the "five" position, palms down.

People

Using both "P" hands, circle them alternately toward the center.

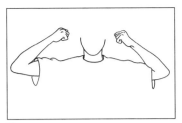

Power

(Flexing the muscles.) With fists clenched, palms facing back, raise both arms and shake them once, with force.

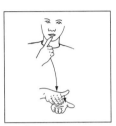

Praise

Hands mime applauding to extol or exalt God. Start with right extended index finger at lips, palm left. Then pat downturned right open hand on palm of upturned left open hand, which is held in front of the face.

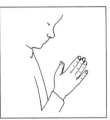

Pray

Place hands palm to palm and draw them toward the body as the head is bowed slightly. Hands are in a position of prayer.

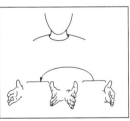

Prepare

Open hands, facing each other and pointing forward, are moved toward the right in several short sweeping motions. Everything is in stacks, all arranged.

Prince of Peace (See **Peace.**)

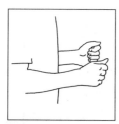

Reigns
The "A" hands, palms facing, move alternately back and forth, as if grasping and manipulating reins.

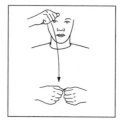

Remember
Place thumbnail of the right "A" on the forehead and then on the thumbnail of the left "A."

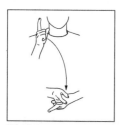

Right
Bring right index finger, held above left index finger, down rather forcefully so that the bottom of the right hand comes to rest on top of left thumb joint.

Risen
Raise right "V" from a palm-up position to a standing position and place it on left palm; signifying lying down and then standing up.

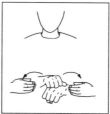

Rock
Strike back of the left "S" with the palm side of the right "A"; place the "C" hands in front of you facing each other, forming the shape of a rock. The fist represents the rock; striking indicates hardness.

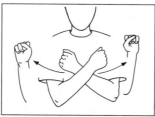

Salvation
Cross wrists with "S" hands, as if wrists were bound; then bring the "S" hands out to the sides, turning them so they are facing forward. (Conveys the idea of being bound and then set free.)

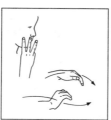

Sea
Sign "water" (strike side of mouth several times with index finger of the "W" hand); then place left hand behind right, palms down; move hands up and down to indicate the waves of the ocean.

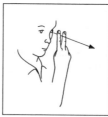

See
Place the "V" in front of the face, fingertips near eyes, and move hand forward. Fingertips point to eyes looking out.

Seek
(Directing the vision from place to place.) Right "C" hand, palm facing left, moves from right to left across the line of vision in a series of counterclockwise circles. The signer's gaze is concentrated; head turns slowly from right to left.

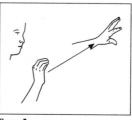

Send
Hold right "and" hand palm out. Then open and move forcefully outward in a throwing motion.

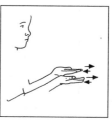

Serve
With both palms facing up, move hands alternately back and forth.

Shine
Open palms, facing each other with tips pointing up, are drawn apart to the sides while the fingers are wiggling.

Silence

Place index finger against mouth, palm facing left; draw both open hands down and toward the side, palms facing down.

Sky

Make a sweeping motion with open hand from left to right, above eye level.

Small

Hold both slightly curved hands out, palm facing palm; push hands toward each other several times.

Son

Sign "male" (grasp imaginary rim of a hat with four fingers and thumb); then place right hand (palm up) in crook of left arm.

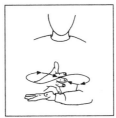

Song

The right "five" hand, palm facing left, is waved back and forth over upturned left arm in a series of elongated figure-eights.

Soul (See **Spirit**.)

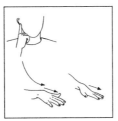

Sound

Touch tip of ear with index finger; direct both "five" hands toward the left, right behind left, palms down. This is to show the ear and the vibrations.

Spirit

The fingers seem to hold something thin and filmy, symbolic of a supernatural being such as the Holy Spirit. Touch thumbs and index fingers of both "F" hands to each other, right hand over left, palms facing. Draw hands apart, lifting right hand in front of chest.

Strength

Both "five" hands are placed palms against chest. They move out and away forcefully, closing and assuming the "S" position.

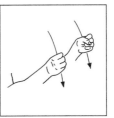

Strong

Bring "S" hands down with force.

Surround

With right index finger, describe a counterclockwise circle around upturned tips of left "and" hand.

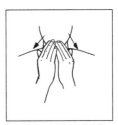

Thank, Thank You

Place the tips of the open hands against the mouth and throw them foward, similar to throwing a kiss. (May be made with one hand.)

Today

(Sign **Now** plus **Day**.)

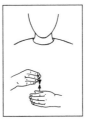 

Trust

Indicates confidence; the hands seem to grab hold of something. Hold right "C" hand a few inches above left "C" hand, palms facing each other, slightly away from the body. Bring hands together and toward the body, changing them into "S" hands as they move.

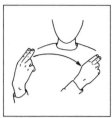

Us
The right "U" hand, palm facing the body, swings from right to left shoulder, an encompassing gesture.

Way
Open hands, fingers pointing forward and palms facing each other; move both hands forward with a slight zigzag motion. (Or, to show that the way of the Lord is a straight way, do not zigzag, but move hands straight forward.)

Weak
Place four fingertips of the right hand in left palm; then bend fingers of right hand. (Signifies being weak in the knees.)

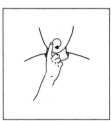

Who, Whom
Describe a circle around pursed lips toward the left with index finger.

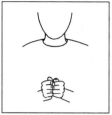

With
Place the "A" hands together, palm to palm.

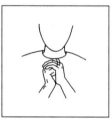

Worship
Place right "A" inside left curved hand; draw hands up and toward you in a reverent attitude. This sign is sometimes also used for "Amen."

Wrong
The "Y" hand touches chin, palm facing in.

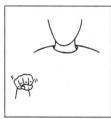

Yes
Shake right "S" up and down in front of you. Agreement is also indicated by shaking the right "Y" up and down. The fist, representing the head, nods in agreement.

You
Point index finger out. For the plural, point index finger out and move from left to right.

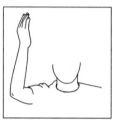

You (Thee)
This directional sign is a natural gesture for the second-person pronoun when it is used to refer to God. Move right open hand from above right shoulder a short distance upward, palm angles left and fingertips pointing up.

Yourself
Direct the "A" hand away from the body in several short quick movements.

Metrical Index

Tune Names

Authors, Composers, Sources

Key Index

Key of Gm

Scripture Index

Songs from Around the World

Songs in Other Languages

Alternative and Duet Accompaniments

Descants

Echo Songs

Orff and Rhythm Instruments

Speech Rhythms

Responsorial Style

Rounds and Canons

Index of First Lines and Titles

Capo Chart

Pianists may find "flat" keys easier to play than "sharp" keys. But the opposite is true for guitarists. Using a capo to clamp the strings allows a guitarist to transpose to a more convenient key. Shortening the strings by one fret (Capo 1) will raise the pitch a half step; clamping on the third fret (Capo 3) will raise the pitch three half steps.

The chart below shows how a capo can be used to play in more convenient keys. For example, by using Capo 3, a song in the key of F (with one flat) can be played as if in the key of D. The resulting sound from the shortened strings will actually be in F. All major and minor chords are listed.

Capo suggestions are made on the bottom right of many song pages. For those songs, find the key signature and key below, add the capo, and play the chords in parentheses. The resulting sound will be in the original key.

Number of flats	Scale degree 1	2	3	4	5	6	7
Key of F capo 3	F (D)	Gm (Em)	Am (F#m)	Bb (G)	C (A)	Dm (Bm)	
Key of F capo 5	F (C)	Gm (Dm)	Am (Em)	Bb (F)	C (G)	Dm (Am)	
Key of Dm capo 5	Dm (Am)		F (C)	Gm (Dm)	A (E)	Bb (F)	C (G)
Key of Bb capo 1	Bb (A)	Cm (Bm)	Dm (C#m)	Eb (D)	F (E)	Gm (F#m)	
Key of Eb capo 1	Eb (D)	Fm (Em)	Gm (F#m)	Ab (G)	Bb (A)	Cm (Bm)	
Key of Eb capo 3	Eb (C)	Fm (Dm)	Gm (Em)	Ab (F)	Bb (G)	Cm (Am)	
Key of Cm capo 5	Cm (Gm)		Eb (Bb)	Fm (Cm)	G (D)	Ab (Eb)	Bb (F)
Key of Ab capo 1	Ab (G)	Bbm (Am)	Cm (Bm)	Db (C)	Eb (D)	Fm (Em)	
Key of Fm capo 1	Fm (Em)		Ab (G)	Bbm (Am)	C (B)	Dbb (C)	Eb (D)